Dialogue and
Critical Discourse

Dialogue and Critical Discourse

Language, Culture, Critical Theory

Edited by

Michael Macovski

New York   Oxford • Oxford University Press   1997

Oxford University Press

Oxford   New York
Athens   Auckland   Bangkok   Bogota   Bombay   Buenos Aires
Calcutta   Cape Town   Dar es Salaam   Delhi   Florence   Hong Kong
Istanbul   Karachi   Kuala Lumpur   Madras   Madrid   Melbourne
Mexico City   Nairobi   Paris   Singapore   Taipei   Tokyo   Toronto   Warsaw

and associated companies in
Berlin   Ibadan

Copyright © 1997 by Oxford University Press, Inc.

Published by Oxford University Press, Inc.
198 Madison Avenue, New York, New York 10016

Oxford is a registered trademark of Oxford University Press

Library of Congress Cataloging-in-Publication Data
Dialogue and critical discourse : language, culture, critical theory /
edited by Michael Macovski.
    p.   cm.
Includes bibliographical references.
ISBN 0-19-507063-1
1. Dialogue analysis.   2. Discourse analysis, Literary.
3. Criticism.   4. Bakhtin, M. M. (Mikhail Mikhaïlovich), 1895–1975.
5. Oral communication.   I. Macovski, Michael.
P95.455.D53   1997
808'.0014—DC20   92-28231

9 8 7 6 5 4 3 2 1

Printed in the United States of America
on acid-free paper

For my parents,
Addie and Al Macovski

Acknowledgments

I want to express my gratitude to the contributors to this volume—for their deep insights into dialogism and for their belief in this collection.

I also thank Cynthia Read, Executive Editor at Oxford University Press, for her initial enthusiasm and continuing faith in the project.

This book is dedicated to my parents, the two people who first inspired—and have always sustained—my dialogue with literature and my love of language.

Last and first, now and always, I thank my wife, Deborah.

Contents

Part II   DIALOGUE BETWEEN WORKS

Part III   DIALOGUE BETWEEN SPEAKERS, READERS, AND AUTHORS

Contributors

Timothy R. Austin is Professor in and Chairperson of the English Department at Loyola University Chicago. His publications include *Language Crafted: A Linguistic Theory of Poetic Syntax* (1984) and *Poetic Voices: Discourse Linguistics and the Poetic Text* (1994).

Don H. Blalostosky is Professor in and Head of the English Department at Penn State University. He has published *Making Tales: The Poetics of Wordsworth's Narrative Experiments* (1984) and *Wordsworth, Dialogics and the Practice of Criticism* (1992), and he is coeditor of *Rhetorical Traditions and British Romantic Literature* (1995).

Caryl Emerson is the A. Watson Armour University Professor of Slavic Languages and Literatures at Princeton University. She is author, most recently, of *The First Hundred Years of Mikhail Bakhtin* (forthcoming 1997), and, with Robert William Oldani, *Modest Musorgsky and Boris Godunov: Myths, Realities, Reconsiderations* (1994). Other areas of interest include Russian music, Pushkin, Dostoevsky, Tolstoy, theories of the novel, and the profession of literary criticism in Imperial, Soviet and post-Soviet Russia.

John P. Farrell, Professor of English at the University of Texas at Austin, is the author of *Revolution as Tragedy: The Dilemma of the Moderate from Scott to Arnold* (1980), as well as essays on Shakespeare, Browning, Dickens, the Brontës, and several contemporary American poets. His essay in this volume is part of a book in progress on Hardy's construction of the Wessex world.

Paul Friedrich is Professor Emeritus of Anthropology, Linguistics, and the Committee on Social Thought, and Associate in Slavic Languages and Literatures, at the University of Chicago. His books include *The Meaning of Aphrodite* (1978), *The Language Parallax* (1986), and *Music in Russian Poetry* (1997).

Shirley Brice Heath, Professor of English and Linguistics at Stanford University, is the author of *Ways with Words* (1983) and, with Shelby Wolf, *The Braid of Literature* (1992). Her research centers on language uses and cultural values across cultures.

Michael Holquist, Professor of Comparative and Slavic Literature at Yale University, is the author of *Dostoevsky and the Novel* (1977), *Mikhail Bakhtin* (1984— with Katerina Clark), and *Dialogism: Bakhtin and His World* (1990).

Michael Macovski is Associate Professor of English at Fordham University in New York City. He is the author of *Dialogue and Literature: Apostrophe, Auditors, and the Collapse of Romantic Discourse* (Oxford University Press, 1994), as well as articles on Emily Brontë, Lord Byron, and the history of publishing.

Rachel May is Associate Professor of Russian at Macalester College in St. Paul, Minnesota. She is the author of *The Translator in the Text: On Reading Russian Literature in English* (1994). She is currently at work on a comparative study of Russian and American nature writing and cultural attitudes toward nature.

Jerome McGann, University of Virginia, has used the dialogue form extensively in his critical work. He writes widely on the literature of the last 200 years and is currently experimenting with digital imaging tools as critical vehicles. The latter work grows out of his current major project, *The Complete Writings and Pictures of Dante Gabriel Rossetti: A Hypermedia Research Archive*.

Gary Saul Morson is Frances Hooper Professor of the Arts and Humanities at Northwestern University. His books include *Narrative and Freedom: The Shadows of Time* (1994), and, with Caryl Emerson, *Mikhail Bakhtin: Creation of a Prosaics* (1990).

John R. Searle is Mills Professor of Philosophy at the University of California at Berkeley. His books include *The Construction of Social Reality* (1995), *The Rediscovery of the Mind* (1992), and *Intentionality: An Essay in the Philosophy of Mind* (1983).

Deborah Tannen is University Professor and Professor of Linguistics at Georgetown University. Her books include *Gender and Discourse* (Oxford University Press, 1994), *Talking From 9 to 5* (1994), *You Just Don't Understand* (1990), *Talking Voices: Repetition, Dialogue, and Imagery in Conversational Discourse* (1989), and *Conversational Style* (1984).

Dialogue and
Critical Discourse

Introduction

Textual Voices, Vocative Texts:
Dialogue, Linguistics, and Critical Discourse

Some Histories of Critical Discourse

The history of critical discourse during the present century is perhaps best described as a pendent history of praxis and genre. If the New Criticism tended to demonstrate its claims on specifically lyric forms, then structuralist, deconstructionist, and historicist theories can be shown to realize their precepts on narrative texts. The choice of such genres derives, of course, from the particular aims and agendas of the critical discourses themselves—from, say, the desire to disinter the lexical ambiguities of lyric language or to locate the *aporia* that belie narratives of ostensible linearity and sequence. Yet if such agendas suggest a critical movement from lyricism to narratology, it is more difficult to explain what might be called the cross-generic form of the last decade, that is, the dissemination and praxis of dialogue. Since the 1981 translation of Mikhail Bakhtin's *The Dialogic Imagination*, the tendency to reconsider the literary text as a nexus of voices—a matrix of interactions extending beyond earlier notions of dialectic, reception, or speech-act theory—has proliferated within both literary and cultural studies. These vocative interactions can be said to persist not only among such traditional entities as author, reader, and character, but more surprisingly among disparate eras, displaced languages, and, above all, socially extant voices. As such, these interactions are less textual than eventual—mediated constructs emerging from specific addresses to and responses from particular persons. They inaugurate a radical shift not only in the historical kinds of discourse studied and practiced, but in the very notions of "subject," "personae," "rejoinder," and "intertextuality."

This volume is accordingly founded on the premise that contemporary critical discourse looks beyond the primacy of the autotelic subject to represent a composite of voices, a convergence that may be simultaneously apostrophic, antiphonal, and agonistic. It represents a cross section of recent dialogic approaches within literary theory, philosophy, and linguistics—and begins to suggest the extension of these approaches within such fields as anthropology, dance, and developmental psychology.[1] It also seeks to develop and refine the critical extensions of Bakhtin's dialogic theory during the last decade, and to imply a variety of related influences—beginning with Habermas, Buber, and Gadamer, and extending to recent perspectives within discourse analysis, psychoanalytic dialogue, and classical rhetoric.[2]

What such approaches collectively embody is the sense of dialogue as a social production, as a form that necessarily revises the prevalent postromantic concept of a single, originary writer and a designated, implied reader. For in this schema both the production and the interpretation of ostensibly original meaning become social acts: collaborative constructions derived from manifold viewpoints. In reconceiving the notion of literary voices, we speak not of a circumscribed artifact, but of a socially constituted action, a dynamic whose methods and objects are neither focal nor discrete, but processive, accretive, and multireferential.

Border Crossings: Dialogue in Literary History

It is this social, extratextual dimension of dialogic discourse that most explicitly distinguishes it from formalist notions of textual influence and response. If dialogue necessarily revises these notions, however, it nevertheless continues to engage other seminal approaches to literary interchange—approaches including post-Freudian theories of literary influence, affectivist theories of reception, linguistic theories of conversational analysis, and philosophical elaborations of speech-act theory.[3] It is not that dialogue supersedes any of these critical schools, nor that their concerns are parallel or even consonant, but that the aggregate of these previous approaches reveals a critical milieu that is prophetic of dialogic thought. In this sense, we can say that dialogue seeks not to subsume previous theories within a single key concept or code, but to recontextualize them. As Bakhtin himself observes in comparing the two, "A context is potentially unfinalized; a code must be finalized. A code is only a technical means of transmitting information, but it does not have cognitive, creative significance" (1986a, 130).

Such a spirit of recontextualization or "creative" exchange can begin to distinguish dialogue's alignments with—and departures from—other concepts of linguistic interaction. In the case of Bloomian models of influential "misprision," for instance, the notion that a given text necessarily alludes to and responds to its precursors anticipates the dialogic concept of "addressivity," in which all discourse partakes of such invocation.[4] According to Bloom's approach, linguistic influence partakes of oedipal rejection, in which a hierarchical text must be continually and fraternally erased. What the post-Freudian model obscures, though, is that such texts can sustain dialogue outside of this hierarchical framework. In this context, literary influence might best be characterized in terms of a conversation, proceeding in spite of any metonymic patricide. Indeed, if the model of patriarchal influence stresses textual succession, its maternal counterpart represents inclusion — a kind of community of voices that more accurately represents dialogic discourse.[5] In applying an overly essentialist model to the process of literary influence, moreover, such revisionary theorists artificially restrict dialogue to a single, metaphorical "family" of discourse (a textual father, son, and absent mother). In so doing, they limit potential exchange to a few conflicted voices, an internecine rhetoric from which extrafamilial voices are arbitrarily excluded.

This process of locating dialogue within the constellation of critical discourse applies equally to reception theory, which in its initial stages also tends to prefigure the premises of dialogic theory. The notion that a text not only implicates readers in a particular way, but that textual meaning itself resides within these readers, anticipates the dialogic notion of meaning as both plurally constructed and socially elaborated. At the same time, however, the precepts of dialogue suggest that readers instantiate meaning in response not only to texts, but to a variety of other voices: extratextual and intertextual, oral and written, present and absent. As a result, linguistic meaning accrues not only in relation to a given reader, but in interaction with this polyphony of both literary and nonliterary voices. If reception theory focuses on the exchanges between a given text and its particular reader, dialogue redefines and extrapolates such interactions as necessarily multireferential and multivocal. Moreover, if such affectivist studies demonstrate how a given text necessarily implicates a reader — in, say, postlapsarian sin or misinterpretation — dialogism includes this implicating process among a plethora of readerly interactions: between text and reader, speaker and reader, reader and reader, and even text and text. The result is an image of an ultimately more eclectic reader, influenced by a wide spectrum of voices, whose affective responses are a product not only of the text that is read, but of other utterances as well, both textual and atextual.

Finally, these dialogic concepts further coincide with recent advances in a last field, discourse analysis, and most particularly with those linguistic studies that apply the field of conversational analysis to literary texts.[6] Such studies hold that many features of oral conversation — including patterned repetition, evocative imagery, and indirect quotation — are elaborated within literary discourse. As a result, these discoursal approaches dovetail with a constitutive dialogic premise: the praxis of tracing dialogic interaction to *actual* voices, and thereby demonstrating how literary dialogue necessarily derives from these heteroglossic sources. What is more, such parallels between dialogue and conversational analysis also apply to the crucial feature of context-dependence, since both fields stress the idea that meaning can be defined only in terms of the immediate social context of a given interaction. What this volume adds to such parallels, however, is the sense that dialogue inevitably extends beyond the limits of real-time conversation — to dialogues that persist across time and space. Thus literary dialogue may often represent interchanges that violate the particular premises of oral conversation, such as constraints on temporality, register, and cohesion within the spoken language.

Revision cum Extension: Recent Formulations and Developments

We have thus far defined what is in itself a "dialogue" between forms of critical discourse—an initially historical comparison that locates dialogic criticism in relation to previous and related modes. Within this schema, the study of dialogue thus serves to recontextualize, extend, and ultimately transmute recent critical notions of misprision, reception, and sociolinguistic interaction. Within the history of critical discourse, then, dialogue is clearly a concept whose time has come, one that also interacts readily with such current concerns as poststructuralist epistemology, feminist critique, and historicized language. It is not surprising, moreover, that several twentieth-century approaches to dialogue would emerge not only from the writings of Bakhtin himself, but in less well-known formulations by Gadamer, Buber, and Habermas.[7] Though such formulations may come up against one another at times, their areas of respective conflict and overlap still enable us to pinpoint the constitutive features of dialogic form. Indeed, the need for a book like the present one arises not in spite of, but because of, such dissension: our purpose is not to obviate one or another of these conflicting approaches but to ensure their interaction. It is not to render disparate voices silent or mute, but to locate and engage their differences.

Such engagements are, in fact, illuminating in themselves. Considering the study of Bakhtin himself, for instance, we should recall that the first translated discussions of his work come under the heading of "intertextuality," the specifically textual referencing of influence and cross-fertilization.[8] Yet while these early formulations of intertextuality have proven crucial, we have also suggested how recent discussions envision dialogic relations as extending well beyond the limits of the text. As Jerome J. McGann (1985) has shown, the textual manifestation of a poem represents only its linguistic dimension; as such, it necessarily omits the poem's operation within a social system, its overall production and reception—what McGann calls the "experience of the poem." In this context, "poetry is itself one form of social activity, and no proper understanding of the nature of poetry can be made if the poem is abstracted from the experience of the poem, either at its point of origin or at any subsequent period" (1985, 21). Hence the abstracted, seemingly self-contained "'text' is not what we should understand as 'a poem.' Rather, what we ought to see is that 'text' is the linguistic state of the 'poem's' existence" (1985, 22). In discussing literature in terms of the contextualized "act," McGann reiterates its ultimately social dynamics, the sense in which the text is an artifactual sign of an ineluctably larger process of social circulation.[9] This emphasis on the "social act," the interactional event, is also apparent in recent revaluations of Bakhtin's early essays. As Gary Saul Morson and Caryl Emerson have demonstrated (1989, 1990), these essays stress the interchange between "acts," as characterized by their particularity or "eventness"—an approach that actually predates Bakhtin's thoughts concerning specifically linguistic interaction or dialogue per se (1989, 6–7).

Hence early emphases on "intertextuality" tend to obscure the socially eventual nature of dialogue, including its specifically atextual associations with the spoken event. They tend to obfuscate what we have identified as the pervasive orality of dialogic discourse—its tendency to encompass, adapt, and interact with various speech forms from everyday life. In Bakhtin's terms, such speech forms are "primary genres," including "certain types of oral dialogue—of the salon, of one's own circle, and other types as well, such as familiar, family-everyday, sociopolitical, philosophical, and so on." It is these primary genres, moreover, that give rise to and interact with such "secondary genres" as "literary, commentarial, and scientific" forms (1986a, 65). For Bakhtin, spoken discourse becomes a kind of germinal wellspring for these primarily written, "secondary" forms. Hence in discussing such secondary phenomena as the essay, the drama, and the sonnet, this volume necessarily looks beyond the intertextuality of voices to the interorality of texts—the spoken origins of textual forms. It holds that dialogue is not merely intertextual but interlingual, hypostatizing relations not only between distant texts but also between discrete rhetorics and idioms—including the diverse political, theological, and economic languages within a single text.

Originary Forms: Orality and Literature

This emphasis on the oral dimensions of written discourse is itself embedded within a historical context, part of a relatively recent movement to disinter the "primary" strata that lie beneath literary forms. Indeed, before the advent of such a movement, the drive to distinguish literary language from spoken discourse motivated a series of linguistic revolutions during the twentieth century—including the Russian Formalist movement that Bakhtin himself sought to challenge. Indeed, Russian formalists, Saussurean structuralists, and Prague Circle grammarians all sought to define what Boris Ejxenbaum referred to as "poetic language," that aesthetic discourse which stands apart from more quotidian forms.[10] More recently, scholars as diverse as Roman Jakobson, Richard Ohmann, and David Lodge have pursued this distinction, seeking to differentiate (in the latter's words) the "writer's medium" from the "virgin" language of origin.[11] Because of this inclination to demarcate the two forms, examining the body of written literature for vestiges of oral form nearly became a lost art, practiced more often by ethnographers and linguists than by literary scholars—and in the latter case limited almost exclusively to studies of epic and ballad.[12] Several literary theorists began, in fact, to resist what they saw as attempts to trace all writing back to its primordially spoken origins. For them, the very *absence* of an individualized "voice" meant that literature could develop and sustain depersonalized connections between written works. Much as previous critical movements had valued metaphysical ambiguity, or the effacement of authorial intention, this one called for the impartiality of the voiceless text.[13]

During the last two decades, however, both literary critics and linguistic historians have shifted the focus away from such divisions between spoken and written language, and turned more often to the features that relate them as mutually reflective, rhetorical modes. Indeed, the critical history of discourse studies during this period is marked by the elision of the spoken/written distinction, prompted by the sense that it is at best misleading and at worst spurious.[14] Such studies have found it enlightening, in fact, to approach the literary text as a *compilation of voices*, as a representation of particular spoken forms. As Barbara Herrnstein Smith has noted, literary discourse posits "not only the representation of speech in drama, but also lyrics, epics, tales, and novels": "[W]hat poems do represent 'in the medium of language,'" she goes on to say, "is *language*, or more accurately, speech, human utterance, discourse."[15]

The chapters in this book begin with this representational relation between "human utterance" and literary discourse. Each assumes that the crucial processes of spoken exchange are represented, extended, and interpreted within the literary text. At the same time, they demonstrate how literary works represent the capacity of vocal exchange to persist, as Mikhail Bakhtin suggests, "in time and in space" — between widely separated speakers, in the form of conscious quotation, unconscious echoes, and even indirect association.[16] It is this colloquy between disparate voices that begins to define the global analogue to spoken exchange, namely, dialogue. As we have noted, the concept of dialogue encompasses not only direct vocal interchange, but relations between the discrete voices of physically distant speakers. Here again, moreover, such relations can also occur between inscribed voices, that is, between represented speakers within a written text. It is this last, textual homology that locates dialogue within the purview of literature, and particularly within literary history. As the chapters in part II suggest, dialogic discourse includes not only the interchange of voices within texts, but interchange *between* texts as well — across discourses separated "in time and in space." I will be returning to such a notion of dialogic form later in this introduction, but for now we should bear in mind that dialogue constitutes a rhetorical extrapolation of vocative form — both spoken and inscribed, intrapersonal and interpersonal, intratextual and intertextual. However persuasive the quest for a discrete literary discourse becomes, it should not obviate what one critic has called "literature's indispensable relationship to the human voice."[17]

Figures of Speech and Speech as Figure:
The Representation of Conversation

That literary texts can be said to represent other discourse types, both written and spoken, amounts essentially to a history of genres. In Barbara Herrnstein Smith's terms, "The various genres of literary art — for example, dramatic poems, tales, odes, lyrics — can to some extent be distinguished according to what types of discourse — for example, dialogues, anecdotes of past events, public speeches, and private declarations — they characteristically represent. Thus, lyric poems typically represent personal utterances . . ." (1978, 8). Although the precise definition of "dialogue" here remains unstated, we must recognize that one of the central types of discourse that literature "characteristically represents" is conversation: the immediate exchange of distinct and often divergent voices. Although we must bear in mind Smith's admonition that literature reconstructs such genres (rather than actually reenacting them), it is equally vital to recognize that literary texts can represent an entire conversational context, including discourse patterns, lexical repair, rhetorical tropes, and speech-act performatives between speakers and hearers.

The writers in this book demonstrate how such linguistic principles of conversation are transposed within literary discourse. Generally speaking, literary studies have tended to leave such transposition unexamined—not because they pass over the speech phenomena within texts, but because there has never been a critical language adequate to the study of such essentially oral features. Apart from recent discourse studies,[18] there is scarcely a vocabulary for delineating the intricate dynamics of spoken forms—no terms for considering what might be called the phenomenology of conversation as a literary figure or technique. The chapters in this book—particularly those in part I—accordingly draw from the fields of discourse analysis and linguistic stylistics in order to suggest what should eventually become a poetics of conversation in literature—an inquiry into the literary enactment of oral modes.

At the same time, the representation of conversation will also reveal as much about discourse forms and orality as it does about literary interpretation. Indeed, in order to translate intrinsically spoken conventions into literary form, authors are necessarily thrown back on seminal questions about discourse genre, pattern, and style. What happens, for example, when authors attempt to translate distinctly oral features of intonation, accent, and dialogue into the silent medium of print? Which qualities of oral discourse are by definition excluded from the writer's repertoire, and which can be transferred? How might writers convey these spoken features, and why would they valorize them? Most crucially perhaps, which characteristics of vocative discourse must be represented as "oral" precisely because they are alien to the epistemological assumptions that underlie all writing? Such questions strike at the very heart of the controversies concerning oral and literary discourse: to address them, we must begin to formulate the noetic relations between speech and writing—relations that amount to a theory of dialogue. We would do well to turn, however, to Bakhtin's own endeavors to situate his work, particularly since he takes pains to contextualize his later writings as a critical response to Russian Formalism.

The Allusive Voice: Bakhtin, Communality, and the Modes of Linguistic Assimilation

Any theory of dialogue must begin with the "utterance," what Bakhtin calls the "unit of speech communication."[19] For within the evolving concepts of dialogue formulated by Bakhtin, interchanges between actual human utterances become a metaphor for the relations between more global, dialogic "voices." Yet this language of the utterance is simultaneously more than a metaphor, more than a linguistic analogy; rather, it expresses the direct link between micro- and macro-versions of dialogue. For instance, much as dialogue necessarily links disparate texts, so too does human conversation echo and reenact previous quotations, sayings, formulas, and tropes. In this context, every conversation is essentially a playing out, a microcosm of dialogue in the world: Bakhtin's "communion of voices" across space and over time is synchronically expressed *within* a given conversation—in the immediate responses, tautologies, echoes, and retellings of direct vocative exchange. To put it another way, we might say that the direct, face-to-face exchange of utterances is an image of that global, universal "conversation" within the collective "speech community"—within the linguistic strata of human discourse.

Bakhtin accordingly presents the utterance as the originary constituent of human discourse. In his formulation such utterances go to make up those "speech genres" or "relatively stable types" that derive from the spoken word. As we have begun to suggest, he then goes on to divide speech genres into two forms, "primary (simple) genres that have taken form in unmediated speech communion," and "secondary (complex) speech genres—novels, dramas, all kinds of scientific research, major genres of commentary, and so forth [which] arise in . . . comparatively highly developed and organized cultural communication (primarily written) that is artistic, scientific, sociopolitical . . ." (1986a, 62). Regarding primary speech genres, for instance, Bakhtin suggests that oral "dialogue is a classic form of speech communication," the genesis of vocative forms (1986a, 72). More significantly, however, he stipulates that secondary genres (including literature) "absorb and digest" the primary, establishing a definitive link between spoken dialogue and primarily written modes. Such written forms are in many cases "a conventional playing out of speech communication and primary speech genres" (1986a, 72). Here again, then, we can say that literary language draws on these primary genres, transposing and reconstructing the rhetoric of spoken forms. Such a reinterpretation or exchange accordingly leaves its mark on a variety of written modes, including literary genres: "Any expansion of the literary language," Bakhtin continues, "that results from drawing on various extraliterary strata of the national language inevitably entails some degree of penetration into all genres of written language (literary, scientific, commentarial, conversational, and so forth) to a greater or lesser degree. . . ." At the same time, this inter-"penetration" between the literary and extraliterary also results in a gradual transformation of communicative discourse, since it "entails new generic devices for the construction of the speech whole, its finalization, the accommodation of the listener or partner, and so forth" (1986a, 65–66).

This "accommodation of the listener or partner" is central both to Bakhtinian theory and to our analysis of literary dialogue. For what Bakhtin calls the "addressivity" of speech genres posits the dynamic reception of any utterance, the continual resounding of dialogic echoes and resonances through a series of respondents. "An essential (constitutive) marker of the utterance," he writes, "is its quality of being directed to someone" (1986a, 95). His theory of dialogue thus defines the word as always already containing its own response: in the context of literary "addressivity," narration necessarily assumes and takes into account its reception. "The entire utterance is constructed," he goes on, "in anticipation of encountering this response" (1986a, 94). What is more, such anticipation includes a narrator's cognizance not only of his auditor's response, but of his own narration as *itself* responding to its rhetorical precursors. In Bakhtin's terms,

Each utterance is filled with echoes and reverberations of other utterances to which it is related by the communality of the sphere of speech communication. Every utterance must be regarded primarily as a response to preceding utterances of the given sphere (we understand the word "response" here in the broadest sense). Each utterance refutes, affirms, supplements, and relies on the others, presupposes them to be known, and somehow takes them into account. (1986a, 91)

Addressivity thus locates the "listener or partner" directly within the dialogic matrix: each narrator both reacts to and generates a corresponding field of verbal resonance.

We must bear in mind, then, the capacity of the utterance to incorporate and reconstitute other voices, for such a concept also suggests how a literary narrator or author might instantiate distant voices within a written text. According to this approach, these distant voices actually become part of the process of speech production: not only does the speaker anticipate his addressee's response, but their individual utterances are actually "aware of and mutually reflect one another" (1986a, 91). In this sense,

[The] speech experience of each individual is shaped and developed in continuous and constant interaction with others' individual utterances. This experience can be characterized to some degree as the process of *assimilation*—more or less creative—of others' words. . . . Our speech, that is, all our utterances (including creative works), is filled with others' words, varying degrees of otherness or varying degrees of "our-own-ness," varying degrees of awareness and detachment. These words of others carry with them their own expression, their own evaluative tone, which we assimilate, rework, and re-accentuate. (1986a, 89)

It is this capacity for the creative assimilation of others' voices—for reworking utterances from even disparate places and times—that illuminates literary interpretations of such genres as autobiography, history, and the bildungsroman. In Bakhtin's terms, "Two utterances, separated from one another both in time and in space, knowing nothing of one another, when they are compared semantically, reveal dialogic relations," even if their themes overlap only tangentially (1986b, 124). Here again, these "dialogic relations" constitute a linguistic matrix or echo chamber, an organic whole that aggregates even estranged voices. "Each word," Bakhtin goes on, "contains voices that are sometimes infinitely distant, unnamed, almost impersonal . . . , almost undetectable, and voices resounding nearby and simultaneously" (1986b, 124).

According to this conception of dialogue, then, a literary narrator or author partakes of a series of dialogic exchanges, both with "nearby" voices embedded in the text, and with previous writers, "infinitely distant" and even "unnamed." In one sense, we can approach the literary text as an artifact of creative "assimilation," of the process whereby an author's utterance "refutes, affirms, supplements, and relies on the others, presupposes them to be known, and somehow takes them into account." Literature becomes a process of reworking, reaccentuating, and reinterpreting the voices of previous characters, prior writers, and divergent aspects of the author's own self.

Dialogue as Nexus: The Evolution of Critical Forms

The need for a book like the present one thus emerges from a series of redefinitions, from an evolution of extensions, developments, and new emphases within the critical study of dialogue. Such developments have begun to challenge previously held interpretations of Bakhtin's central formulations—to distinguish dialogue most particularly from such fields as dialectic rhetoric, doctrinal Marxism, and the overzealous valorization of the carnivalesque.[20] At the same time, this volume also endeavors to reveal and develop several rarely discussed dynamics inherent within dialogic language, including not only its widely hermeneutic and ontological effects, but its potential for agonistic exchange—an aspect that Bakhtin himself was loathe to acknowledge.[21]

In putting forth an eclectic concept of dialogue, then, this volume thus attempts to be both revisionary and prophetic, contributing both to the continual retelling of literary history and to the enactment of new critical forms. For the proliferation of dialogic discourse has not only recontextualized these critical forms, but diversified them as well—giving rise not only to new approaches but to an essentially new genre of critical engagement. I refer here to the recent resurgence and restructuring of dialogic criticism, a form that seeks to represent the multiplicity of current criticism in terms of discrete voices within a single text. Whether such a form encompasses a single author's disparate views, or the distinct perspectives of separate commentators, it marks the revitalization of a critical mode that has remained effectively dormant since the classical era. In works of the last two decades by Stephen Greenblatt, Geoffrey Hartman, Michel Foucault, and Alan Liu,[22] the recovery of this mode defines a contemporary discourse that is simultaneously plural and discrete: one that allows for both the multivocal perspective of critical reinterpretation and the personalized commitment of the individual voice. In the present volume these genres are most directly represented in chapters by Jerome J. McGann (Anne Mack and Jay Rome) and Don H. Bialostosky; yet the essentially dialogic nature of related critical forms is apparent throughout the collection.

This volume focuses, then, on the three interlocking dimensions of dialogue we have outlined: part I delineates dialogic interactions between voices of a single text; part II traces such exchanges on an intertextual level; and part III locates both kinds of exchange in the dialogue between speakers, authors, and readers. As we have noted, however, such divisions are more a matter of relative emphasis than exclusivity; indeed, the interpenetration between each of these dialogic modes is what defines the very term. Yet the foregoing groupings prove revealing when we begin to compare the particular focus and approach toward dialogism of each essay.

In part I ("Dialogue within Works"), for instance, Timothy Austin stresses how the dialogue between poetic voices within Percy Shelley's "Ozymandias" simultaneously re-creates a larger, extratextual dialogue with history. In chapter 1, "Narrative Transmission: Shifting Gears in Shelley's 'Ozymandias,'" Austin focuses on the dialogue among the sonnet's overlapping voices—the points of view implied by figures like the narrator, traveler, sculptor, author, and reader. What these voices have in common, he suggests, is the attempt to represent Ozymandias's history as an artistic construct, abstracted from actual events. In tracing the sonnet's critical evolution, for example, Austin shows how Shelley subverts the reader's ability to locate the sources, allusions, and identities behind both the Egyptian king and the traveller who tells his story. Throughout the lyric, both alleged reportage and fictional narration turn out to be "historically elusive and factually unreliable." Yet what such elusiveness reveals, Austin suggests, is the relativity of artistic endeavors to re-create history, to effect a dialogue with temporality. For such dialogues with the past must perpetually reinvent the historical figures they depict—must continually, in the sculptor's terms, re-"tell" and re-"read" their subjects.

Indeed, much as the traveler's historical narration turns out to be suspect, the sculptor's ability to represent the same events comes up against a parallel slippage. In portraying ekphrastic art with terms like "tell" and "read," Shelley not only stresses the narrative nature of artistic imitation but also calls into question the entire process whereby such narration attempts to represent history—to sustain dialogue with the redacted past, with former voices. Such narration is finally a matter of not facticity but fluidity: poetic dialogues with history must, again, be cyclically re-created, rather than inscribed within the constraints of chronological recapitulation. Even direct quotation is shaped and revised by such dialogic processes as poetic translation and artistic license. Narration in general—and historical narration in particular—must necessarily "refashion what it seems only to repeat."

In chapter 2, "The Power of Speech: Dialogue as History in the Russian *Primary Chronicle*," Rachel May develops this concept of dialogue as simultaneously intratextual and transhistorical. In her discussion of the *Primary Chronicle*—a Slavic text that covers sociopolitical events of Kievan *Rus'*—May suggests that the tendency for such medieval history narratives to incorporate direct speech signifies more than its common designation as a mere dramatic device or structural feature. Instead, she argues, the use of such direct quotation testifies to the cultural power of speech during this period, in that performative phrases, forced quotation, and false attribution become synecdoches for political force.

This force manifests itself most effectively, for instance, when one character deceives another into repeating a toast, grant, or order that carries a different meaning in another context. In such cases, May shows how the power of various speakers derives from their ability to manipulate clashes between literal and conventional meanings. For these characters, speech *is* action: dialogue embodies power because of its status as an intentional agent, an arbiter of events. In May's terms, "A hierarchy of 'powers of speech' emerges: at the top stand those who speak their own words and realize them in action, as well as those who put words in others' mouths; then come those who are silent; and last those whose speech is either ineffective or has undesired results." Within such a hierarchy, then, the right and ability to speak— as well as to interpret hidden meanings—confers authority for a host of characters, including warriors, rulers, and even a speaking God. As a result, displays of eloquence tend to legitimize both religious prophets and political leaders. In terms of dialogic modes, the speech acts that authorize such figures take many forms, including treaties, wills, toasts, betrothals, and other oral agreements. On a religious level, they encompass such testaments as baptisms, prayers, confessions, prophecies, and vows.

May then goes on to discuss how the historian-chronicler also partakes of dialogue, both with the reader (or listener) and with past voices. "By invoking the words of powerful or saintly characters from the past," she suggests, "the chronicler is himself engaging in a kind of dialogue with those luminaries." Then, in the final section of her essay, May brings her argument to bear on several larger issues concerning the textualization of orality, the legitimization of vernaculars, and the narratization of history. Here, she discusses the *Primary Chronicle* as a transitional form between oral and literate cultures. In this context, her argument casts light on such questions as the narrative depiction of spatiality, the temporal uses of "shifters," and the affective use of deictics to shift the reader (or listener) into the dialogic space of the speaking character. At the same time, such oralistic features also illuminate the dialogic foundation of the *Chronicle's* political discourse, as demonstrated in passages where the envoys quoted are regarded as dialogic embodiments of the rulers they represent. May then extends this approach to the oralistic dimensions of historical narrative, including the uses of formulaicity, memorableness, and interpolated speech acts. In so doing, she is able to situate the chronicle's narrative form and distinctive style within several contemporary theories of historiography and translation. Ultimately, she argues, the chronicle's status as a written document serves to subvert the oralistic, performative power it sets out to represent.

Chapter 3, John P. Farrell's "Crossroads to Community: *Jude the Obscure* and the Chronotope of Wessex" shares May's concerns with how dialogue can instantiate both physical space and historical redaction. Farrell begins with Bakhtin's concept of the chronotope, that "time-space" locus which, by focusing narrative events or "materializing time in space," enables the "concretizing of representation." Farrell then applies the concept to Thomas Hardy's *Jude the Obscure*, in which the county of Wessex embodies this chronotopic locus. As Jude moves from Christminster to Aldbrickham and finally to "Elsewhere," his Wessex travels come to represent both his own alienation as a solitary consciousness and the thematic yearning for return in the novel. Such returns are also figured in the many crossings, crossroads, and intersections throughout the novel, as characters cross and recross their own paths, their historical pasts, and the pasts of other characters.

Jude's ultimate response to both his isolate self and his failed returns is a kind of global dialogism. This final, intersecting dialogue is not only topographic and historiographic, but also linguistic and intertextual—encompassing Jude's relations to such voices as the novel's ironic narrator, its Father Time character, and even the mytho-historical figures of Tristram and Job. Indeed, Jude's dialogized voices (and texts)—his world's "Hebraic, Hellenic, Arthurian, Gothic, Victorian, and modernist striations"—constitute a response to the monologic narrative of the novel. In the end, writes Farrell, "Jude himself becomes a crossroads," as his solitary self-dissolution comes up against the dialogic recognition of a "communal consciousness"—a "social construction that resists the . . . alienation of the Victorian socio-economic state."

This reapplication of dialogism to the sociological and spatial becomes, in Paul Friedrich's "Dialogue in Lyric Narrative," chapter 4, an extension to the cross-generic and grammatical. Bakhtin, of course, begins many of his generic characterizations of dialogism with the novel and then goes on to complicate the dialogic paradigm with a series of other "novelized genres." In much the same way, Friedrich begins by defining lyric poetry in terms of its relative paucity of quoted dialogue, and then complicates this generic distinction by characterizing the fundamentally dialogic dimensions of various lyric forms. Whereas most lyric poetry incorporates dialogism by addressing an implicit "you," several intermediate forms create parallel effects by either representing conversation (as in the eclogue) or including indirect or partial vestiges of address (as in the "addressed monologue"). Friedrich brings out much of this generic expansiveness by playing upon the exchange between the "deep, underlying" sense of dialogism (Bakhtinian, anthropological, and so on) and the "overt," conversational representation of quoted dialogue (empirical, practical, and pragmatic).

The relatively rare appearance of this latter, literal dialogue within lyric poetry leads Friedrich to focus on two nineteenth-century poets distinguished by their combination of both traditionally lyric modes and more dialogic forms: Robert Frost and the Russian lyricist, Nikolay Nekrasov. Both poets manage to blend—and exploit the tension between—the usual lyric, in which the author's voice normally strips language of individual intentions and voices, and the novel, in which multiple voices intersect within a dialogized "ideological center." For instance, whereas Frost, in a poem like "The Death of the Hired Man," introduces dialogism by denoting multiple interlocutors, Nekrasov, in "Orina, the Soldier's Mother," achieves a parallel effect by exploiting Russian suffixes that variously connote kinship, collectivity, second-person reference, and pastoral interchange.

Both poets choose to include types of emotionality, colloquialism, and voice that are normally deemphasized within lyric forms; they do this by incorporating diverse kinds of modal shifts into their poetry—including those interrogative, imperative, subjunctive, hortatory, and minatory moods that "at least create the illusion of cutting through the relatively artificial or high-flown language of lyric poetry." (At its most intense level of feeling, however, much lyric poetry—even that of Nekrasov—dispenses with several grammatical markers of this modal emotionality, as demonstrated by Friedrich's analysis of the Russian affective suffixal system.) At the same time, Friedrich notes that these modal switches into dialogism also entail "a shift from communication between a lyric 'I' and an addressed 'you,' into a minidrama, where at least two represented interlocutors are exchanging quoted words in a kind of reenactment." Ultimately, such shifts into lyric dialogism involve two opposing movements: they draw readers closer to the text by sociolinguistically approximating characters, and they simultaneously distance readers through the use of dramaturgical modes.

In part II ("Dialogue between Works"), the intratextual dialogics of part I are again crucial, yet they are mirrored and expanded by an emphasis on parallel intertextual dialogues—on exchanges that reach between works or, in Bakhtin's words, "across time and space." In chapter 5, "Dialogics of the Lyric: A Symposium on Wordsworth's "Westminster Bridge" and "Beauteous Evening," for instance, Don H. Bialostosky traces both the intra- and intertextual dimensions of these two celebrated sonnets. He begins by pointing out the tendency of both the New Critics and their present inheritors to ignore precedent utterances rather than responding to and revoicing them within their literary arguments. Much as the New Critics envision the lyric as an isolated poetic voice, so their critical precepts tend to neglect the prior interpretive accounts of the poems they discuss. Using the rhetorical model of the symposium, then, Bialostosky links or dialogizes seven separate readings of the two sonnets into a kind of intertextual conversation—an "*account* of previous utterances on a topic selected from a larger field." He thus situates these apparently divergent readings within a dialogic matrix, one that interpolates their specific responses to one another.

Bialostosky's symposium form does not lend itself to ready summation, but its place in this collection becomes clear when we rehearse its complex argument. He initially points out how Cleanth Brooks's reading of "Westminster Bridge" misses the personified assumptions behind the concept of "paradox." Unlike Brooks, he sets up a social, dialogic definition of paradox in which the "dox" (posited belief or opinion) is variously crossed, supplanted, and supplemented by the implied voices in Wordsworth's sonnets. Bialostosky then extends this social, response-based approach by contrasting it with Michael Riffaterre's reading of Wordsworth. For Riffaterre, the language of "Westminster Bridge" strikes the reader as the individual's specific, semiotic "idiolect" interacting with the broader "sociolect." For Bakhtin, however, such a sociolect cannot be divorced from the individual's idiolect since, in his terms, the "'I' can realize itself in discourse, only when dependent on the 'we'"—a "we" that is "concrete, filled with specific content and accented as an individual utterance." This "I," too, manifests itself not in terms of abstract semiotic codes and superfluous grammatical features but, instead, in relation to the poetic speaker's actual situation and responses—to the varying "overtones" and full richness of "living human speech."

Bialostosky then turns to the Chicago School and begins by contrasting Bakhtin's concept of "speech performance" as an object of poetic imitation with R. S. Crane's subordination of such speech in favor of feeling, moral choice, or action. He also contrasts the Chicago critics' uneasiness about discussing poetic "theme" with Bakhtin's focus on the term as the full, concrete sociohistorical scope of an utterance (as opposed to the isolated, reproducible linguistic elements that constitute its "meaning"). In Norman Maclean's view, for instance, such linguistic elements are made to fit a procrustean, reproducible "meaning," while missing the Bakhtinian "theme" of the poem as a response to a particular characterized child, presented in a genre similar to that of "Anecdote for Fathers" and "We Are Seven."

Bialostosky next uses Bakhtin to resist Kenneth Burke's analytical reliance on rhetorical reductions, grammatical categories, and poetic stasis. He opposes Burke's bilateral distinction between "scene" (generally the "non-verbal") and "agent" (the "verbal") to Bakhtin's focus on the poetic "*product of the social interaction of three components:—the speaker* (author), *the listener* (reader), *and the one of whom* (or of which) *they speak* (the hero)." This approach enables Bialostosky not only to question the verbal/nonverbal dichotomy but also to explicate Bakhtin's tripartite purview—one that recognizes the material voices of speaker, listener (such as the child in "Beauteous Evening"), and hero, who in this sonnet is actually the "irreducible otherness" of holy language.

Bialostosky then revoices Charles Molesworth's rhetorical approach to "Westminster Bridge" and suggests that one must examine not only Wordsworth's republican ideology of the time but also the *language* of this ideology, as manifested in the public voice of the poet's political sonnets. By bringing out the dialogic possibilities of such rhetorical readings, moreover, Bialostosky is able to reconsider the speaker's utterance as a Bakhtinian speech genre with the city as its hero, fellow citizens as its listeners, and God as its addressee. Finally, Judith W. Page's feminist interpretation of "Beauteous Evening" maps Wordsworth's privatistic concerns onto the same poetic elements, so that the "adult speaker becomes a father evading 'his particular responsibilities to his illegitimate daughter Caroline,' his religious language becomes 'patriarchal religious language,' and his closing gesture becomes one of placing 'Caroline in the hands of God—a substitute father for the father Wordsworth knows he will never be' or even, in consigning her to 'Abraham's bosom,' symbolically killing the child."

Bialostosky's dialogue among critical texts is again refigured in Deborah Tannen's dialogue among linguistic ones—that is, among sociolinguistic schools that recall and reframe Bakhtin's concerns with quotidian language, echoic interchange, and the interaction of oral and written genres. In chapter 6, "Involvement as Dialogue: Linguistic Theory and the Relation between Conversational and Literary Discourse," Tannen first considers why, in their search for a model of linguistic theory, literary theorists have turned to transformational grammar rather than to the language fields of discourse analysis, linguistic anthropology, and sociolinguistics in general. In fact, she argues, it is these latter fields that support, extend, and elaborate upon Bakhtin's theories, far more than does the dominant paradigm of generative approaches to language.

Tannen accordingly discusses the work of several contemporary sociolinguists, philologists, and language philosophers whose approaches both resonate with and expand upon Bakhtinian concepts. She explains how, in the same way that Bakhtin challenges his contemporary linguists' overemphasis of Saussurean system and theoretist faith, Paul Friedrich and others question the formalist overreliance on rule ordering, discrete units, and context-free analysis. She also describes how Gary Saul Morson and Caryl Emerson's discussion of Bakhtin's emphasis on "the everyday, the ordinary" invokes current sociolinguistic concerns with everyday language use rather than sentence-based grammars. In much the same way, she traces how Bakhtin's concepts of interactive utterances and cross-fertilizing speech genres resonate with A. L. Becker's discussions of "remembered prior texts."

Tannen then extends this comparative analytic to a host of other linguistic approaches. She shows how Bakhtin's doubts about the Humboldtian derogation of real-life, contextual features accords with the work of Dell Hymes, John Gumperz, and Shirley Brice Heath—all of whom argue for the crucial role of language's communicative and cultural contexts. She also demonstrates how Bakhtin's ideas about traditional and other preexistent speech genres reflects directly on concepts of linguistic formulaicity discussed by Dwight Bolinger, Wallace Chafe, Adam Makkai, and herself. Finally, she analyzes how Bakhtin's valorization of not one speaker but his or her relation to other participants in speech communication parallels the work of anthropological linguists such as Frederick Erickson, Thomas Kochman, Ron and Susan Scollon, and herself.

Tannen goes on to analogize her own findings on the relation between ordinary conversation and literary discourse to Bakhtin's discussion of how oral "primary genres" are "absorbed" and "digested" by "secondary genres" such as novels and theater. "Fictional dialogue seems 'real' by a process of synecdoche," she argues, as "literary conversations echo both other literary conversations and remembered conversations from real life." For Tannen, this oral-literary connection is further exemplified by what she calls cross-genre "involvement strategies"—that is, listener and reader involvement deriving from such features as repetition, details, rhythmic ensemble, "constructed dialogue," and audience participation in sensemaking. She then concludes by applying this model to both literary and conversational re-creations of the same event, as seen in the recorded conversations and published stories of the Greek writer, Lilika Nakos.

Tannen's dialogic linkage between literary and oral modes also accords with my own liaison between Byron's specifically poetic voices and the oral gossip, rumor, and cant of the Regency. In chapter 7, "'The Bard I Quote From': Byron, Bakhtin, and the Appropriation of Voices," I argue that the self-exiled Byron actually conjures these distant voices—as well as the written texts of his critics—by instantiating an expatriate dialogue within his own poetry. Such a dialogue deploys a multivoiced, polyphonic style in order to represent three discrete kinds or "levels" of discourse, which together constitute the dialogic strata of *Don Juan*. On the first level, Byron's narrative dialogism serves to represent the divergent and rifted aspects of the Byronic self. This layered selfhood is most apparent in the character Juan who, in one sense, is no more than the sum of the voices around him, an aggregate of reported stories—so that as the poem ends he has been constituted by the vocal "fame" which has accrued about him. For Byron, however, such dialogism sustains not only self-consciousness but ongoing self-criticism; it enables him both to separate and to listen to his remarkably divergent selves, within the context of ontological interchange.

On the second level, Byron's dialogism enables him to *reconstruct* and encounter the language of his literary contemporaries by representing them as poetic discourse. Such poetic voices come to emblematize collective judgment, what Byron variously refers to as "circulating scandals," "public feeling," and, most cogently, personal "fame." When Byron brings such voices into *Don Juan*, they become the literary equivalent of his contemporaries' rumor, hearsay, and cant—so that the poem itself becomes a rhetorical arena for both the reproduction and the parody of belletristic discourse. Yet by repeating this discourse himself, Byron also demonstrates that such scandals are nothing more than a reiteration of voices; indeed, repetition renders them predictable, habitual, and ultimately unremarkable.

Finally, on the third level, dialogic modes enable Byron to represent the entire scope of what he often refers to as Regency "Society," manifested in the casuistic voices of gossip and critique. By re-creating and parodying the discourse of this society, Byron can appropriate it, delimit it, and even begin to rise above it. In another sense, however, Byron has also joined the discourse of his milieu: he has fashioned this literary world in his own image. For by voicing the mockeries and complaints of his detractors, he necessarily introduces his own retort, juxtaposes both invective and rejoinder—and thereby places himself in *dialogue* with Regency voices. In recreating the discourse of the "Society" he has abandoned, he paradoxically reenters it on his own terms. In this context, Byron specifically designs his dialogism for a rhetorical inclusiveness of his readers—creating a text that anticipates, incorporates, and conjures its own response. This polyphonic design also mandates a series of hermeneutic processes, including communal interpretation, Horatian argument, and Socratic dialogue.

Chapter 8, "Marxism, Romanticism, and Postmodernism: An American Case History," addresses some of the same dialogic interactions between text, society, and Byron's readers. In it, Anne Mack and Jay Rome (!) offer a piece of ongoing critical dialogue that asks whether Marxist thought—with its emphasis on societal contradiction, radical change, and an at times strict historical determinism—can be reconciled with its image within American literary studies, an institution that has traditionally stressed hermeneutic pluralism, reformist change, and critical ambiguity. That is, what happens to Marxist thought when it becomes a variable value, a new formalism, another method or set of analytical tools?

The authors go on to apply this critical dualism to a critique of Jerome J. McGann, whose work bears crucial affinities with and departures from Marxist thought. For McGann, literary works are essentially events, acts of representation that in turn involve specific investigative procedures. As a result, criticism's structure resembles a "double helix, an interconnected investigation of the textual history of the work, on the one hand, and the reception history on the other." What is more, each of these "operations, according to McGann, always and inevitably reveal a Bakhtinian heteroglossia," with manifold voices composing the linguistic "text," its material "versions," global constitution, and reception history. It is this complex interaction, moreover, that marks literary events not merely with classic Marxist "contradictions" and Hegelian determinacy but with "patterns of congruence and incongruence, consequence and inconsequence"—the fractal "determinacy of atomization and randomness." And as dynamic social processes—acts or "deeds of language" within society—these literary events are by definition neither autonomous, nor disinterested, nor linguistically self-contained.

Thus the dialogic interaction between a work's textual and reception histories comes to constitute the social subject of literary study. The authors then go on to allegorize this social process—to perpetuate the critical activity of the social subject—by presenting two acts of interpretation that illustrate McGann's view of the social text. The first of these, on Byron's "Fare Thee Well," suggests that the complex meanings of the poem reveal themselves only in the context of its socially situated dialogue—its "bibliographical, productive, and reception histories." In particular, Byron's multiple voices in producing the poem, as well as the multiple audiences it reaches, instantiate a social text that is finally beyond any originary poet's control. Finally, the second act of interpretation embedded in the dialogue addresses the opening passage of Robert Frost's "Stopping by Woods on a Snowy Evening." Here, the authors query both Frost's "multiplied text"—encompassing its grammatical variants, diverse contexts, and readers' textual codes—and the Bakhtinian communicative exchange and heteronomy of the poem.

In part III ("Dialogue between Speakers, Readers, and Authors"), we find many of the same forms of dialogue under consideration, yet with an even greater emphasis on contemporary, real-life speakers, investigators, and readers—readers of, for instance, Kafka and Bakhtin, as well as of the English essay. Hence in chapter 9, "The Essay in English: Readers and Writers in Dialogue," Shirley Brice Heath again traces the dialogic contextualization of what amounts to the social text, though her own paradigm stresses both the historical genesis and the present readership of the English essay. For Heath, moreover, this dialogism inheres in the essay's early connections with other interactive genres, particularly the letter and the journal. By rehistoricizing the genre, she demonstrates how, in variants like the scientific essay, the "elemental form . . . lay in the earlier letters of those correspondents who had used letters for debates, comparative observations, and reports on experiments."

Heath's analysis thus serves to link the historical trajectory of the essay with the social and economic development of conversation. Both emerge as the "product of the leisure of the higher social classes and of a cultural confidence engendered by power in society's institutions of governance and finance." Likewise, both essayists and conversationalists rely not on rhetorical closure but on digression, observation, and an Emersonian openness and intimacy that enables an audience to enter their respective dialogues.

In Bakhtin's terms, then, the essay abjures the "semantic finiteness and calcification" of fixed, "authoritative discourse." As a result, the genre's historical form is necessarily at odds with its pedagogical incarnation in the twentieth century—a version in which specialized, methodical authority subverts the conversational, "back-and-forth" movement of the form's multiple voices. Despite this multiplicity, however, Heath goes on to stress what she terms the "semantic unity" of such diverse voices, a "boundedness" that persists even amongst "contradictory or sharply divergent" personae.

For Michael Holquist, though, this social multiplicity of voices has also tended to raise the specter of cultural relativity. In response, his "Bakhtin and Beautiful Science: The Paradox of Cultural Relativity Revisited," chapter 10, expands on a central precept of dialogism—what Bakhtin terms the "outsideness" required to understand a foreign culture—in order to confront the vexed problem of relativity. Holquist ultimately delineates the extremes of this problem, locating us between the endless regress of cultural difference and the colonialist essentialism of authority.

Holquist's answer to this dilemma is to focus on the human body as the locus of cultural investigation, as a heuristic encompassing Bakhtin's lifelong fascination with both the historical "situatedness of perception" and the overall nature of the biological sciences. Only the human body—the sign paradoxically representing both cultural communality and individual uniqueness, particularity, and historicity— can offer that combination of "sameness and difference" necessary to anthropologi- cal understanding. Such a somatic sign not only instantiates the paradox of cul- tural relativism but also offers the kind of third-party "outsideness" that "will let us distinguish between various cultures effectively and coherently." It provides a "rela- tive universal"—the "gift of our own otherness."

The foundation of this somatic capacity for distinguishing between cultures arises from the fact that, by virtue of its inherent separateness, the human body must encounter, perceive, and eventually come to know the world through application of the scientific, experimental method. Despite Anglo-American reservations about such a method, Holquist demonstrates how revolutionary Soviets in general—and Bakhtin in particular—use it to model the interactive, qualitative, indeterminate, and value-discrimination aspects of culture. Deprived of such a method, we are con- demned to the kind of "utmost localization" represented by Kafka's "In the Penal Colony," where the torture of the state and the tyranny of writing imprison offend- ers in a horribly particularized space and time.

This problematization of dialogic concepts, implications, and constraints also lies at the heart of chapter 11, John R. Searle's "Conversation as Dialogue." Here, Searle considers how the clearly defined, constitutive, and constrained rules that govern speech acts might be applied to dialogue—to the series of actions that constitute con- versation. Inasmuch as conversation extends beyond the single speech act to a series of statements and rejoinders, Searle begins by asking which speech acts actually an- ticipate, and even determine, particular responses. This approach to what Bakhtin terms the "addressivity" of the utterance leads him to analyze how speech acts might specifically constrain the scope of possible appropriate responses, as appears to occur with bets, invitations, and what linguists often call "adjacency pairs"—including ques- tion/answer, greeting/greeting, and offer/acceptance or rejection.

Searle then goes on to examine several current theories of dialogue within this definitional context, starting with Grice's four maxims of conversation, particularly that of "relevance." Such maxims, he suggests, instantiate no *constitutive* constraints on conversational responses—that is, they provide no constraints determined by the fact that a given sequence of utterances is a conversation. Instead, any possible constraints emerge only in relation to a particular speaker's (or hearer's) shifting aims for a given conversation. Searle then turns to the work of ethnomethodologists like Sacks, Schegloff, and Jefferson, whose seminal article proposes a set of "recur- sive rules" for the dialogic phenomenon of turn-taking in conversation. He finds, though, that such statements actually function as not rules but descriptions, since they never play a causal role in the production of conversational behavior. No in- terlocutor actually follows such rules and, indeed, real-life conversation often pro- ceeds without any rules at all. For Searle, "A statement of an observed regularity, even when predictive, is not necessarily a statement of a rule."

In the end, Searle shows that we cannot apply the kind of constraints that gov- ern speech acts to conversations, since the latter are governed by a completely ex- ternal, nonconstitutive constraint—namely, the particular purpose of a specific dialogue. Searle further demonstrates that conversational purpose, intentionality, and relevance—concepts that could potentially constrain some useful rules of dialogue—actually depend upon an infinite regress of "background" presuppositions, prior intellectual capacities and collateral information not represented in the conversational structure itself. Such presuppositions are, again, nonconstitutive. Ultimately, neither semantic contents nor the interaction of these lexically based contents can delimit a rule-based poetics of dialogue.

This concern with dialogic constraints, rules, and definitions also informs chapter 12, the last chapter of the volume, Gary Saul Morson's and Caryl Emerson's "Extracts from a *Heteroglossary.*" Yet the *Heteroglossary* is also more than a set of definitions. Unlike a dictionary, it actually conjures us to reconsider many of Bakhtin's key concepts—including dialogue, polyphony, and heteroglossia—and acts to clarify the rampant misunderstandings that continue to obfuscate them. It addresses the particularly problematic nature of interpreting Bakhtin, stemming from his use of divergent definitions and neologisms, from works translated by different people at different times, and from the notorious controversy of disputed authorship involving Bakhtin, Voloshinov, and Medvedev.

Central to such misunderstandings is Bakhtin's multilayered idea of polyphony, "arguably his most original and counterintuitive concept," and the one that, in his terms, "has more than any other given rise to objections and misunderstanding." Morson and Emerson take pains, in fact, to distinguish *polyphony*, which emerged from Bakhtin's thinking about authorship and responsibility in the 1920s, from *heteroglossia*, which arose from his essays on the theory of the novel in the early 1930s. Whereas heteroglossia refers to the "diversity of speech styles in a language," the concept of polyphony encompasses an approach to narrative, a theory of creative process, and a representation of human freedom. In Bakhtin's terms, the polyphonic author is like "Goethe's Prometheus," who "creates not voiceless slaves (as does Zeus) but *free* people capable of rebelling against him."

Morson and Emerson provide a similarly illuminating distinction between Hegelian (and Marxist) *dialectics* and Bakhtin's often misunderstood concept of *dialogue*. "Dialectics is," for instance, "a manipulation of moribund abstractions; dialogue is a kind of interaction that requires live and unfinalizable people"—so that (unlike dialectic) "it requires at least two different people and two irreducibly different perspectives." Developing this latter concept, they explain how dialogue differs from tropes, ambiguity, disagreement, logical contradiction, and the "alternation of speakers (in life or in a drama), with mere 'compositionally expressed dialogue.'" Instead, the authors offer three concurrent though differing definitions of dialogue. The first definition applies to all utterances, in that they assume at least two participants, an orientation to previous utterances, and a shape determined from the outset by both speaker and listener (whether present or potential). The second definition involves parody and other "double-voiced" utterances; and the third denotes a "vision of truth" that "can only be represented by a conversation," by "something that by its very nature demands many voices and points of view."

The authors go on to reconsider and clarify a host of Bakhtinian concepts, including potential meanings, semantic possibilities, and intentional potentials; third person; truth of one's own self-consciousness versus secondhand truth and evalua-tion; innerly persuasive discourse or word; first and second stylistic lines of the European novel; and unnovelistic novel.

As a whole, then, these chapters argue for a redefinition of literary meaning—one that is communal, interactive, and vocatively created. They demonstrate that literary meaning is not rendered by a single narrator, nor even by a solitary author, but is incrementally constructed and exchanged. It is not so much conveyed as accrued over time and space.

Notes

1. The implications of dialogism for such fields as anthropology, psychology, and dance have been respectively treated by Maranhao (1990), Shotter (1992), and Croce (1989, 1988).

2. Within the field of discourse analysis, one finds such extensions of Bakhtin's theo-ries in, for instance, Tannen (1989); within the study of classical rhetoric, see Maranhao (1990) and, less directly, Swearingen (1991). For potential applications within the field of psychoanalysis, see Leavy (1980).

3. Among the many post-Freudian theories of influence, see, for instance, Bloom (1975, 1982), as well as Paulson's (1983) analysis of Wordsworth's overarching forebears. Related linguistic studies include Carter and Simpson (1988), Tannen (1989), and Goodman (1971). Finally, the philosophical approaches of Habermas (1979), Searle (1969), Petrey (1990), and Geis (1995) bear at least indirectly on many of the dialogic implications noted in this introduction. For related reception studies, see note 18.

4. For Bakhtin's analysis of addressivity, see "The Problem of Speech Genres," 94–95, 91; for Bloom's notion of misprision, see *The Anxiety of Influence*, esp. chapter 1.

5. For more on the feminist implications of dialogic theory, see both Kristeva (1969) and Bauer and McKinstry (1991).

6. See Austin (1989), as well as notes 3 and 4 above.

7. Fogel (1985), for instance, points out the interactional approaches of these theo-rists; see esp. 7, 221, 224–26, 236–37.

8. For examples of the first approaches to such intertextuality, see Kristeva (1969), Barthes (1981), and Riffaterre (1978, 1980).

9. McGann (1985) begins his analyses as a response both to Bakhtin's essay "Discourse in Life and Discourse in Art" and to *The Formal Method in Literary Scholarship*. While more recent scholarship has challenged the supposition that Bakhtin wrote the latter work—see Morson and Emerson (1989, 1990)—the general theories and principles cited by McGann are clearly part of Bakhtin's overall concept of literary interaction and social dialogue.

10. Ejxenbaum (1926, 9); also quoted in Pratt (1977, 4).

11. Pratt (1977, 22). In her first chapter Pratt traces the evolution of these twentieth-century literary movements to set "poetic language" apart from spoken discourse. In lin-guistic circles, however, the same period saw a focusing on the spoken word, with written language characterized as both derivative and secondary (see Saussure [1966], Sapir [1921], and Bloomfield [1933], as discussed in Chafe and Tannen [1987, 383]). More recently, the *relation* between the two forms of discourse has been the focus of more descriptive research by Havelock (1963), Goody (1977), Chafe (1982), and Ong (1982). Finally, Banfield (1982) constructs a more formal linguistic model to distinguish between spoken discourse and a particular literary style, *style indirect libre*.

12. See, for example, Lord (1960).

13. For instances of this literary movement, see Derrida (1973, 1978). Other theoretical studies include Kneale (1986) and Porter (1986).

14. For examples of such conclusions, see Hirsch (1972, 260) and Fowler (1970, 183–84), as quoted in Smith (1978, 206–207 n.4). For recent research that compares the two forms of discourse descriptively, see such linguistic studies as Biber (1988), Tannen (1982), and Heath (1983).

15. Barbara Hernnstein Smith (1978, 24, 25); see also Bialostosky's (1984, 98) analysis of Smith's distinction.

16. Bakhtin (1986b, 124).

17. Wesling (1981, 81).

18. See, for instance, Austin (1989), Tannen (1989), and Quasha (1977).

19. See Bakhtin (1986a, 73). In presenting this synoptic view of Bakhtin's theories, I stress his later essays as the most developed formulations of the concepts of "addressivity" and "assimilation." For earlier perspectives on these concepts, see Bakhtin (1984).

20. See Morson and Emerson (1990), esp. pp. 49–50, 55–57, 132–33; 34–35, 44, 85–87, 107–12, 266–68, 297–98, 460–62, 467.

21. For analyses of the agonistic, even coercive, potential of dialogic forms, see Ong (1981), Fogel (1985, 1–38), and Macovski (1994, 3–40); on the potentially hermeneutic and ontological operations of dialogue, see Macovski (1992, 99–169).

22. See Liu (1989, 500).

Works Cited

Austin, Timothy. "Narrative Discourses and Discoursing in Narratives: Analyzing a Poem from a Sociolinguistic Perspective." *Poetics Today* 10:4 (Winter 1989): 703–28.

Bakhtin, Mikhail. "The Problem of Speech Genres." In *Speech Genres and Other Late Essays*, translated by Vern W. McGee, edited by Caryl Emerson and Michael Holquist. Austin: University of Texas Press, 1986a.

———. "The Problem of the Text in Linguistics, Philology, and the Human Sciences: An Experiment in Philosophical Analysis." In *Speech Genres and Other Late Essays*, translated by Vern W. McGee, edited by Caryl Emerson and Michael Holquist. Austin: University of Texas Press, 1986b.

———. *Speech Genres and Other Late Essays*. Translated by Vern W. McGee. Edited by Caryl Emerson and Michael Holquist. Austin: University of Texas Press, 1986c.

———. *Problems of Dostoevsky's Poetics*. Translated and edited by Caryl Emerson. Minneapolis: University of Minnesota Press, 1984.

Banfield, Ann. *Unspeakable Sentences*. London: Routledge and Kegan Paul, 1982.

Barthes, Roland. "Theory of the Text." In *Untying the Text: A Post-Structuralist Reader*, edited by Robert Young. London: Routledge and Kegan Paul, 1981.

Bauer, Dale M. and Susan Janet McKinstry, editors. *Feminism, Bakhtin, and the Dialogic*. Albany: State University of New York Press, 1991.

Bialostosky, Don H. *Making Tales: The Poetics of Wordsworth's Narrative Experiments*. Chicago: University of Chicago Press, 1984.

Biber, Douglas. *Variation across Speech and Writing*. Cambridge: Cambridge University Press, 1988.

Bloom, Harold. *Agon: Towards a Theory of Revisionism*. New York: Oxford University Press, 1982.

——. *The Anxiety of Influence: A Theory of Poetry*. New York: Oxford University Press, 1975.

Bloomfield, L. *Language*. New York: Holt, 1933.

Buber, Martin. *I and Thou*. New York: Scribners, 1970.

Carter, Ronald, and Paul Simpson. *Language, Discourse, and Literature: An Introductory Reader in Discourse Stylistics*. Boston: Unwin Hyman, 1988.

Chafe, Wallace. "Integration and Involvement in Speaking, Writing, and Oral Literature." In *Spoken and Written Language: Exploring Orality and Literacy*, edited by Deborah Tannen. Norwood, N.J.: Ablex, 1982.

Chafe, Wallace, and Deborah Tannen. "The Relation between Written and Spoken Language." *Annual Reviews in Anthropology* 16 (1987): 383–407.

Croce, Arlene. "Cotillon (ballet review)." *New Yorker* 12 December 1988, pp. 143–45.

——. "Mark Morris Goes Abroad" and "Grand pas Classique." *New Yorker* 16 January 1989, pp. 61–64.

Derrida, Jacques. *Speech and Phenomena, and Other Essays on Husserl's Theory of Signs*. Translated by David B. Allison. Evanston: Northwestern University Press, 1973.

——. *Writing and Difference*. Translated by Alan Bass. Chicago: University of Chicago Press, 1978.

Ejxenbaum, Boris M. "The Theory of the Formal Method." In *Readings in Russian Poetics: Formalist and Structuralist Views*, translated by I. R. Titunik, edited by Ladislav Matejka and Krystyna Pomorska. Cambridge: MIT Press, 1971.

Fogel, Aaron. *Coercion to Speak: Conrad's Poetics of Dialogue*. Cambridge: Harvard University Press, 1985.

Foucault, Michel. *The Archaeology of Knowledge*. Translated by A. M. Sheridan Smith. New York: Pantheon Books, 1972.

Fowler, Roger. "The Structure of Criticism and the Language of Poetry." In *Contemporary Criticism*, Stratford-upon-Avon Studies no. 12, edited by Malcolm Bradbury and David Palmer. London: Edward Arnold, 1970.

Gadamer, Hans-Georg. *Dialogue and Dialectic*. New Haven, Conn: Yale University Press, 1980.

——. *Truth and Method*. London: Sheed and Ward, 1979.

Geis, Michael L. *Speech Acts and Conversational Interaction*. New York: Cambridge University Press, 1995.

Goodman, Paul. *Speaking and Language*. New York: Random House, 1971.

Goody, J. *The Domestication of the Savage Mind*. Cambridge: Cambridge University Press, 1977.

Greenblatt, Stephen. *Renaissance Self-Fashioning: From More to Shakespeare*. Chicago: University of Chicago Press, 1980.

Habermas, Jurgen. *Communication and the Evolution of Society*. Boston: Beacon Press, 1979.

Hartman, Geoffrey H. "The Interpreter: A Self-Analysis." In *The Fate of Reading and Other Essays*. Chicago: University of Chicago Press, 1975.

Havelock, E. A. *Preface to Plato*. Cambridge: Harvard University Press, 1963.

Heath, Shirley Brice. *Ways with Words*. Cambridge: Cambridge University Press, 1983.

Hirsch, E. D., Jr. "Three Dimensions of Hermeneutics." *New Literary History* 3 (1972): 245–61.

Kneale, J. Douglas. "Wordsworth's Images of Language: Voice and Letter in *The Prelude*." *PMLA* 101 (May 1986): 351–61.

Kristeva, Julia. *Semeiotike: Recherches pour une semanalyse*. Paris: Seuil, 1969.

Leavy, Stanley. *The Psychoanalytic Dialogue*. New Haven, Conn: Yale University Press, 1980.

Liu, Alan. *Wordsworth: The Sense of History*. Stanford, Calif.: Stanford University Press, 1989.

Lord, Albert B. *The Singer of Tales*. Cambridge: Harvard University Press, 1960.

McGann, Jerome J. *The Beauty of Inflections: Literary Investigations in Historical Method and Theory*. New York: Oxford University Press, 1985.

Macovski, Michael. *Dialogue and Literature: Apostrophe, Auditors, and the Collapse of Romantic Discourse*. New York: Oxford University Press, 1994.

Maranhao, Tullio. *The Interpretation of Dialogue*. Chicago: University of Chicago Press, 1990.

Morson, Gary Saul, and Caryl Emerson. *Mikhail Bakhtin: Creation of a Prosaics*. Stanford, Calif.: Stanford University Press, 1990.

————, editors. *Rethinking Bakhtin: Extensions and Challenges*. Evanston, Ill.: Northwestern University Press, 1989.

Ong, Walter J., S.J. *Fighting for Life: Contest, Sexuality, and Consciousness*. Ithaca, N.Y.: Cornell University Press, 1981.

————. *Orality and Literacy: The Technologizing of the Word*. New York: Methuen, 1982.

Paulson, Ronald. *Representations of Revolution, 1789–1820*. New Haven: Yale University Press, 1983.

Petrey, Sandy. *Speech Acts and Literary Theory*. New York: Routledge, 1990.

Porter, James I. "Saussure and Derrida on the Figure of the Voice." *MLN* 101 (1986): 857–894.

Pratt, Mary Louise. *Toward a Speech Act Theory of Literary Discourse*. Bloomington: Indiana University Press, 1977.

Prince, Gerald. *A Dictionary of Narratology*. Lincoln: University of Nebraska Press, 1987.

Quasha, George. "Dialogos: Between the Written and the Oral in Contemporary Poetry." *New Literary History* 8 (1977): 485-506.

Riffaterre, Michael. *Semiotics of Poetry*. Bloomington: Indiana University Press, 1978.

————. "La Trace de l'intertexte." *La Pensee*, no. 215 (1980): 4-18.

Sapir, E. *Language: An Introduction to the Study of Speech*. New York: Harcourt-Brace, 1921.

Saussure, F. de. *Course in General Linguistics*. Translated by W. Baskin. New York: McGraw-Hill, 1966.

Searle, John R. *Speech Acts: An Essay in the Philosophy of Language*. London: Cambridge University Press, 1969.

Shotter, John. "Bakhtin and Billig: Monological versus Dialogical Practices." *The American Behavioral Scientist* 36:1 (September/October 1992): 8-21.

Smith, Barbara Herrnstein. *On the Margins of Discourse: The Relation of Literature to Language*. Chicago: University of Chicago Press, 1978.

Swearingen, C. Jan. *Rhetoric and Irony: Western Literacy and Western Lies*. New York: Oxford University Press, 1991.

Tannen, Deborah. "Oral and Literate Strategies in Spoken and Written Narratives." *Language* 58 (1982): 1-21.

————. *Talking Voices: Repetition, Dialogue, and Imagery in Conversational Discourse*. New York: Cambridge University Press, 1989.

Wesling, Donald. "Difficulties of the Bardic: Literature and the Human Voice." *Critical Inquiry* 8 (Autumn 1981): 69-81.

PART I

DIALOGUE
WITHIN
WORKS

Narrative Transmission

Shifting Gears in Shelley's "Ozymandias"

I enjoy reading [*Rip Van Winkle*] and [appreciate] the novelty of the
format. But is it just a novelty? Why does all this structure exist? Why not
just have the story itself?

Bertram Bruce,
"A Social Interaction Model of Reading"

As the interests and concerns of theoretical linguists have changed and expanded
over several decades, their colleagues in literary studies have shown themselves adept
at finding ways to turn new insights in linguistic science to good account in the
analysis of literary language. Structuralist and transformationalist paradigms in turn
provided fertile ground for literary applications; phonological, morphological, syntactic, and semantic analyses contributed to a steadily growing body of essays and
monographs by students of the language of literature. One could have predicted,
therefore, that the more recent emergence within linguistic theory of a focus on
discourse in everyday contexts, including specifically the study of both conversation and narration, would lead in due course to assessments of the relationship
between spoken discourse and literary works.[1]

The potential for work of many kinds in this general area of interaction is striking. One approach considers "natural" discourses as they appear in literary texts of
various genres: for example, dialogue in drama, conversation in fictional prose and
in poetry, and speech in the more exclusively literary form of the dramatic monologue. A second examines literary works in their entirety as contributions to a wider
discourse directed by their respective authors either to known addressees or to a
general audience, their "readership." Where a particular text involves narration, its
methods can be compared with those typical of oral, or at least nonliterary, narratives. Where dialect, or cant, or gender-marked language appears, variationist methods can be employed to suggest functions served by such specialized languages in
literary as in (or as contrasted with) everyday contexts.

Acknowledging that the innovative emphasis in linguistic theory on discourse-level phenomena opens up many new avenues for the analysis of literary language represents but a preliminary step, however. Even exploiting some of those opportunities by undertaking discourse-based analyses of specific literary texts constitutes at best half of the story. For, as with all applications of linguistic methods in criticism, there will remain the challenge of integrating the results of linguistic investigation with other, nonlinguistic material in the search for a satisfying overall assessment of the work under consideration. Some years ago I argued vehemently that interpretive claims advanced on the basis of close linguistic (in that instance, syntactic) analysis should not be regarded as privileged a priori over those whose origins lay, for example, in biographical, historical, psychoanalytical, or feminist theory (1984, 130–31). The burden of convincing one's readers of the plausibility, coherence, and explanatory power of one's reading of a text, I insisted, weighs just as heavily on linguistic critics as on their colleagues from other intellectual backgrounds. Since that time I have become if anything still more convinced that linguistic analysis by itself (and, indeed, linguistic analysis *of any particular kind* if unsupported by parallel work from a different subarea of the discipline) will usually generate far less striking interpretive insights than analysis that is illuminated and informed by an understanding of other aspects of the work being studied.

The discussion that follows is therefore methodologically eclectic by design. It certainly employs several different approaches that would fall within most definitions of "discourse theory." But it also utilizes some straightforward, sentence-level syntactic analysis and some Jakobsonian discussion of formal patterning. From nonlinguistic fields I have borrowed ideas (or, more often, accepted challenges) formulated in the first instance by biographers and historians. What emerges, I hope, is not just a convincing reading of a much-loved text badly in need of refurbishment, but also an example of how discourse analysis can contribute in vitally important ways to a literary debate that also embraces several other critical points of view.

H. M. RICHMOND'S DESCRIPTION OF Shelley's "Ozymandias" as "a familiar and impressive poem" (1962, 65) epitomizes the not-so-benign condescension bestowed by most critics on this sonnet. Among the works of a poet most admired for his bold experiments and emotional fervor, the very strengths that make "Ozymandias" easily accessible to a broad readership have led to its virtual omission from serious studies of Shelley's poetry. Lacking the zealous indignation and ad hominem attacks of political satires such as "The Mask of Anarchy," for example, this text is often viewed as their pale shadow, Shelley's characteristic antiauthoritarian rhetoric muted in this instance both by the historical remoteness of his subject and by the restrictive nature of the sonnet form. For other commentators, attracted to Shelley by the bold formal experimentation of "Lines Written among the Euganean Hills" or "Stanzas Written in Dejection," the only mildly unconventional rhyme scheme in "Ozymandias" appears a feeble gesture toward artistic originality. Even the historical context in which the poem was written contributes to its reputation for solid (or stolid) respectability. Composed as part of a poetic parlor-game between Shelley and his good friend (but undistinguished poet) Horace Smith during the late autumn of 1817, "Ozymandias" belongs to the awkward period of "gloom and indecision" (Holmes 1974, 406) that intervened between the emotional drama of Shelley's court battle with Harriet for custody of their children and his equally traumatic decision to leave England for Italy in March 1818.

Flanked in the corpus by the inflammatory *The Revolt of Islam* on the one hand, and by "Julian and Maddalo" on the other, "Ozymandias" has at best been accorded passing mention in most comprehensive accounts of Shelley's achievements. Richard Holmes does call it "the finest sonnet he ever wrote" (1974, 410) but, as W. Van Maanen insists, such superlatives must be placed in the narrow context of "the sixteen sonnets Shelley wrote." After all, Van Maanen continues, the poem contains many apparent flaws: "[Its] opening line is almost too prosaic; the eighth line is clumsy and obscure; some of the rhymes are false" (1949, 123). And so "Ozymandias" has slipped virtually unchallenged into a quiet backwater of the poetic mainstream, constantly reanthologized by editors attracted to it, one suspects, precisely because it delivers a typically Shelleyan message in a conveniently short work while also avoiding the complexities of thought and style evident in so many of the more acclaimed texts.

For one persistent group of literary bloodhounds, however, "Ozymandias" has offered a continuing challenge. The scent they follow is laid in the very first line of the poem (the line that Van Maanen criticizes as "almost too prosaic"): "I met a traveller from an antique land." Led by J. Gwyn Griffiths in 1948, a band of literary historians have struggled in a series of notes, remarks, and replies to pin down the identity of Shelley's unnamed "traveller."[2] Their discoveries, to which I shall return later, range from the intriguing and insightful to the wildly speculative. Their discussions have, however, remained coldly antiquarian throughout, uninvolved with the emotionally fiery core of the sonnet as it is encountered by readers unaware, for the most part, of the intellectual and social history of early-nineteenth-century England.

I propose to draw on some of the better insights from each of these broad categories of critical treatment of this text and to construct from them a richer and, I believe, more satisfying reading. I shall employ some conclusions that follow quite straightforwardly from various contributions to the debate about the identity of the traveller in support of a radical revision of the thematic structure of "Ozymandias." That reassessment in turn will enable us to reevaluate some of the text's apparent technical imperfections and to reconceive "Ozymandias" as a sophisticated and even daring poetic creation. The key to achieving that ambitious goal lies in various aspects of the poem's discourse structure.

WE MAY BEGIN BY EXAMINING a passage that spans the first and second quatrains of the poem, a passage often misinterpreted or misremembered even by those who, like Richmond, would probably claim to have been "familiar" with it for many years:

> Near them, on the sand,
> Half sunk, a shattered visage lies, whose frown,
> And wrinkled lip, and sneer of cold command,
> Tell that its sculptor well those passions read
> Which yet survive, stamped on these lifeless things,
> The hand that mocked them, and the heart that fed.
>
> (3–8)

The verb *tell* that begins line 6 takes as its syntactic subject the several unattractive features of the "shattered visage" of Ozymandias's colossus: its "frown, / And wrinkled lip, and sneer of cold command." Since features (or *expressions*) such as these are normally taken to "express" human emotions—anger, sorrow, amusement—the reader might expect the direct object of *tell* in this context to enumerate some such emotions: These features *tell* (of) Ozymandias's disdain, contempt, pride. . . . And this is indeed roughly what many readers believe Shelley to have written. In fact, however, the syntactic direct object of *tell* is itself a proposition: "*that* its sculptor well those passions read / Which yet survive. . . ." Shelley focuses, that is, not on the emotions themselves, but on their realization by an anonymous stonemason and, more particularly, on the striking effectiveness with which that rendition was accomplished.[3] Not, of course, that Ozymandias's emotions are immaterial, for they still appear syntactically as the direct object of *read* in the crucial clausal complement to *tell*. Their impact upon the traveller, nevertheless, comes at second hand and can exist at all only as a result of the sculptor's inspired artistry:

| OZYMANDIAS'S PASSIONS | ←——→ | SCULPTOR'S RENDITION | ←——→ | TRAVELLER'S EXPERIENCE |

The elaborately patterned syntactic and semantic form of line 6 emphatically foregrounds Shelley's concern with the sculptor's role. One formal linguistic arrangement places the two all-important, semantically complementary verbs of transmission (*read* and *tell*) at opposite ends of the line, bracketing the mention of the sculptor himself and thus emphasizing his role as mediator:

> *Tell* that its sculptor well those passions *read*
> └————————————————————┘

At the same time, in a poem that makes heavy use of internal as well as end rhymes (for example, the series *land / stand / sand / command / hand / Ozymandias / sands*), line 6 also divides neatly into five-syllable half-lines, *tell* this time patterning with *well* to stress the excellence of the sculptor's workmanship:

> *Tell* that its sculptor *well* those passions read
> └————————————┘

Yet a third formal configuration depends on the metrical balance Shelley achieves by setting artist and subject on either side of the word that evaluates their successful collusion, so to speak, in the creative act:

> ˘ ´ ˘   ˘ ´ ˘
> its sculptor   *well*   those passions

A reading of this crucial line that is sensitive to these interlocking patterns in its linguistic form demands that we pay attention as much to the active contribution of the artist as to the passive role of Ozymandias himself.

We may also note in passing that, despite the passage's exclusive concern (in terms of reference) with the art of monumental statuary, Shelley has chosen in line 6 to employ verbs associated primarily with *verbal* communication at both levels of this complex sentence (*tell* and *read*) rather than selecting either medium-neutral terms (such as *express, render,* or *convey*) or others specifically associated with the visual arts (such as *depict, show,* or *portray*). We shall have reason to return to this observation later.

A second striking feature of the long sentence that occupies lines 3–8 of this poem is the contrast it sets up between two widely separated time frames:

> whose frown
>
> And wrinkled lip, and sneer of cold command
>
> Tell that its sculptor well *those passions read*
>
> Which yet survive, stamped on *these lifeless things,* . . .

At the ends of lines 6 and 7, Shelley again employs parallel metrical templates, this time with the purpose of inviting the reader to contrast a chronologically distant but vibrant past with the more proximate but comparatively colorless present.[4] Again, too, he deploys additional linguistic resources to enhance the precision and the impact of his point. The suffix *-less* appears on three occasions in this sonnet, each time in the context of the statue's ruined remnants (rather than in that of its original magnificence), each time in phrases that stress the extreme aridity of the wreck and its surroundings: *trunkless, lifeless,* and *boundless* (of the "bare, . . . lone and level sands"). Linked morphologically, this series stands in marked contrast to the life-affirming vocabulary associated throughout the poem with the characters and events of the earlier epoch (*mocked, fed, hand,* and *heart*). At the same time, in a conventional but deliberate way, Shelley also relies on deictic demonstratives to establish the temporal separation of the periods he describes, denoting the traveller's present with proximal deictics and the sculptor's time frame with distal ones. Besides the contrast already noted in lines 6 and 7 ("*those* passions" versus "*these* lifeless things"), the inscription on the pedestal is referred to as "*these* words,"[5] while the phrase "*that* colossal wreck" in line 13, though it seems at first to break from the distribution I have suggested by referring to the ruin (a contemporary object) with a distal demonstrative, actually reconfirms it. The most plausible semantic analysis of that phrase, I submit, takes *that* to modify *colossal* rather than *wreck,* giving us the paraphrase "the wreck of that colossus" by analogy with "that *colossus's* wreck." If this sense is granted, then a consistent scheme of temporal deixis is indeed preserved throughout the poem.

In lines 3 to 8 of "Ozymandias," then, Shelley describes how the physical remnants of a statue can transmit, even in decay, the artistry of an earlier, more vital era to the denizens of a later, less lively age. It is the artistic accomplishment of such "transmission," I stress again, at least as much as the spirit itself of that distant time, that the wreck conveys. While the passions have indeed "survive[d] . . . / The hand that mocked them," that survival is expressed only as a rider to the testimony that provides the central focus for this sonnet: the speaker's recognition that the "sculptor well those passions read." The sculptor's triumph is portrayed not as mechanical visual re-creation, not as the journeyman fashioning of a waxworks dummy, but as an original act committed by an artist whose gift is to "read" and to "tell" rather than just to mimic his subject. It is in that interplay of a text and an interpreter—implied by the reading metaphor and then cleverly driven home by the tension between the archaic sense of *mocked* meaning merely "copied" and its modern, more evaluative sense, "made fun of"—that what is most "telling" emerges. Inevitably, too, it is the product of that fusion that alone "survives" to be "read" by those who later encounter the artifact outside the context of its original creation.

That Shelley should have advanced such a radical critique of the role of the artist will surprise nobody familiar with his views on poetic theory expressed in such prose treatises as the "Preface" to *Prometheus Unbound* and the "Defence of Poetry." That the unnamed sculptor should effectively usurp Ozymandias's own role as the primary agent merely affirms, after all, the function of all artists as the true but "unacknowledged legislators" of worldly affairs (Ingpen and Peck, 1927, 7:140). What I am suggesting by way of departure from such familiar ground is that it may be appropriate to adopt this perspective in reconsidering this particular text, a text whose very obvious political message has generally overshadowed what I believe is its second (but by no means secondary) concern with the nature of artistic creativity.[6]

THUS FAR I HAVE CONCENTRATED ON Shelley's presentation of the artistic "event" that occupies the central position in "Ozymandias." We may now shift our focus, however, to an earlier section of the text and to the nameless traveller whose account of that distant event this poem purportedly relates. The full intricacies of the historical and critical debate about the traveller's identity will rapidly tire those who attempt to follow its every twist and turn; still, the question at its core is far from trivial. It might well be argued that Shelley's already striking description of Ozymandias's statue could only have benefited had he simply foregone the adumbrated account of its provenance in line 1 of the poem. One must in fact concur with William Spanos when he rates as "a very real interpretative and critical problem" the question of "why Shelley presents the tale . . . within the framework of a contemporary conversation and what artistic value is achieved by doing so" (1968, 14). Yet how are we to arrive at a solution to Spanos's "problem" unless we first establish some apparently basic information about that "framework of . . . conversation," and more specifically about the identities of the participants?

A number of commentators who have attempted this fundamental task assume the first-person narrator of the whole poem ("*I met* . . .") to be Shelley himself and the first line to have been intended literally.[7] Accordingly, they have sought to associate the traveller with some specific figure from early-nineteenth-century Britain; candidates have included several members of Shelley's immediate circle and perhaps a half-dozen antiquarians and adventurers whose exploits the poet might plausibly have learned about in the press or by attending public lectures. Minutely examining contemporary travelogues, scholars in this group have championed individuals such as Medwin (Griffiths 1948, 84) or Pococke (Richmond 1962, 68), the details of whose prose accounts might explain the precise combination of particulars that we find in Shelley's poetic rendition. Johnstone Parr (1957) even reproduces early archaeologists' maps, illustrations, and photographs to amplify his discussion of their probable influence on "Ozymandias." A recurring problem for the members of this school of thought, however, is that the statue of Ramesses II, remnants of which lay scattered in the desert sands in 1817, had been ill-treated by the elements. As Parr explains, "[In] Shelley's day the face . . . was so obliterated that no one could have discerned a 'frown,' a 'wrinkled lip,' or a 'sneer of cold command'" (1957, 32–33). No (literal) traveller whom Shelley had (literally) met, that is, could (honestly) have included such details in his account of what he had seen.

A second group of scholars have argued that the traveller should in any case be seen as a figure whom the poet had "met" only in a literary sense.[8] Initially, the most popular contender in this second category was one Diodorus Siculus (Diodorus the Sicilian), the Greek author of a world history characterized by the *New Columbia Encyclopedia* as "uncritical and unreliable," who lived during the first century B.C. We may credit Griffiths (1948) with being the first to point out Shelley's probable indebtedness to Diodorus, an association which is now uncritically enshrined in notes appended to "Ozymandias" by such frequently consulted authorities as Neville Rogers (1968, 468–69) and the editors of the *Norton Anthology of English Literature* (1979, 2: 690 n.8). But a number of challenges have since been mounted to the claim that Diodorus was Shelley's *direct* source. Several articles have shown that the relevant passage from Diodorus's history had already been translated into English repeatedly by Shelley's day. Possible intermediaries range, in fact, from Sir Walter Raleigh to the fourth (1810) edition of *The Encyclopaedia Britannica* (Notopoulos 1953, 442–43; Parr 1957, 34–35). Unfortunately, no hard evidence supports any one of these pretenders conclusively, so that James Notopoulos's confident assertion, "it is unlikely that Shelley read Diodorus in 1817" (1953, 442), actually rests on little more than the widely approved but probatively irrelevant judgment that Diodorus's *opus magnum* makes for "dull and anything but attractive reading" in the original (Van Maanen 1949, 124).

The strongest evidence in favor of identifying the traveller with Diodorus (whether directly or as mediated by an English translator) lies, in fact, within the text itself. For Diodorus describes the statue of Ozymandias in an unblemished, unweathered form—a form, that is, in which facial expression would indeed have been discernible. He also mentions prominently the hubristic inscription on the pedestal that Shelley likewise placed at the climax of his sonnet. Conversely, however, the dismembered legs and torso that Shelley describes do not accord well with Diodorus's account of a "work of art" in which, "despite [its] great bulk, neither crack nor flaw can be seen" (Murphy 1964, 63; cf. Griffiths 1948, 84). The disposition of the "trunkless legs" and of the "shattered visage" partially buried in the sand recall instead the nineteenth-century travelers' reports of the "Ramesseum" adduced by Parr and his colleagues. We appear, in short, to have reached an impasse. Neither Diodorus writing before Christ's birth nor some nineteenth-century explorer can adequately fill the traveller's shoes. The former, though in a position to report the presence of a "frown" or a "wrinkled lip," could have done so only in the context of a statue still intact (and, as a simple matter of historical fact, reported no such things); the latter would have seen only a wrecked statue altogether devoid of identifying facial features.

This standoff would indeed be troubling if we were committed to the view that "Ozymandias" is a simple political parable, Shelley's poetic cautionary tale to hubristic monarchs. The lessons of history necessarily lose much of their impact where the reliability—indeed, the very existence—of the purported historian is thrown into doubt. As I suggested earlier, however, Shelley repeatedly invites the reader to detect in this sonnet a second theme: the complex rôle played by the artist in recording and relaying historical events and characters. In this context, our inability to locate the traveller unambiguously in "real" historical time need neither surprise nor frustrate us. Our view of the "real" Ozymandias has already been distorted, however minimally, by the lens of the sculptor's "reading" and re-"telling" of that dictator's "passions." When the traveller, who faces the equally daunting challenge of transforming what he witnessed visually into words in order to (re)transmit it as a narrative, turns out to be historically elusive and factually unreliable, we merely find ourselves removed one additional step from a historical "reality" long since lost to us. Extending our previous conception of the poem as depicting a chain-of-transmission, we realize that adding one further link to that chain serves only to reveal the weakness of them all:

| OZYMANDIAS'S PASSIONS | ⟷ | SCULPTOR'S RENDITION | ⟷ | TRAVELLER'S EXPERIENCE | ⟷ | READER'S INTERPRETATION |

We may—indeed, we should—both note and learn from the ironic contrast between Ozymandias's vainglorious boasting and the ignoble fate of the colossus he ordained, Shelley insists in this poem. But in doing so, he also points out, we will be assuming that all of the intervenient artists who have "reported" either the tyrant's deeds or his appearance (whether verbally or visually) have "well . . . read" their respective originals. Absent such an assumption, the poem veers from exemplum to fable across a dividing line that is at best blurred and at worst simply nonexistent.

THIS LINE OF ARGUMENT may seem to depend too heavily on a literal-minded and picayune reconstruction of the background of a figure, the traveller, whom Shelley mentions only briefly and in an ostensibly prefatory sentence. I have already met this objection in part both by echoing Spanos's call for *some* rational explanation for Shelley's inclusion of those opening remarks in the first place and by suggesting in response that the unreliability of the traveller as a narrator rather effectively foreshadows that of the sculptor in the second quatrain. I now want to consider a further implication of our newfound skepticism about the traveller: the light it casts on the (at first glance, equally transparent) function of the other participant in the framing discourse, the individual who speaks in the text as "I."

In his admirably plain-spoken essay on "Ozymandias," Spanos astutely points out an assumption common to the work of all the contributors to the debate about the identity of the traveller described in the preceding section of this chapter. Each of those commentators, that is, takes as given "the conventional equation of author and speaker" (1968, 15). Spanos attributes the widespread, if tacit, agreement among scholars on this point to the equally "conventional [critical] perception . . . that the Romantics, especially Shelley, were committed to the personal lyrical mode" (14), but we might choose to apply his point more broadly. Surely, one might argue, it would be unreasonable to blame *any* reader for making that same assumption when the sonnet he or she is reading, a work unquestionably authored by Shelley, opens with the blunt first-person assertion "I met a traveller"?[9] I can see the naive appeal of this argument, yet I share Spanos's unease with the notion that that *initial* identification must necessarily hold sway throughout our reading (and subsequent rereadings) of this or any other poem.[10] It might be unwise to dismiss too quickly Spanos's suggestion that we need to adduce some "*authentic artistic* function" (14; my italics) for the first-person narrator in "Ozymandias," whether that function involves interpreting the narrator as Shelley himself or reconceiving him as some other speaker.

Spanos's own response to the task he set himself exploits the wide temporal and cultural gulf that separated Shelley's immediate audience from the historical figure of Ozymandias. He proposes that the text's "I" is not Shelley in propria persona but a figure loosely representative of nineteenth-century European civilization. The traveller, he argues, represents the contrasting Eastern culture. By means of the anecdote he tells about Ozymandias, Spanos suggests, the traveller hopes to induce the narrator to apply lessons learned from the collapse of another once-dominant civilization to the similarly precarious plight of the narrator's own. This interpretation is certainly stimulating. I propose to take a somewhat different direction, however, combining Spanos's useful cautiousness about the transparency of Shelley's narrator with a striking feature of Diodorus's antecedent text that has, so far as I can tell, been overlooked by all previous commentators.

Examination of the original text of Diodorus's history reveals that even Diodorus never actually saw the ruins of the Ramesseum that he carefully described for posterity. Even he was only repeating at second hand a description he had himself culled from the pages of a prior Greek chronicler, Hecataeus of Abdera, who had written two centuries before him:

> And it is not only the priests of Egypt . . . who corroborate what we have said, but also many of the Greeks who traveled to Thebes in the days of Ptolemy . . . and who wrote books on Egyptian history: Hecataeus is one of these.
>
> Now Hecataeus tells us that ten stades from the oldest tombs . . . there stands a monument to the king named Osymandias [*sic*]. (Murphy 1964, 62 and n. 99)

Let us set this discovery in the context of my previous discussion. We have already seen that no contemporary of Shelley's could reliably have reported as the traveller does on the frown, lip, and sneer so vital to our understanding of the importance of the statue that appears in his sonnet. Now (by his own confession so to speak) even

Diodorus forfeits his eligibility for that role, leaving the shadowy Hecataeus as the only known firsthand witness. But if Hecataeus is to be the traveller (and setting on one side for a moment the previously mentioned problem that in Shelley's poem the statue is described as a ruin), a new potential traveller/narrator alignment emerges: might not the first-person narrator ("I") be Diodorus, the whole poem representing, so to speak, a freewheeling versified paraphrase of Diodorus's own text?[11] Or again, in the most radical interpretation of all, could we not posit as the narrator an unnamed contemporary of Hecataeus, some Greek citizen of the *third* century B.C., who could literally have "met" Hecataeus and heard what he "said" (as neither Diodorus nor Shelley could)?

Before the complexities of the alternatives I am laying out grow too dizzying, it may be useful to build on a crucial feature of "Ozymandias" noted by Von Rainer Lengeler: "Das Sonett baut sich im wesentlichen aus drei ineinandergeschachtelten Fiktionsebenen auf, die durch das Ich, den Reisenden und Ozymandias in der Rolle des Sprechenden bezeichnet werden" [The sonnet is constructed essentially out of three narrative layers boxed one within another, which are characterized by the I, by the traveller, and by Ozymandias in the rôle of speaker] (1969, 537; my translation). Adopting a simple technique proposed by Bertram Bruce (1981, 287), we may diagram Lengeler's three "Fiktionsebenen" as shown in Figure 1-1, which represents "Ozymandias" as a complexly layered narrative. At each level (easily referenced by the number in the top right-hand corner of the relevant box) we find both a narrator and an auditor (or at least a recipient) of the narrative whose content is specified in the box labeled with the next highest integer. Level 3 thus specifies, for instance, the communicative event discussed at some length earlier in this chapter, in which the traveller reads the sculptor's complex message off the statue's features.[12] It is at level 2 that the traveller verbalizes that whole experience, presumably for the benefit of the narrator, and at level 1 that the narrator conveys his version of events to us, the readers.

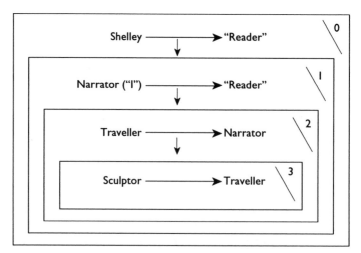

FIGURE 1-1. Narrative Layering in "Ozymandias"

Such a formalization of the text's narrative complexities permits a more precise discussion of the rôles of given participants at, or between, narrative levels. It pinpoints, for example, Spanos's mistaken inversion of those rôles in his statement that "the sculptor is to Ozymandias what the traveller is to the speaker in the framework" (1968, 15). For while the speaker (whom I have been calling the narrator) is a recipient at level 2, Ozymandias does not feature as a participant of *any* kind, let alone as a recipient, at any level in this poem; at most he is the pretext (and pre-text) for the sculptor's level-3 discourse. Despite its usefulness in correcting such minor inaccuracies, though, we must recognize that Figure 1-1 defines only the *intra*textual relations in this short poem. Our current challenge in seeking to establish whether any *extra*textual references can be substantiated is to search out candidates who, taken together, will satisfy the historical constraints that circumscribe the author (level 0), the narrator (levels 1 and 2), and the traveller (levels 2 and 3).

Adopting "the conventional equation of author and speaker," we might take Shelley to be both the author of the whole text and the narrator at level 1. If Shelley is indeed the level-1 narrator, then candidates for the traveller—as we have seen— include Diodorus, Hecataeus, or one of Shelley's contemporaries. If, however, Shelley's role is restricted to level 0 and it is Diodorus who speaks as "I" at level 1, then Hecataeus remains a candidate for the traveller's spot. If, finally, the narrator is an anonymous third-century Greek citizen, Diodorus is eliminated altogether from the chain of narrative transmission described in the poem (though not, of course, from the real-world sequence of narrators that lies behind the text).

At this point it is important to stress that none of this speculation in any way affects the important conclusions reached earlier in this discussion. No proliferation of research into possible historical sources for the narrator, that is, can overcome the one fundamental obstacle to a unified historical identification of the traveller: the paradox that, in order to report as he does, a historical traveller would have to have lived at a time when the statue of Ramesses was shattered but not yet featureless, and that no such time has been recorded. My intention in spelling out in such detail the many additional uncertainties that pervade every level of this text is rather to reflect what Shelley himself must certainly have been aware of, whether he had read Diodorus's history in the original or in translation: namely, that his own sonnet would repeat yet again a story whose roots lay over two thousand years in the past and whose previous tellers had served as at best imperfect transmitters of some original "reality." Spanos utilizes the doubt that he casts on the equation of Shelley with the narrator to broaden the impact of this poem's *political* message. Without denying the usefulness of his argument, I propose that the lack of a well-focused "I" in this sonnet also reinforces Shelley's *literary* theme: the inevitability of slippage in renarrations of history and the importance of recognizing this creative dimension to what too often and too easily passes for objective reportage.

IF INDEED ONE GOAL of the octave of this sonnet is to probe, indirectly and implicitly, the whole concept of narrated experience, then that theme (just like the explicit political theme that parallels it) comes to a head in its sestet. In a poem where historical time has begun to seem almost infinitely flexible and where secondhand knowledge is apparently the best that one can hope for, the quotation marks that herald Ozymandias's boastful inscription, "My name is Ozymandias . . . ," offer at first a welcome if belated foothold. Direct quotation, after all, enjoys a very special status in narration (see Tannen 1989, 106–8). A direct quotation is presumed to preserve perfectly the linguistic shape of its original — including even such inherently relative, and thus vulnerable, features as tense, modality, deixis, and pronominal reference. In this text, furthermore, Shelley seems particularly eager to encourage this assumption; neither *heard* nor *read*, the words of the inscription are said merely to "appear." *Whoever* "I" is in this text, therefore, and *whoever* the traveller may be, the words on the pedestal, unlike the statue itself, are surely immune to the weathering effects of both meteorological and narrative storms?[13]

If Griffiths is right, it was J. H. Fowler in his notes on *Palgrave's Golden Treasury* who first drew public attention to the fallacy inherent in the preceding argument when he noted that "if the inscription was in hieroglyphics, it would have been unintelligible in Shelley's time, the key being only found by Champollion in 1822" in the form, of course, of his decipherment of the Rosetta Stone inscriptions (Griffiths 1948, 80–81). This is not to accuse Shelley of blatant fabrication; Diodorus and Hecataeus, writing in Greek, represent the intervenient stages by which Ozymandias's words were in fact transmitted to Shelley's contemporaries, and (as I noted earlier) Shelley did retain the general tone and contents of the inscription that they reported. But this does not altogether resolve the challenge to the integrity of those "quoted" lines. For not only have the words that appear in lines 10 and 11 of Shelley's "Ozymandias" been translated at least twice (from hieroglyphics into Greek and from Greek into English), but, as Van Maanen points out (1949, 124), they have also been considerably paraphrased in the process. Someone has taken the decidedly cryptic words recorded by Diodorus ("if anyone wishes to know how mighty I am and where I lie, let him surpass any of my works," in Edwin Murphy's [1964] scholarly translation) and fashioned a far more morally tendentious (and doom-laden) text: "Look on my works, ye Mighty, and despair!" The voice we recognize here is surely that employed by Shelley in such rabble-rousing verses as *The Mask of Anarchy* or "Men of England" and not that which one might encounter in the dusty pages of some ancient history book. While Shelley has borrowed from his sources both the notion that some words are inscribed on the base of the statue and the references in that text to the *mighty* and to *works*, his use of quotation marks is quite misleading if viewed from a historical standpoint.[14] The unbroken line of verbatim repetition that they imply cannot be confirmed by consulting the sources available to us (as they were also to Shelley and to his contemporaries). Where the external discourse markers most insistently assert historical accuracy, in fact, Shelley has inveigled his most unmistakably Shelleyan presence.[15]

Our recognition of Shelley's hand (among others) at work in crafting the received text of Ozymandias's "utterance" leads inexorably to another, still more disconcerting observation. For the famous initial words of that inscription, just like the opening line of the poem itself, are couched in the first person: "*My* name is Ozymandias. . . ." Who, then, is *this* speaker who indulges in the very fundamental discourse function of self-naming? We have mounting evidence that his authenticity as a historical figure—and thus the literal veracity of the words ascribed to him—rests on very insecure foundations. Conceding that point, we might still, with only a minor reorientation of our perspective, install the sculptor's *representation* of the tyrant as the speaker. If we pause for a moment to reflect on the entire scene that Shelley has described, though, this fallback position also loses its initial appeal. The legend, after all, appears on a plinth that supports nothing even remotely resembling a human speaker. We see only "two vast . . . legs of stone"; the head, with its organs essential to both language and speech faculties, lies some way off, "half sunk." The closer we look, in fact, the harder it becomes to discern exactly who could qualify as a "speaker" here.

A still more intriguing challenge is presented when we move to the second line of the reported inscription. "Look on my works," the first-person speaker demands. If the previous line's act of self-naming failed for lack of a well-defined speaker, the peremptory imperative in this one creates parallel problems by referring to "works" that it is impossible for the reader to locate in either the linguistic or the physical context that Shelley has provided. A conventional explication of the poem would naturally claim that Shelley's point lies precisely in the fact that "[nothing] beside remains"; Ozymandias's bombast evaporates *because*, in the absence of any "works" to be "looked on," his command is fatally flawed as an act of discourse—an infelicitous directive that the reader cannot possibly fulfill.[16] But by what right are we now counting the inscription as representing Ozymandias's words? As I have already argued, we would stand on safer ground if we attributed the whole artwork to the sculptor who fashioned it, an attribution openly fostered by Shelley in the sonnet's octave. To pursue this line of argument to its conclusion and to associate the sculptor with the first-person speaker in line 11 who invites us to look on "his" works might at first seem absurdly farfetched; our reluctance to accept that interpretation is perfectly natural and is closely allied to our earlier, equally intuitive resistance to any suggestion that the narrator of the entire sonnet might not in fact be Shelley himself. Yet we have already established that the sculptor is, in an important though nonobvious sense, an "utterer" of the statue as a whole. It was he who "read" Ozymandias's features and it is his handiwork that "tells" the traveller all that he knows about the pharaoh. By extension, when it comes to the words within the quotation marks, even though each of the narrators featured in our extended chain-of-transmission had some hand in shaping the words that we read today, it was the sculptor who, as first in line, wielded particularly significant power with regard to their content. We can never know what Ozymandias actually said when he commissioned the statue, since we read at best a copy of a copy of a copy of the words he spoke. For all we can tell, Ozymandias may never have authorized either the monument or the text beneath it; those words could just as easily represent an entirely original contribution of the sculptor's own devising, concocted either with or without the tyrant's blessing and by no means necessarily reflective of the "true" character of the historical Ramesses II. Like every amanuensis from Moses on the mountaintop to Boswell, in effect, the sculptor can rely on the almost boundless trust of his readership in the accuracy of what may or may not by any means be an accurate transcription.

If we once accept the possibility that line 11 invites the "mighty" to look upon the sculptor's works rather than upon those of his royal model, a new irony emerges. Time has certainly devastated Ozymandias's kingdom, but, to add insult to injury, his achievements have been significantly outlasted by the sculptural creation of one of his socially inferior contemporaries, perhaps even one of his own subjects. Whatever the glories and accomplishments of this "King of Kings," we now know him by name alone; it is the *un*named sculptor's monument that survives and it is his skill as a master of his craft that the traveller can still appraise. In a very real sense, in fact, the sculptor's "hand" has "mocked" Ozymandias, exploiting the power conferred by the acts of narration and quotation to hurl the tyrant's boastfulness (whether ever verbalized or not) back in his face.

Let us step back for a moment, though. We should not forget poet Robinson Jeffers's characterization of all sculptors as "*foredefeated* / Challengers of oblivion" ("To the Stone-Cutters," lines 1–2; my italics).[17] Even our sculptor's "works" were doomed from the beginning to long-term decay, a fact that renders his moral victory over Ozymandias temporary at best. Significantly, it is an inscription, hardly the aspect of any sculptor's work that we would isolate as displaying his greatest skills, that seems to have survived time's ravages better than the directly representational, purely sculptural parts of the work. "Telling," it would appear, works best in the medium of language to which it bears a direct, rather than only a metaphorical, relation. And even in this respect, our belief that the sculptor's work has endured may, like a desert mirage, vanish upon closer inspection. The states of the "trunkless legs" and of the "shattered visage," after all, are *described* to us, whereas the text of the inscription, by being *quoted*, materializes magically before our eyes in seemingly pristine condition. The sculptor's chiseled letters may in fact have grown worn and chipped, but so long as the abstract linguistic form that they realize can still be discerned, the repetition (or effectively re-creation) of that form by each individual who reads them will miraculously restore them to their "original" clarity. Yet again, we perceive the peculiar and magical power of quotation and of narration to refresh and to refashion what it seems only to repeat.

All of which brings us back one last time to the realization that what we read in "Ozymandias" are still in the final analysis the words of one Percy Bysshe Shelley. I have no wish, certainly, to dispute that it greatly enriches our appreciation of this poem to hold in balance two distinct readings of line 11 in which the speakers are respectively Ozymandias and the sculptor. Each of those superimposed readings follows with impeccable logic from the analysis that this chapter has presented. But we cannot overlook the fact that Shelley himself also "utters" the words "quoted" in lines 10 and 11, emending and versifying them in the process; nor can we evade the conclusion that the lines that precede and follow them incontrovertibly also represent *his* "works." Shelley has turned the material he inherited from various sources to his own ends, confounding historical accuracy in the service of his own political agenda. He has both refurbished and, in the process, refashioned the faded inscriptions of an ever-receding line of historical speakers. It is in part *his* voice that we hear harmonizing with theirs in line 11; the words "Look on my works, ye Mighty, and despair" ring true also as his own defiant and derisory gesture in the face of the rebuffs he had experienced in 1817 at the hands of authority, respectability, and conservatism. What is most remarkable of all, he has accomplished all of this while simultaneously drawing the reader's attention to his own subversive act.

As Don Bialostosky remarks in chapter 5, Bakhtin regarded poetry as typically monologic. Read monologically, as a political set piece, "Ozymandias" will probably never rise above the status of "impressive familiarity," to paraphrase Richmond. Its value to literary and social historians either as evidence of sociopolitical trends or as material on which to practice their detective skills seems already to have been largely exhausted. But linguistic analysis of several different kinds can combine to reveal Shelley's sonnet as in part "literary" in the sense that it addresses issues integral to the very act of composing an original text. By framing his account of the desert scene in a conversational context; by underdefining that context in such a way as to invite ultimately frustrating speculation about its participants; by subtly redirecting readers' attention away from the statue's original and towards its creator; by emphasizing in particular a "direct quotation" that thoughtful reflection inevitably reveals as less than word for word; and, finally, by twice employing the first person in contexts that seem at first transparent yet ultimately develop troubling opacities—by all these means, Shelley injects a second theme into his poem. "*Caveat lector,*" he warns; narratives, even those that ostensibly relate historical and autobiographical material, are still texts created by their authors in ways that fatally compromise their historicity. Worse still (from the historian's standpoint), the insertion of discourse markers such as quotation marks that should signal faithful adherence to historical "truth" in actual fact constrain the author no more tightly than their omission elsewhere in the text.

This second way of reading the text might be described as dialogic, using that term in the second of the three senses defined by Morson and Emerson in their "Heteroglossary" in chapter 12. Rather than being, like parody, "double-voiced," however, this text is multivoiced, its many voices paired in a bewildering and finally ineluctable array of possible speaker/hearer, writer/reader, author/narrator, and narrator/traveller configurations. To what extent Shelley himself recognized this "potential meaning" (again, see the "Heteroglossary") in his sonnet we can never know, although I alluded earlier to his well-documented interest in the influence of creative artists in shaping historical and political events. With or without his conscious direction, though, there can be no doubt that "Ozymandias" challenges several of our most basic assumptions about certain kinds of literary texts: that lyrical poems are generically monologic (a position also most effectively challenged by Don Bialostosky's contribution to this volume); that their first-person narrators invariably and exclusively present the firsthand experience of their authors; that representational art represents anything more objectively "real" than the artist's own skill at his or her trade; and that direct quotation constitutes in any sense "a neutral conduit of objectively real information" (Tannen 1989, 108).

Such a broadened reanalysis of "Ozymandias" fulfills, I submit, my objective of raising this sonnet's reputation as a complex and mature work in the Shelley canon. It depends, by all means, on a sophisticated sensitivity to the subtleties of discourse and of conversation. Like most of our linguistic faculties, that sensitivity is, I would claim, present in each and every reader and thus plays some part in her or his sub-conscious appreciation of any poem. My purpose in this chapter has been to draw out that knowledge for conscious examination; to allow it to interact with more conventional (and thus more readily accessible) judgments about imagery, theme, and historical context; and thus to bring into question whether the most obvious and accepted reading of a text much maligned and condescended to by traditional criticism is by any means exhaustive.

ACKNOWLEDGMENTS   For helpful discussions of the material addressed in this chapter, I am grateful to Steven Jones, Michael Macovski, and the members of a 1988 graduate seminar in stylistics at Loyola University, Chicago. Naturally, any errors, whether of material fact or of good judgment, remain my own. The text of "Ozymandias" I use throughout this discussion is the one contained in Ingpen and Peck's 1927 edition of Shelley's *Collected Works*, vol. 2.

Notes

1. For a discussion of the developments in theoretical linguistics alluded to here, see Tannen (1989); for their literary implications, see Toolan (1990).

2. This sequence of contributions to the critical literature is excellently described and documented by Mary A. Quinn (1984, 49 n.1).

3. Von Rainer Lengeler, in an excellent discussion of this sonnet, makes the same point: "Diese Bruchstücke aber künden nicht von dem historischen Ozymandias, sondern von der Kunst des unbekannten Bildhauers" [These fragments, though, reveal not the historical Ozymandias but the skill of the unknown sculptor] (1969, 538; my translation).

4. I am, of course, begging a number of questions here in referring so freely to "present" and "past"; for the moment these should be read merely as relative, not as absolute, terms. It will be precisely the purpose of later sections of this chapter to reconsider their appropriateness in the context of the sonnet as a whole.

5. I recognize, of course, that the demonstrative here is primarily cataphoric, its referent being the quoted material that immediately follows in lines 10 and 11. Nonetheless, the vividness of that direct quotation is significantly reinforced, it seems to me, by the use of "these" in a context where proximal deixis has already become firmly associated with the contemporary, rather than with a past, era. I shall return to this point later.

6. I must in fairness exempt from this sweeping generalization Lengeler's (1969) short but thoughtful analysis of "Ozymandias" as a narrative creation.

7. As Spanos's (1968) reference to "a *contemporary* conversation" reveals, he himself belongs among this first group.

8. I have already noted Shelley's use elsewhere in this poem of terms usually confined to verbal communication ("tells," "read") to describe processes that are in no sense linguistic. May we not see in this employment of "met" the obverse situation, a nonlinguistic term being used to describe what may in fact have been a literary rather than a face-to-face encounter? Elsewhere, Shelley certainly uses the verb *meet* in such a figurative sense. In the following lines from "Epipsychidion," the encounter narrated can only be viewed as a highly abstract spiritual experience: "She *met* me, Stranger, upon life's rough way, / And lured me towards sweet Death." (Ingpen and Peck, 1927, 2, 359, 72–73; my italics).

9. This is not the place in which to discuss in detail the extent to which genre may influence readers' judgments in the area of first-person narration. Clearly, though, stand-up comics who open their acts with words such as "A funny thing happened to me on my way to the club" are not expected to be speaking autobiographically in the strictest sense; nor do novels, even if written in the first person, seem to be expected to reflect the author's own sentiments directly. As Spanos implies, however, lyric poems, and sonnets even more typically, do tend to be regarded uncritically as vehicles for the poet's own thoughts and emotions.

10. Indeed, I have argued elsewhere (Austin 1989) that the first-person narrator of William Wordsworth's "Resolution and Independence" is not in fact Wordsworth himself but a projection of Samuel Taylor Coleridge's beliefs and emotions—a conclusion I reached only after reading the poem in its full context as one contribution to an extended poetic debate between those two poets.

11. I find it tantalizing, at the very least, that Diodorus's characterization of Hecataeus should refer to him as one of those "Greeks who *traveled* to Thebes . . . and wrote books."

12. In Figure 1-1, I have substituted the sculptor for Lengeler's "Ozymandias in der Rolle des Sprechenden" at level 3 for reasons that should be evident in light of the preceding discussion.

13. Lengeler, once again, notices both the importance of direct quotation in Shelley's poem and the paradox that it appears precisely when we reach the most deeply embedded—and thus arguably the most fictive—narrative level. The conclusion that he draws from this observation differs radically from my own, however. He alleges (and I shall shortly explicitly deny) that when we finally reach that quotation, "[wir hören] nun gewissermassen Ozymandias selber sprechen" [we now hear, as it were, Ozymandias himself speaking] (1969, 536; my translation).

14. In this connection, we may return to an observation I commented on in note 5: Shelley's insistence that "on the pedestal *these* words appear," when viewed in the context of his characteristic association of proximal deictics with *present* time, also suggests that we should regard "those words" as being anchored in the *past* less firmly than we might otherwise have expected.

15. This is not the only respect in which it is finally Shelley's artistic vision—rather than the impersonal testimony of history—that controls the reader's experience of this poem. I devoted considerable space earlier to discussing the facial features of Ozymandias's statue and the probability that they would have been evident to witnesses in 300 or 100 B.C., but not to those in A.D. 1800. In a fascinating footnote, D. W. Thompson explains that such questions are in effect moot: "We now know that the Egyptians did not sculpture their kings in such fashion. The face in the sonnet is not that of an Egyptian king, but that of Shelley's tyrant, a Godwinian monarch whose character has been ruined by court-life" (1937, 63). Indeed, as Thompson goes on to point out, the model for Shelley's Ozymandias lies not in Egypt, nor even in London, but in the descriptions of other, patently unhistorical kings that pepper the Shelley canon (he cites, for example, *The Revolt of Islam*, canto 5, stanza 23, and *Prometheus Unbound*, act 3). In visual image as in verbal quotation, therefore, Shelley's apparent interest in matters historical cannot be relied on to ensure the accuracy with which he reports the details of his subject.

16. Such an approach neglects the fact that at least one "work" of Ozymandias *is* still available for inspection: the statue itself, ruined though it may be. Perhaps, then, Ozymandias's claim to a lasting legacy is not entirely groundless even if what survives is a comparatively unimpressive ruin that hardly justifies the title "King of Kings."

17. One inevitably recalls also the triumphant promise of another great sonneteer to his lover: "you shall shine more bright in these contents / Than unswept stone, besmeared with sluttish time" (Shakespeare, Sonnet 55, lines 3–4).

Works Cited

Abrams, M. H., ed. *The Norton Anthology of English Literature*, 4th ed. 2 vols. New York: W. W. Norton, 1979.

Austin, Timothy R. *Language Crafted: A Linguistic Theory of Poetic Syntax*. Bloomington: Indiana University Press, 1984.

———. "Narrative Discourses and Discoursing in Narratives: Analyzing a Poem from a Sociolinguistic Perspective." *Poetics Today* 10, no. 4 (1989), 703–28.

Bruce, Bertram. "A Social Interaction Model of Reading." *Discourse Processes* 4 (1981): 273–311.

Griffiths, J. Gwyn. "Shelley's 'Ozymandias' and Diodorus Siculus." *Modern Language Review* 43 (1948): 80–84.

Holmes, Richard. *Shelley: The Pursuit*. London: Weidenfeld and Nicolson, 1974.

Ingpen, Roger, and Walter E. Peck. *The Complete Works of Percy Bysshe Shelley*. 10 vols. New York: Charles Scribner's Sons, 1927.

Lengeler, Von Rainer. "Shelleys Sonett Ozymandias." *Die Neueren Sprachen* 68 (1969): 532–39.

Murphy, Edwin, trans. *Diodorus "On Egypt."* Jefferson, N.C.: McFarland, 1964.

Notopoulos, James A. "Two Notes on Shelley: (2). Shelley's 'Ozymandias' Once Again." *Modern Language Review* 48 (1953): 442–43.

Parr, Johnstone. "Shelley's *Ozymandias*." *Keats-Shelley Journal* 6 (1957): 31–35.

Quinn, Mary A. "'Ozymandias' as Shelley's Rejoinder to Peacock's 'Palmyra.'" *English Language Notes* 21, no. 4 (1984): 48–56.

Richmond, H. M. "Ozymandias and the Travelers." *Keats-Shelley Journal* 11 (1962): 65–71.

Rogers, Neville, ed. *Shelley: Selected Poetry*. Oxford: Oxford University Press, 1968.

Spanos, William V. "Shelley's 'Ozymandias' and the Problem of the Persona." *CEA Critic* 30 (1968): 14–15.

Tannen, Deborah. *Talking Voices: Repetition, Dialogue, and Imagery in Conversational Discourse*. Cambridge: Cambridge University Press, 1989.

Thompson, D. W. "Ozymandias." *Philological Quarterly* 16 (1937): 59–64.

Toolan, Michael J. *The Stylistics of Fiction: A Literary-Linguistic Approach*. New York: Routledge, 1990.

Van Maanen, W. "A Note on Shelley's *Ozymandias*." *Neophilologus* 33 (1949): 123–25.

The Power of Speech

Dialogue as History in the Russian Primary Chronicle

For the modern reader, medieval histories have an endearingly theatrical quality because they tend to emphasize direct speech and dialogue in place of reported action. Nowhere is this tendency more apparent than in the Russian *Primary Chronicle (Povest' vremennykh let)*, which covers political and social events of Kievan Rus' from the ninth to early twelfth centuries. It is a striking feature of this work that the narrator almost never speaks for the characters. The episodes, written by a largely unnamed succession of monks, are peppered with quotations in the first person and present tense, which lend a dramatic cadence to the entire work. Readers now are inclined to see this feature as merely a quaint medieval narrative device, or perhaps as the amateur historian's primitive attempt to produce a good yarn at the expense of historical accuracy.[1] The use of direct speech in the *Primary Chronicle*, however, carried far more meaning in the medieval context than we are inclined to ascribe to it from a modern vantage point. The shift from primarily oral to highly literate culture has brought with it a change in the perceived force of speech, in which the semantic content of what is said is far more important than the nature of the communicative act, especially in historical writing.[2] The types of speech acts that predominate in the *Primary Chronicle* are sufficiently different from those in modern histories to warrant close scrutiny, for they offer a key to understanding both the chronicle's aesthetic construction and its exploration of how power is established and exercised.

Dialogue in the *Primary Chronicle*

Much of the chronicle follows a familiar narrative rhythm: each episode begins by introducing the characters, setting, and conflict; this leads into a pivotal dramatic scene, which is followed by a description of the results or an evaluation of the action. What distinguishes this pattern from ordinary narratives is that the pivotal event is most often a speech or dialogue.[3] What is more, these tend to be made up of classic performative speech acts, that is, sentences that accomplish actions by their very utterance: promises, betrayals, threats, invitations, treaties, proposals, and so on. They are indicated linguistically either by an introductory phrase, such as "He said" (*reče*), or simply by an abrupt shift into the present tense and first person. (The use of tense and person shifters or of such deictic expressions as "here," "now," or "this" is, incidentally, the only way to signal direct speech in medieval Slavic manuscripts, which mostly lack punctuation.[4]) In effect, the narrator appears to yield the floor to the characters for the crucial moments of the story. To use further terminology from speech-act theory, we can say that the narrator is confined to a *constative* role, fitting his words to the world, while the characters engage in *performative* speech, changing the world by their words.[5]

The narrative pattern I just described is repeated over a hundred times in the chronicle. The entry for the year 980 offers a good example of the rhythm that results:[6]

> In the year 6488. Vladimir came to Novgorod with the Varangians, and he said to Yaropolk's deputies, "Go to my brother and say to him, 'Vladimir is advancing upon you, prepare to fight him.'" And he remained in Novgorod.
>
> And he sent to Rogvolod in Polotsk, saying, "I want to take your daughter for my wife." So [Rogvolod] said to his daughter, "Do you want to marry Vladimir?" She said, "I do not want to pull off the boots of a slave's son; I want Yaropolk instead."[7] For Rogvolod had come from abroad and he held power in Polotsk. . . . And Vladimir's men returned and reported to him the whole speech of Rogned, daughter of Rogvolod, the prince of Polotsk. Vladimir then gathered many warriors . . . and came to Polotsk and killed Rogvolod and his two sons and took [Rogvolod's] daughter as his wife.
>
> And he marched upon Yaropolk. Vladimir came to Kiev with many warriors, and Yaropolk could not withstand him, and he shut himself up in Kiev with his people and with Blud. . . . But Vladimir sent to Blud, commander of Yaropolk's army, with false words: "Be my ally. If I kill my brother, I will place you in my father's stead, and you will receive much honor from me. For it was not I who began to fight my brothers, but he. I have attacked him out of fear of that." And Blud said to Vladimir's envoys, "I will be your ally and friend." Oh evil human lie! As David says, "A man who ate of my bread has raised a lie against me." . . .
>
> And so Blud betrayed his prince, having received great honor from him. Blud remained with Yaropolk under siege but, deceiving him, he often sent to Vladimir encouraging him to storm the city, intending to kill Yaropolk at that time, since he did not want to do it openly in front of the citizens. Blud could not kill him, and so he invented a scheme, persuading him not to venture out of the city into the fray. Blud said to Yaropolk, "The Kievans are sending to Vladimir, saying, 'Storm the city, we will give up Yaropolk to you.' You must flee the city." And Yaropolk heeded him

and fled, and he shut himself up in the town of Rodnia . . . while Vladimir took Kiev and laid siege to Rodnia.

And there was a great famine in Rodnia. . . . And Blud said to Yaropolk, deceiving him all the while, "Do you see how many soldiers your brother has? We cannot defeat them. Make peace with your brother." And Yaropolk said, "So be it." And Blud sent to Vladimir, speaking thus: "Your plan has come to fruition, for I will bring Yaropolk to you and you prepare to kill him." Hearing this, Vladimir went to the hall of his father's castle with his soldiers and his retinue. And Blud said to Yaropolk, "Go to your brother and say to him, 'Whatever you give me, I will accept.'" Yaropolk set off, but Variazhko said to him, "Don't go, Prince, they will kill you; flee to the Pechenegs and take your army." But he did not heed him. And Yaropolk went to Vladimir, and when he went through the doors, two Varangians impaled him on their swords. Blud closed the doors and did not allow [Yaropolk's] men to go after him. And thus Yaropolk was killed. . . . (90, 92)

In each episode of this entry the narrator identifies the main players and the location of the action, and then the characters take the floor to determine the nature of the drama. In the first scene Vladimir challenges Yaropolk, which effectively initiates the struggle between the two brothers. The second scene (which describes events that transpired a few years earlier, and serves therefore to explain one cause of the brothers' enmity) hinges upon Vladimir's proposal of marriage and Rogned's refusal. In scene three Vladimir and Blud make their clandestine agreement. In the last two scenes Blud uses his cunning to persuade Yaropolk to give himself up.

Each of these oral confrontations leads to a violent outcome, but it would be wrong to see them as merely catalysts to action. The speeches are significant actions in their own right. First, linguistic philosophers would see a marriage proposal, a challenge, and an alliance as verbal acts, accomplished when—and only when—the words are spoken by those who have the authority to speak them. Second, in a more anthropological sense, the presence and manner of speeches in the chronicle reveals more about the hierarchy among the various characters than do the outcomes of the battles. Vladimir's boldness and initiative establish him as a powerful leader; Rogned's refusal shows her sense of self-worth and her father's importance (although it would seem that she is subsequently punished for boasting); Vladimir's brother, Yaropolk, only speaks to agree with his general, Blud, which demonstrates his weakness, while Blud is able to confer as an equal with Vladimir. Blud's strength, in fact, comes largely through speech, since he is powerless to kill Yaropolk himself, but nevertheless is able to talk the prince into stepping into his trap, even over the good advice of a trusted counselor. And, finally, no one speaks directly to the lesser characters, such as envoys and retainers, except to give them messages to pass on to others; communication with minor players is reported by such constructions as "He ordered them to fight." As D. S. Likhachev points out, speeches here belong to "not nameless figures, but historical personages" (1952, 95).

If the chronicler seems to have a keen sense of the dramatic value of quoted speech, he shares the device liberally with his characters. There are several instances of embedded quotations, in which one actor puts words into another's mouth or repeats the speech of a third party. Vladimir's initial communiqué to Yaropolk takes this form, when he tells Yaropolk's envoys, "Go to my brother and say to him, 'Vladimir is advancing upon you, prepare to fight him.'" The fact that he not only issues a challenge but causes it to be spoken by Yaropolk's own deputies testifies to his power. Another character who uses this device is the treacherous Blud, who persuades Yaropolk to flee Kiev by quoting treasonous speeches on the part of its citizens. Yaropolk readily believes him, for the culture of the time depends upon the accurate relaying of messages (witness the number of times messages are delivered by third parties in this entry alone). The fact that Blud abuses this trust by fabricating the speeches is weighty testimony to his lack of scruples. Finally, in Rodnia, Blud not only tells Yaropolk to surrender to Vladimir, but tells him what to say, namely, "Whatever you give me, I will accept." This statement is intentionally ambiguous: Yaropolk is to believe he is merely suing for peace on Vladimir's terms, while everyone else (including Yaropolk's faithful adviser Variazhko) knows he is asking for death. Blud's treachery, therefore, consists not only in delivering Yaropolk into Vladimir's hands but in humiliating Yaropolk by making him speak words whose performative meaning he does not understand. A hierarchy of "powers of speech" emerges: at the top stand those who speak their own words and realize them in action, as well as those who put words in others' mouths; then come those who are silent; and last those whose speech is either ineffective or has undesired results.

The ability to flaunt verbal conventions and play upon the difference between literal and conventional meanings is also a valued skill in the chronicle, and Blud's prowess at it places him in powerful company. The most accomplished practitioner of this art is Olga, Vladimir's grandmother. In 945, after the Derevlians kill her husband, they send envoys to ask Olga to marry their prince. She replies,

> "I like what you say, for I cannot resurrect my husband now. But I want to honor you in the morning before my people, so now you return to your boat and remain there with proud bearing, and in the morning I will send for you and you say, 'We will not go on horseback, nor will we go on foot, but carry us in our boat' and they will carry you in the boat." (70)

Meanwhile, of course, Olga has a great pit dug for them. She sends her bearers to get the Derevlians in the morning, and the latter repeat their lines perfectly. She has even provided a script for the Kievan bearers, who grumble, "We do this against our will; our prince is killed and [Olga] wants to marry your prince." But when the scene is played out, the bearers drop the boat into the pit and bury the Derevlians alive. In effect, Olga has crafted an elaborate death scene for her enemies, complete with stage directions ("with proud bearing"). She clearly is powerful enough simply to have the visitors killed, but she chooses instead to make a ritual of it. In so doing, she exhibits her verbal authority to full advantage: like Blud, Olga humiliates her enemies by subverting their power of speech; like Vladimir, she sees her own words realized in action, and this combination places her among the prophets and the gods.

Olga manipulates verbal conventions in other ways as well. In 955 the Byzantine emperor makes her a proposal of marriage; she replies that she cannot marry him until she is baptized, and that she will only be baptized by his hand. "After she was baptized, the emperor called her and said to her, 'I want to marry you.' But she replied, 'How can you marry me, when you have baptized me yourself and called me "daughter?" That is against the Christian law, as you know'" (74, 76). The emperor is forced to admit defeat, and he bestows many gifts upon Olga for her cleverness. The conflict of literal and conventional meanings, which Olga so adroitly exploits, recurs as a theme throughout the chronicle, pitting the clever, bold, and unscrupulous against the traditional and lazy. Emile Benveniste claims that such modern French phrases as *Je vous souhaite la bienvenue* and *Je vous conseille de le faire* have lost their performative function, in which the "bidding" and "advising" really denoted the primary actions on the part of the speakers, and have become instead banalities. "Degraded as they are to simple formulae, they must be restored to their primary meaning in order to recover their performative function" (1966, vol. 1, 271, my translation; see also Felman 1980, 21). Benveniste's argument, although it has the ring of a modern discovery, is but the rediscovery of a very old theme, aptly illustrated by a scene in the chronicle from the year 1066. Here, a Greek officer is sent to Prince Rostislav "with treacherous intent": "When Rostislav was drinking alone with his retainers, the officer said, 'Prince, I want to drink to you.' (*Khochiu na tia piti.*) So [the prince] replied, 'Drink'" (180). The officer proceeds to drink to the prince and then offers him a cup with poison in it, killing him. Thus, the prince gives the order for his own death by making the formulaic response to a formulaic toast. For him, the semantics of this exchange have been lost, and the officer takes advantage of that fact, interpreting the words literally while knowing that the prince will not do the same. Ordinarily a toast carries the illocutionary force of wishing someone good health, but the officer certainly harbors no such wish. In effect, he subverts the conventional performative function that the exchange has acquired in favor of "returning the formula to its original sense," because he literally does wish to drink to the prince. An even more literal reading of his words unearths an underlying pun, for his proposal is very like the formulaic challenge to battle: "I want to attack you" (*Khochiu na vy iti*: literally, "I want to go against you"); the toast could mean, "I want to drink against you." Like Olga, the Greek officer speaks the truth, but it is a truth based upon his own interpretation of the words, and communication is intentionally subverted. The prince, in accepting the toast as an empty formality, plays straight into the officer's hands.

The play on verbal convention in this episode links it to the theme of authority and responsibility that informs much of the chronicle. The prince is the only one who can authorize the toast, but the officer manipulates him into doing so without thinking. Benveniste points out that there can be no speech *act* without authority (1966, 273). Indeed, in the chronicle, the ability to perform speech acts is often synonymous with authority, resulting from it and constitutive of it at the same time. The chronicler stresses again and again that the privilege to act through speech must be exercised with care and deliberation, for when it is taken lightly—as here, or among the Derevlians, or in the frequent cases of broken oaths and alliances—it brings nothing but trouble.

The power of words to change the course of events extends beyond simple, face-to-face dialogue in the chronicle. Within the religious context, prayers, confessions, baptisms, and vows are the farthest thing from empty rituals: they are the crux of the matter, ends in themselves. Olga, presumably still governed by pagan pragmatism despite her conversion, uses this fact in refusing the hand of the Byzantine emperor. More thoroughly Christian characters are less opportunistic. When Boris and Gleb fall victim to their brother's perfidy in 1015, they do not resist, they simply pray. And their prayers prove, in the long run, to be mightier than their slayers' swords, because they bear witness to the martyrs' piety and secure them sainthood.

Words occasionally take on magical powers that are effectively independent of the individual speakers who utter them. In the year 1072 the relics of Boris and Gleb are brought to a new church for interment:

> Kissing Boris' relics, [his nephews] laid them in a stone coffin. After that, they took Gleb in a stone coffin and put it on a sled, and grabbing the ropes, they moved it. When they got to the doors [of the church], the coffin stopped and went no farther. And they ordered the people to call out, "Lord, have mercy," and [then the nephews were able to move] it. (194)

Thus, the speaking of the formula changes the physical world by removing the spell from the coffin.

Prophesies, too, can have a world-changing effect, although they are more complex speech acts than mere incantations.[8] In itself, a prophesy is a revelation of God's truth; the deity is brought to life and the speaker's status is enhanced by the act of speaking this truth. Werner Kelber writes of Christian prophets that "they speak the sayings not as mere human words, but as the words of Jesus, and not of the Jesus of the past, but in his present authority" (1983, 202). Thus prophets are near the apex of the speech-act hierarchy, for their words are divine. Bearing this out is the fact that prophesies usually come true in chronicles: the world sooner or later conforms itself to the prophet's words, often over the stubborn resistance of the people concerned:

> Oleg had asked the soothsayers, "What will I die from?" And one soothsayer had said, "Prince, from the horse that you love and ride on, from it will you die." Having taken this to heart, Oleg said, "I will never mount it, nor will I see it again." And he ordered that it be fed and not brought to him, and for several years he did not see it. . . . And in his fifth year [in Kiev], he remembered the horse. . . . And he called the head stableman and said, "Where is my horse . . . ?" And the stableman replied, "It has died." Oleg laughed and upbraided the soothsayer, saying "The soothsayers do not speak the truth, but only lies." And he ordered that his [current] horse be saddled. "Let me see its bones." And he came to the place where its bare bones and bare skull lay and dismounted, laughed, and said, "Is this the skull that is to bring me death?" And he set his foot on the skull, and a snake crawled out of the skull and bit him on the foot. And because of that he fell ill and died. (52, 54; year 912)

Here, too, verbal traditions conspire against the boastful Oleg: the inexorable prophesy and the fatal mistake of trying to thwart it. Oleg takes the soothsayer's words at surface value and, like Prince Rostislav, the Derevlians, or the Greek emperor, he must suffer for his inability to interpret their hidden meaning. This is in itself a formulaic story in which hubris and blindness to linguistic nuance go hand in hand. Traditionally, the power of prophesies lies not only in their prescience but in their special relationship to language: like poets and riddlers, prophets can demand of their audience intense engagement in the interpretive process and therefore can play off conventional and literal meanings against one another. As we have seen, this is one of the chronicle's most prized powers.

Oleg's death scene is followed by a commentary in which the reader is cautioned not to be surprised that even pagan prophesies can have magic power. Once Christianity is firmly ensconced as the primary religion, however, the conditions governing the effective utterance of prophesies become much more strict. In 1071 Prince Sviatoslav's emissary, Yan, is pitted against some pagan magicians:

> They said to Yan, "Our gods inform us that you cannot do anything to us." He said to them, "Your gods are lying to you." But they said, "We shall stand before Sviatoslav, and you can do nothing." Yan ordered that they be beaten and that their beards be shaven. [They continue to resist and he orders them gagged and bound.] . . . And Yan said to them, "Now what do your gods say to you?" They said, "Now our gods say we will not get away from you alive." And Yan said to them, "Then your gods have told you the truth." (190)

The would-be prophets are forced to change their words to suit the reality they face, thus admitting their own impotence and, what is more, the weakness of their gods. This exchange could be read as a textbook discussion of the "felicity conditions" upon the prophetic speech act (that is, the standards of necessary authority and proper performance that permit a speech act to be effective). Yan systematically proves that he, and not the pagan magicians, is the arbiter of "the truth," thereby gutting any claim they might make to being endowed with prophetic authority.

If eloquence is a sign of power in the chronicle, silence is surely the lot of the powerless.[9] Yaropolk's inability to speak for himself (in the lengthy passage cited earlier) is a clear demonstration of his weakness, although he at least retains the moral high ground of the betrayed. In a later passage in the chronicle it is the betrayers who are stricken speechless, as a sign of their moral degradation. The year is 1097, which for the chronicler is the very recent and therefore vivid past. Two cousins, Sviatopolk and David, have been plotting against a third, Vasilko, and they are stalling for a chance to seize him while he is a visitor in Kiev:

> And [Vasilko] came with few retainers to the prince's home, and Sviatopolk came out to meet him, and they went into an outbuilding, and David came and they sat down. And Sviatopolk spoke first, saying, "Stay for the holiday." And Vasilko replied, "I cannot stay, brother. I have already sent the carts on ahead of me." David, meanwhile, sat as if struck dumb. And Sviatopolk said, "At least have breakfast, brother!" And Vasilko promised to stay for breakfast. And Sviatopolk said, "You sit here, and I'll go get things in order." And he went out, while David and Vasilko remained sitting there. And Vasilko tried to converse with David, but David had neither voice nor hearing, for he was in the grip of horror and had treachery in his heart. Having sat a while, David said, "Where is my brother?" They said to him, "He's standing in the vestibule." And getting up, David said, "I'll go after him, and you, brother, sit

here." And getting up, he went out. And as soon as David left, [the guards] seized Vasilko. . . . (250)

Sviatopolk makes some attempts at conversation, although he mostly repeats earlier invitations (this passage is preceded by a lengthy account of the conspirators' attempts to persuade Vasilko to stay for Sviatopolk's name-day celebration) or simply reports on what he is doing. David is completely unable to speak to Vasilko, and only opens his mouth to get himself out of the room. Unlike other princely figures in the chronicle, these two have lost the power to change events with words; their treachery reduces them to silence or empty small talk. The whole episode is marked by frequent repetition of oral formulae ("Don't go," "Sit here," and the friendly use of the vocative "Brother"), which enhances the sense of hollow desperation and moral impotence on the part of the conspirators. In the aftermath of this scene, the cousins have Vasilko tortured, blinded, and imprisoned, but later they release him and he goes on to distinguish himself by his eloquence, both in private conversation with the chronicler and in a subsequent battle scene. Thus, the conspirators overpower him, but they do not silence his voice; if anything, they increase its righteous power.

The relationship between language and power motivates the narration of many individual scenes, but it also serves as a general theme for the chronicle as a whole. The first speech in the work appears in the opening entry, which is an encapsulated Old Testament history of the world. Significantly, it is about language (it comes during the story of the Tower of Babel), and it is spoken by God: "Lo, this is one people and one tongue" (24).[10] That this episode is singled out for detailed treatment, while the rest of the Old Testament is condensed into a few paragraphs, immediately identifies it as thematically central; the references to linguistic unity and responsible communication are not meant to be lost on the reader.

The fact that God speaks in the chronicle places subsequent speakers in authoritative company, and the fact that His words are delivered in the Old Slavic of the chronicler also lends legitimacy to the whole endeavor of writing in the Slavic language, an issue hotly disputed in church dogma in the tenth century. Later on in the chronicle, this topic is addressed explicitly by the pope (whose pronouncement is also given in Slavic): "Let the words of the book be fulfilled, that 'All tongues shall praise God'" (42; year 898). This clearly marks the chronicle as a self-conscious attempt to establish the historical and religious standing of the Slavic vernacular.

The question of the proper use of language for political and social ends is just as important as these theological debates. The correct forms for treaties, wills, and oral agreements are quoted at length. Speech acts confer legitimacy upon rulers: before his death in 1054, Yaroslav the Wise summons his sons and says, "The throne of Kiev I bequeath to my eldest son, your brother Iziaslav. Heed him as you have heeded me. . . ." This is the best example of a performative speech act (of the classic "I hereby" form) in the chronicle; it also carries strong thematic weight, as succession struggles underlie many of the work's most tragic scenes. The most notorious entry in the chronicle is the "Invitation to the Varangians" of 862, in which the

Slavic tribes inhabiting the regions near Kiev send to the Varangians, saying, "Our land is large and fruitful, but it lacks order. Come reign and rule over us" (36). However legendary the story may be, it clearly represents an attempt to legitimize the power of the Kievan princely family, and the source of such legitimacy is the spoken request.

Thus, nearly the entire chronicle can be said to be about speech acts. What is more, in the context of twelfth-century *Rus'*, such a work itself represented a special kind of speech act. Medieval literature was usually written to be read aloud, and even if there was no audience, readers in early literate society probably sounded the work out slowly, rather than scanning it mentally as we would.[11] The absence of punctuation marks or word breaks would have encouraged such an approach. They tend to bring the work much closer to a simple recording of sound than to a primarily visual means of communication. In the case of the chronicle, there were other factors as well that distanced it from what we ordinarily think of as literature. It was written in small increments over a long period of time, there is no single author, and many of the coauthors are unnamed; the idea of a unified point of view or an author/narrator division is difficult to sustain.[12] As a result, the chronicle must have seemed less like a physical entity, a book, than like an ongoing story, an action.

The *Primary Chronicle* and Oral Culture

The overwhelming prevalence of direct speech at every level in the *Primary Chronicle* justifies consideration of the work as a document of the transition from oral to literate culture.[13] Writing was introduced into the Slavic world at the end of the ninth century, and this chronicle is among the earliest known indigenous written works.[14] Many early entries draw heavily on legends, presumably of oral origin. Moreover, the emphasis on speech acts as historically significant events is fully consistent with oral tradition. Walter Ong argues that as we come to rely on print we lose the sense of speech as action:

> The fact that oral peoples commonly and in all likelihood universally consider words to have magical potency is clearly tied in, at least unconsciously, with their sense of the word as necessarily spoken, sounded, and hence power-driven. Deeply typographic folk forget to think of words as primarily oral, as events, and hence as necessarily powered: for them, words tend rather to be assimilated to things, "out there" on a flat surface. (1982, 32–33)

Seen from the viewpoint of a primarily oral culture, then, many events of the chronicle are more easily understood. The verbal dueling that seems merely colorful to a modern reader, such as Oleg's fatal boasting, Yan's argument with the pagan soothsayers, and Olga's desire to put words into her enemies' mouths, are grand assertions of power. This is true not only when the speeches change the course of events; it is inherent in the very act of speaking. The use of deictics, such as "I," "here," and "now," serves to shift the reader (or listener) into the time and space of the speaking character, who becomes the center of the world for that moment. By invoking the words of powerful or saintly characters from the past, the chronicler is himself engaging in a kind of dialogue with those luminaries. What is more, buttressed as he is by church doctrine and hindsight, he can freely praise or condemn their actions.

In a primarily oral culture, the speaker-addressee relationship is the only effective communicative context;[15] an "objective" orientation, based on universally accepted standards (such as maps) is difficult to attain. Two peace negotiations in the early eleventh century demonstrate the problem of conveying spatial relations in writing. In 1024 Mstislav addresses Yaroslav, whom he has just defeated in battle at Listven' (northeast of Kiev), and says, "You are the elder brother; you take the throne in your Kiev, but let me have this side [of the Dniepr River]" (162). Since we know who is speaking and where he is located, it is easy to interpret the meaning of "this side." Interpretation is more difficult when there is no identifiable speaker. In the next entry (1026), we read: "Yaroslav gathered many warriors and went to Kiev, and he made peace with his brother Mstislav at Gorodets [which is across the Dniepr from Kiev—RM]. And they divided the Russian land between them along the Dniepr: Yaroslav took this side, and Mstislav the other" (162). In order to understand this passage, the reader must know that the chronicler was writing in Kiev and for him, "this" side was where Kiev stood, even though the agreement was forged on the far side of the river. The presumption that the reader can pinpoint the author in space marks this work as closer to oral than to literate tradition.

Along with the change from orality to literacy and from overtly relative to supposedly objective narrative constructions has come the emergence of a new attitude toward historical speech: we view spoken words as mere vessels of meaning, important for the content they convey, rather than as events that, in effect, confer power upon the speaker by their utterance. As a result, modern historical narrative shies away from reporting first-person speech acts, except for eyewitness accounts (important as "facts," not as performances) or colorful or idiosyncratic turns of phrase (Churchill's witticisms, for example). Twentieth-century accounts of the events related in the chronicle, while relying heavily on that document for information, almost never use the speeches, which have come to seem whimsical and unhistorical to us. For example, George Vernadsky's rendition of the battles between Vladimir and Yaropolk contains only one direct quotation, Rogned's refusal of Vladimir's marriage proposal, and that is included strictly out of cultural interest, because it was taken from an epic poem on the same theme (Vernadsky 1948, 57).

It is wrong, however, to dismiss the use of speech in the medieval chronicle as symptomatic of a primitive notion of history. The distinction between "empirical" and "fictional," or between "historic" and "mimetic" that Scholes and Kellogg bring to bear in their analysis of Thucydides (1966, 60–62) betrays a modern bias that may obscure the motives behind earlier historical endeavors. For the Kievan chronicler, at any rate, the content of the speech may have been no more significant than the act of speaking.[16] Even if the actual historical figure had said nothing at a given juncture, the presence of a speech in the chronicle places the speaker in a certain relationship to other people and to the surrounding world, and the dynamics of such relationships are legitimate subjects for historians of any period.[17] Furthermore, to the extent that major themes within the chronicle—in particular, internecine strife and legitimation of rulers—were every bit as pressing at the time of writing, repetition of conciliatory speeches, oaths of allegiance, and the like in the present tense may have been the chronicler's own attempt at incantation or self-fulfilling prophesy. As Brian Stock comments in *The Implications of Literacy*, oral rituals could be absorbed into early literate culture without losing their force: in law, for example, "the ritual was the bond" (50).

That the chronicle form differs significantly from modern historical narrative is indisputable; Hayden White rightly stresses the former's strict chronological ordering and lack of narrative closure as deficiencies where the telling of a story is concerned (1987, 16). However, his claim that truly "narrativizing" histories represent events as "speaking themselves," while chronicles do not, is troublesome, at least with regard to the *Primary Chronicle*. Here, events quite literally speak themselves: the characters are permitted to pronounce the crucial statements, and their speeches are what make things happen, not the chronicler's exegetical remarks (although, of course, his editorial influence in choosing speeches and making them rhetorically forceful is undeniable). By contrast, a modern scholar only indulges in dramatizations of events when explicit sources are available, and the constant reference to these sources serves less to have the stories "speak themselves" than to turn the reader's attention back to the historian and the prevailing rules of historical scholarship.

Modern scholars appear to be uncomfortable with direct speech not just as a source of historical information but as a formal device as well. The only complete translation of the *Primary Chronicle* into English was published in 1953 by the Medieval Academy of America and based on a 1930 translation by Samuel H. Cross, revised by O. P. Sherbowitz-Wetzor. This translation renders the vast majority of the direct quotes indirectly (that is, in third person and past tense). For example, where the original entry for the year 980 reads, "And Blud said to Yaropolk, 'Go to your brother and say to him whatever you give me I will accept'" (92), the Cross version is, "Blud next induced Yaropolk to appear before his brother and express his readiness to accept any terms he might offer" (93). For all its bookishness, this style reads smoothly to the modern ear and the editors were clearly satisfied as long as factual information was being retained (although there are also numerous outright inaccuracies in the Cross version). However, the importance of speech *as speech* is lost, as is the sense of power that comes through speech. In this case, for example, Blud's sophisticated use of double entendre becomes, in Cross's rendering, simply another act of treachery.

Even in those scenes where speech primarily serves a dramatic rather than a constative purpose, the translator still limits himself to giving the content. The episode of the blinding of Vasilko (1097, cited earlier in my essentially literal translation) receives the following treatment from Cross:

> David sat silent as if struck dumb, till Svyatopolk invited Vasil'ko to breakfast with them, and Vasil'ko accepted. Then Svyatopolk said, "Remain seated here a moment while I go out and make a certain disposition." He thus went out, leaving David and Vasil'ko alone together. Vasil'ko tried to open a conversation with David, but there

was no voice nor hearing in him, for he was afraid, and had treachery in his heart. After he had sat awhile, he inquired where his cousin was. The answer was given that he was standing in the vestibule. David then rose and asked Vasil'ko to remain seated while he sent in search of Svyatopolk. He then stood up and went thence. When David had thus gone out, others seized upon Vasil'ko. . . . (189).

The facts are not missing from Cross's version, but the effect is very different. In the original, the speeches bring the action into the present tense ("Where is my brother?") and the first person ("I'll go after him"). They also emphasize the awkwardness of the face-to-face contact: for example, both Sviatopolk and David address their cousin Vasilko as "brother" in the friendly manner, while plotting against him. Cross conveys the basic content of the speeches but omits terms of address and other dramatic frills. In his account, David's inquiries seem rational and even nonchalant, while in the original they are excruciating outbursts in the midst of strained silence. The fact that Cross could have felt this passage to be equivalent to the original shows how distant he was from a sense of speech as action. No doubt, he believed he was spurring the action along (after all, in our culture action is often opposed to dialogue, not seen as inherent in it), but he ultimately sacrificed much of the chronicle's impact.

Thus, for the chronicler, historical speech had a power that it has since lost. To assert that this is entirely a culturally determined change, however, would be to detract from the stylistic force of the work, which is admirably suited to its special purpose. By using simple parataxis instead of more complex syntactic structures, the chronicler achieves a directness that brings the characters and their interactions into relief and gives their moral examples a compelling immediacy for the reader (or listener). The great prototype for this style is, of course, the Bible, of which Nancy Partner writes, "Once a stylistic embarrassment to educated pagan converts, [it] became the model for a new, emotional and powerful style whose connections were not causal or temporal but somehow 'vertical,' linking earthly events to the divine will" (1977, 198). The Bible, however, was translated into unadulterated Old Church Slavic, a high-church language distinct from the vernacular; the chronicle, by contrast, makes use of a mixture of the two languages, which allows for formal experimentation and a kind of dialogue between audience and character at a more accessible level (Worth 1984, 245). The resulting diglossia is still fairly circumscribed by conventions on the use of the church language in particular, and further restricted by the formulaic nature of many episodes; by interspersing first-person speech and simple narrative, the chronicler achieves a higher degree of heteroglossia than would otherwise be possible.

The force of the chronicle's style may also have been enhanced by the fact that it mimicked a familiar form of medieval oral communication in which envoys carried messages between leaders. The way these are described suggests that envoys repeated speeches verbatim, in the first person, as if they themselves were but a recording medium or, as D. S. Likhachev suggests, a proxy for the original speakers: "The envoy spoke in the name of the one who had sent him as if at the moment of speaking he were that sender."[18] (Note, for example, the following construction from 980: "And Blud said to Vladimir's envoys, 'I will be your ally'"

[Likhachev 1947, 90]. He uses the second-person singular, as if he were addressing Vladimir himself.) In the social context of the tenth and eleventh centuries, then, there must have been tacit acceptance of a pure communicative voice which the chronicler, like the ambassador, could adopt.[19] This contrasts markedly with present-day historical discourse which, according to Roland Barthes, always has an extra layer of communicative complexity in the form of the historian's act of utterance. The "shifters" that indicate this act, he writes, "[complicate] the chronological time of history by bringing it up against another time, which is that of the discourse itself and could be termed for short the 'paper-time'" (1981, 10). This applies equally well to modern readings (and translations!) of the chronicle, but perhaps not to its early reception, when shifting time and person was a standard communicative approach.

A further advantage of the chronicle's style—particularly in its use of dramatic dialogue and short episodes that crescendo to a world-changing speech act—is that it aids memory and, perhaps, helps the reader to follow the rapid changes of scene and players necessitated by the episodic structure. Although the recording of the text presumably obviated the need for individuals to retain all the information in their heads, the prevailing concept of history was still an oral one in which memory served as the source and memorableness as the goal. According to H. Marshall Leicester, Jr., "What is remembered [in oral cultures] is what the society has *structured as memorable*: the traditional, the formulaic, the orthodox. What lasts is not what an individual does, but what everybody knows" (1987, 21). The characters' speeches are not, by and large, especially eloquent or original; they are formulae whose meaning lies in the speaker and the context, in their memorableness. They may also have offered an accurate reflection of prevailing oral patterns: Likhachev mentions in his introduction to the *Primary Chronicle* that short, pithy speeches were a necessity—and a litmus test of leadership skills—in a culture that depended on envoys carrying messages in their heads, sometimes over very long distances (1978, 16–17).

It cannot be said that liberal use of dialogue was original with the chroniclers; they need only have taken their model from the historical passages of the Old Testament (Samuel and Kings are good examples). Other European chronicles also use this style, although rarely to such a degree as the Slavic one, or with such verisimilitude.[20] Likhachev points out, moreover, that speech in Byzantine chronicles is almost exclusively monologic and lacks the liveliness of dialogue in the *Primary Chronicle*.[21] Even among Slavic writings of its own period the *Primary Chronicle* stands out. Nestor's *Life of Theodosius* (1080s) and the *Tale of Boris and Gleb* contain some dialogue and a great many biblical quotations, as does Vladimir Monomakh's *Instruction* (1117), but here speeches tend to reflect the characters' inner states or to report and describe experience, rather than to change the course of events. (In the case of the hagiographic works, this is partly explainable by the monastic glorification of prayerful silence and the avoidance of worldly influence.) The contrast, then, between the use of speech in these works and in the *Primary Chronicle* mirrors the constative-performative contrast between language as an instrument of truth and knowledge, on the one hand, and language as a means to an end, on the other (see Felman 1980, 27). Unlike the hagiographers, the chroniclers were thoroughly pragmatic in their approach to narrative.

The *Primary Chronicle* takes its authority from the spoken word: first from God's word, and later from the speeches of princes and other leaders. However, the chronicle is a written document that ultimately serves to undermine the very speech-act force that it sets out to codify. Even when the manuscript was read aloud, the immediacy and world-changing quality of the speaker-addressee relationship was lost, because the written words were unchangeable. Benveniste rightly points out that a performative act cannot be repeated or reported by a third party without losing its performative status and becoming a constative utterance (1966, 273; see also Felman 1980, 21). Once history is recorded, then, it becomes a set of "facts"; we read the *Primary Chronicle* today for information or cultural insights, not to revive the force of the words as actions. The content of the speeches has become paramount, even though we know that they were at best approximations to what, if anything, was actually said. (The "Invitation to the Varangians," perhaps a mere device of oral-formulaic storytelling, has engendered endless scholarly speculation and heated political debate as to the origins of the Russian ruling family, for example.[22]) Although the narrator within the text temporarily yields performative authority to the characters, taking up only the ostensibly constative role, in the long run this narrator has the ultimate performative power—the power to create a history, presumably with political ends in mind, out of legend and collective memory.

ACKNOWLEDGMENTS   I wish to thank William Mills Todd III, Mary Louise Pratt, Ernest R. May, Joseph van Campen, Jehanne Gheith, Thomas P. Hodge, Michael Macovski, and the late Edward J. Brown for their provocative and helpful suggestions.

Notes

1. As Richard Vaughan puts it, "The sort of manipulation, selection, even invention, to which the past was subjected in the middle ages shows that, even if some medieval historians accepted the notion of God's plan at work in history, they did not scruple to revise that plan in the light of their own needs" ("The Past in the Middle Ages," *Journal of Medieval History* 12, no.1 [March 1986]: 11).

2. Nancy Partner comments that "the admittedly simple relationship between history and fictional narrative has not been much explored, perhaps because literary critics do not find medieval histories aesthetically interesting and historians deplore what they consider an illicit and improper connection" (1977, 195).

3. In this respect, medieval Russian writing showed similarities to other European writing of the time. Karen Pratt remarks of Old French romances, "Around sections of dialogue are constructed what modern critics frequently designate as 'scenes' (a term which usefully underlines the dramatic nature of much medieval narrative)" (1989, 213).

4. The issue of the linguistic construction of direct and indirect speech in the *Primary Chronicle* could be the subject of a lengthy study by itself. There are very few instances of true *indirect* speech in this work, which has suggested to some that the abun-

dance of dialogue might have been syntactically necessary, rather than stylistically motivated. Joseph van Campen, for example, makes the interesting point that if indirect speech in modern Russian preserves the tense shifters of the direct quotation, it is possible that Old Russian preserved the person shifters as well (personal conversation, 22 July 1988). However, examples can be found in contemporary works, such as Nestor's *Life of Theodosius*, of indirect speech that uses third-person constructions: ". . . poklonisja emu sъ slьzami, moljasja emu da by u nego bylъ" (literally, "he bowed to him in tears, beseeching him that [he] might stay with *him*" [rather than "that {I} might stay with *you*], 237); "I zapovedavъ suščimъ s nimь, da dopravjatь têlo ego vъ manastyrь . . ." ("And commanding those who were with him that *they* take *his* body to the monastery," 250). From "Nestor's *Life of Theodosius, First Abbot of the Cave Monastery*," *Anthology of Old Russian Literature*, edited by Ad. Stender-Petersen (New York and London: Columbia University Press, 1966), 230–77.

5. The distinction is put in these terms by Stanley Fish in his study of *Coriolanus* as a play about speech acts. "How to Do Things with Austin and Searle," *Modern Language Notes* 91 (1976): 983–1025.

6. Translations from the *Primary Chronicle* in this chapter are my own. Where possible, I have attempted to retain the original syntax, although this sometimes results in awkward constructions in English. The edition from which these passages are taken is in *Pamiatniki literatury drevnei Rusi, XI–nachalo XII veka*, ed. L. A. Dmitriev and D. S. Likhachev (Moscow: Khudozhestvennaia literatura, 1978), 22–277. This text renders the chronicle in modern type, with abbreviations filled out and word breaks and punctuation marks inserted. It also includes a translation into modern Russian, which I have consulted for my own translation. The fact that direct quotations are clearly punctuated in this version of the text but not in the original should not be taken as a sign that direct speech is somehow read into the chronicle by modern readers. All the quotations are discernible in the original, due to the use of first-person or present-tense constructions, or because of the presence of deictic terms. In fact, it is possible that some sentences that lack these indicators were also intended by the chronicler as direct speech, but they cannot be so identified today.

7. George Vernadsky writes, "To draw off the boots of her husband was one of the symbolic acts of the bride in the Old Russian marriage ceremony" (1948, 57). Vladimir and Yaropolk had the same father, but Vladimir's mother had been a servant of his paternal grandmother Olga; see Cross and Sherbowitz-Wetzer translation (1973, 241 n.69).

8. Grateful acknowledgment is due Mary Louise Pratt for pointing out the special nature of prophesies within the realm of speech acts (private conversation, 20 July 1988).

9. Monks, by contrast, valued silence above all. (Theodosius is extremely strict with monks who are heard to be chatting together, for example, and vows of silence are common.) It is ironic that the chroniclers who used speech so well in their writing were products of a monastic environment.

10. The original text is more ambiguous than this, for the Old Slavic term for language (*jazykъ*) is also used to mean "tribe" or "people." In fact, one authoritative translation into modern Russian gives this as, "*Vot rod edin i narod edin*," or, roughly, "Here is one stock (creatures of one origin) and one people." I prefer to be guided by the traditional translations of the Old Testament, which refer explicitly to language.

11. Writes Albert Lord, "H. J. Chaytor has told the fascinating story of medieval man's laborious reading aloud of manuscripts, making them out letter for letter and word for word" (1960, 220). See also Ong (1982, 119).

12. Scholes and Kellogg maintain that the ironic distance between author and narrator is possible only in written narrative, while "traditional, oral narrative consists rhetorically of a teller, his story, and an implied audience" (1966, 53). The chronicle seems to be a hybrid, an oral-type narrative in which a number of different tellers take turns adding episodes.

13. Dennis Seniff gives an interesting discussion of diglossia in medieval works, based on the mingling of oral and textual or written aspects. Among the former he includes direct address and exhortation; use of proverbs, comedy, and popular tales; and references to words, sounds, silence, reading, hearing, speaking, and so on, all of which are abundantly present in the *Primary Chronicle*. Textual aspects include biblical elements, references to lists and geographical sources, and commentary on the literary process, which are also present here, if to a lesser degree (1987, 153).

14. Although the monk Sylvester signed and dated his version in 1116, the earliest extant manuscript is from 1377, known as the Laurentian redaction.

15. Walter Ong's discussion of the "verbomotor lifestyle" is illuminating in this regard (1982, 68–69).

16. Riccardo Picchio says the following about the "open tradition" of Old Russian authorship, but it could hold just as well for internal quotations: "The idea that 'true words' were not the individual property of any human was based on the assumption that such words could only come from above" (1984, 252). There is evidence that literacy brings a shift in the whole concept of what constitutes a quotation. The formulaic nature of oral composition not only aided but constructed memory: Ong claims that oral cultures feel less need for verbatim memorization than literate ones (1982, 64–65).

17. This is not to say that the speeches are all fabricated. Likhachev writes that "the Russian chronicles show striking accuracy in conveying words spoken in the historical circumstances, and they preserve the formulae correctly" (1947, 114).

18. Likhachev (1947, 118). Likhachev also notes that this convention led both senders and receivers of messages to ignore the envoys' presence and act as if they were speaking directly to one another (1952, 96–102).

19. For the monks writing the chronicle, this must have allowed both a desirable degree of self-effacement and a gratifying sense of vicarious power.

20. See, for example, Gregory of Tours's sixth-century *History of the Franks* or the thirteenth-century Icelandic sagas of Snorri Sturluson. Oral narrative tends to be rich in dialogue, too, as evidenced by Jan Vansina's account of Kurumba legends (1985, 72–73).

21. Of speech in the *Primary Chronicle* Likhachev writes, "This is not book-talk but true oral speech, closely reflecting words that were actually spoken. It is precisely in its use of direct speech that the chronicle displays its connection to life itself" (1947, 114). See also Likhachev (1952, 93–102).

22. See, for example, the discussion of the "Norman theory" in Nicholas Riasanovsky, *A History of Russia*, 3d ed. (New York: Oxford University Press, 1977), 25–28.

Works Cited

Primary Sources

Povest' vremennykh let. In *Pamiatniki literatury drevnei Rusi*, edited by L. A. Dmitriev and D. S. Likhachev. Moscow: Khudozhestvennaia literatura, 1978.
The Russian Primary Chronicle. Translated and edited by S. H. Cross and O. P. Sherbowitz-Wetzer. Cambridge, Mass.: Mediaeval Academy of America, 1973.

Secondary Sources

Barthes, Roland. "The Discourse of History." In *Comparative Criticism. A Yearbook*, edited by E. S. Shaffer. Cambridge: Cambridge University Press, 1981.

Benveniste, Emile. *Problèmes de la linguistique genérale*. 2 vols. Paris: Gallimard, 1966.

Crosby, Ruth. "Oral Delivery in the Middle Ages." *Speculum* 11 (1936): 88–110.

Eremin, I. P. *Literatura drevnei Rusi*. Moscow: Akademiia nauk, 1966.

Felman, Shoshana. *The Literary Speech Act*. Translated by Catherine Porter. Ithaca, N.Y.: Cornell University Press, 1980.

Fish, Stanley E. "How to Do Things with Austin and Searle: Speech Act Theory and Literary Criticism." *Modern Language Notes* 91 (1976): 983–1025.

Kelber, Werner H. *The Oral and Written Gospel*. Philadelphia: Fortress, 1983.

Leicester, H. Marshall. "Oure tonges *différance*: Textuality and Deconstruction in Chaucer." In *Medieval Texts and Contemporary Readers*, edited by Laurie A. Finke and Martin B. Schichtman. Ithaca, N.Y.: Cornell University Press, 1987.

Levinson, Stephen, *Pragmatics*. Cambridge Textbooks in Linguistics. Cambridge: Cambridge University Press, 1983.

Likhachev, D. S. *Vozniknovenie russkoi literatury*. Moscow and Leningrad: Akademiia nauk SSSR, 1952.

———. *Russkie letopisi i ikh kul'turno-istoricheskoe znachenie*. Moscow: Akademiia nauk, 1947.

———. "Velichie drevnei literatury." In *Pamiatniki literatury drevnei Rusi*, edited by L. A. Dmitriev and D. S. Likhachev. Moscow: Khudozhestvennaia literatura, 1978.

Logan, Richard D. "A Conception of the Self in the Later Middle Ages." *Journal of Medieval History* 12 (1986): 253–68.

Lord, Albert B. *The Singer of Tales*. Cambridge: Harvard University Press, 1960.

Magnusson, Magnus, and Hermann Palsson. "Introduction" to Snorri Sturluson, *King Harald's Saga*. Hammondsworth, England: Penguin, 1976.

Ong, Walter J. *Orality and Literacy*. London: Methuen, 1982.

———. "Orality, Literacy, and Medieval Textualization." *New Literary History* 16, no.1 (1984): 1–12.

Page, Norman. *Speech in the English Novel*. London: Longman, 1973.

Partner, Nancy F. *Serious Entertainments: The Writing of History in Twelfth-Century England*. Chicago: University of Chicago Press, 1977.

Picchio, Riccardo. "The Impact of Ecclesiastic Culture on Old Russian Literary Techniques." In *Medieval Russian Culture*, California Slavic Studies no. 12, edited by Henrik Birnbaum and Michael S. Flier. Berkeley and Los Angeles: University of California Press, 1984.

Pratt, Karen. "Direct Speech—A Key to the German Adaptor's Art?" In *Medieval Translators and Their Craft*, Studies in Medieval Culture 25, edited by Jeannette Peer. Kalamazoo, Michigan: Western Michigan University, Medieval Institute Publications, 1989), 213–46.

Pratt, Mary Louise. "Toward a Speech Act Theory of Literary Discourse." Ph.D. diss., Stanford University, 1975.

Sadock, Jerold M. *Toward a Linguistic Theory of Speech Acts*. New York: Academic Press, 1974.

Scholes, Robert, and Robert Kellogg. *The Nature of Narrative*. New York: Oxford University Press, 1966.

Seniff, Dennis P. "Orality and Textuality in Medieval Castilian Prose." *Oral Tradition* 2, no. 1 (1987): 150–71.

Spiegel, Gabrielle M. *"Pseudo-Turpin,* the Crisis of the Aristocracy and the Beginnings of Vernacular Historiography in France." *Journal of Medieval History* 12 (1986): 207–23.

Stetsenko, A. N. *Slozhnosochinennoe prediozhenie v drevnerusskom iazyke.* Tomsk, Russia: Izdatel'stvo tomskogo universiteta, 1962.

Stock, Brian. *The Implications of Literacy.* Princeton, N.J.: Princeton University Press, 1983.

Traugott, Elizabeth Closs, and Mary Louise Pratt. *Linguistics for Students of Literature.* New York: Harcourt, 1980.

van Dijk, Teun A., ed. *Discourse and Literature.* Amsterdam: John Benjamins, 1985.

Vansina, Jan. *Oral Tradition as History.* Madison: University of Wisconsin Press, 1985.

Vaughan, Richard. "The Past in the Middle Ages." *Journal of Medieval History* 12 (1986): 1–14.

Vernadsky, George. *Kievan Russia.* New Haven, Conn.: Yale University Press, 1948.

White, Hayden, *The Content of the Form.* Baltimore: Johns Hopkins University Press, 1987.

Worth, Dean S. "Toward a Social History of Russian." In *Medieval Russian Culture,* California Slavic Studies no. 12, edited by Henrik Birnbaum and Michael S. Flier. Berkeley and Los Angeles: University of California Press, 1984.

Crossroads to Community

Jude the Obscure *and the* Chronotope of Wessex

Time and space merge here into an inseparable unity, both in the plot itself and in its individual images. In the majority of cases, a definite and absolutely concrete locality serves as the starting point for the creative imagination. But this is not an abstract landscape . . . no, this is a piece of human history. . . . Therefore the plot . . . and the characters do not enter it from outside, are not invented to fit the landscape, but are unfolded in it as though they were present from the very beginning.

> M. M. Bakhtin,
> "The *Bildungsroman*"

Remembrance, return, and repetition are eerie experiences in Thomas Hardy. Peter Casagrande points out that "the 'truth'" Hardy attempted to exhibit in *The Return of the Native*, his most tellingly titled book, "is the law of nature that he had contended with from the beginning—that all is change and all change decay. . . . Thus homecoming and its attendant hope of personal and social renewal must be seen as futile and destructive, even unnatural" (1982, 127). J. Hillis Miller has recently read Hardy's marked emphasis on repetition as a Freudian scenario: "[E]ach man or woman moves forward through life repeating an unsuccessful attempt to reach again a seemingly lost primal unity" (1982, 135). Yet the echoings, recollections, and reformations that emerge so readily in Hardy's novels have another kind of quality as well. They give dimension to the environment and substance to the figures of the fiction. Hardy's novels seem filled with the spirit of Tennyson's Tithonus who, knowing the cruelty of the gods, longs for death and yet comes immensely alive and present to himself in the act of telling his story. What enables Hardy to maintain in his novels his sense of both dissolution and resurgence is the rivalry of voices and speech genres that register in the narrative and echo throughout the thickly textured world in which the characters move and communicate "as though they were present from the very beginning."[1] The point may be illustrated by what is probably the best-known commentary on *Jude the Obscure*. Hardy's friend Edmund Gosse concluded his review of the novel testily:

> One word must be added about the speech of the author and of the characters of
> *Jude the Obscure*. Is it too late to urge Mr. Hardy to struggle against the jarring note
> of rebellion which seems growing upon him? . . . What has Providence done to Mr.
> Hardy that he should rise up in the arable land of Wessex and shake his fist at his
> Creator? . . . We wish he would go back to Egdon Heath and listen to the singing of
> the heather. And as to the conversations of his semi-educated characters, they are
> really terrible. Sue and Jude talk a sort of University Extension jargon that breaks
> the heart.[2]

Gosse gives away his perception of the dialogized discourse of the narrator who
is not only the fist-shaking adversary of the Creator but the voice of the Creator as
well, just as he is also the demiurge in "the arable land of Wessex" which for Gosse,
who has clearly been there, and the narrator in his demiurgic utterances, is a place
more suited to singing than fist shaking. Moreover, Gosse performs the service of
embodying the very voice of social privilege at which Jude and Sue shake their fists
as they attempt to ingrain their own discourse with the deep traditions of their culture before that culture breaks their hearts. All of these positions, voices, and
coexistences form a social heteroglossia the effect of which is often to reconstitute
and reprise both actions and utterances as they cross in space and time through
alien territories. Hardy's repetitions and returns point as much to dialogic interaction as to states of dissolution.

An implicit social analysis is involved in this distinction. The dissolved self is
located by Hardy in a social structure that reifies human relationships and leaves
each person alone and exposed to a metaphysics of "fate," "Crass Casualty," and
"Purblind Doomsters." Nothing in the institutional context or the sedimentary
cultural discourses that attend individual lives supports any de-reifying process or
effect. From this perspective the world looks to Hardy just as he described how the
British Museum Reading Room looked to him one March afternoon in 1888:

> Souls are gliding about here in a sort of dream—screened somewhat by their bod-
> ies, but imaginable behind them. Dissolution is gnawing at them all, slightly ham-
> pered by renovation. In the great circle of the library Time is looking into Space.
> Coughs are floating in the same great vault, mixing with the rustle of book-leaves
> risen from the dead, and the touches of footsteps on the floor.

Hardy had already begun thinking of *Jude* when he made this note,[3] and the note
in fact anticipates the bleak estrangements, dead letters, decaying selves, and
coffined culture that the fist-shaking narrator of *Jude* invites us to see. Supremely
abstract Time looks into utterly unmarked Space; all sounds are hollow; all selves
disintegrate.

But Hardy's novels are never set in such objectified environments. They are set
in the great chronotope he called Wessex. Wessex has pretty much remained the
preserve of enthusiastic scene-spotters and eminent historians of regional realism,
but this domain of Hardy's fiction is much greater than the sum of its local parts.
And while recent critics like Faurot and Moore have devised productive new approaches to Wessex, I have invoked Bakhtin's concept of the chronotope because it

seems especially germane to the uses Hardy makes of the distinctive world in which he sets his fiction. Chronotope (literally "time-space") refers, Bakhtin says,

> to the intrinsic connectedness of temporal and spatial relationships that are artistically expressed in literature. . . . In the literary chronotope, spatial and temporal indicators are fused into one carefully thought-out, concrete whole. Time, as it were, thickens, takes on flesh, becomes artistically visible; likewise, space becomes charged and responsive to the movements of time, plot and history. This intersection of axes and fusion of indicators characterizes the artistic chronotope (1981, 84).

Chronotope is thus something like what an older critical discourse referred to as milieu, but it is to milieu as the forest floor is to an earthtone carpet. For the sumptuous implications and applications of Bakhtin's concept I must refer the reader to the detailed discussions by Holquist (1990) and Morson and Emerson (1990). At the moment, my appropriation of the chronotope for the purpose of re-reading Wessex is limited to four points. The chronotope can, very simply, refer to ways in which spatial and temporal elements in a narrative are thematized, such as in the figure of the crossroads that we so often find in Hardy's novels. More pervasively, the chronotope may be understood as an inclusive term for the intricate temporal relations of story and discourse as they form themselves within the space of a narrative text. But the chronotope is also the dialogic interaction of time and space where human spaces are densely sedimented with layers of historical time which are themselves conceived in dialogic relation with one another. Finally, there are chronotopic perspectives that emerge from the reflections of one narrative's inevitable associations with the time-spaces formed by other narratives that are contemporary with it. In Hardy's case, one form of chronotopic dialogism is quite deliberate since, as I will suggest, Wessex is a reconstruction of the Arthurian chronotope that so preoccupied Victorian writers.

In the Wessex chronotope, time does not stare blankly into space but inscribes it. Hardy constructs his world much in the manner in which Bakhtin sees Scott constructing his: "For [Scott] each clump of land was saturated with certain events from local legends . . . but, on the other hand, each event was strictly localized, condensed in spatial markers. His eye could see time in space" (1986, 53). Bakhtin also develops a key point that relates the phenomenon of the chronotope to the social analysis that Hardy's construction of the Wessex chronotope implies:

> The chronotope makes narrative events concrete, makes them take on flesh, causes blood to flow in their veins. An event can be communicated, it becomes information. . . . Thus the chronotope, functioning as the primary means for materializing time in space, emerges as a center for concretizing representation, as a force giving body to the entire novel. All the novel's abstract elements . . . gravitate toward the chronotope and through it take on flesh and blood, permitting the imagining power of art to do its work. (1981, 250)

Conceived in this way Wessex becomes a place where social being and social construction resist the objectifications and alienations of the Victorian socioeconomic state. In Scott's novels, the chronotope is offered as virtually an image and a ground of presumptive solidarity. A similar tendency is one of the most powerful and privileged motives in the nineteenth-century novel, coming to resonant expression in the early novels of George Eliot. For Hardy, the case is much more problematic. He cannot completely reconstruct Eliot's knowable communities as a foil to the hegemony of the socioeconomic state. In Hardy's world, even bedrock tends to be cracked. Yet Wessex, though never so immediately knowable as Eliot's world, is no less endowed with the structures of communal life. Wessex reflects a social environment too intimate, too many-dimensioned, too dialogically active to be dominated by a formation as bloodless as the bureaucratized Victorian state. Even in *Jude the Obscure* Hardy's Wessex "is a concrete and visible world of human space and human history" (1986, 42) that, by its very nature, resists erosion either by irony or ideology. And although within Hardy's narrative voice we can always hear his Reading Room abstractions, the narrator also patiently cultivates "points of view, consciousnesses, voices" (Bakhtin 1984, 93) as an ensemble that reconstructs the experience of solidarity.

The dialogic reverberations that penetrate the deep strata of narrative discourse in *Jude* represent a counterstatement to the dead letters that litter the novel's text. Jude suffers and dies amid those reverberations, but he nonetheless retains his sense of connection and concreteness because of them. The conflicts and tensions inherent in this claim can only be sorted out if we make the effort to follow Jude in his chronotopic journey. It would seem, in some respects, that Jude's journey is a hopeless affair, a diagram of the dissolved self. Bakhtin, in a passage on Tolstoy, describes what might be taken as the exiguous achievement of Hardy's dialogization:

> Tolstoy's discourse harmonizes and disharmonizes . . . with various aspects of the heteroglot social-verbal consciousness ensnaring the object, while at the same time polemically invading the reader's belief and evaluative system, striving to stun and destroy the apperceptive background of the reader's active understanding. (1981, 283)

But Jude himself resists this narration of his journey. Jude remains on the boundary of discourse, between his own discourse and another's. He does not so much seek a road as a crossroads; indeed, it is his sense of crossed roads that establishes his sense of community or, as he would call it, "fellow-feeling."

On one of their walks together Jude and Sue "crossed a main road running due east and west—the old road from London to Land's End. They paused, and looked up and down it for a moment, and remarked upon the desolation which had come over this once lively thoroughfare, while the wind dipped to earth and scooped straws and hay-stems from the ground" (110). A moment before, Jude had cut "a long walking-stick for Sue as tall as herself, with a great crook, which made her look like a shepherdess" (110). The scene illustrates what happens at the crossroads in *Jude the Obscure*. Both the narrator's discourse and the discourse of the characters are woven into a past that, in turn, infuses the present with a new life just as the wind in this pastoral scene stirs the hay-stems. Jude and Sue intersect with forms of love and life that are both beyond their reach and yet within their range. The desolation, of course, is ominous, but the narrator does not "stun and destroy the apperceptive background" that enables the reader to perceive the history of emotions that animate Jude and Sue and reanimate the scene. Moreover, this episode itself forms a crossroads with many other episodes in the novel. Jude and Sue meet for the first time "at the cross in the pavement which marked the spot of the Martyrdoms" (81). Later, at another critical point, Jude wanders "unconsciously . . . to a spot called The Fourways" and falls to thinking "what struggling people like himself had stood at that Crossway, whom nobody ever thought of now. It had more history than the oldest college in the city. . . . He began to see that the town life was a book of humanity infinitely more palpitating, varied, and compendious than the gown life" (96).

The crossroads is one of the basic tropes in *Jude* and it reflects the crisscrossed, heteroglossic nature of the text we are reading. The figures who appear at the crossroads are inevitably diminished by their belatedness, as Jude is struck "by impish echoes of his own footsteps" (70) when he tours Christminster. But the crossroads, as indeed the text, is the environment where heteroglossia is dialogized. The figure crossing the crossroads fills the ghostliness of the past with a specific context and accents the utterance of history with a particular and renewed consciousness of its presence. "Like all newcomers to a spot on which the past is deeply graven he heard that past announcing itself with an emphasis altogether unsuspected by, and even incredible to, the habitual residents" (70). Such encounters, which appear both in the text and *as the text*, have the effect of diminishing the diminutions of the ironic narrator while crossing the alien word of the Victorian socioeconomic state with a language of communal consciousness. That language also belongs to the narrator and we hear it in his very preoccupation with constructing crossroads.

Indeed, it is important to realize that the narrator in *Jude the Obscure* speaks in several voices because he is himself a crossroads figure. The very act of constructing a text involves him in the same complex struggle between the spirit and the letter that reflects itself so often in the puzzled actions of the main characters. The narrator projects himself as the figure who, on the one hand, devised the novel's bitter epigraph, "The letter killeth," and, on the other hand, as the modern tragedian who keeps searching among the novel's vast array of inscriptions, quotations, notes, codes, cultural discourses, and, most importantly, its own poignant utterance for the completing spirit that giveth life. The relations of the letter and spirit form one of the primary dialogic dimensions of the novel, enabling us to perceive the double-voiced narrator seeking his direction at the crossroads where irony and tragedy intersect. And these roads intersect with all other roads in the novel.

To follow Jude's journey is to follow these crossroads, to be crossing from one ideologeme to another. The scheme of the whole novel, which Hardy once described as a "quadrille" (F. E. Hardy 1962, 273), can be laid out as a crisscross. All four of the main characters begin their novelistic lives in or near Marygreen. They all travel, but at different times, to Christminster. Then each moves on from Christminster to live somewhere else. But having dispersed from Christminster, they all ultimately return to it, or through it, crossing their own tracks and each other's as they do, ironically growing more emotionally estranged as their paths reconnect. For Arabella, Sue, and Phillotson, the returns are accompanied by retreats into hardened, finalized forms of themselves, roads to nowhere or cul-de-sacs of identity. Sue declines into dogma. Phillotson—who once opened himself, remarkably, to the alien discourse of another, internalized it, and acted dialogically—yields to patriarchy and self-propaganda. Arabella, who even had once mustered sufficient spirit for a little religious conversion, learns nothing and ends, where she began, as a heartless sham. Each of the three discovers, and lays active claim to, his or her own worst self. But Jude remains on the road.

In Bakhtin's understanding, the chronotope "is the place where the knots of the narrative are tied and untied" (1981, 250). For Hardy, Wessex is the chronotope where the roads of the narrative are crossed and recrossed. Jude is always affected by a Wessex topography that is also a Wessex historiography. All roadways in Wessex are covered with signs. All systems of roads are covered with other systems. This novel, for example, makes the railway network a critical new feature of the chronotope, a point of moral departure (as when Sue leaves Phillotson and meets Jude at a train station) and historic arrival (as when Father Time makes his entry "in the gloom of a third-class carriage" [218]). All of the roads and road systems carry the heteroglossic and intertextual traffic of Wessex. There is, however, a key crossroads, the very point at which Jude's journey begins, that is especially worth surveying.

Jude takes his first step toward Christminster when, as a child, he ventures out on a northeastward road hoping to catch a glimpse of the distant city. The path he takes

> was a public one, . . . climbing up [a] long and tedious ascent . . . till the track joined the highway by a little clump of trees. . . . Not a soul was visible on the hedgeless highway . . . and the white road seemed to ascend and diminish till it joined the sky. At the very top it was crossed at right angles by a green "ridgeway"—the Icknield Street and original Roman road through the district. (17)

The road north leads to Christminster; the Roman road leads all the way southwest to Cornwall. The road north takes Jude to the city of light; the old Roman road carries the traveler to the site of passion. Jude never travels to Cornwall, but he is always shadowed, nonetheless, by Tristram, Mark, and the two Iseults. The Wessex chronotope is indelibly and expressively inscribed by the signs and traces of the Arthurian romances, and in this novel the central romance is the story of Tristram.[4] I can offer only a few words about the Tristram allusions here since, in this study, I am more concerned with the chronotopic than the intertextual issues in *Jude*.[5] The crossroads at the hedgeless highway reminds us that Jude is never really going in just one direction as though he were in the grasp of something like Father Time's "steady mechanical creep" (219). His movement is multiple. It is centered by both the intersections and the collisions in the novel of knowledge and passion, chivalry and socialism, Camelot and Christminster, history and fiction. Though Jude is barred from the colleges, he is immersed in the chronotope. Wessex remains heteroglot; as such, it retains the discourse of communal consciousness among its social languages.

Jude's story is enacted at the northeastern edge of Wessex; Tristram's story begins at the southwestern edge. Hardy had been to the southwestern edge—on the very significant occasion when he met Emma Gifford (whom he married in 1874) — and had composed one of his earliest and finest poems to commemorate the event, "When I Set Out for Lyonnesse" (1870), his first appropriation of the Tristram story. Fifty-three years later, near the very end of his life, he was still fascinated by the story and wrote *The Famous Tragedy of the Queen of Cornwall* which was staged, according to his own direction and drawings, on a set modeled after the Great Hall of Tintagel Castle. We can recognize the chivalric romance as an intertext in *Jude* by observing how Phillotson, as a surrogate father, plays King Mark to Jude's Tristram, an allusion brought to its sharpest focus when Jude has to "give away" Sue to Phillotson on the day of their wedding. Hardy rearranged the relations of the two Iseults, Sue and Arabella, but he maintained in Sue and Jude the intense, completely hopeless relationship of Tristram and Iseult of Ireland (a relationship critically influenced by Hardy's strange, life-imitating-art reprise of the Tristram story when he met Florence Henniker, the model for Sue, in Ireland).[6] Perhaps the most telling motif that Hardy imports from the romance is the "love-philter." But this becomes the concoction of a quack physician produced in earnest only at the end of the novel. The drugs binding Jude to Sue and Jude to Arabella are present, already a feature of human nature, from the beginning (though the Tristram-like effects of a magic potion are sustained in Jude's predilection for drink). Undoubtedly the most poignant connection between the romance and the novel comes when Jude lies dying, muttering Sue's name. Sue does not come. Hardy is recalling not only the romance itself but the deathbed scenes in Arnold's and Swinburne's retellings of the story.

But the Tristram story is cited here not so much as a literary source as for the way in which its axial position helps us to read Jude's journey in Wessex. The Wessex chronotope keeps Jude anchored in a social space that does not — because it cannot — obliterate the images of human solidarity that both Camelot and Christminster, especially in their Victorian versions, persist in evoking. Jude struggles to ally himself with dreamy conceptions of both love and knowledge, to become their true knight. He is beaten back both by his own delusions and by his tormentors. All of his trials, however, expose concrete stratifications of the world in which he moves: Jude's idealizations never cancel the particular web of social, historical, and discursive terrains that make a space for his own voice and consciousness. Even the splintering of the social self that Jude experiences, as he seeks institutional affirmation of his thoughts and passions, takes place within the illuminations and consolations of a still knowable world.[7] The compassionate authorial voice underneath the voice of the ironic narrator is always heroicizing Jude's obscurity.

The first four chapters of *Jude the Obscure* give us an account of Jude's childhood in a form that rehearses the trials of attenuated communication and connection that he will suffer so sharply in the maturing of his experience. In these same chapters, the ironic narrator acts as the pitiless colleague of Jude's tormentors. Phillotson abandons Jude; his aunt Drusilla explains to him that "It would ha' been a blessing if Goddy-mighty had took thee too, wi' thy mother and father, poor useless boy" (12); Farmer Troutham punishes him; and the quack Vilbert betrays him. In each case Jude is made to feel both his own deprivations and the indifference of

others to the hidden spirit within him. The narrator joins in the rout of Jude's expectations and affections by bestowing on him the gleaming image of Christminster
while treating it, in the main, as an atmospheric trick: "The air increased in transparency . . . till the topaz points . . . were faintly revealed. . . . The spectator gazed
on and on till the windows and vanes lost their shine. . . . The vague city became
veiled in mist. . . . The foreground of the scene had grown funereally dark, and near
objects put on the hues and shapes of chimaeras" (19).

The narrator thus stages what will be the repeated scene of Jude's injuries as Jude
tries and fails to possess the objects of his desire. Though this narrator has something in common with all Jude's tormentors, he is most like Farmer Troutham. He
characteristically arrives on the scene to turn the instruments of Jude's labors against
him. Jude's "dazed eyes . . . beheld the farmer in person, the great Troutham himself, his red face glaring down upon Jude's cowering frame, the clacker swinging in
his hand" (14). The narrator's clacker is ironic discourse. The novel is always reminding us of a close parallel between the gray mists that engulf Jude's golden images
and the killing letter that obliterates the spirit's utterance. The narrator's manipulation of this parallel is clear in this scene. Jude, tired of driving the birds away from
their prospective dinner, makes the signal discovery of "a magic thread of fellow
feeling" uniting his life with that of the birds (14). But the narrator is always at hand
to undo magic threads whenever they manifest themselves. Not only is Jude struck
with his own rattle, "till the field echoed with the blows," but the clacks resound
"from the brand-new church tower just behind the mist" (15). The language of the
clacker, amplified by the mystifications of institutional consciousness, overwhelms
Jude's word ("Eat, then, my dear little birdies") and proclaims the hegemony of
the narrator's ironic discourse.

By sending Troutham to cut the "magic thread of fellow-feeling," the narrator
performs a kind of erasure or attenuation that typifies the moves of the discourse.
The practice begins with the novel's rubric: "The letter killeth." However, the effect of these cuts, attenuations, and erasures in the novel is often to prompt the reader
to supply the missing voice and missing magic threads. They can be discovered in
the wider, heteroglot world of the chronotope where the narrator's own voice is
dialogized and where the letter is drawn into dialogue with the spirit.[8]

Jude ends his journey by reciting from Job, thus returning, as though in a great
circle, to the prophetic menace of Farmer Troutham. The narrative order of the
novel can always be seen as controlled by the same oppressive circular structure
observed by the Reading Room philosopher. The late appearance of Father Time,
for example, is yet another construction of action moving in a pointless circle. Father
Time is pointedly called "little Jude" and he acts not only as Jude's descendant, but
as his replacement, an unglossed figure of the destiny already inscribed in Jude's
life from the beginning but one that he naively refuses to read. We are offered this
view through numerous proleptic allusions to Father Time in the scenes recount-
ing Jude's childhood. Jude's face is said to wear "the fixity of a thoughtful child's
who has felt the pricks of life somewhat before his time" (11); Jude comes to think
that "Nature's logic was too horrid for him to care for" (17); he even wishes "that
he had never been born" (27). It is clear that Father Time's startling intrusion into
the narrative is legitimized by his direct descent from the Jude of the opening chap-

ters who at one point senses that "all around you there seemed to be something glaring, garish, rattling [that] hit upon the little cell called your life, and shook it, and warped it" (17). The circle is complete.

But Jude refuses to be trapped within the bitter circle of the narrator's irony. His dream of Christminster, his passionate appropriation of the texts he reads, his craftsmanship and fellowship as a worker, his dialogic encounters with those whom he loves and those he opposes, the deeply layered world in which he moves with its Hebraic, Hellenic, Arthurian, Gothic, Victorian, and modernist striations, all dialogized in him, form an answering language that the arctic ironies of the narrator cannot suppress. The truncated text from 2 Corinthians that prefaces the novel is, after all, followed by a novel that, precisely, overcomes the monologic reduction of Paul's words and restores the crisscross of the letter and the spirit. The letter killeth, but the novel giveth life.

Hardy's representation of the conflict between monologic reduction and dialogic encounter occurs pervasively in the novel, especially in the dialogues of Sue and Jude. Sue is always attempting to shed one or another doctrine and arrive at a unitary truth, while Jude, though often attempting to follow Sue's lead, keeps juxtaposing and counterposing ideas and voices that are for him coexistent. "At moments he stood still by an archway, like one watching a figure walk out; then he would look at a window like one discerning a familiar face behind it. He seemed to hear voices, whose words he repeated as if to gather their meaning" (311). The general form of this conflict is strikingly illustrated in the novel's account of Father Time. Jude tries to give Father Time something of his own spirit; Sue, to her terrible cost and sorrow, gives him a set of abstractions. That Father Time is tossed between the letter and the spirit is clear from the wobbly fit he makes with the prevailing style and tone of the text. His own consciousness is devoid of any dialogic interplay with the world around him. He is named not for the chronotope but for the Reading Room:

> Children begin with detail, and learn up to the general; they begin with the contiguous and gradually comprehend the universal. The boy seemed to have begun with the generals of life, and never to have concerned himself with the particulars. To him the houses, the willows, the obscure fields beyond, were apparently regarded not as brick residences, pollards, meadows; but as human dwellings in the abstract, vegetation, and the wide, dark world. (220)

Father Time is in the grip of a consciousness that will turn murderous under the inadvertent prompting of Sue's bleak lectures on human fate. But Father Time as a symbolic figure mirrors the double-sidedness of the narrative that contains him. For while his own consciousness is monologic, he is in his human relations a site of meanings that reflect the consciousnesses of others. When he is found hanging, the narrator writes of his place in the lives of Jude and Sue: "The boy's face expressed the whole tale of their situation. On that little shape had converged all the inauspiciousness and shadow which had darkened the first union of Jude, and all the accidents, mistakes, fears, errors of the last. He was their nodal point, their focus, their expression in a single term" (266). The very abstractness of the boy's outlook is, in the end, subordinated to the crisscrossed, thickly textured writing on his face.

As a character, then, Father Time undergoes a transformation that corresponds to the most important transformations in the novel itself: he is gathered within the text's semantic sphere and takes on "the *form of a sign* that is audible and visible for us" (Bakhtin 1981, 258). The doctrinal reduction of the novel's intricate chronotope to a "wide, dark world" of meaningless fate cannot survive the novel's devoted attention to intersections and nodal points.

Bakhtin argues that without temporal-spatial expression, even abstract thought is impossible. "Consequently, every entry into the sphere of meanings is accomplished only through the gates of the chronotope" (1981, 258). Through those gates Jude walks. He is denied admission to the colleges of Christminster and to the squalid little system of privileges they control, but he refuses to be denied the sphere of meanings that his own affection for Christminster represents. Christminster does not validate Jude: Jude validates Christminster. "'Still harping on Christminster—even in his cakes!' laughed Arabella. 'Just like Jude. A ruling passion. What a queer fellow he is, and always will be'" (248). Arabella does not see that Jude's sustained passion returns to Christminster the dialogic standing that its socioeconomic imperatives have been obscuring.

The structure of the novel traces Jude's effort to rediscover the intersections of the letter and the spirit of which Christminster is itself the preeminent instance. The first five "Parts" map Jude's movements from one town or village to another in a sequence that reflects the weave of his desires and disappointments. We follow him from Marygreen to Christminster, where he finally gives up his dream of being accepted at one of the colleges. By now he also has lost Sue. "Deprived of the objects of both intellect and emotion, he could not proceed to his work" (97). But he almost immediately reclaims both of these objects by relocating to Melchester (Salisbury) and pursuing an ecclesiastical career and a submerged relationship with Sue. After Sue's marriage the action is centered at Shaston (Shaftesbury), where Phillotson has a school. Shaston represents a great change for Jude. He cannot follow Sue there, but his passion for her makes him realize he cannot follow his ecclesiastical career either. The collapse of all Jude's dreams is associated with Shaston just as Shaston itself is associated with a collapse of its own dreams that followed the Dissolution:

> Shaston, the ancient British Palladour . . . was, and is, in itself the city of a dream. Vague imaginings of its castle, its three mints, its magnificent aspidal Abbey, the chief glory of South Wessex . . . all now ruthlessly swept away—throw the visitor, even against his will, into a pensive melancholy. . . . To this fair creation of the great Middle-Age the Dissolution was, as historians tell us, the death-knell. . . . The natural picturesqueness and singularity of the town still remain [but] are passed over . . . and one of the queerest and quaintest spots in England stands virtually unvisited today. (158)

Shaston reflects Jude's own dissolution and his deepening sense of obscurity. He finally burns his books, feeling he is unworthy of any high spiritual pursuit because of his social place and his persistent, illicit passion for Sue. Moreover, it is at Shaston that Sue sees how burdened Jude is by his effort to be constant to his vision: "You are Joseph the dreamer of dreams, dear Jude. And a tragic Don Quixote. And sometimes you are St. Stephen, who, while they were stoning him, could see Heaven opened. O my poor friend and comrade, you'll suffer yet" (163). And Jude does suffer. However, the question posed by the novel's structure is whether he suffers dissolution, whether, like Shaston, he is reduced to an obscure and "passed over" memorial of his once great purpose.

The next stage of Jude's journey, "Part Fifth: At Aldbrickham and Elsewhere," represents a decisive shift whose implications have been blurred in critical readings of the novel. Jude, now accompanied by Sue, sets out to find a deliberate and assured obscurity. Aldbrickham (Reading) is an industrial town intruding upon the border of "Upper Wessex" and as far from the connecting social patterns that have formed Jude as we can imagine. It is at Aldbrickham that Father Time joins his wandering parent. Aldbrickham represents a place of nearly complete alienation. It is the social equivalent of Father Time's epistemological blankness. All of the voices that mix and resound in Wessex, all of the identifying markers, all of the crisscrossed roads come to silence and anonymity at Aldbrickham. The change is registered in the attitude of the narrator: Aldbrickham is never described, and is given no texture whatever. Even more significant is the next development. Jude and Sue travel to an "old town" in Upper Wessex that "*may be called* Stoke-Barehills" (228; my italics). The narrator himself begins to have difficulty in detecting the obscure corners to which the characters move. Though an old town, Stoke-Barehills is all built over with "modern chapels, modern tombs, and modern shrubs" (229). The place is the site of the Great Wessex Agricultural Show "whose vast encampment spreads over the open outskirts of the town like the tents of an investing army. Rows of marquees, huts, booths, pavilions, arcades, porticoes — every kind of structure short of a permanent one — cover the green field" (229). Jude has now come to a place exactly the reverse of Christminster in both its architectural and chronotopic quality.[9]

There is one place left for Jude to inhabit in this journey toward the dissolution of his dream: Elsewhere. No place in the novel is so pertinently named. "Whither they had gone nobody knew, chiefly because nobody cared to know. Any one sufficiently curious to trace the steps of such an obscure pair might have discovered without great trouble that they had enter[ed] on a shifting, almost nomadic life" (244–45). There is a world Elsewhere, but it is only a geographical expression. It is quite beyond the horizon of Jude's chronotopic imagination. Bakhtin has proposed that true dialogic relations "are possible only in relation to a hero who is a carrier of his own truth, who occupies a *signifying* (ideological) position. If an experience or a deed does not pretend to some *signifying power* . . . but only to *reality* (evaluation) then the dialogic relation can be minimal. . . . I must find myself in another by finding another in myself" (1984, 286–87). These are the conditions denied at Aldbrickham and Elsewhere. What Jude confronts in his nomadic life are the conditions of "a special type of inescapably solitary consciousness" (1984, 288) that Bakhtin attributes to capitalism and that Hardy, more specifically, locates in the dissolution of the communal consciousness that is only felt and understood when true dialogic relations remain possible.

Jude ultimately resists Elsewhere by deciding to return to Christminster: "it is the centre of the universe to me, because of my early dream: and nothing can alter it. Perhaps it will soon wake up and be generous" (254). Though it is at Christminster that Jude faces his greatest sufferings, he recovers there his "signifying power." The institutional negations of his dream cannot dissolve his crisscrossed, interoriented relation to Christminster. We see this in Jude's initial act when he returns to the city of spires. He adds his own voice to the voices that have echoed in its chief streets. Years earlier, when he walked among those streets for the first time, the gathered voices of the luminaries who had studied there came to him on the wind and the luminaries made "him comrades in his solitude" (65). On his return to the city Jude steps into the place of public orator and articulates for his working-class audience both their view of his failure and his view of Christminster's failure. Weighted though his experience is with suffering in the past and suffering to come, Jude has escaped "solitary consciousness" by yet again finding the magic threads of fellow-feeling. These threads only appear at the much-traveled and heavily marked crossroads of social heteroglossia where claims of both the spirit and the letter remain openly contested. Jude's return from Elsewhere to Christminster is a return from "the wide, dark world" to "the sphere of meanings." This is why, even as Jude suffers his terrible tragedy, he continues to move, while in the city, closer and closer to its heart: "Michaelmas came and passed, and [they] were in lodgings . . . nearer the centre of the city" (305); "[a]fter Christmas, . . . he shifted his lodgings to a yet more central part of the town" (316). From this place, as he is dying, Jude joins the chorus of Christminster voices, quoting Job in counterpoint to the students' hurrahs. In doing so, he forms the last and most poignant crossroads of the text.

"'When I am dead,' he told Arabella, 'you'll see my spirit flitting up and down here among these'" (312). Jude cannot imagine himself as end-stopped. He says that he can see "those spirits of the dead again, on this my last walk, that I saw when I first walked here" (312). These spirits do not appear in Elsewhere. They emerge for Jude because he has internalized them and has reproduced his own utterance in relation to theirs. He tells the crowd on his return that "eight or nine years ago when I came here first, I had a neat stock of fixed opinions, but they dropped away one by one and the further I get the less sure I am" (258). In making his dialectical departure from the Christminster sages, he is entering into dialogical relation with them and is bearing their word, as bureaucratic Christminster failed to do, to the crossroads of the city. Jude himself becomes a crossroads. The multiple languages and accents that intersect in Christminster intersect in him.

The deathbed scene amplifies the same "signifying power." For on his deathbed Jude's utterance includes, not only the voice of the sacred texts that he has internalized, but the voice of the chivalric texts as well. His tragedy is figured as both Job's and Tristram's. The unanswering deity to whom his Jobian words are addressed, and the unaccommodating lover to whom he murmurs for water, mark the distinctively fearful isolation to which Jude has come. At the same time, from the scene of isolation Jude's utterance carries across the whole Wessex chronotope from its spiritual boundary to its secular boundary, once again juxtaposing the discourses of Cornwall and Christminster, passion and knowledge, fiction and history. Only within the heavily inscribed world of Wessex can these discourses encounter each other. Elsewhere, they are silenced or obscured. As Jude dies in Christminster, he also penetrates the deep strata of his own discourse, obscuring the ironic narrator in the process and recollecting the knowable community which he entered, not from the outside, but as one who belongs as though he "were present from the very beginning."

Notes

1. The quoted phrase, repeated from the epigraph to this chapter, appears in M. M. Bakhtin, *Speech Genres and Other Late Essays* (1986, 49). Other works by Bakhtin cited in this chapter are *The Dialogical Imagination* (1981) and *Problems of Dostoevsky's Poetics* (1984).

2. A portion of Gosse's review is reprinted in the Norton Critical Edition of *Jude the Obscure* (1978, 39), edited by Norman Page.

3. The note appears in Florence Emily Hardy, *The Life of Thomas Hardy 1840–1928* (1962, 206). This work, originally published in two separate volumes, was actually written by Hardy himself. For the chronology of the novel's composition, see Page, ed., *Jude the Obscure* (1978, ix).

4. Hardy's use of the Arthurian romances and his interest in Victorian versions of them have begun to be studied; see Basham (1984), and Pinion (1986, 159–60). Hardy's use of the Tristram and Iseult story was first observed by Sherida Yoder in a paper written for Julien Moynahan at Rutgers University in 1974 (Moynahan 1977, xviii–xix). Also see Clark and Wasserman (1979). Rabiger also notes Tristram parallels in Hardy's works (1989, 90–100).

5. The intertextual relations of the Tristram and Iseult story in works by Tennyson, Arnold, Swinburne, Hardy, and Mary Elizabeth Braddon are the subject of a longer study in progress from which I have used some passages here.

6. For the essential details, see Pinion (1986, 152–55) and Millgate (1982, 335–41, 353–55). In May 1893 Hardy and his wife visited Ireland where their host was the lord-lieutenant. The lord-lieutenant's sister, Florence Henniker, then in her late thirties and the author of three novels, was hostess. Hardy was infatuated at once. Henniker's husband, a soldier, was stationed at Portsmouth. When the Hardys returned to England, Henniker crossed the Irish Sea with them. Hardy, at work on *Jude* by this point, attempted to engage Henniker in, minimally, a very serious flirtation.

7. Raymond Williams identifies his concept of the "knowable" community in *The Country and the City* (1973), a book basic to our understanding of the social text in Victorian literature. I discuss both Williams's work and Victorian ideas and images of community as *telos* more fully in my essay on *Wuthering Heights* (Farrell 1989). In addition to Williams, see Gregor (1974), Miller (1970), and Meisel (1972). All of these studies see a division in Hardy of a sort that is, roughly speaking, epitomized by Irwin and Gregor: "Emphases change, but the basic pattern remains. In form, a contemplative narrator broods over a community evoked in loving detail; in substance, the narrative is structured by major conflicts" (1977, 11).

8. Saldívar reads the crisscross in *Jude* as chiasmus, "whose own figural logic both asserts and denies referential authority" (1983, 622). Though I take a different view, I am much indebted to Saldívar's subtle essay.

9. See Bakhtin's discussion of relationships among competing chronotopes: "The general characteristic of these interactions is that they are *dialogical* (in the broadest use of the word). But this dialogue cannot enter into the world represented in the work, nor into any of the chronotopes represented in it; it is outside the world represented, although not outside the work as a whole" (1981, 252).

Works Cited

Bakhtin, M. M. *The Dialogic Imagination: Four Essays.* Translated by Michael Holquist. Edited by Caryl Emerson and Michael Holquist. Austin: University of Texas Press, 1981.

——. *Problems of Dostoevsky's Poetics.* Translated and edited by Caryl Emerson. Minneapolis: University of Minnesota Press, 1984.

——. *Speech Genres and Other Late Essays.* Translated by Vern M. McGee. Edited by Michael Holquist. Austin: University of Texas Press, 1986.

Basham, Diana. "*Jude the Obscure* and *Idylls of the King.*" *Thomas Hardy Society Review* 1, no. 10 (1984): 311–16.

Casagrande, Peter J. *Unity in Hardy's Novels: 'Repetitive Symmetries.'* Lawrence: Regents Press of Kansas, 1982.

Clark, S. L., and Julian N. Wasserman. "Tess and Iseult." *Thomas Hardy Society Review* 1, no. 5 (1979): 160–63.

Farrell, John P. "Reading the Text of Community in *Wuthering Heights,*" *ELH* 56 (1989): 173–208.

Faurot, Margaret. *Hardy's Topographical Lexicon and the Canon of Intent: A Reading of the Poetry.* New York: Peter Lang, 1990.

Gregor, Ian. *The Great Web: A Study of Hardy's Major Fiction.* London: Faber, 1974.

Hardy, Florence Emily. *The Life of Thomas Hardy 1840–1928.* London: Macmillan, 1962.

Hardy, Thomas. *Jude the Obscure.* Edited by Norman Page. New York: Norton, 1978.

Holquist, Michael. *Dialogism: Bakhtin and His World.* London: Routledge, 1990.

Irwin, Michael, and Ian Gregor. "Either Side of Wessex." *Thomas Hardy after Fifty Years.* Edited by Lance St. John Butler. Totowa, N.J.: Rowman, 1977.

Meisel, Perry. *Thomas Hardy: The Return of the Repressed.* New Haven, Conn.: Yale University Press, 1972.

Miller, J. Hillis. *Fiction and Repetition: Seven English Novels.* Cambridge: Harvard University Press, 1982.

——. *Thomas Hardy: Distance and Desire.* Cambridge: Harvard University Press, 1970.

Millgate, Michael. *Thomas Hardy: A Biography.* New York: Random House, 1982.

Moore, Kevin Z. *The Descent of the Imagination: Postromantic Culture in the Late Novels of Thomas Hardy.* New York: New York University Press, 1990.

Morson, Gary Saul, and Caryl Emerson. *Mikhail Bakhtin: Creation of a Prosaics.* Stanford: Stanford University Press, 1990.

Moynahan, Julien. "Editor's Introduction." *The Portable Thomas Hardy.* New York: Viking Penguin, 1977.

Pinion, F. B. "*Jude the Obscure*: Origins in Life and Literature." *Thomas Hardy Annual* 4 (1986): 148–64.

Rabiger, Michael. "Hardy's Fictional Process and His Emotional Life." In *Alternative Hardy*, edited by Lance St. John Butler. New York: St. Martin's Press, 1989.

Saldívar, Ramón. "*Jude the Obscure*: Reading and the Spirit of the Law." *ELH* 50 (1983): 607–25.

Williams, Raymond. *The Country and the City.* New York: Oxford University Press, 1973.

Dialogue in Lyric Narrative

Introduction: A Paradox

> All truth is dialogue.
>
> Robert Frost (Cook 1958:164)

All lyric poetry is dialogical because the poet, no matter how solipsistic he intends or claims to be, is actually engaging or attempting to engage someone else, an interlocutor. Despite this inevitably dialogical situation, comparatively little lyric poetry, as contrasted with epic or dramatic poetry, contains actual quoted, literal dialogue. The deep structure is always dialogic, whereas the surface structure is only rarely so.

On one side of the paradox, that poetry is "essentially dialogical," we find many variations: dialogue, for example, that is implicit, subliminal, or even unconscious. To begin with the classic case of apostrophe, the poet starts off with, "I love the dark race of poets / and yet there is also happiness," and continues in this apparently monologic form for a half-dozen lines until the rhetorical turn, when he says, "We can live here, Cristina, / we can live here," that is, "I can live with you to/with whom I have been talking (in my imagination)" (Simpson 1983, 22); here the apostrophe marks the eruption of climactic emotion.

A second, less obvious example of indirect or partial dialogue in lyric poetry is the so-called addressed monologue where the poet is mainly declaring a sudden realization of his own, while, almost as a matter of form, ostensibly addressing some-body else. A pat example of this is Fet's "What a night! Transparent is the air, and still," which is followed by a protestation of love that seems to stand by itself and to backstage almost out of sight the faceless and relatively insignificant interlocutor (Gustavson 1966, 172–73). I could go on with dozens of subtypes of partial or latent dialogue in lyric poetry, but all would suggest that the poet, or lyric addressor, is always somehow addressing someone, and moreover that this expressive address is the essential function of the lyric voice (Jakobson 1960, 356–58).

Let us turn to the other side of the paradox, lyric that presents dialogue. Perhaps the most clear-cut exception, on the one hand, is the eclogue, a classical subgenre of the pastoral set in the country (bucolic, idyll) and representing a conversation between two or more persons that is often at least implicitly critical of society (see, for example, Preminger, Warnke, and Hardison 1974, 212). Modern eclogues (since the early eighteenth century) often include characterization and a narrative line. Perhaps the strongest example of represented dialogue, on the other hand, is also one of the earliest. The Old Testament Song of Songs, a sustained conversation between two lovers, or between bride and groom, is presented directly, without narrative bracketing, and hence at a universal level quite different from the social and historical marking of most explicitly dialogic poetry. It shows how the emotion that is conveyed by dialogue can draw the reader/listener into the text. The poem has suggested many readings, but, like most lyric poetry, it is saliently about love and death, where death usually means some yearning or nostalgia for someone who has passed away (Pope 1977). The gist of the dialogic stratum in poetry is not erotic — that would be too simple — but some more generic idea of affect that includes love, sensuality, tenderness, agape. I will return to this idea later.

Before moving to the next section, let me interject that I also weighed other, strongly dialogical lyric poets in the balance, and have them in mind even while focusing on the perhaps optimal contrast between Frost and Nekrasov. These other dialogical poets include Akhmatova, Robert Browning, Dante, Dickinson, Donne, Hardy, the author of parts of the *Poetic Edda*, the Job poet, Pope, Tsvetaeva, Tu Fu, Virgil, a number of minor eighteenth-century English poets (Lonsdale 1984), and, finally, Wordsworth and Pushkin (to whom, respectively, Frost and Nekrasov owed a great deal).[1] Enormously revealing dialogical materials are contained in Frost's long, unrhymed, loosely blank verse narrative poems, notably in *North of Boston*, which, however, tend to be neglected today in favor of "Design" and other short, relatively monophonic lyrics. Now let us get down to our two cases.

Two Dialogic Poets Par Excellence: Frost and Nekrasov

> I alone of English writers have consciously set myself to make music out of what I call the sound of sense.

> Robert Frost (1964:79)

As exceptions to the general rule of the paucity of dialogue in lyric, there stand two poets whose work is full of it: Frost and Nekrasov. To remind you of Frost and introduce many of you to Nekrasov, a brief digression, tilted toward the issue of dialogue, seems in order. Robert Frost was born in 1874, not in New Hampshire, but in San Francisco. Until adolescence he "never read a book," as he put it, preferring to travel about with his garrulous politician father and commune at home with his Scottish mother (who also read him Scott, border ballads, and selections from *Ossian* [Thompson 1964, 69]). When he was eleven the family moved back to his father's hometown of Lawrence, Massachusetts. Robert finally entered school, eventually read a book, published his first poem at sixteen, and graduated from high school two years later as the class valedictorian and star Latinist. At eighteen he studied a few months at Dartmouth and thereafter two years at Harvard, before beginning to farm a thirty-acre, one-horse farm near Derry, New Hampshire, which he continued to do for ten years while writing poetry and intermittently teaching psychology and Latin (including Virgil) at local colleges. Those are the relevant essentials for his dialogue masterpieces. Less important for now are the subsequent points about his family life and tragedies, his sojourn in England, and his emergence as national bard, symbolized by his role at President Kennedy's inauguration three years before his death in 1963. I note the peculiar facts of his late and limited education and his immersion throughout his formative years in three drastically different dialects: of San Francisco, Scotland, and Lawrence; and that he then not only acquired but actually studied the dialect of southern Vermont and New Hampshire farmers—listening to their "sentence sounds," as he called them, making extensive notes, and casting the waves of their intonation into his variously tight iambic and loose, intonationally rising feet. The actual idiolect of one farmer, Charles Hall, was crucial to Frost's creative process (Munson 1977, 34–35). Yet, as Karki (1979) remarks somewhere, a dialogue by Frost is not a tape recording.

A second poet with an enormous amount of actual dialogue in his lyric narrative—where, indeed, it is often preponderant—is Nikolay Nekrasov. Nekrasov was born in central Russia in 1821, of a mother who, while not actually Polish, as is usually claimed, was born in Warsaw, had studied the language (Courbet 1948, 7; Birkenmayer 1968), and, while her son was still a youth, familiarized him with it as well as with Russian poetry and the values of both traditions. The poet played with peasant children on the isolated estate, and had continuous contact with peasants until he went off to St. Petersburg at age sixteen, where, because of dire circumstances (his father refused to support his studies), he failed to get admitted to the university and eventually studied only one year as an auditor (Birkenmayer 1968, 17–19). For several years he mingled with the bottom echelons of society: lower-class urban speech ways, like peasant ones, became second nature. This, again, is the essential background to his dialogic masterpieces, and I need not expatiate here on his subsequent, celebrated career as a journalist, editor, publisher, poet, and leader of the radical or "civic" branch of the intelligentsia—climaxed in a way at his funeral in 1877 where Dostoyevsky pronounced him to be as high as Pushkin or Lermontov, to which many in the radicalized crowd cried out, "Higher, higher!" For us, the other, critical aspect of his work was that, as if to supplement his deep, primary knowledge of folk Russian, Nekrasov continued to study peasant speech, making notes after conversations, and so forth. The poem "Orina, the Soldier's

Mother," to which I return below, was not only based on experienced conversation, but several times, while on hunting trips, the poet made detours in order to check once more the actual wording of the bereaved, old peasant woman — "to not be false," as his sister put it (Chukovsky 1971, 531). Moreover, he assiduously studied the remarkable compendia of Russian words, proverbs, folktales, riddles, and songs that kept emerging during his mature years (notably Dal's dictionary); his major critic and commentator (Chukovsky 1971) feels moved to prove that Nekrasov's knowledge of peasant brogue was based more on experience than on secondary sources. Let us now turn to three analytical factors that seem crucial when it comes to dialogue in lyric narrative.

Critical Analytical Factors

Dialogue

> The possibilities for tune from the dramatic tones of meaning struck
> across the rigidity of a limited meter are endless.
>
>   Robert Frost (Pritchard 1962, 56)

I can speak of dialogue or the dialogical in lyric poetry, but what do I mean? I am referring, on the one hand, to a number of abstract considerations: to the axiom or assumption that all speech and language originates on an impulse to communicate, now or eventually, with other human beings (Bakhtin 1983, 279); to what has been called the dialogic emergence of culture (Tedlock and Mannheim, 1995) (to which I addend "the dialogic emergence of poetry"); to response or the anticipation of response as the great supporting mechanism; or to an abstract characterization of the lyric poet as intentionally sharing, as at a reading, or unconsciously aspiring to be overheard; it is in these senses that lyric poetry, so peculiarly intense, is always at its roots dialogical. By "dialogue," on the other hand, I refer to the fairly colloquial and literal meaning of any conversation or similar exchange between two or more interlocutors, to two or more people using natural language in a definite space and time (Friedrich 1995, 34–36). This would correspond roughly to the etymological sense of the Greek *dia*, "between" (also "through, across"), plus *legesthai*, "speak," which suggests that we coin the term "between-speak" for these variously practical, pragmatic, and empirical senses. This chapter, then, focuses on the interplay, counterpoint, and dialectic between, on the one hand, the deep, underlying sense of dialogical and, on the other hand, the overt representations of dialogue, of between-speak.

Psychosociolinguistic Differentiation

> They call me a New England dialect poet. . . . It was never my aim to
> keep to any special speech. . . . What I have been after from the first
> consciously, is tones of voice.
>
>   Robert Frost (Cox 1966, 81)

In a gem of a poem of only twelve lines, Josephine Miles (1986, 50) effectively represents a rapid-fire exchange between four differentiated speakers: a truck driver, a resentful chauffeur ("Pull her up my rear end," "leave me handle my own car"), an usher, and a bystander ("Give her the gun"); there is also a contrast in formality between the truck driver, who addresses the chauffeur as "Mac," and the usher, who says "sir." These varied levels of language distinguish the speakers in the poem from one another (Kennedy 1986, 50). The poem, called "Reason," runs as follows:

> Said, Pull her up a bit will you, Mac, I want to unload there.
> Said, Pull her up my rear end, first come first serve.
> Said, Give her the gun, Bud, he needs a taste of his own bumper.
> Then the usher came out and got into the act:
> Said, Pull her up, pull her up a bit, we need this space, sir.
> Said, For God's sake, is this still a free country or what?
> You go back and take care of Gary Cooper's horse
> And leave me handle my own car.
>
> Saw them unloading the lame old lady,
> Ducking out under the wheel and gave her an elbow,
> Said, All you needed to do was just explain;
> *Reason, Reason* is my middle name.

It would take an actor, or better, four actors to do full justice to the dialogic potential of this poem.

To turn to larger canvases, hundreds of lines of colloquial conversation are conveyed in the regular sonnets of Pushkin's *Eugen Onegin*, and, 160 years later, Vikram Seth in *The Golden Gate* made the same "Onegin stanza" the vehicle of quite different conversations between his Silicon Valley characters (while signally failing, however, to differentiate the speakers à la Pushkin and Frost). Skill at such sociolinguistically charged poetry resembles the dialectal skill of prose writers such as Twain, with his "seven Pike County dialects" in *Huckleberry Finn*, except that one must also satisfy the demands of line, meter, rhythm, and even rhyme; in other words, a stereotypically prosaic feature must be melded with the formalism of the poem to create an inner tension that is unique to dialogic poetry (Friedrich 1991).

Perhaps the most obvious fact about poems like these is that they typically characterize the speakers and situate them, the poem, and the poet within a historically, socially, and psychologically differentiated universe—because the poet exploits the resources of phonics, diction, and style to achieve various kinds of marking of the participants in the represented speech situation.

Such psychosociolinguistic differentiation puts great demands on the poet. To begin he or she must differentiate the interlocutors, not only through linguistic cues but also, to [some?] extent, worldview and personality—as in the Miles poem. The meter and rhyme of a dialogic poem, for example, might be expected to differ significantly from the surrounding, descriptive passages, and it usually does. Our obvious expectation would be for the conversational part to be less regular, and it often is. But right away note that this conventional expectation of regularity is often frustrated by the poet for the sake of some mood or freshness. In Frost's poem called

"Paul's Wife," the loggers do not ask Paul, "How's the wife?" as they would in real life, but use the metrically more regular and rhetorically more marked, "How is the wife, Paul?" Such metrical regularity, imposed in part on dialogue, has the effect not only of marking the discourse, but of creating various kinds of irony (for example, understatement, mockery, or parody).

The unexpected marking of dialogue in lyric narrative is often accentuated in the surprisingly large number of poems with conversations within conversations — what I would call embedded or encapsulated dialogue. In another poem by Frost called "The Runaway," two men are observing a colt that has grown frisky at the falling snow and one of them remarks, quoting the speech, as he imagines it, of the mare mother of the colt, who exclaims, "'Sakes! / It's only weather!,'" which is immediately followed in the Frost line by the man's inference of the colt's reaction, "He'd think she didn't know!" In the Nekrasov poem, "Orina, the Soldier's Mother," a half-dozen critical, emotionally powerful lines consist of the bereaved, quoted mother quoting her son. Such encapsulation or embedding of dialogue within dialogue intensifies and deepens the dialogically oriented emotions in question.

The sociolinguistic differentiation of dialogue through idiolect or situation reaches an extreme in Nekrasov's "The Peasant Children," where no less than nine peasant lads speak a line or two each as they peek between the cracks in the barn wall at the apparently sleeping hunter (Nekrasov, obviously), and his dog:

Listen! again a whisper!

First voice
"A beard!"

Second voice
"A gentleman, they said. . . ."

Third voice
"Quiet you-all, you devils!"

Second
"Gentlemen don't have beards — moustaches."

First
"But his legs are long, just like poles."

Fourth
"And look, on his cap — a watch!"

Fifth
"Hey, big deal!"

Sixth
"And a golden chain. . . ."

Seventh
"Probably they cost a lot?"

Eighth
"It shines like the sun!"

Ninth
"And there, the dog — a big one, a big one!
Water's even running down his tongue."

> *Fifth*
> "A rifle! And look: double-barrelled,
> the lock's engraved. . . ."
>
> *Third (fearfully)*
> "He's looking!"
>
> *Fourth*
> "Be quiet, it doesn't matter, let's stay a bit, Grisha!"
>
> *Third*
> "He'll beat us!"
>
> My spies took fright
> And dashed away. . . .

The poet's problem of making individual protagonists clearly distinguished in the mind of the reader is maximized in poems like this by the total or near-total absence of props and other externals such as you have on stage to tell you who is doing the talking; in this case, I must admit that, if they were not identified by numbers, I would lose track of which lad was speaking. More generally, the whole question of the subtle interaction between degrees of metricality and degrees of conversationality in lyric poetry remains largely unexplored.

Modal Dialectic

> You may string together words without a sentence sound to string them
> on just as you may tie clothes together by the sleeves and stretch them
> without a clothes line between two trees but—it is bad for the clothes.

> Robert Frost (Thompson 1964, 111)

A more complex problem than those of sociohistorical situatedness and sociolinguistic differentiation is what I would call modal dialectic. Again, I mean this, in the first place, in the fairly concrete sense of grammatical moods; the theses of description, in the indicative mood, alternate with the antithetical dialogic texts that often bring in other moods, or consist entirely of them (a point to which I return below). There is enormous variation here. Some poems such as Frost's "The Witch of Cöos," and parts of entire traditions such as ancient Tamil love poetry (Ramanujan 1967) or much contemporary Irish folk poetry, may consist entirely of overt dialogue (and the role of the dialogic is quite different in such cases). In other poems or entire traditions overt dialogue may be absent, although actually suggested. Between the extremes of the maximally or totally dialogic and the minimally dialogic or cryptodialogic, there are many intermediate degrees. In many poems a single word or short utterance or utterances, often an apt proverb, projects, like the tip of the iceberg, above the descriptive surface. The most moving example of the latter, to my ken, is Frost's poem, "'Out, out—,'" where the sister's call, "Supper!," with all its warm and nurturing connotations, is quickly followed, after the boy is mutilated by the power saw, by the boy's cry, "Don't let them cut my hand off— / The doctor, when he comes. Don't let him, sister!" And then Frost goes on, with a reversed first foot: "So. But the hand was gone already," and continues so until the boy's death. The fact that the title, in quotation marks, itself refers back to an "addressed monologue" in Shakespeare further enhances the dialogical intensity of this poem.

The bulk of poems that are being called dialogic here exemplify other intermediate degrees, mixing considerable amounts of dialogue with other, nondialogic text, sometimes in about equal proportions, and it is with this sort of poem and, in particular, with the phenomenon of switching between dialogue and nondialogue, that I am mainly concerned. Often enough the dialogue part, evocative of real people speaking naturally, is the point of cathexis for the reader, or better, of catalysis for the whole poem—where it comes together and then takes off.

This remains a more general point about the role of dialogue: we view poesis as processes in the mind of the poet, and of the reader-listener, and in the constantly emerging text, and in other emerging texts in the same or other relevant traditions, and the changing realities to which the texts and, through them, the poet refer or at least allude. We have a model that includes not only a Platonic mimetic model, a realist model, and a communication model, but all cogent models. The text of the poem is dynamic and climactic in these terms and exists in a universe of interlocking matrices or models, which are activated or catalyzed and made to interresonate by dialogue.

Practicum 1: The Russian "Affectives"

> You buried yourselves in translations instead of dialogue because it was safer to audit elsewhere than to listen to your own people.
>
> Aaron Fogel

The speech quoted in dialogue, although it need not be so, is usually more colloquial than the contiguous lyric text—in the sense that it contains a higher rate of parataxis, asyndeton, abbreviated forms, and the like. Entire subsections of the language can be emphasized; in English, for example, the use of contracted forms employing 're, 't, and 's (so conspicuous in Frost, often with metrical motivation) increases. It can also be the case that entire subsections of the language are omitted or categorically deemphasized. One of the most striking cases of this concerns what I am calling the Russian "affectives" (usually called "diminutives"). This is actually a highly dynamic system that interrelates two dimensions: (1) diminutive versus augmentative, and (2) endearing or "hypercharistic" versus pejorative. Many degrees along both dimensions are signaled by an enormous number of simple and complex affixes with what has been called an "intensely expressive and familiar character" (Ubegaun 1963, 83). In fact, the more realistic and contemporary analysis of Wierzbicka (1992) smashes the reductionist-structuralist components of traditional grammar and uses at least forty-seven (undefined) semantic components (for example, "jocular, teasing, warm," and so forth) in order to construct propositional, pragmatic definitions of over a dozen major affective suffixes, many of them with many subtypes. This affective suffixal system is more richly evolved in Russian than in any other Slavic language or, apparently, any language in the world—although, as regards frequency, some other languages, such as the Spanish of Mexican peasants, are analogous. Much of the imagination-boggling Russian (and, more generally, East Slavic) system was appropriated by Russian-area Ashkenazic Yiddish and contributes to the expressivity of that language (Stankiewicz 1985).

Let us look at some instances. The dimensions of diminutive and endearing, for example, are signaled by a number of suffixes such as *-ik*: *nos*, "nose," yields *nósik*, "little nose" (fairly standard when speaking to a child). Many words have over a half-dozen suffixed forms in regular use: *golová*, "head," yields *golóvka*, and so forth. Russian has some eighteen variations on the theme of "father": *pápa, pápochka* . . . (Gerhart 1974, 21–26), while English has about seven. The sheer number of these expressive suffixes varies and may be very great: the colloquial speech of the city of Penza has not only *-ik* and other, familiar items, but a grand total of eighty expressive suffixes of some sort (Wierzbicka 1992, 2). The system is perhaps most dramatically illustrated by the five main variants of Christian names, as follows (six if we include the French here since the literary culture in question was bilingual):

Anna   *Asya* (dim.)   *Asen'ka* (hyperchar.)   *Annushka* (pop.)   *Aska* (pej.)
Pavel   *Pavlik* (dim.)   *Pasha* (hyperchar.)   *Pavlusha* (pop.)   *Pashka* (pej.)

The sheer rate of use (not to be confused with number of forms in the system) is highest when speaking to children or in peasant speech; here the diminutives are so frequent that the plain, unadorned form often has to be regarded as the emphatic or marked one; if—to stay with "nose" as above—you told a four-year-old child to wash his *nos* rather than his *nósik*, a threat or disapproval might be implied. In sum, at least three factors are involved: large numbers of suffixes and suffixal combinations, high rates of usage and contexts of usage, and richness of nuance in expressive meaning.

Much of the system is brought into play in the "realistic" or popular poets. Krylov (1769–1844), one of the founders of Russian poetic realism, often displays "an abundance of peasant idioms, vocabulary, and suffixes (affectionate and diminutive)"; "the use of diminutive suffixes lends a certain lyricism," according to the major Krylov scholar (Stepanov 1973, 141–42). Actually, there is in Krylov enormous variation in the role and frequency of diminutives. In "The Crow and the Fox," the first fable in his first book of fables, we find ten diminutives in the total of twenty-six lines, especially where the fox, trying to entice the crow, speaks to the "dear little dove" with "dear little eyes" and "dear little feathers" and a "dear little nose [beak]" and a "dear little voice"; here we see the ironic and satirical potential of diminutives. Many of Krylov's fables have only two or three diminutives, and a great many have none at all, even when there is a conversation between two fabulesque characters (who, as Potebnya noted in a brilliant simile, are very like the pieces in a chess game). The diminutives in Krylov, then, are not so much an ethnographic mirror of peasant reality as a resource for realistic strategies which include hypercharacterization in the ethnographic portrayal of dialogue.[2]

The strongest positive examples of using these suffixes are Nekrasov's poems, notably "Who Had It Good in Russia?," with thousands of such forms, and his two-page poem, "Orina, the Soldier's Mother," already alluded to above. The latter purports to represent an actual dialogue between a sympathetic hunter who has stopped for the night, and an old peasant woman whose son, after being cruelly punished in the tsarist army (tortured through flogging, one guesses, with undertones of diffuse homosexual sadism), comes home and in the course of ten days pines away and dies. In this poem we find thirty-one affective affixes spread over twenty-nine quatrains, or more than one per quatrain. Beyond the raw statistics we can make some generalizations about the functions of the affective suffixes in this and perhaps other similar poems: (1) they are bunched near the beginning to set the tone; (2) many formulaic affectives are used for proper names and objects that are typically denoted in this way (*kruchínushka* for "sorrow," for instance); (3) unusual, minimally formulaic affectives are used for highly expressive effect—for example, *bolyóchonyok*, "sick," is rhymed with *mokrókhonyok*, "wet," when depicting the sick son spitting blood into his handkerchief. In terms of both structure and rate, once again, Nekrasov's use of the affective system is artful to a high degree, and subtly calculated.

Let me illustrate the above with a more or less "literal" translation of two stanzas of this poem:

> Barely alive in the autumn night
> We are returning from the hunt
> And, glory be to God, arrive
> At last year's lodging place.

> "Here we are! Hullo, old girl!
> How come you're frowning, *kúmushka*—
> You didn't start to think of death?
> Chuck it! It's an idle thought [*dúmushka*].

Note *kúmushka* with the affective suffix *-ushka*; the basic word *kum* (here the feminine *kumá*), is the untranslatable kinship term for the godparent of a child or the parent of a godchild (the same as *compadre/comadre* in Spanish; it can also be read as "friend," or as the archaic "gossip" in the same sense). Note that "thought" (*dúma*) also gets expanded expressively to *dúmushka*.

> "Have hard times come on you?
> Speak up, maybe I'll shake them off for you,"
> And Orinushka went on to tell
> Me of her great sorrow.

Her "hard times" or "sorrow, woe," *kruchína*, is in the formulaic suffixed form *kruchínushka*, and the character herself takes this same affective suffix *'o*, a suffix that conveys "not so much endearment as a kind of pity, of feeling sorry for people" (Wierzbicka 1992, 29; 1997).[3] After the young man has died, the poem concludes:

> And he expired just like a little candle [*svéchenka*]
> Of wax, before the icon. . . .
> Few words, but of grief a little river [*réchenka*]
> Of grief a bottomless little river.

Thus the poem ends with two rhymed affectives, the second of which is repeated.

The affective suffixal system is part of a much larger one that includes the following as components:

1. The kinship terms, especially those used for address (see *pápa* above), or that also serve as labels for more comprehensive categories (*dédushka*, "grandfather," but also, in familiar contexts, "old man").
2. The pronouns, especially the familiar, second-person pronoun *ty* and the pragmatic rules for its use, and the massive implications of such use (Friedrich 1979, 3–126).
3. A set of derived, possessive nouns ending in *-in*, which are especially frequent with kinship terms (for example, *pápin*, "Dad's").
4. The set of nouns that is pluralized with *-(y)ata*, which, in turn, includes "child," birds and wild animals, and also little devils (I made up "little wood spirit," *lesyáta*, and it was accepted by natives).
5. The various collectives that are also part of the larger affective system; for example, Russians doing things together in twos are referred to, almost obligatorily, not by the sheer number word (*dva*), but by collectives that correspond roughly to "twosome" (for example, *vdvoyóm*; the same holds for "three" and "four").

Clearly, this is not the place to set forth the full rules for these and related forms and the patterns of their interconnections, but it is the place to mention that all of these forms and patterns are part of a morphological codification of a human universe that is relatively informal, affective, emotionally charged, and close to what is in some sense "natural"—the family, the house yard, the wilds. Indeed, the existence of this morphologically coded intimate or primal universe is one of the most distinctive issues in Russian language and culture.

A striking and fascinating fact, toward which I have been heading, is that the various components in this primal, emotion-charged system, so diagnostic of Russian, are strongly, almost categorically, *avoided* in lyric poetry, and this is particularly true of the affective suffixal system. The fairly canonical anthologies by Obolensky (1976) and Markov and Sparks (1967), for example, contain almost no such affectives except for poems by poets such as Krylov, Nekrasov, and Mayakovsky, who specialize in grass-roots speech (and in *Eugene Onegin*). Even Nekrasov, as the great Chukovsky has shown in detail (1971, 216–59), actually *deleted* hundreds of thousands of "real" colloquialisms from early drafts. In the "Orina" poem just discussed, the affectives are practically absent at the climactic points, as when the young man, naked, is being inspected by the recruiting general, and during the death scene when he is hallucinating about his former tormentors: you dispense with affectives at the moments of life-or-death truth.

The highly structured avoidance of the affective suffixes is contrapuntally related to the goals of emotional intensity in lyric poetry and is a significant latent tension in Russian high poetry—a conflict between form and emotional implication—a structured silence that is broken by dialogue in lyric narrative that, for example, is socially and historically situated in the culture of peasants or the culture of children (Chukovsky 1960).[4]

Conclusion: Inner Tension / Outward Expression and Levels of Involvement

> The principal object . . . was to choose incidents and situations from common life, and to relate or describe them . . . in a selection of language really used by man, and, at the same time, to throw over them a certain colouring of the imagination.
>
> William Wordsworth, *Lyrical Ballads*

I began with a seeming paradox: that all lyric poetry is at least implicitly dialogic, whereas little lyric poetry contains actual dialogue. The discussion has brought not an answer or a resolution but another, deeper paradox, this one not seeming but real. It does not answer anything but I hope it improves our understanding or at least our appreciation of the issue.

As some of the preceding data show, a significant amount of dialogue in lyric narrative is concerned with exclamation, interjection, questioning, and the like — or in other, grammatical, words, with the interrogative, imperative, subjunctive, hortatory, minatory, and similar moods, or in more general terms, with a switch into a more emotional mode.

These modal switches in reported dialogue can have the prime effect or at least create the illusion of cutting through the relatively artificial or high-flown language of lyric poetry to a relatively real language such as real people use in real speech; of seeming to ground lyric discourse in life as lived, or at least actually spoken of; of inviting the reader-hearer to the sounds of real voices of exclamation, greeting, and anguish — often enough limited to a word, a phrase, or one or two sentences: "Don't let them cut it off," cries the boy. There is a change in the dialogic relation between the reader-hearer and the text (and, implicitly, the poet) because language brings them closer to each other. Thus surface dialogue achieves a new and compelling subjectivity, and approximation or involvement that is highly linguistic (Tannen 1989).

These same modal switches, however, also entail a shift from communication between a lyric "I" and an addressed "you," into a minidrama, where at least two represented interlocutors are exchanging quoted words in a kind of reenactment; in other words, the shift goes from the superficially monologic or hypothetically dyadic mode into a minidramatic one that builds a new level of complexity into the poem. This restructuring of dimensions is drastic in terms both of classical genre theory and in terms of semiotic theory — like the effect of a character on stage who suddenly starts to address the audience, or the switch, not dealt with in this chapter, from the narrative dialogue of a play into the language, often formally monologic, that can stand as pure lyric; Shakespeare, obviously, is the author whose work most frequently contains such shifts.

At one level, the switch to minidrama has the effect of setting off the poet from the reader-hearer; indeed, it may simulate a sort of objectivity where the poet and the audience join in listening to "between-speak" between third parties who typically are socially and historically situated — granted that these others are creatures of the poet's fancy, they still are part of the suspension of belief for a time and are "out there" being heard. This dramaturgical aspect of lyric dialogue puts a middle term before the poet and the reader-hearer and hence a sort of distance between these two participants in the speech situation.

One thing that makes the dialogue poems of Frost and Nekrasov work aesthetically is the way they integrate what I earlier dubbed "linguistic involvement," which moves the reader toward the text, with dramaturgical distanciation which superficially creates a space between the poet and the audience. The tension generated by both putting off and drawing in, by the contrary pulls of centripetal, sociolinguistic approximation and superficially centrifugal, dramaturgical distanciation contributes to the special power of these poems. The great difficulty of integrating such linguistic approximation/involvement and dramaturgical distanciation in a *lyric context* also accounts or may help to account for the relative rarity of dialogue in the high style of lyric narrative and in high lyric poetry more generally—at least in Russian and English.

I have just posited and argued for a dynamics or even dialectic of approximation versus distanciation. At a more deeply dialogical level, however, the experience of seeming to share a minidrama draws the poet and his or her audience together— whether they are eavesdropping on an amusing exchange or witnessing a horrifying rural tragedy. This drawing-together is reminiscent of the way two people become closer through contemplating a Rembrandt painting, or an oratorio in a cathedral, or an expanse of natural beauty. The most powerful example of dramaturgical approximation in Russian poetry that I know of is the end of Nekrasov's long and greatest poem, "Frost, Red Nose," about a peasant woman who gets lost in the forest and freezes to death: "[T]he terrible cold the Red Nosed Frost personifies at the outset mysteriously changes into heat . . . in the course of this dialogue. Similarly, the sovereign and mysterious power that he wields as he 'strides' through the woods yields to expressions of tenderness and love" (Gregg 1986, 45).

Such lyric minidramas, then, resolve or transmute the overt conflict between the thesis of linguistic approximation and the antithesis of dramaturgical distanciation—not only resolve but transcend the conflict as the poem moves into a new level of relationship between four of the main components in the poetic situation: (1) the addressor has been drawn closer to the reader; (2) the addressee or reader has grown more empathetic to the poet and more involved in the text; (3) the text of the message has become more accessible and, in most cases, more emotionally charged; (4) the language code itself has emerged in the new guise of a subcode that is closer to conversation and life as lived (Bühler 1990; Jakobson 1960). Thus the "dialogue in lyric poetry" fundamentally alters the nature of that poetry, not by making it necessarily better or more powerful—nothing is more powerful than great, albeit nondialogue poetry—but by changing the dimensions of the poetic situation and the relations between those dimensions.

Let me ground these concluding abstractions about distanciation and approximation with a final, more practical generalization. A feature shown by Frost and Nekrasov is that neither has fared well in translation and, related to this problem, that neither has fared particularly well outside his own speech community of English and Russian. This is surely one reason Frost never won the (much-coveted) Nobel Prize, and that Nekrasov, although ranked with Pushkin, Blok, and other great Russians, is hardly known outside Russia—probably some of you readers have never heard of him. One major reason for the failure to achieve dialogue across languages is the critical aesthetic role and the sheer quantity of dialogue in their lyric narrative, much of it highly idiomatic, nuanced, and attuned to the maximally local sounds of a New Hampshire farmer or peasant women in Central Russia.

Practicum 2: "The Death of the Hired Man"

> I will develop this quality until it becomes not my weakness but my strength. I will prove that conversation can be poetry.

> Robert Frost (Thornton 1937, 7)

One of the ultimate dialogic poets is Robert Frost, but in peculiarly specific ways that include his practically scientific attitude to "actual speech": "I ventured to make poetry out of tones that . . . from the practice of other poets are not usually regarded as poetical" (Frost 1964, 191). This was part of a more general "scientific" position (shared by Wallace Stevens incidentally) that "'things' like stars are 'there' for consciousness to work on and with" (Brower 1963, 178). His position of scientific realism about stars and tones (Bhaskar 1978) was articulated in terms of a complex theory of the sounds, tones, and accents of conversation which I can only suggest here by reference to his idea that the poet is an overhearer (someone overhearing and re-creating conversation), and that a sentence in poetry must do more than convey a meaning of words, "it must convey a meaning of sound" (Frost 1966, 6); sentence sound, the sound of sense, ear writer and ear reader are some of the key components in this original aesthetic.

Frost's scientific realism was also fully integrated with a partly classical model of the dialogic and of dialogic genres. While it is methodologically erroneous to set up a table of genres and fit each of his poems into its box as Lynen does (1960, 117–30), it is indispensable to note the genre-specific fact that Frost's more dialogical poems range from surface monologues ("A Servant to Servants") to near- or emerging monologues ("The Witch of Cöos"), to literal dialogue ("Mending Wall"), to dialogue between three or more persons ("Hired Man"). These multiple options, in turn, intersect with degrees of pastoralism (rural to urban, and so on), and run from highly philosophical dialogue ("West-Running Brook") to minimally philosophical imagery and narrative ("Out, out—"). Many of his dialogues in "The Death of the Hired Man" interweave drama, character study, idyll, and short story, as well as harking back to a dialogic genre in which Frost was steeped: the eclogue. "I first heard the voice from the printed page in a Virgilian eclogue and from Hamlet" (Cox 1966, 109). Eclogic elements are certainly basic to "The Death of the Hired Man," and we know that Frost knew Virgil's eclogues, had studied and taught them, and was deeply inspired by them. But to simply call this and similar poems eclogues, or worse, "Georgics," in the manner of Pound (1914: 127–30) and others, is to miss the polymathean synthesis of Frost's achievement and to commit the methodological error of taxonomic reductionism noted above.

One of the ultimate dialogical poems in the world, but in Frost's world in particular, is "The Death of the Hired Man," a minidrama in the above sense, but also because the "action is felt to be happening in the present" (Lynen 1960, 110). It is about a hired man, a salient social type in rural New England at the time, who has returned to the closest he knows to home, and to two people he hopes will take him in. It appeared in 1914, while the poet was still sojourning in England, one year after his first collection and as part of his second, *North of Boston* (ten of the twenty-one poems in this volume are decidedly dialogical, but there was a sharp drop in dialogue in his later volumes and his oeuvre as a whole).

"The Death of the Hired Man" shifts between interlocutors many times, and between different degrees of lyric intensity, and, in some metaphorical sense, includes the author and the silent, feminine moon as additional partners to the speech event. It is written in unrhymed, fairly regular iambic pentameter, with some extra syllables, a highly variable caesura, many spondees (for emphasis), and also reversed feet—as in the first two lines, each of which, strongly alliterated, introduces a main character (in media res, as is typical of Frost): "Mary sat musing by the lamp-flame on the table, / Waiting for Warren. . . ." She runs down the darkened corridor to meet him with the words "Silas is back" and "Be kind," thus introducing early on the themes of mercy and compassion that she represents. Husband Warren then speaks twenty lines, prosaic as is his wont, including an intensifying quote within a quote from the hired man that, as if an icon to his stubbornness, is put in trochees that buck the iambics. Warren, on the other hand, stands initially for the sort of justice Silas should get for going off so often at harvest time when he was needed. Warren and Mary then altercate gently about whether to take Silas in; there may be some tension between the two. Mary describes how Silas is "a miserable sight, and frightening, too," "huddled against the barn door fast asleep; he's worn out, he's asleep beside the stove"; her speech, as all critics note, is hesitant, slow, relatively broken and repetitive, heavy with pity. She defends Silas's offer to ditch a meadow, a symbol of his need for self-respect (a central value in rural New England and Calvinist cultures more generally). Also, he has been muttering obsessively, pathetically about a college student with whom he worked last summer. Here Mary, the intercessor, rises for the first time into a more intense lyricism, which includes these lines:

> . . .You know how they fought
> All through July under the blazing sun,
> Silas up on the cart to build the load,
> Harold along beside to pitch it on.

Here "Frost's form in the dramatic eclogue thus inclines to the lyric as his lyric figure inclines to the dramatic," or "these lyric expansions in Frost's eclogues fulfill the dramatic impulse and give it meaning, serving a purpose similar to a choric speech in Shakespeare" (Brower 1963, 165; also see Pritchard 1962, 38–56).

Mary depicts Silas's fantasies of once again arguing with student Harold and proving to him that how to build a load of hay or "to find water with a prong is as much a feat as learning Latin." (We who know recognize that the college student is somehow Latinist Frost himself. Incidentally, I must interrupt the analysis of the poem to note an extreme case of the reader's response being determined by personal factors: as an adolescent, I studied Latin, pitched hay and built hay loads, argued with the hired man under the blazing sun, and once watched a water-witch, apple branch in hand, locating our artesian well, only two hours' drive from Frost's Derry, New Hampshire; but this poem works without such personal understandings.) To continue, Warren not only admits in his grudging way to Silas's skill at building loads of hay, but rises to a lyricism that balances Mary's:

> He bundles every forkful in its place,
> And tags and numbers it for future reference,
> So he can find and easily dislodge it
> In the unloading. Silas does that well.
> He takes it out in bunches like big birds' nests.
> You never never see him standing on the hay
> He's trying to lift, straining to lift himself.

To which Mary replies for another paragraph or so at a slightly higher pitch of lyricism, including, "And nothing to look forward to with pride, / And nothing to look forward to with hope." Then, for the first of two times, Frost himself seems to break into the trialogue, becoming a fourth interlocutor, and introducing the fifth, the silent moon, which interacts with Mary, who is portrayed as stereotypically feminine (spreading her apron, reaching for the vine strings):

> Part of a moon was falling down the west,
> Dragging the whole sky with it to the hills.
> Its light poured softly in her lap. She saw it
> And spread her apron to it. She put out her hand
> Among the harplike morning-glory strings,
> Taut with the dew from garden bed to eaves,
> As if she played unheard some tenderness
> That wrought on him beside her in the night.
> "Warren," she said, "he has come home to die:
> You needn't be afraid he'll leave you this time."

In Bakhtinian terms, moments like this and indeed the whole poem stand somewhere between two poles: (1) the usual lyric where the direct, unconditional voice of the author "strips all aspects of language of the intentions and accents of the people" (Bakhtin 1975, 110–11), and, on the other hand, (2) the novel or short story, where many linguistic and/or stylistic planes intersect, not in the author's voice but an 'ideological center'" (Bakhtin 1981, 42–90). But poet Frost, with a different angle on the matter, put it, "Lyric will be piled on lyric till all are easily heard as sung or spoken by a person in a scene—in character, in a setting" (Lynen 1960, 128). Finally, building on the dialogical tradition as a whole, I would put it: Frost in this poem has achieved a fusion of the dialogic and the purely lyric so perfectly that the latter is taken into the former in a resolution that the tension between lyric/dialogue calls for.

Mary and Warren go on arguing, weaving in the comparison of Silas to a stray hound. Warren picks up on "Home" in what everyone has recognized as a climax in the minidrama: "'Home,' he mocked gently, / 'Yes, what but home?'" and compares Silas to a stray hound. Then comes the Frostian aphorism (which became part of my family culture): "Home is the place where, when you have to go there, / They have to take you in." Mary counters with, "I should have called it / Something you somehow haven't to deserve," thus ringing in again, not only her compassion (in the intonation of "something" and "somehow"), but also what self-respect and belonging can mean to a homeless man. Warren then gestures in an analogue to Mary reaching for the vine: "Warren leaned out and took a step or two, / Picked up a little stick, and brought it back / And broke it in his hand and tossed it by," and describes Silas's alienation from his bank-director brother down the road (whom Silas will not approach because of self-respect and who probably would not take him in if he did). And so the poem rises toward its heights with, inter alia, the note that the only way Si (Warren has softened to "Si") ever hurt anyone was the pain he caused Mary at seeing him so old and broken, so pathetic. In the closing lines we see the dark, iconically feminine trinity of cloud, moon, and Mary, a trinity of "man's fate and mortality," emerge as a substitute for the higher trinity of Christianity. To conclude, then, Mary persuades Warren to go and look at Si.

> ". . . You mustn't laugh at him
> He may not speak of it, and then he may,
> I'll sit and see if that small sailing cloud
> Will hit or miss the moon."

> It hit the moon.
> Then there were three there, making a dim row,
> The moon, the little silver cloud, and she.

> Warren returned—too soon, it seemed to her—
> Slipped to her side, caught up her hand and waited.

> "Warren?" she questioned.

> "Dead," was all he answered.[5]

ACKNOWLEDGMENT   I want to thank members of the "Poetry and Poetics across Cultures" workshop (University of Chicago) for their comments after a presentation on October 29, 1990, and likewise the participants in the MLA session on "Dialogue in Literary Narrative" on December 28, 1990—and Deborah Tannen for inviting me to participate in the latter.

Notes

An expanded version of this chapter appears in my *Wordsworth, Dialogics and the Practice of Criticism* (Cambridge: Cambridge University Press, 1992).

1. Other poets who exercised a primary influence on Frost's dialogicality included Chaucer, Shakespeare (whom he read in the 1890s), Robert Browning (who remained a favorite), and Hardy (who taught him "the good use of a few words" [Karki 1979, 11–16; Sharma 1981, chap. 1]).

2. To bring home these points for the English reader, here is the total of diminutives in the Krylov fable (which was modeled on the French version of La Fontaine's fable): *kusóchek* 'little piece of cheese'; *blizyókhonke* '[the fox ran up] a little close'; *plutóvka* 'the rascal'; *golúbushka* 'dear little pigeon'; *glazki* 'dear eyes'; *perúshki* 'dear feathers'; *nósík* 'dear nose (beak)'; *golosók* 'dear voice'; *svétik* 'dear light'; and *plutóvka* 'repeated'.

3. In this same brilliant analysis, Wierzbicka concludes about *-ushka* that it "can be combined with words encoding abstract existential concepts" such as grief, freedom, work, death, thought, care, strength, or fate (I omit the Russian here except to note that it includes our *dúmushka*). And later: "All these facts suggest that the expressivity encoded in the suffix *ushka* . . . seems to reflect an important feature of Russian folk philosophy, which views the human condition as pitiful and which encourages both resignation and compassion" (1992, 29). On these expressions, see also Stankiewiez 1957.

In Pushkin's *Eugene Onegin*, 3.32, we read of Tatyana that, after writing her love letter, "Her poor head [*golóvushka*] shoulderward she has inclined," to which stilted translation Nabokov comments: "a kind of compassionate diminutive (from *golóvka*), often used in plaintive folk songs" (1975, 2:397).

4. The avoidance of affectives is part of a more general pattern: the language of lyric poetry in Russian, as in many traditions, is relatively decorous. The affective and other parts of "primal" language are blocked on social and psychological grounds. Beyond this, there is a general avoidance in lyric poetry of forms that are inherently too violently emotional, which resembles the categorical exclusion of obscenities even from much realistic literature; such quotidian or standardized emotionality would conflict with the special kinds of emotionality that lyric poetry typically seeks.

The general misperception of the relation between lyric poetry and the affective system is illustrated by C. M. Bowra, who knew a lot about the theory and practice of Russian poetry: ". . . its large vocabulary, its affective diminutives, fit it [the Russian language] for poetry" (1947, xiv). The above discussion of affectives in Nekrasov intersects in small part with the section on Nekrasov in Friedrich 1997.

5. Robson and others have questioned the role of the moon in the poem as extraneous and so forth (1966, 752–53). This is part of a more general critical anomaly in Frost criticism, most of which appeared during the heyday of variously behaviorist, empiricist, and even positivistic points of view and hence neglected his deeply mythological stratum. Be it added that, in this intellectual climate, Frost's claim or suggestion to be capturing and representing real speech and real dialogue contributed greatly to his meteoric and extraordinary critical reception.

Works Cited

Bakhtin, M. M. *The Dialogic Imagination: Four Essays*. Translated by Michael Holquist. Edited by Caryl Emerson and Michael Holquist. Austin: University of Texas Press, 1983.
———. *Questions of Literature and Aesthetics*. Moscow: Khudozhestvennaya Literatura, 1975. (In Russian.)
Bhaskar, Roy. *A Realist Theory of Science*. Atlantic Highlands, N.J.: Humanities Press, 1978.
Birkenmayer, Sigmund S. *Nikolaj Nekrasov: His Life and Poetic Art*. The Hague: Mouton, 1968.
Bowra, C. M. *A Book of Russian Verse*. London: Macmillan, 1947.
Brower, Reuben A. *The Poetry of Robert Frost: Constellations of Intention*. New York: Oxford University Press, 1963.

Bühler, Karl. *Theory of Language: The Representational Function of Language.* Translated by Donald Fraser Goodwin. Amsterdam: John Benjamins, 1990.

Chukovsky, Kornej. *Masterstvo Nekrasova.* Moscow: Khudozhestvennaya Literatura, 1971.

———. *Ot Dvukh Do Pjati.* Moscow: Sovetskij Pisatel', 1960.

Cook, Reginald L. *The Dimensions of Robert Frost.* New York: Holt, 1958.

———. "Emerson and Frost: A Parallel of Seers." *New England Quarterly* 31 (1959): 201–17.

Corbet, Charles. *Nekrasov: L'Homme et le poete.* Paris: Institute d'Etudes Slaves de Université de Paris, 1948.

Cox, Sidney. *A Swinger of Birches: A Portrait of Robert Frost.* London: Collier Macmillan, 1966.

Friedrich, Paul. "Catalysis and Synthesis in Life-Changing Dialogue." In Tedlock and Mannheim, 1995, 33–53.

———. *The Language Parallax.* Austin: University of Texas Press, 1986.

———. *Music in Russian Poetry.* New York: Peter Lang Press, 1997.

———. "Polytropy." In *Beyond Metaphor: The Theory of Tropes in Anthropology*, edited by James Fernandez. Princeton, N.J.: Princeton University Press, 1991, 17–56.

———. "Structural Implications of Russian Pronominal Usage." In *Language, Context, and the Imagination: Essays by Paul Friedrich*, edited by Anwar S. Dil. Stanford, Calif.: Stanford University Press, 1979, 63–126.

Frost, Robert. *Interviews with Robert Frost.* Edited by Edward Connery Lathem. New York: Holt, 1966.

———. *North of Boston.* London: Nutt, 1914.

———. *The Poetry of Robert Frost.* Edited by Edward Connery Lathem. New York: Holt, Rinehart and Winston, 1974.

———. *Selected Letters of Robert Frost.* Edited by Lawrence Thompson. New York: Holt, 1964.

Gerber, Philip L. *Robert Frost.* Boston: Twayne, 1966.

Gerhart, Genevra. *The Russian's World. Life and Language.* New York: Harcourt Brace Jovanovich, 1974.

Gregg, Richard. "Dar'ia's secret; or, What happens in *Moroz, Krasnyi Nos.*" *Slavic Review* 45, no.1 (1986): 38–49.

Gustavson, Richard T. *The Imagination of Spring: The Lyric Poetry of Afanasy Fet.* New Haven, Conn.: Yale University Press, 1966.

Jakobson, Roman. "Concluding Statement: Linguistics and Poetics." In *Style in Language*, edited by Thomas A. Sebeok. Cambridge: MIT Press, 1960.

Karki, Mohan Singh. *Robert Frost. Theory and Practice of the Colloquial and Sound of Sense.* Aligarh, India: Granthayan, 1979.

Krylov, I. A. *Works.* 2 vols. Edited by N. L. Stepanov. Moscow: Pravda, 1956. (In Russian.)

Kuzma, Gregg, ed. *Gone Into if Not Explained: Essays on Poems by Robert Frost.* Lincoln, Nebr.: Best Cellar Press, 1976.

Lonsdale, Roger. *The New Oxford Book of Eighteenth-Century Poetry.* New York: Oxford University Press, 1984.

Lynen, John F. *The Pastoral Art of Robert Frost.* New Haven, Conn.: Yale University Press, 1960.

Markov, Vladimir, and Merrill Sparks. *Modern Russian Poetry.* New York: Macgibbon and Kee, 1967.

Miles, Josephine. "Reason." In *An Introduction to Poetry*, edited by X. J. Kennedy. Boston: Little, Brown, 1986.

Moore, Marianne. "The Fox and the Crow." In *A Marianne Moore Reader.* New York: Viking Press, 1961.

Morson, Gary Saul, and Caryl Emerson. *Mikhail Bakhtin: Creation of a Prosaics.* Stanford, Calif.: Stanford University Press, 1990.

Munson, Gorham B. *Robert Frost: The Study of Sensibility and Good Sense.* New York: George H. Doren, 1972.

Nabokov, Vladimir. *Alesandr Pushkin.* 2 vols. Princeton, N.J.: Princeton University Press, 1975.

Obolensky, Dmitri. *The Heritage of Russian Verse.* Bloomington: Indiana University Press, 1976.

Pope, Marvin. *Song of Songs.* New York: Doubleday (Anchor), 1977.

Pound, Ezra. "Modern Georgics." *Poetry: A Magazine of Verse* 5 (1914): 127–30.

Preminger, Alex, Frank J. Warnke, and O. B. Hardison, Jr. *Princeton Encyclopedia of Poetry and Poetics.* Princeton, N.J.: Princeton University Press, 1974.

Pritchard, William H. "*North of Boston*: Frost's Poetry of Dialogue." In *In Defense of Reading*, edited by R. A. Brower and R. Poirier. New York: E. P. Dutton, 1962, 38–56.

Ramanujan, A. K. *The Interior Landscape. Love Poems from a Classical Tamil Anthology.* Bloomington: Indiana University Press, 1967.

Robson, W. W. "The Achievement of Robert Frost." *Southern Review* 2 (1966): 735–61.

Simpson, Louis. "Luminous Night." In *People Live Here: Selected Poems 1949–83.* Brockport, N.Y.: Boa Editors, 1983.

Sharma, T.R.S. *Robert Frost's Poetic Style.* Delhi: Macmillan India, 1981.

Stankiewicz, Edward. "The Expression of Affection in Russian Proper Names." *Slavic and East European Journal* 1(1957): 196–210.

——. "The Slavic Expressive Component of Yiddish." *Slavica Hierosolymitana* 7 (1985): 177–87.

Stepanov, Nikolay. *Ivan Krylov.* New York: Twayne, 1973.

Tannen, Deborah. *Talking Voices. Repetition, Dialogue, and Imagery in Conversational Discourse.* Cambridge: Cambridge University Press, 1989.

Tedlock, Dennis, and Bruce Mannheim, eds. *The Dialogic Emergence of Culture.* Urbana: University of Illinois Press, 1995.

Thompson, Lawrence. *Robert Frost: The Years of Triumph 1915–38.* New York: Holt, 1970.

Thornton, Richard, ed. *Recognition of Robert Frost.* New York: Henry Holt, 1937.

Ubegaun, B. O. *Russian Grammar.* Oxford: Clarendon Press, 1963.

Wierzbicka, Anna. "Personal Names and Expressive Derivation." Chap. 7 in *Semantics, Culture, and Cognition.* New York: Oxford University Press, 1997.

——. "Russian Personal Names. The Semantics of Expressive Derivation." Unpublished manuscript (1992).

PART II

DIALOGUE BETWEEN WORKS

Dialogics of the Lyric

A Symposium on Wordsworth's "Westminster Bridge" and "Beauteous Evening"

In his afterword to the comprehensive collection of essays *Lyric Poetry: Beyond New Criticism*, Jonathan Arac remarks with some impatience that "so many essays from such diverse concerns agree to ignore so much important work."[1] Arac's complaint about these essays could be applied to many others that have accumulated on the topic of "the lyric" or "the poem" since the New Critics discovered how to produce critical essays as responses to isolated lyric poems. Such critical essays have exhibited "the stability of organization and the capacity to engender successors" that M. H. Abrams takes as the marks of a genre in his essay on the greater romantic lyric, and they also share with the lyric genre he describes a model of the relation between a speaker and the object that provokes his discourse: put a romantic poet in front of a natural scene or a New Critic in front of a lyric poem and discourse will be produced without need to posit any prior conversations or any other interlocutors.[2]

The genre of the New Critical essay, then, like the lyric genre it interprets, tacitly agrees to ignore precedent utterances and to stage the encounter of an already informed mind with its object. Were it to polemicize with previous views or to shape itself as a contribution to a discussion already under way, it would be less likely to meet New Critical criteria like those set by the editors of the volume going beyond New Criticism—"that each essay work from at least one specific text" (Hosek and Parker 1985, 353) and that the essays "bring contemporary theoretical questions to bear on the interpretation of specific lyric traditions and poems" (14). Critics with their given theories, like poets with whatever notions they happen to carry with them, will produce characteristic kinds of utterances when they respond to the poems before them and "agree to ignore so much important work."[3]

This agreement about genre will produce many interpretations of poems without clarifying theoretical disagreements or adjudicating their diverse consequences in practice. The accumulation of essays produced on this model will testify to its generic "capacity to engender successors," but it will not result in an articulated conversation. The pile may be added to, but it won't add up. Arac notes that the New Critical emphasis on the isolated lyric poem has been replaced in the recent collection with an emphasis on the "intertextual" relations between poems or poets, but the critical practice he describes and criticizes seems not to have taken this emphasis to heart as it applies to the intertextual relations among critics.

Arac tries to supplement this lack by providing some of the history of the discussion the essayists neglect in their "tactical" (1985, 352) deployment of ideas about the lyric. He reconstructs, for example, the intertextual relations between Bakhtin and Kristeva out of which the term "intertextuality" itself emerged, and he highlights the differences between personalizing and impersonal uses of the term (348–50). His afterword produces a history and imagines a potential context for essays that typically apply theories to poems.

But while the genre of the "afterword," in which Arac has more than once written,[4] makes its writer responsive to the essays that precede it as they need not have been responsive to one another or to other previous work, its limits prevent it from overcoming the inarticulateness of accumulations of critical essays. It must characterize trends instead of responding to specific arguments, call attention to omissions instead of working out their implications, and depend on prior reading of the other essays instead of revoicing them as they figure in its own argument. An afterword can call attention to the inarticulateness of the collection of essays it follows, but it cannot fully make it articulate.

These limits are shared, with few exceptions, by all the genres available for articulating and addressing what has already been written. Introductions, afterwords, annotated bibliographies, reviews, and review essays are all much smaller and much less prominent than the works to which they respond. A situating paragraph at the beginning of an essay, a three-page review of a three-hundred-page book, or Arac's ten-page response to over three hundred pages of text containing twenty-one essays accurately represent the usual proportions. The reviewing genres are also typically set apart from the "original contributions" in opening chapters or paragraphs, review sections (sometimes in smaller print), or notes, even though both "originality" and "contribution" make sense only in a conversation that can remember what has already been said and recognize what now needs saying.

Bakhtin's emphasis on the dialogic character of all discourse ("intertextuality" is Kristeva's word, not his) can perhaps help us to restore not only the lyric poet but also the critic-essayist to awareness of the conversation from which their generic habits have abstracted them. If, as he claims, *all* utterances are shaped as responses to and anticipations of other utterances, then the lyric poet supposedly singing in splendid isolation and the critic supposedly closeted alone with the poem will both be found to have company. If, as he also claims, all objects of discourse are always already invested with discourse, then the lyric poet's beloved and the lyric critic's poem do not wait speechlessly for the poet and the critic to articulate them; they themselves have already spoken and been spoken for. J. Hillis Miller, who has raised the New Critical essay's neglect of prior critics into a principle and carried it out in his practice, characterizes the tradition of the text's interpretation by others as "an opaque mist or . . . an impenetrable thicket of thorns around the sleeping beauty"[5] through which the critic-prince, in effect, penetrates to have a direct encounter with the text itself, but Bakhtin, who uses the same figures of "obscuring mist" and entanglement to describe the object of discourse already involved in previous discourse, also admits the contrary figure of the "'light' of alien words," and he does not imagine that either the critic or the work can be separated from the conflicting discourse in which they have been constituted.[6]

Bakhtin's premises can lead us to recognize in both poems and essays the hidden dialogues that shape their discourse, but they can also guide us toward creating critical (perhaps by way of poetic) genres that integrate responses to our object of discourse with responses to the others who have spoken about it and articulate those responses more comprehensively and self-consciously than the New Critical essay allows. The symposium, one of the dialogic genres Bakhtin associates with the tradition of Menippean satire, offers itself for these purposes.[7] It is not to be imagined, however, as a group of essays solicited for oral presentation and published as a collection but, on the model of Plato's *Symposium*, as an *account* of previous utterances on a topic selected from a larger field of available utterances by a narrator. Involved with the topic and affiliated with or opposed to previous speakers, the narrator of a symposium tells what he or she thinks "most worth remembering" and responds to it in his or her own terms or in the terms of his or her hero.

This generic model informs my present discourse, which constructs a symposium from among several critical essays that have chosen to demonstrate their theories of the lyric or of poetry in readings of one or both of two canonical Wordsworth sonnets, "Composed upon Westminster Bridge" and "It is a beauteous evening, calm and free."[8] These two poems have provoked characteristic readings from critics representing several of the major schools of thought in modern American criticism, just as the topic of love provoked typical responses from representatives of the principal intellectual professions of Plato's day. Cleanth Brooks turned to both poems in the opening gambit of his New Critical classic, *The Well Wrought Urn*; Norman Maclean chose one of them to illustrate his Chicago school analysis of a lyric poem; Kenneth Burke used both to take dramatistic exception to Maclean's reading; Charles Molesworth chose "Westminster Bridge" for a rhetorical reading; J. Hillis Miller selected it for a deconstructive one; and Michael Riffaterre used it to illustrate his intertextual semiotic reading. Most recently Judith W. Page has made "It is a beauteous evening, calm and free" the chief exemplar in her feminist analysis of Wordsworth's "Calais sonnets."[9] Though their essays remain true to form in paying little or no explicit attention to precedent utterances on the poems, their complex potential interrelations may be brought, as Bakhtin says, "by means of a dotted line to the point of their dialogic intersection" (1984, 91).

In bringing out those points of connection among them, however, I will not be standing outside their dialogue but in its midst, organizing my presentation of their words and responding critically to their claims in order to bring out the value of the position with which I myself identify. As Apollodorus comes forward as an unabashed lover of Socrates and arranges his account of the symposium to bring out the superiority of his hero's discourse on love, so I here identify myself with Bakhtin's dialogics and shall attempt to demonstrate its value in interpreting lyric poetry, even as I represent the views of the other symposiasts. Bakhtin did not address himself to the poems that concern me, and his most extensive published comments on the lyric (narrowly conceived) treat it as a monologic foil to the dialogic novel (1981, 275–88), but his works on language, literary form, poetic discourse, and the novel repeatedly supply me with comments and perspectives that inform my criticism of the critics and my readings of the poems. I do not, however, like Plato's Apollodorus, save my hero's discourse for last but draw on it as I report and respond to what each of the others has said.

Beginning with Brooks's New Critical reading and Riffaterre's semiotic sophistication of it, I then take up Maclean's Chicago school reading and Burke's dramatistic critique of it, and finally examine Molesworth's rhetorico-political, Page's feminist, and Miller's rhetorico-deconstructive readings. Each of the first two pairs constitutes short connected lines of discussion in which the second writer follows the first, but neither line attends to the other's readings. The last two writers enter the discussion as sui generis contributors explicitly affiliated with no predecessors, but both reveal important connections to the others. Though I do not pursue a single thesis through all of my engagements with them, I believe that each engagement highlights a significant resource of modern criticism and an important implication of Bakhtin's dialogics. Neither a New Critical essay nor a series of unrelated refutations, this symposium as a whole discovers previously unrecognized affinities and oppositions among its participants, elaborates a dialogic theory of lyric poetry and critical discourse, and illuminates Wordsworth's poems.

Dialogics of Paradox: Cleanth Brooks and New Criticism

Brooks opens *The Well Wrought Urn* (1947/1975) with readings of Wordsworth's sonnets because Wordsworth — poet of direct self-expression and simple poetic diction — is a hard case for Brooks's now-familiar thesis that "the language of poetry is the language of paradox." Brooks claims, nevertheless, that both sonnets are "based upon . . . paradoxical situation[s]" and that the Westminster Bridge sonnet gets its power from "the paradoxical situation out of which [it] arises" (3–5), but he does not say what he means by "the language of paradox" or "paradoxical situation." Whatever he means, he makes the situations in Wordsworth's sonnets sound paradoxical through the language he uses to describe them.

In the one, "the poet is filled with worship, but the girl who walks beside him is not worshiping . . . yet . . . the innocent girl worship[s] more deeply than the self-conscious poet who walks beside her" (4). Brooks here presents "Beauteous Evening" as if its paradox were in the situation itself, not in the perspective of the speaker, as if the paradoxical contrast between the speaker's worship and the girl's lack of it were impersonally reversed by a revelation of the truth of the girl's deeper inner worship. In the other poem, Brooks makes the paradox one that the speaker himself registers as a surprising discovery: he expects that only nature can "wear the beauty of the morning," but he declares in what Brooks calls "almost shocked exclamation" that "'*Never did sun more beautifully steep / In his first splendour*, valley, rock, *or* hill'" than now it steeps, of all things, London (1975, 6).

These ways of talking suggest a distinction between paradox as an utterance taken to be inconsistent or self-contradictory on its face and paradox understood as an utterance contrary to someone's opinion, that is, between impersonal or "objective" paradox intelligible in itself and socially relative or dialogical paradox intelligible only to one who knows the "dox"(*doxa*), or "opinion," against which the paradox (*paradoxos*, "contrary to expectation") plays. In his eagerness to demonstrate the pervasiveness of paradox, however defined, Brooks does not examine the distinction between these interpretations of paradox implied by his descriptions of the two poems, and he takes for granted the objective understanding. The dialogical view of paradox, however, would question the objective understanding and the distinction itself. It would insist that *some* "dox," either tacitly assumed as dialogizing background or verbally represented within the poem itself, is the necessary ground of a dialogic phenomenon like paradox. There can be no reversal of or play on expectation without an expectation, and no expectation without *someone* to expect it, even if *everyone* expects it and the expectation therefore goes without saying.

Because Brooks does not reflect on the dialogical model of paradox implicit in his description of "Westminster Bridge," he also does not consider the various ways that paradox relates to dox, that is, the ways in which by-opinions respond to or relate to the opinions off which they play. Bakhtin analyzes a large class of discourse oriented to other discourse, as paradox is oriented to "dox" or even to "orthodox," but he recognizes also both "diverse forms of interrelationship" and "various degrees of deforming influence exerted by one discourse on the other" (1984, 199). Brooks's position gains what power it has by calling attention to all kinds of byplay in poetry under the rubric of "paradox," but it gives little help in discriminating those forms and degrees of byplay—those relations of dox and paradox—Bakhtin elaborates.

Brooks's reading of "Westminster Bridge" thus recognizes a speaking person who feels compelled by a striking impression of London to reverse his usual opinion of it. But Brooks underestimates the radical relation of dox to paradox the poem depicts. The speaker expresses not just Brooks's "sense of awed surprise" at the discovery that "man-made London is a part of nature too" (1975, 6); he gives unreserved testimony to the power of the scene before him against the claims of anything else the earth has to show or of any moment he has known of natural illumination. Indeed, the shock to the speaker's usual assumptions is so great that he seems to cast off his usual identity and to stand for the moment outside it, ecstatically rejecting that dull-souled perspective that could pass this experience by and testifying to an experience of calm in this vision deeper than any he has ever seen or felt. If the position he declares stands paradoxically toward his usual opinion, the tone in which he declares it is that of the convert who has turned decisively away from blindness toward the light of revealed truth. He preserves the memory of his former view not as a standard to which the new experience unexpectedly conforms but as a reminder of the dullness of soul from which the present revelation has freed him. The speaker's paradoxical utterance in this case *supplants* the dox against which it shaped itself but preserves that dox as the reminder of what he imagines he has transcended.

A different relation between dox and paradox holds in "Beauteous Evening." If we set aside Brooks's impersonal description of it and read it dialogically as a speaking person's utterance, the relation of the speaker's dox and paradox is mediated by his failed attempt to share his sense of the evening's holiness with the child with whom he is walking. The dox, the initially posited opinion of God's immanence in the evening, meets a resistance in the child's indifference to the invitation to listen to the sound of the "mighty Being" the speaker hears. In the paradoxical sestet, the speaker finds a way to preserve his own sense of that Being's power by positing a secret inner relationship between God and the child to explain away the child's outward nonparticipation in the worshipful posture the evening provokes in him. Here the paradox is not a *replacement* of the posited dox but a *supplement* to it, a compensation for its failure to include the child. It can be taken, I think, neither as a simple continuation of the poem's initial worshipfulness nor as an unexpected reversal of the speaker's and the child's apparent relations to God, but as a recovery from embarrassment. The speaker, carried away with his sense of the evening, has invited the child to enter into something unsuited to her, and like the father in "Anecdote for Fathers" he covers his embarrassment at the awkward discovery of his mistaken manner of address with affectionate declarations and compensatory imaginings. The speaker's appeal for "choral support" from his child-companion is disappointed;[10] the assurance of his worshipful tone is threatened. But with a pause in his discourse lasting for perhaps several moments beyond the fulsome full stop of "everlastingly," he reasserts himself in his affectionate condescension toward the child and his exalted recuperation of her failure to share his evaluation of the evening. He does not adopt a view that she could share but reasserts the presence of the power she has not acknowledged and even exalts her relation to that power over his own in a delicate self-abasement in keeping with his initial worshipfulness.

If, as Bakhtin claims, "the fundamental condition of lyric intonation is *unhesitating confidence in the sympathy of the listeners*," then this lyric poem moves in the direction of what he calls "lyric irony," which expresses "social conflict" through the "meeting in one voice of two embodied evaluations, and their interferences and interruptions" (1983, 25). Though the child says nothing, her lack of response registers her implicit evaluation of the situation and provokes a changed tone from the speaker. Furthermore, the relation of religiously sophisticated adult and unsophisticated child is a social relation like the one in "We Are Seven" that calls the sophistication itself into question and provokes the adult to offer a sophisticated account of the child to explain away its apparent unorthodoxy. The adult's religious paradox here, like the adult's physical explanation of the child's ignorance in "We Are Seven," functions to protect his orthodoxy.

The paradox in "Beauteous Evening," then, works to preserve the speaker's fundamental opinion, while the paradox in "Westminster Bridge" gains its power by contradicting the speaker's expectation. Both relations of paradox to dox could be given rather ponderous abstract names from Bakhtin's taxonomy of discourse types: "Beauteous Evening" could be described as unidirectional double-voiced discourse, the second part of which is an active type of discourse in hidden dialogue with the child's implied contradictory evaluation of the evening. That is to say, the sestet continues the evaluative direction of the octave by attributing to the child a stand-point consistent with the narrator's desires, even as it implicitly answers the child's implied contradictory standpoint. "Westminster Bridge" could be categorized as vari-directional double-voiced discourse parodically representing and rejecting the speaker's now-transcended view of London as a successfully exorcised dullness of soul (1984, 199). Both poems are double-voiced in that they enact a relation between two opinions, but the voices are in agreement—despite resistance—in "Beauteous Evening" and in opposition in "Westminster Bridge." The awkwardness of Bakhtin's terms compared to the grace of Brooks's unexamined "language of paradox" should not obscure the gain Bakhtin's locutions make in precise discrimination over Brooks's blanket term.

My dialogic reading, however, has not rejected Brooks's claim that paradox operates in these poems: instead, it has reinterpreted the grounds of paradox as social and recognized the functions of paradox as varied. These lyric poems, like many of Wordsworth's best-known lyrics, work not as the expression of single or simple voices but as responses to other voices within or outside the speaker. The experiences of London or of the beauteous evening reveal their power not just in the speaker's direct response to them but in his response to other opinions of them. The speaker's impassioned paradoxical utterances are provoked not just by things, but by the social world of other utterances that evaluate them; not just by the phenomenal world of nature or naturelike London, but by the doxical world of social relations, values, and words.[11]

Dialogicality and Intertextuality: Michael Riffaterre and Semiotics

The statement with which I have just concluded sounds like the premise of an essay by Michael Riffaterre (1984) that also takes up the "Westminster Bridge" sonnet and Brooks's reading of it. Riffaterre explores the kind of literary mimesis that refers not from "words to things" but "from words to words, or rather from texts to texts" (142). Riffaterre emphasizes the reference of words to words over the reference of words to things just as I emphasize the shaping of words "not just by things but by the social world of other utterances." But despite our similar language and the similar structures of our assertions, several important differences compel me to distinguish my dialogics from Riffaterre's semiotics of the lyric.[12]

Most important is a difference like the one Arac observes between impersonal and personalizing understandings of "intertextuality." Though both Bakhtin and Riffaterre posit other words necessary to understand the words of any given poem, Riffaterre imagines those words as an intertext—"a corpus of texts, textual fragments, or textlike segments of the sociolect that shares a lexicon and, to a lesser extent, a syntax with the text we are reading" (142). Bakhtin, however, posits the dialogic figure of the speaker whose words sound against the dialogizing background of other people's words. Riffaterre's term "sociolect" appears to emphasize the same social understanding of language that I have emphasized, but again his definition objectifies and depersonalizes the dialogic social world of interacting opinions and voices, when he defines a "sociolect" as "language viewed not just as grammar and lexicon but as the repository of society's myths . . . themes, commonplace phrases, and descriptive systems" (160n). Riffaterre's "sociolect" here treats social myths and commonplaces on the same linguistic model it uses for grammar and lexicon, again without imagining the dialogic world of speakers *appealing* to those commonplaces and *invoking* those myths in specific social situations.[13]

When Riffaterre describes "Westminster Bridge" as the kind of text that "owes its descriptive power to an intertext that it negates while compelling the reader to remain fully aware of that intertext" (149), his point once again resembles my claim that "the speaker's paradoxical utterance supplants the dox against which it shaped itself but preserves that dox as the reminder of what he imagines he has transcended." Riffaterre's "intertext" has the same role in his model as "dox" has in my terms or "dialogizing background" has in Bakhtin's, but while Bakhtin and I imagine the represented speaker interacting in his utterance with the opinions of others, Riffaterre's impersonal formulation imagines a text acting on an actual reader by means of an intertext.

Riffaterre's reader interprets the poem, then, not by re-creating a speaker's utterance as it responds to other utterances but by recognizing how the idiolect—which he defines as the "individual's specific semiotic activity" (160n)—interacts with the sociolect. In "Westminster Bridge" the reader discovers the poem's idiolectic evaluations of London in two ways. First, the poem uses "positive markers" in the "extolment lexicon" (151) to transfer to London the "descriptive features characteristic only of Nature herself" (152). Second, the poem negates one negative marker in the usual language applied to the city—the "smoke" whose negation in the word "smokeless" preserves what Riffaterre calls a "trace left by the intertext at the surface of the text displacing it" (153). For Riffaterre, the words work on the reader, without reference to anyone's use of them and without reference to the things they describe, because they have ambiguous places in textual codes that necessarily operate in the reader's mind (cf. Riffaterre, 142, 154, 159). Riffaterre, then, treats evaluation as if it were a matter of a word's place among other words in a social lexicon, as, for instance, "'garment' has the plus sign, as opposed to *cloak*, with its minus sign" (151). He treats "surprise," which, like Brooks, he finds in the poem, not as the speaker's response to the reversal of his expectations but as an objective relation the reader must recognize between the connotations of the city in the sociolect and its connotations in the idiolect. He attributes "emotion" not to the speaker's response to London but to the poem's use of a device like repetition, which he calls a "codified, well-established sign for emotion" that the reader must decode as such (156).

Riffaterre does not specify the emotion to be decoded from the repetition he points to in the line, "Ne'er saw I, never felt, a calm so deep!" To do so I think he would have to go beyond decoding. He would need to acknowledge the "I," that appears for the first time in the poem in this line, as significant for more than the fact that it is a pronoun "not repeated" (156). It is a pronoun that is unprecedented, like the experience it acknowledges. The "I" in this line evokes a specific person testifying that his experience of London at this moment surpasses in the depth of its calm any other experience of calm he has ever known. The tone of this testimony—conveyed more by word order in relation to metrical stress and by position in the line than by *choice* of words—is emphatic and unequivocal. The reversed word order of "Ne'er saw I" with "Ne'er" at the head of the line, the repeated "Ne'er . . . never," the stress on "saw" and "felt" as well as on "calm" and "deep," make this experience for the one who exclaims it more than the transfer to London of Riffaterre's "descriptive features characteristic only of Nature herself" (152). What this speaker emphatically declares he sees and feels is more intense and less "obvious" than Riffaterre's statement of "the lesson we are supposed to learn . . . : that London has beauty . . . equal to nature's" (150).[14]

A "semiotic mechanism" (150) that can account for the poem's communication of no more than this is inadequate, and a reader who can be satisfied that this is all there is to communicate has let his theory reduce the poem to a commonplace. Brooks too fails to mention the line I have been concerned with and misses, as Riffaterre does, the emphatic point that the speaker experiences this moment's calm as an instant surpassing anything he has known in nature or anywhere else, for that matter, but Brooks at least imagines a speaker and hears his tone of "almost shocked exclamation" (6). The very looseness of Brooks's terms and the slippage they permit him between "the language of paradox" and "paradoxical situation" leave him free to abandon his apparently objective linguistic model when a poem like this one seems to demand attention to the tones of its speaker's utterance. Riffaterre's more systematic linguistic approach leads him to diminish the speaker to a superfluous grammatical feature appropriated by the reader (154, 159) and to diminish tone to an objective plus-or-minus relation between sociolect and idiolect. Riffaterre provides an emblem for this impoverished notion of tone in the photographic metaphor he chooses for the relation of sociolect to idiolect. He writes, "The complementarity of sonnet and sociolect resembles the correspondence between a photograph and the negative it has been developed from: developing requires a reversal of tones, an exchange of black for white" (153). Brooks at least hears, though he cannot account for, the tones that mark the speaker's profound response to the scene before him and to his own and others' mistakenly low expectations of its value. Riffaterre finds the "power" of the poem, such as it remains for him, in its objective substitution of what he calls "a positive structure for its negative homologue," and he relishes the simple mechanical beauty of its shift of minuses to pluses, of black tones to white (154).

Bakhtin gives us an account of tone that preserves objectivity without abstracting itself from the speaker's situation and identifying with a mechanically decoding reader's perspective. For Bakhtin, an utterance, like an enthymeme, always has two parts, the verbally realized part and the implied part, the speaker's words and the understood situation they respond to and resolve. Sounding much like Riffaterre, he asserts that "implied evaluations" of these understood situations "are not . . .

individual emotions, but socially determined and necessary acts," but he goes on to find a place for the "I" that Riffaterre minimizes when he adds, "*Individual emotions can only accompany the fundamental tone of the social evaluation as overtones*—the 'I' can realize itself in discourse, only when dependent on the 'we'" (1983, 12).

The "we" here that provides the dialogizing background for a given individual utterance is not, however, an "it," a "sociolect" abstracted to represent the stereotyped values of a society, but a specific community of others whose prior utterances and potential responses provoke, situate, and make the utterance intelligible, a "dialogized heteroglossia, anonymous and social as language, but simultaneously concrete, filled with specific content and accented as an individual utterance" (1981, 272). However commonplace or conventional those individually accented utterances may appear to the observing linguist or historian, they will have impinged on the speaker as the words of significant precursors and listeners, and they will have shaped the speaker's tones (and the properly situated reader's interpretation of them) more subtly than Riffaterre's theory would allow.

The contrast between Bakhtin's metaphors for tone and Riffaterre's photographic figure can stand for the difference between their theories. Bakhtin's musical figure of "overtone" permits the intonation to "freely undergo deployment and differentiation within the range of the major tone" (1976, 102). And his visual figure epitomizes, in its difference from Riffaterre's, the difference in the range of values his theory permits us to recover: he writes, "*The commonness of assumed basic value judgments constitutes the canvas upon which living human speech embroiders the designs of intonation*" (1976, 103). Even if Riffaterre let his photographic figure transfer shades of grey from negative sociolect to positive idiolect, it would still be less interesting than the intricate and colorful tonal designs to which Bakhtin's figure and his theory direct our attention.

Theme and Meaning: Norman Maclean and the Chicago School

It is not accidental that Bakhtin's dialogics has something to say to Riffaterre's semiotics and Brooks's poetics: Bakhtin shaped his argument in response to the tradition of abstract objectivist linguistics Riffaterre follows and to the related tradition of Russian formalist poetics Brooks's New Criticism resembles.[15] It should not surprise us, then, that Bakhtin's criticism of language conceived apart from its functioning in utterance and of a poetics too exclusively preoccupied with literary language should itself resemble the Chicago school's criticism of the New Critics' linguistic assumptions—the Bakhtin school and the Chicago school offer analogous critiques of analogous formalisms.

As we will see, however, the different unifying principles Bakhtin and the Chicago critics invoke and the different conceptions of genre they depend on make their different responses more consequential than their similar situations. Bakhtin frames his criticism of formal linguistics and poetics in terms of what his translator calls the difference between *theme* and *meaning*. "Theme" or "thematic unity" is Bakhtin's name for the "significance of a whole utterance . . . *taken in its full, con-*

crete scope as an historical phenomenon"; it is not in his usage reducible merely to the subject or topic of discourse. "Meaning" is his term for those abstract linguistic elements "of the utterance that are *reproducible* and *self-identical* in all instances of repetition," elements like phonemes, dictionary definitions, or Riffaterre's "texts" that are constant in the linguistic system but tonally indeterminate in any instance of their use.[16] In his critique of formalist poetics, Bakhtin formulates the relation between theme and meaning in this way:

> The thematic unity of the work is not the combination of the meanings of its words and individual sentences. . . . Theme always transcends language. Furthermore, it is the whole utterance as speech performance that is directed at the theme, not the separate word, sentence, or period. . . . The theme of the work is the theme of the whole utterance as a definite sociohistorical act. Consequently, it is inseparable from the total situation of the utterance to the same extent that it is inseparable from linguistic elements.[17]

The thematic unity of an utterance, then, is its unity as an utterance of a given kind in a specific situation, and we make sense of it not as we identify independently reproducible linguistic elements or relatively constant common topics of discourse.

To account for how we do grasp the themes of utterances in life or in literature, Bakhtin posits speech genres and our capacity to invent and re-create them. If we cannot grasp themes in the same way that we identify phonemes or topoi out of context, then we must have available to us not only a repertoire of familiar situations and the utterances they provoke but also a capacity to imagine unfamiliar situations and the utterances that resolve them. We come to any work of literature already in full possession of "a series of inner genres for seeing and conceptualizing reality," with a repertoire of familiar themes. We as individuals may be "richer or poorer in genres, depending on [our] ideological environment." But literature itself "occupies an important place in this ideological environment" and its genres can "enrich our inner speech with new devices for the awareness and conceptualization of reality" (1978, 134), for the re-creation and discovery of the themes of utterances.

These questions of genre and of a unifying principle of the poetic whole not reducible to its linguistic elements also arise in R. S. Crane's Chicago school critique of Brooks's New Critical theory. Crane's Brooks indeed comes closer to the theoretically consistent Riffaterre in his reliance on a "single principle, essentially linguistic in its formulation" than to my own theoretically inconsistent but practically insightful Brooks.[18] But the position Crane opposes to the one he attributes to Brooks shares the emphases on genre and on the poem as finished whole that I have just drawn from Bakhtin. Here is Crane coming to his point:

> [A] poet does not write poetry but individual poems. And these are inevitably, as finished wholes, instances of one or another poetic kind, differentiated not by any necessities of the linguistic instrument of poetry but primarily by the nature of the poet's conception, as finally embodied in his poem, of a particular form to be achieved through the representation, in speech used dramatically or otherwise, of some distinctive state of feeling, or moral choice, or action, complete in itself and productive of a certain emotion or complex of emotions in the reader. (1952, 96)

Everything in this passage before the phrase "in speech" agrees with Bakhtin's critique of the "formal method" of the Russian formalists, but in that phrase Crane shows his Aristotelian colors and goes on to subordinate speech as medium to a nonverbal object of imitation: feeling or moral choice or action. Crane does not recognize *utterance* or "speech performance" (Bakhtin 1978, 132) as itself an object of imitation. He recognizes only plot and its analogues as organizing principles of a poetic whole, and he denigrates an explanation of a poem that resorts to "an inconsequential and unmoving 'theme'" (1952, 100).[19]

Crane quotes with contempt the same word "theme" that Bakhtin's translator chooses as the name for Bakhtin's valorized unifying principle, but these conflicting evaluations of a single word would not surprise the dialogic theorist who expects "a constant struggle of accents in each semantic sector of existence" (Bakhtin 1973, 106). Crane himself, however, might have been surprised or displeased by the more positive tone one of his Chicago colleagues gives the word. Norman Maclean (1964) offers a paradigmatic analysis of Wordsworth's "Beauteous Evening" as one of several "poems by Wordsworth that treat much the same 'theme'—poems in which Wordsworth represents what he believes is involved in the discovery of God" (138). Maclean too places the word "theme" in quotation marks that betray his uneasiness in using it, but theme nevertheless plays a significant part in Maclean's "Analysis of a Lyric Poem."[20]

Maclean's attempt to discuss "the whole poem as some kind of unit in itself" (131) links his effort with both Crane's and Bakhtin's emphasis on unifying principles. Like Bakhtin, he situates his reading by distinguishing it from reductions of the poem to language or to subject matter. Maclean defines himself against a formal analysis preoccupied with prosodic rules and "individual figures of speech," on the one hand, and a biographical criticism that reads the poem as a discourse on the poet's life, addressed to his illegitimate child Caroline and through her to her mother Annette, on the other (131–33).[21] Maclean goes on to divide his own analysis of the poem into two parts that correspond closely to Bakhtin's division of meaning from theme. First, he attempts to discover the poem's parts at the material levels of prosody, syntax, and signification of its words. Second, he tries to account for the relationship of those parts as both an imitation of a developing course of feelings and thoughts and as a treatment of a recognizable Wordsworthian theme.

Maclean does not pretend that he can recognize the poem's unifying principle in the same way that he can identify its syntactic and prosodic parts, but he does not see how much his account of the meanings of the parts already depends upon his thesis about the theme of the whole. He points, for example, to the poem's departure in its second quatrain from normal Petrarchan rhyme scheme and to the poem's division into "three syntactic entities" as signs that the plot of the poem divides into three parts, but neither rhyme scheme nor syntax yields unambiguous divisions. This syntactic division of the poem further suggests to him an intimation of plot movement from "breathlessness, to exaltation, to meditation" (134), because he finds "breathlessness" in the four independent clauses without conjunctions in the first part, "exaltation" in the "apostrophe" of the second part (though not in the apostrophe of the third part), and a "more cognitive" meditative tone in the dependent clauses and participial phrases of the last part (133–34). But apostrophes are not devices at the level of syntax, and it must be clear that the other speculations drawn ostensibly from syntax are again, like the division of the poem Maclean proposes, tonally indeterminate in themselves without an implicit hypothesis concerning the utterance in this particular context. Unconjoined clauses are not necessarily breathless any more than dependent clauses and participial phrases are necessarily reflective.

Just how far his hypothesis about the whole guides Maclean's account of its parts becomes clear in his reading of its semantic elements, of the words not only as indices of the shifting objects of the poet's attention but also as evidence of his response to those objects, of his feelings and thoughts about them (134). Maclean draws on such evidence most crucially in his account of the first part of the poem in which he argues, for reasons I will make clear in a moment, that the poet responds to the evening "as a sensory being" (135). His argument hangs on the claim that "'beauteous' in its strict meaning is to be distinguished from 'beautiful' in that it is more sensory in its connotations." But it is hard to imagine a "strict meaning" for such a word in the first place and impossible to find warrant for this connotation in the *OED*, where "beauteous" is distinguished not as sensory but as poetic or literary in its usage. In defense of his claim, Maclean goes on to argue still more implausibly that the remaining lines of the first part, even after its speaker's characterization of the evening as "holy" and his comparison of its quiet to that of a nun, "as yet . . . record only the poet's sensory impressions" (135). Only when the sun, at the end of the first part, is said to "brood" does Maclean admit an "activity the course of which cannot be traced by sensory perception" (136). Though he acknowledges the religious connotations mobilized in this part by the words "heaven" and "holy," he insists that it "is improper as yet to read the lines as affirmations on the part of the poet that the evening literally has religious signification" (135).

Why, though the utterance is shaped by a reverent response to the evening from the outset, should Maclean press the connotations of "beauteous" into such unlikely service while he minimizes the mutually reinforcing connotations of "holy" and "heaven" as well as the religious provenance of the simile? Because, as his introduction of "Tintern Abbey" at this point makes clear, he has abstracted a Wordsworthian plot movement "from sensation, to thought, to an understanding of the powers and limitations of thought" (138) from his reading of that most Wordsworthian of poems, and he tries to fit this sonnet's movement into a similar pattern. His syntactic and prosodic divisions of the poem and his tonal interpretation of its syntax follow from this model of its genre.

The generic repertoire to which Maclean has turned for his model of the poem's overall movement is a doctrinal plot pattern abstracted from "many other poems by Wordsworth that treat much the same 'theme'" of what the poet "believes is involved in the discovery of God" (138). My own recourse to generic analogues in "Anecdote for Fathers" and "We Are Seven" locates the thematic similarity not in the divisions of their common religious subject matter but in the participants of their common discursive situations. These poems depict adults who give accounts of exchanges between themselves and children similar to the exchange depicted in the sonnet between speaker and child. In both the poems I look to, the adult's attempt to bring a child to share his adult view is met with frustration, and the frustration is itself resolved by compensatory explanations in the retelling of the encounters. The theme that defines these verbal interactions as a whole is, like the theme of the sestet of "Beauteous Evening," the adult speaker's response to his abortive effort to bring a child to share his adult perspective.

Unlike the personal anecdotes in which the speaker recapitulates his exchange with the child in responding to it, however, the sonnet depicts the response as a final stage in a continuing exchange. Accomplished with less effort and with only the briefest pause after the provoking encounter, the speaker's response in the sonnet resolves his embarrassment smoothly, without the need to dwell on the exchange and go through it again as the speakers in the anecdotes must do. But the effectiveness and ease of the compensatory gesture does not make it any less such a gesture.

A generic hypothesis about the poem shapes not only Maclean's but my own reading of its elements, but his attempt to describe the movement of the poem as an internally necessary plot development revelatory of a familiar Wordsworthian "theme" finally reduces the sonnet to a reproducible Wordsworthian meaning, though he had wished "to explain as exactly as possible its uniqueness" (138). The sonnet's theme, in Bakhtin's sense, escapes him, because he is committed to distinguishing the poem's unifying action from its verbal embodiment, while Bakhtin, as I have noted, looks for a unifying theme in the embodied verbal interaction itself. Maclean's Wordsworthian genre posits an internal plot of sensation, feeling, and thought externalized in language; the dialogic genre I have suggested recognizes in the speaker's utterance an emotional and thoughtful verbal response not just to God in the evening but to the child at his side.

Dialogics and Dialectic: Kenneth Burke and Dramatism

Kenneth Burke's (1962) response to Maclean's essay and to the Chicago school mini-manifesto of which it was a part is both a model for and an admonition to my own symposium. Burke responds more explicitly to the Chicago position than any of the other writers I am examining respond to the other positions against which they define their own. His dialectical program commits him to make his way "through the cooperative competition of divergent voices" (253), much as my dialogic practice commits me to engage the other voices that constitute the "social dialogue surrounding" (Bakhtin 1981, 278) the two sonnets and the lyric genre that concern me. But Burke's dialectic also proceeds, as he himself recognizes, by "reduction of one terminology to another." If, as he says, "any word or concept considered from the point of view of any other word or concept is a reduction" (Burke 1962, 96), then Burke's reading of philosophy, poetry, and criticism in terms of his dramatistic pentad is clearly a reductive project, and I am compelled to ask myself whether the dialogic reading of other critics I have undertaken is reductive as well.[22]

To give a dialogical account of how one terminology affects the terms of another terminology it represents, I must supplement Burke's premise that "any word or concept considered from the point of view of any other word or concept is a reduction" (1962, 96) with Bakhtin's assertion that "the dissolution of the reported utterance in the authorial context is not—nor can it be—carried out to the end. . . . The body of the reported speech remains detectable as a self-sufficient unit" (1973, 116). The addition of Bakhtin's premise makes the relation between reporting and reported speech not an unresisted reduction of one word to another's terms but an "*active relation* of one message to another" (116) in which, though the reporting context has power to distort or diminish or reduce the reported word, the reported word has independence sufficient not only to reassert itself but, in some cases, to achieve parity with or even power over the voice that reports it. Though dialectical reduction of another's words to one's own terms is a possible move, perhaps even a strong temptation, in dialogic exchange, it is not the necessary or ultimate form of such exchange. In principle, it is not even a possible form, since the other word maintains its intransigent autonomy even when the dialectic makes every effort to negate and transcend it.

Burke himself shows some embarrassment at his reductive treatment of the Chicago critics when he acknowledges that he may appear to have invoked them merely to insist that "these authors ply their trade under the trade-name of 'dramatism' rather than 'Aristotle'" (Burke 1962, 481–82). But he nevertheless declares that he could affirm "nearly every particular observation that Mr. Maclean makes about the sonnet . . . if he but gave it the pointedness that would derive from an explicit recognition of the 'dramatistic' element in his vocabulary" (476), and he takes the occasion of Maclean's analysis of the sonnet to submit it and the lyric genre to his own dramatistic analysis.

Wordsworth's two sonnets figure in Burke's analysis of the lyric at two levels: as illustrations of the dialectical opposition of the lyric to the dramatic and as illustrations of the "scene-agent (or lyric) ratio" (233) within Burke's dramatistic terminology itself. In Burke's dialectic, if action is the essence of drama, stasis or rest is the essence of lyric. Burke points to both Wordsworth sonnets to illustrate this claim. "A typical Wordsworthian sonnet," he writes, "brings out this methodological aspect of the lyric (its special aptitude for conveying a *state* of mind, for erecting a moment into a universe) by selecting such themes as in themselves explicitly refer to the arrest, the pause, the hush. However, this lyric state is to be understood in terms of action, inasmuch as it is to be understood as a state that sums up an action in the form of an attitude," whether attitude is taken as incipient action, as a culmination of action, or as a substitute for action (475–76). Of "Westminster Bridge" he writes, "The imagery is of morning, so there is incipience. But it is not the incipience of the internal debate, arrested at the moment of indecision prior to a decision from which grievous consequences are inevitably to follow. Nor is it a retrospective summary. It just *is*, a state of mind that has come to rest by reason of its summarizing nature. . . . It has conveyed a *moment of stasis*" (246).

But in both sonnets, as we have seen, the speakers acknowledge opinions different from the ones they assert, and they deny those opinions forcefully. If this is not the debate of a dramatic character on the verge of tragic action, it is surely the dialogue of a mind with its own opinions or with the opinions suggested by the behavior of others. Who said that earth *had* anything to show more fair than the beauty the speaker sees in London? Who suggests that the child's lack of solemn thought *should* be interpreted as a sign of her nature's distance from divinity? The speakers' active answers to the voices that suggest these opinions make their "states of mind" dynamic engagements with resistant opinions rather than static expressions of "perfect lyric mood" (Burke 1962, 246). The child's presence with the speaker in the scene of "Beauteous Evening" (a presence Burke does not notice) and the effect of her behavior on his utterance brings this lyric so close to dramatic monologue that it seems less to exemplify "lyric mood" than dramatic interaction. The dialectical opposition of genres Burke proposes seems, in the example he has chosen, to collapse into an extension of the dramatic domain.[23]

At the level of dramatistic analysis itself, Wordsworth's sonnets figure for Burke as illustrations of "the scene-agent (or lyric) ratio" (233). In this ratio., the quality of the background or setting or situation is transferred to the agent contained in that setting. Burke uses "Beauteous Evening" as a "perfect instance of the scene-agent ratio treated theologically. . . . The octave is all scene, the sestet all agent. But by the logic of the scene-agent ratio, if the scene is supernatural in quality, the agent contained by this scene will partake of the same supernatural quality. And so, spontaneously, purely by being the kind of agent that is at one with this kind of scene, the child is 'divine'" (8).

Though he claims to be convinced by Maclean's three-part division of the sonnet, Burke twice describes it in this two-part pattern that conforms to the scene-agent ratio (8, 474–75). Both times he emphasizes the spontaneous, unproblematic character of the transfer of divinity from scene to agent, completely ignoring the speaker and the speech performance through which he accomplishes it. He takes the scene as it is *described* in the octave as given rather than as thematized in someone's utterance and takes the transfer of divine qualities from scene to child as an impersonal grammatical pattern rather than as an active invention uttered to counter a contrary impression. It is true that such an invention might more properly fall, not under the grammatical analysis to which the scene-agent ratio belongs, but under Burke's rhetorical analysis, for it seems to be one of those rhetorical devices that have what he calls "a 'you and me' quality about them, being 'addressed' to some person or to some advantage" (xix). But Burke offers the grammatical analysis itself in its artificial separation from his other analytic perspectives as if its terms and their ratios were more "basic forms of thought" (xvii) than the speaker or listener of rhetoric and dialogics. "Scene" in Burke's grammar tends to be as patent, impersonal, and objectively constraining as "sociolect" in Riffaterre's, and the mediating work of a speaker on which my dialogics rests is in principle reducible for both of them to abstract grammatical categories. From my point of view, however, rhetoric and dialogics are more fundamental than grammar, and the most "objective" grammatical categories always carry more casuistical baggage in any instance of their use than Burke is ready to admit.

In Burke's grammar, for instance, the category of "scene" is meant to be an open functional place that does not beg the question of how a given philosophical casuistry interprets it, but it tends in Burke's actual use to be opposed to agent as the *"non-verbal in general"* to the *"verbal in general."* Though he recognizes that "the ground of any particular verbal action must be a complex of verbal and non-verbal factors" (103), and he calls for attention to words both in their "nature as words in themselves *and* [in] the nature they get from the non-verbal scenes that support their acts" (482); it is clear even from this passage that Burke thinks of "scene" or situation as primarily extrinsic and nonverbal, while he attributes to words in themselves a nature of their own apart from their relation to scene or situation.

Bakhtin's dialogics places utterance in a different relation to a differently understood "*non-verbal context*" than Burke's dramatism (1983, 11). Most importantly, it focuses not on an agent acting alone in a scene but on a speaker whose speaking is the "*product of the social interaction of three components—the speaker* (author), *the listener* (reader), and *the one of whom* (or of which) *they speak* (the hero)" (1983, 17). Speaker and listener share (and author and reader must create and re-create) an unspoken context of common "*spatial purview*," "*common knowledge and understanding of the circumstances*," and "*common evaluation* of these circumstances" (1983, 11). They share these factors, however, not as a commonly recognized "external cause of the utterance" but as "*essential constituent part[s] of its sense structure*" (1983, 12), not merely as an external visible scene but as an intelligible utterance, part of which is verbally realized and part of which is unspoken but implied.

Bakhtin's common "spatial purview," then, is not the manifest scene of drama that would be there even if the action were not taking place but a taken-for-granted aspect of the material world that the speaker's utterance responds to and resolves for both speaker and listener—the world implied by the speaker's deictics, assumed in the speaker's pronouns, and taken for granted in the speaker's enthymemes. The listener for whom the utterance is intelligible does not sit in the position of the objective dramatic spectator outside the action and the scene in which it takes place (and outside Burke's dramatistic pentad as well), but instead participates in the situation that provokes the speaker's utterance and shares the speaker's understanding of what need not be said.[24]

Though Burke intends his dramatistic perspective to recover a properly human interpretation of human action against those scientistic perspectives that reduce action to motion, it preserves the external and objectified stance of those scientistic models and fails to account for the place of spectators (or listeners) in relation to the scenes they observe or the actions they interpret. Bakhtin's dialogic model of utterance not only places speaker and listener in "*real, material participation in one and the same section of being*" (1983, 11), but it also makes the object of discourse participate in that world. The hero belongs to the same social world as speaker and listener either as a speaker in his or her own right or as a topic of the discourse of other speakers in the same world. The situation provocative of utterance includes the hero not just as part of a nonverbal scene in which the speaking agent acts but as an already articulate or articulated other whose words provoke the speaker's words.

The religious language of "Beauteous Evening" may be understood in these terms not just as a Burkean terminology, an agency manipulated by the speaker to describe the evening, but as a voice of religious power shaping the speaker's perception of it. What makes the speaker perceive a calm evening and call it "holy" is a social language of holiness associated with his belief in God, whose power the speaker registers, asserts, and preserves in his utterance. Even when we take the speaker and the child, his listener, into account, as Burke does not, we still cannot account for the speaker's utterance as a relation between him, the child, and the evening scene. It is God whose felt presence in the evening moves the speaker to describe it as he does and whose power, even as it is not acknowledged by the child, compels him to assert His unapparent presence for her. God is the hero of the sonnet and the religious language in which He is known to believers like the speaker makes the "scene" expressive for the speaker as it would not be to one who did not share that belief and its language. That the child who shares his spatial purview does not share the religious language in which he evaluates the scene provokes him to draw further on the resources of that language to account for her obliviousness. For the speaker the religious language of his utterance celebrates the power of God not only to inform the scene but even to account for the child who does not recognize God's power explicitly or respond to the language in which the speaker invokes Him. Again, in another Burkean context—that of "the rhetoric of religion"—this account of the poem might be perfectly acceptable, but it nevertheless challenges the terms of his dramatistic grammar and the reading he has derived from them.

A good dramatistic casuist might still try to reduce the speaker's religious language under the heading of "agency" to an instrument with which the speaker describes the scene and resolves his problem about the child, but the speaker at least would not imagine himself manipulating a "God-term" so much as he is responding in socially appropriate language to evidences of God's presence. Bakhtinian dialogics, however, acknowledges the power of languages to shape our individual uses of them and personifies the sources of those languages as autonomous "heroes," where Burke's dramatism would reduce languages to manipulable terminologies and demote their sources to "agents." Dialogics will direct our attention toward the irreducible otherness in those languages, where dramatism would teach us to perform their reduction to familiar ratios. In practice we will always be choosing to follow one of these lessons, as I have chosen in this section to hold Burke to the idiosyncrasies of his readings and the habitual interpretations of his terms instead of "placing" him and Bakhtin in his (or someone else's) grammatical terms.

Rhetoric and Dialogics: Charles Molesworth and the Ideological Horizon

Had Burke chosen to treat Wordsworth's sonnets in his rhetoric rather than his grammar of motives, that engagement would surely have been different from the one I have just worked through, but another critic provides a rhetorical reading of "Westminster Bridge" that can stand in for Burke's and provoke an engagement in its own right as well. Charles Molesworth (1977), without explicit reference to Burke, shares important terms and interests with him as indeed he implicitly shares terms and interests with the other three critics I have so far introduced into my symposium.

He situates his argument, however, not in a tradition of critical arguments but in a context of biographical and historical information on the personal circumstances surrounding the sonnet's composition and the changing character of Wordsworth's political views. Though at one point he mentions a "formalist criticism" (272) to which he opposes his own inquiry, he does not call his overall position "rhetorical." Instead he repeatedly characterizes specific topics and observations in his discourse as "rhetorical," and I have chosen to highlight them as his characteristic moves to bring out his distinctive contribution to the critical symposium I am constructing. More than any of the other critics I have considered, Molesworth allows the theoretical implications of his essay to emerge from his practice rather than thematizing his theory and illustrating it (or failing to illustrate it) in his practical criticism. He does not, then, announce, nor can we hold him to, a theoretical agenda, but even as I have tried to preserve Burke's idiosyncrasies from identification with his theory, I want to bring out a theoretical theme for my own purposes from Molesworth's rich polytopic responses to the sonnet.

The theme Molesworth does announce—"The Republican Structure of Time and Perception"—does not subordinate all of his responses to the sonnet, but it does subsume his principal observations on both the rhetorical devices in it and their function in its overall rhetorical "argument." Molesworth argues that the poem is not just an observer's response to an uncommon visual scene but a citizen's response to an image of his city, resonant with "civic tones" (269). The terms in which the speaker sees London show traces of "Wordsworth's republican sentiment" (269) that reveal not the city made over in terms of natural beauty, as Brooks and Riffaterre read the poem, "but natural spectacle redrawn in the terms of civic grandeur" (269). Though he concedes that "we do not come away from the poem with a sense of its argument" (266), his accomplishment is to highlight its argumentative features and to define its "fullest argument" for its "fullest audience" (273) as a citizen's "'pointing with pride'" (270) to the revealed majesty and power of his city. The speaker's utterance described in this way not only bears witness to his regenerated view of his city but also teaches "a propaedeutic lesson" to his fellow citizens (272)—it also, I can note, allows itself to be characterized as a Bakhtinian speech genre with the city as its hero and fellow citizens as its listeners.

Though Molesworth enumerates his share of formal devices without clear rhetorical functions, he emphasizes the poem's argument in a way that permits him to notice and account for "devices" beyond the reach of Riffaterre's sociolexical analysis or Maclean's prosodic, semantic, and syntactic categories. He can hear "civic tones" in the regal diction of "majesty" (269). He can point out several "rhetorical negation[s]" (264) in the poem and see them "in the earnest service of forcefully stating [the poem's] higher affirmations" (263). He can recognize in the second line that "a virtual viewer is disposed of in order to establish the correct audience for the scene, and, presumably, for the poem as well" (264). He can account for the "figure of speech" of the "mighty heart" in the last line, in which he says "the city is not only . . . humanized but individualized, made over into a single subsistent agent, and one, furthermore, as the adjective 'mighty' tells us, with heroic scope and power" (266).[25]

This last formulation resonates in our context with overtones suggestive of both Burke and Bakhtin. Indeed, Molesworth's restatement of the point could lack nothing of the dramatistic explicitness Burke found wanting in Maclean's reading: "What ordinarily is witnessed as the scene of heroic action has taken over the role of heroic agent" (Molesworth 1977, 269). The effect of scene on speaker has transformed the scene into an agent whose "mighty heart . . . lying still" is felt as power or incipient action. That the city as agent is a personified hero recalls Bakhtin's autonomous hero as a participant in the speaker's discourse. The "civic tones" Molesworth hears in the speaker's description are to this poem what the religious tones are to "Beauteous Evening." They are the expression of a social language of political values impressed upon the speaker by the power of the city as the language of religious reverence was impressed upon the speaker in the other poem by the sense of God in the evening. They are felt in the language of or about the hero of the poem that shapes the speaker's response to his subject, the "republican sentiment[s]" that influence not, I think, the speaker's "acts of . . . perception" (269) but his utterance in response to the scene he witnesses.

In characterizing the speaker's sentiments as a "republican structure of feeling" (269), Molesworth attempts to ground his reading of the poem in a historical ideological formation that will permit us to recognize its resonance, but he has some difficulty constructing what Bakhtin calls "the ideological horizon" (1978, 17) in which the poem participates. He reaches toward a reconstruction of Wordsworth's "political views," on the one hand, and toward an ideal construction of "the republican imagination," on the other, combining Wordsworth's historical party affiliations and his present economic behavior with classical Roman stereotypes of republican virtue (268–69). Molesworth attempts here to identify an objectified nonverbal "structure of time and perception" characteristic of the republican position that accounts for the verbal devices of the poem, but he misses an opportunity to identify a *language* of political sentiment in Wordsworth's explicitly political poetry that helps to locate the language of "Westminster Bridge" within the same ideological horizon those poems define.

Molesworth begins his essay by calling attention to Wordsworth's composition in 1802 of political sonnets he published in 1807 under the heading "Sonnets Dedicated to Liberty," and he places "Westminster Bridge" among a group of "other sonnets not on directly political subjects" composed at the same time (261), but he barely returns to the political sonnets to discover evidence not just of Wordsworth's political ideology at the time but of the language in which that ideology appears, turning instead to the poet's life and opinions to construct his account of the "immediate situation" (262) of the poem's composition.

But the contemporary composition of those political sonnets is surely an important part of that situation, and the public voice they assume and the language they deploy are surely more significant to the dialogic situation of "Westminster Bridge" than the poet's marriage plans, his magnanimous settlement of an old debt, or even his identification with the Girondist platform some years before. Wordsworth indeed suggests an association between "Westminster Bridge" and the regularly dated and situated sonnets of the "Liberty" group by making it the only dated sonnet of the "Miscellaneous Sonnets" in the 1807 gathering and one of two to specify its place of composition.[26] Molesworth cites one passage from one of the political sonnets, "To Toussaint L'Ouverture," to show Wordsworth making "political heritage" become "natural environment" (271), but this rather abstract figurative move is not as close to the language of "Westminster Bridge" as several passages from other poems.[27]

In "Composed by the Sea-side, near Calais, August 1802" Wordsworth says that the Evening Star that shines on England should look "on her banners, drest / In thy fresh beauty," using a figure close to "This City now doth like a garment wear / The beauty of the morning" in an utterance that overtly glorifies the nation. The opening and closing terms of "Westminster Bridge," "Earth" and the "mighty heart," are brought together in another sonnet reminding his former companion Jones of the experience they shared of the festival in Calais on the anniversary of the fall of the Bastille: "The antiquated Earth, as one might say, / Beat like the heart of Man" ("To a Friend, Composed Near Calais, On the Road Leading to Ardres, August 7th, 1802"). Here the transfiguration of Earth into a human heart marks the apogee of the poet's political hopes for the French Revolution, and the recapitulation of that figure in the overall development of "Westminster Bridge" marks a recovery of those hopes now revealed not in action in France but in potential in the transfigured capital city of England. The evocation of Milton's great patriotic contemporaries in "Great Men have been among us" portrays them as knowing how to recognize the national virtues the poet recognizes in the London of "Westminster Bridge":

> They knew how genuine glory was put on;
> Taught us how rightfully a nation shone
> In splendor: what strength was, that would not bend
> But in magnanimous meekness

Here the capacity to recognize national glory and splendor is what the great patriots knew and have taught their later countrymen like the poet. It may even be that the capacity to recognize national strength not in its martial exercise but in its voluntary self-restraint may resemble the speaker's capacity in "Westminster Bridge" to recognize that strength in its utter repose.

One might wish to locate the ideological horizon of these political poems themselves in relation to the discourse of other ideological spheres of contemporary social life—political debate or patriotic harangue or party manifesto—or even in relation to the republican discourses of a classical education, but one would not reach a point at which one could abstract a republican ideological formation or structure independent of those discourses with which one could then explain the poems. The dialogic perspective finds confirmation for Molesworth's reading of "Westminster Bridge" in the voices of Wordsworth's political sonnets and might lead us to discover wider resonances of his political language in other social discourses, but it would urge Molesworth to change his title from "The Republican Structure of Time and Perception" to "The Republican Voice in 'Westminster Bridge'" and to seek his evidence not in the facts of the poet's life but in his other poetic and prose voices and the social languages they embody. The evidence I have gathered from Wordsworth's political sonnets would suggest a further change of title to "The Patriotic Voice in 'Westminster Bridge'" or even "The Nationalistic Voice in 'Westminster Bridge,'" for the poem's language celebrates the nation without specifying its constitution.[28]

By locating the poem in "the tradition of epideictic verse" (269) Molesworth's rhetorical perspective reveals the city as the hero the speaker celebrates, not just in visual but in political glory, but it also raises the question, To whom is the poem on the bridge addressed? Molesworth hears in the mixing of the poem's lyric and political voices a "conflict in the poet's sense of audience" (271). Because the speaker, unlike the speaker of "Beauteous Evening," is alone, the poem's rhetorical genre is a problem. It contains "more than a hint of a moral suasion" and yet it seems closest in genre to the "diary entry," a kind of counterpart to Dorothy's journal entry on the experience from which the poem is drawn (271). The speaker seems to speak "to all the occupants of these 'very houses'" he describes (271), but his utterance in "its fullest argument" for "its fullest audience . . . speaks to citizens as well as observers, . . . to the ages as well as to the moment" (273). Molesworth does not look to the one direct address of the poem—the exclamatory "Dear God!" in the thirteenth line—to locate the poem's addressee and situate its utterance (he ignores it in his close reading of the line on p. 266 and cites it as evidence of something else on p. 270). But the speaker's testimony, his bearing witness to the vision of London he beholds, seems properly addressed to God by whom the speaker swears to what he beholds. The utterance gains its authority for any humbler witness, any fellow citizen, partly by neglecting to address him or her. It is not, as Molesworth suggests, that "the poet escapes from the demands of suasion by the pellucidity of his observations" (271) but that he reveals the power to which he attests by his complete attention to it and his appeal to God as his witness. An address to any particular others would, as the speaker in "Beauteous Evening" discovers, open his testimony to question, neglect, or contradiction. But the address to God certifies the utterance on the highest authority instead of attempting to share it or to confirm it from another's experience.

As Bakhtin recognizes in talking about the "specific gravity of rhetorical speech," "the stronger the feeling of hierarchical eminence in another's utterance, the more sharply defined will its boundaries be, and the less accessible will it be to penetration by retorting and commenting tendencies from outside" (1973, 123). The rhetorical perspective, then, will be particularly suited to an utterance like this one in which the alternatives of retort and comment are closed off and the speaker presents himself and his experience for admiration or emulation. But the dialogic perspective, whose affinity to the rhetorical Bakhtin clearly recognizes (see Bakhtin 1981, 268–69, 280), encompasses not only this hierarchical "*declaratory* word" (1973, 159) but also the more vulnerable and responsive dialogized word. Dialogics can learn much from the "great external precision" (1981, 269) of rhetorical analysis of conventional speech forms and figures and much from the analysis of determinate rhetorical situations as well, but it cannot limit its purview to those situations or accept those forms as fixed. The voices of the Western lyric tradition are closely allied to the rhetorical tradition whose terms have shaped not only the criticism but the production of lyric poetry from classical times even to those recent romantic times in which the tradition has been feared lost.[29] But a rhetorical criticism of lyric utterance remains likely to reduce precedent voices to objectified structures or responding voices to silence unless it is conversant with the dialogic possibilities it traditionally rules out.

Dialogics and Feminist Critique: Judith W. Page and the Women in Wordsworth's Life

Judith W. Page's (1988) feminist reading of "Beauteous Evening" brings out the voices of silenced women in that sonnet and reveals the affinity that others have noted between dialogic criticism and feminist critique.[30] Like Molesworth, Page situates the poem she is reading in a context of biographical and historical information, and also like him she does not emphasize the theoretical implications of her critical terms.[31] In examining the relations between Wordsworth's "public and private concerns" (189), however, she does not, like Molesworth, use private information to substantiate public rhetorical stances but reads public language as a refiguring of private conflicts, reviving without recalling biographical readings like those against which Maclean defined his Chicago school reading (see note 19 above). By focusing not on a single sonnet but on what she calls the "Calais Sonnets," written in August of 1802 during a critical month in Wordsworth's domestic life, Page reads the language of both public and private poems as utterances shaped by the same domestic situation.

Page opens her argument with a synopsis of this situation: "In August of 1802, when Wordsworth was about to marry Mary Hutchinson, he went to France with his sister Dorothy to settle affairs with his former lover Annette Vallon and their illegitimate daughter Caroline" (189). To read "It is a beauteous evening, calm and free" as an utterance provoked by these circumstances is to specify the social relations represented in the poem not just as those between an adult male and a female child but rather as those between a father and his illegitimate and soon-to-be-abandoned daughter. It is also to wonder about her mother, "Annette, the woman who has temporarily impeded his [the father's] marriage . . . [as] an unacknowledged presence in the poem" (197).

These specifications—drawn, it should be remembered, not from the text of the poem alone but from letters and Dorothy Wordsworth's journal entries that reveal the circumstances of its composition—reconfigure the tone and theme of the utterance and heighten perception of its dialogic interaction. The adult speaker becomes a father evading "his particular responsibilities to his illegitimate daughter Caroline," his religious language becomes "patriarchal religious language," and his closing gesture becomes one of placing "Caroline in the hands of God—a substitute father for the father Wordsworth knows he will never be" or even, in consigning her to "Abraham's bosom," symbolically killing the child. The tone of "Listen!" in the sixth line of the poem becomes not a generalized apostrophe as Maclean suggested or an attempt to call the child to share the speaker's perception, as I earlier suggested, but a "command" to the child to attend to her father and her Father. The closing account of her relation to God is not just the speaker's compensation for his embarrassed failure to get the response he sought from the child but the father's act of "appropriating the authority of voice to himself" and telling "the girl who she is and where she lives and what her limitations are" (199). As an utterance addressed in specified circumstances to an auditor whose responses are registered not in her own voice but only through the speaker's account of her, the poem takes on generic affinity not to Maclean's model of "Tintern Abbey" or to my own models of "We Are Seven" and "Anecdote for Fathers," but to the "dramatic monologue." Page finally values the poem not for its rhetorical suppression of Wordsworth's "private self and anxieties" but for its powerful revelation of them (199–201).

The power of that revelation depends, however, not just upon the poem but upon the stability and primacy of the scene in which Page places it. The ocean-side scene must become "Calais," the speaker "Wordsworth," the child "Caroline," and Dorothy, Annette, and Mary must be standing in the wings. The text Page constructs gives convincing specificity to these figures and constrains the symbolic action in the scene it specifies with what appears to be an overwhelming dramatistic scene/agent ratio, but the verbal artifact of the sonnet, taken in itself or even in relation to the other sonnets composed under the same circumstances, does not demand, though it cannot resist, this reading. As discourse in art rather than discourse in life, the poem allows the construction of an ambivalent dialogic relation between its speaker and the child he addresses; as discourse in the life re-created in Page's argument the poem seems wholly determined by the circumstances that occasioned it.

Responsibility and Indeterminacy:
J. Hillis Miller, Deconstruction, and the Ethics of Reading

No recent critic has argued more vigorously against the determinacy of poetic language, or indeed of language in general, than J. Hillis Miller. He has promoted his deconstructive celebration of indeterminacy under the banners of both the "rhetorical" and the "dialogical," though he does not make either term explicit in the essay (1971) in which he deconstructs "Westminster Bridge." Nevertheless, I shall query him in that essay about how his ideas and his practices of rhetorical and dialogical criticism compare with those I have already presented, because his demonstration of the sonnet's indeterminacy involves the same methods and effects he elsewhere calls by those names. In another essay he calls "rhetorical" analysis "the investigation of the role of figurative language in literature";[32] the effect he names "dialogical" involves, among other things, the production of indeterminate "vibrating resonances" between alternative meanings "which can never be stilled in a single monological narrative line."[33] Since his reading of the sonnet both focuses on figurative language and discovers indeterminate resonances, an approach to his theory through his practice in this essay is not inappropriate.

Miller's deconstructive work also enters the purview of my symposium at another level. The "ethics of reading" he has advocated has made neglect of other critics into an ethical principle that gives precedence to the "imperative" of "the words on the page" over his "ethical responsibilities toward students and colleagues, and the whole institution of literary studies."[34] If we find Miller's ethics of reading compelling, we will have no ground for complaint at critics' neglect of previous critics' work and no need for the Bakhtinian dialogics of criticism I have been elaborating in this symposium. Miller has enacted his ethics of reading in solo readings of a number of romantic lyrics that have previously been widely discussed by other critics. His reading of "A slumber did my spirit seal," which has provoked a strong rejoinder from M. H. Abrams, does not invoke the widely known critical controversies surrounding the poem,[35] and his reading of Wordsworth's sonnet "Composed upon Westminster Bridge" does not notice any of the previous engagements with it. His staged encounter between himself and the sonnet does not explicitly register any relations between his voice and the voices of other critics who have written about it, but I shall show how closely his deconstructive reading of the sonnet reiterates an earlier New Critical reading and, at the same time, fails to demonstrate either the power of Miller's deconstructive criticism or the necessity of his ethics of reading.[36]

Miller's reading of "Westminster Bridge" acknowledges an aspect of apparent unity and straightforward meaning in the poem, what Miller calls "an undeniably mimetic dimension [that] . . . is not to be dismissed or transcended by further interpretation" (304). In this aspect the poem represents the objects of the cityscape in the smokeless air and the poet's "subjective reaction" (304) of calm corresponding to the calm he perceives. Like Maclean, Miller imagines what is imitated not as utterances but as "extra-linguistic realit[ies] . . . , whether mental or physical, [that] are presumed to have existed outside that language and not to depend on it for their existence" (305).

Miller goes beyond this mimetic reading to bring out the indeterminateness of the language of "Westminster Bridge" in what he would call a rhetorical analysis of its use of negatives and its pattern of metaphors. He attends to the negatives, explicit and implicit, more closely than any of the other readers I have considered, claiming that each negation "creates a shadowy existence for what is denied," even an evocation of "such dullards" as would not be moved by the beauty of the city (305). Like Riffaterre, however, Miller consigns the figure of the speaker to his mimetic reading and so does not take the interplay of the negations and what they negate as a speaker's gestures situating his utterance in a field of other utterances, its paradox as a response to some dox. But he does not go on as Riffaterre does to read the negations as the idiolect's determination of its relation to a sociolect. Instead, Miller believes the negations create "the presence of what they deny" as "a shimmering mirage lying over their explicit assertions" (306), an unresolved "suspens vibratoire" (303) that contributes to the overall "dialogical" effect of irresolution in the poem. Miller represents the negations not as Bakhtinian signs of hidden dialogue with other utterances in the dialogizing background but as language that has the power to call up in the foreground other language that interferes with what it is saying—what he elsewhere calls the "interference of the dialogical with the monological" ("Ariachne's Broken Woof," 60).

Miller's "rhetorical" analysis reads the metaphors in the sonnet to the same "dialogical" effect. He concentrates on the "personification of the city as a sleeping human figure" and discovers a "point of radical ambiguity" in the discrepancy between what he makes of the last two lines—that the city appears to be asleep in the thirteenth line but dead, "like a corpse," in the final one. Having suggested this reading, Miller accepts it as the basis for further implications. First he reasons that the city is "like a corpse because there are no human consciousnesses present within it," and then he notices that the speaker's own consciousness paradoxically violates the condition of human absence that gives the scene a calm like nature's. The "oscillation" that arises between this "rhetorical" reading and the mimetic one that it supplements but does not transcend is for Miller "the characteristic endpoint of any careful reading of Wordsworth's best poems" (306–7). In this "dialogical" suspense "between mimesis and emblem, between imitative form and creative form," he writes, "the images of the poem hang balanced" (309). Miller has produced this suspended "dialogical" effect without voices, dialogue, and meaning by using a "rhetorical" criticism that lacks concepts of speaker, audience, and occasion. He creates indeterminacy by choosing not to inquire into determinants.

But he also creates unwarranted determinacies by choosing not to inquire into alternative readings. He does not answer Burke's or Molesworth's sense of incipience in the poem, for example, a reading that might point toward the awakening of the mighty heart that now lies still. Nor does he entertain the common metaphorical senses of "heart" as the vital center of the nation or as the seat of courage and feeling or simply as a person, senses for which lying still would not necessarily imply morbidity. He does not look for verbal parallels in Wordsworth's other poems where he would have found these lines that question the inevitability of his reading: "Yet pure and powerful minds, hearts meek and still, / A grateful few, shall love thy modest Lay."[37] These still hearts are alive, just not agitated.

Indeed the trick of Miller's reading is to literalize the vehicle of the heart as an individual person's physical organ whose stillness may seem relatively unambiguous. But even without the technology of cardiac stimulation, we may recognize that a heart lying still *may* suggest various states of suspended animation—the love-song convention is but one example. Miller, whose critical principles open his reading to language without contextual limits, creates the final indeterminacy of the poem by uncritically determining this figure and then reasoning from the determination he has made to paradoxical conclusions. He has not made his reading answerable to the specific linguistic diversity he repeatedly celebrates in general.

But has this obliviousness to alternative readings "made possible new insights into what is going on" in this particular work (Miller 1980, 610)? When Miller gives precedence to the "imperative" of "the words on the page" over his "ethical responsibilities toward students, colleagues, and the whole institution of literary studies," has he retrieved anything for those students and colleagues and for that institution that they would otherwise have lacked (Miller 1980, 613)? In the case of "Westminster Bridge," Miller gives us very little that David Ferry did not give us in his 1959 reading of the sonnet.[38]

Not yet having heard of the deconstruction of metaphysics, Ferry arrives at a reading that anticipates Miller's main insights by exaggerating the New Critical "tension" between "'surface' and 'deeper' meanings" into a "hostility" (12). Just as Miller preserves the difference between mimetic and emblematic or imitative and creative readings of the sonnet, so Ferry offers "dramatic" and "symbolic" readings. In his "dramatic" reading Ferry touches first on the description of London, focusing on the same details Miller does in his mimetic reading, and then presents the speaker's attitudes toward these objects, Miller's "subjective reaction." Ferry's symbolic reading overlooks the negations Miller emphasizes in his "creative" reading, but it zeroes in on the same figure of the heart lying still in the last line and reads it to very much the same effect, choosing the same shocking word, "corpse," to make the point memorable.[39]

Ferry writes, "the last line of Wordsworth's sonnet suggests that the city is not merely sleeping but dead, its heart stilled. The poet looks at London and sees it as a sort of corpse and admires it as such, welcomes a death which is the death of what the city has come to stand for in his symbolic world" (14). Like Miller, Ferry takes the death of the city as the absence of human beings from the scene, and like him also Ferry catches the ironic twist this reading produces: "the 'death' the poet is so pleased to witness is the death even of those properties in himself by which he responds so wonderfully to the city at this particular moment" (14–15). Miller writes, "The poet shares in a calm which can only exist if he is absent. He is both there and not there, as if he were his own ghost" (307). Finally, like Miller, Ferry does not permit this symbolic reading to supplant the dramatic one; instead he juxtaposes them to produce a paradox—"that one of the great representatives of our human powers of articulation should be himself a lover of silence" (15). Miller phrases a comparable paradox in somewhat more elaborate terms: "The forms of articulated speech or melody make the unworded blast of the original word available by turning it into definite tones or speech, and at the same time they limit it, transform it, obscure it, veil it over, traduce it by translating it" (302). Both these paradoxical formulations set the articulated against the inarticulable, devaluing the mimetic "surface" of the poem in the light of the depths revealed in Ferry's symbolic "aspect of eternity" (12) or Miller's deconstructionist abyss.

I have pressed home the closeness of Miller's reading to Ferry's not merely to assert Ferry's claim to acknowledgment and to discredit Miller's claim to novelty. Two men trained at Harvard at the height of New Criticism's influence in the late 1940s and early 1950s might well have assimilated the same critical languages and reading strategies,[40] and in any case my point is not just to reaffirm the scholarly obligation of doing one's homework. This obligation sends one to the critical archive to give due credit to others who have anticipated one's own reading or idea, but it does not urge one to formulate one's reading or idea in response to the voices that have already spoken or to discover its affinities and oppositions in the public discourse one is proposing to enter. It is a conservative duty of respecting established intellectual properties rather than a radical enterprise of producing new intellectual property through active appropriation of others' words and ideas. Dialogics calls attention to critics' neglect of their predecessors not merely to convict them of failure to meet their obligations but to make them answerable to the cosmopolitan critical community that enables and challenges their readings.

The issue that provokes me at the end of my own engagement with the critics I have addressed (knowing that I have still left others out of account altogether[41]) is that Miller's neglect of other critics in his deconstructive practice is as programmatic as attention to other critics in my dialogic practice. Miller ignores the work of others not just because he tacitly accepts the generic limitations of the New Critical essay but because he explicitly believes that their work is irrelevant to his own encounters with the language of literary texts.

I have already quoted from a passage in Miller's response to Vincent Leitch in which Miller opts for his obligation to the language of the text in preference to his responsibilities to students, colleagues, and institutions (1980, 613). At a conference on the Yale school several remarks by and about Miller suggest a similar opposition of the text to the critics.[42] After offering his unsubstantiated judgments of the readings of several critics in a recent symposium on Matthew Arnold, Miller writes:

> Adjudication of differences here is of course possible only by a response to that call, "Back to the texts!," which must be performed again and again in literary study. Nothing previous critics have said can be taken for granted, however authoritative it may seem. Each reader must do again for himself the laborious task of scrupulous slow reading, trying to find out what the texts actually say rather than imposing on them what she or he wants them to say or wishes they said. (1984, 28)

At first listening, these may sound like unexceptionable scholarly commonplaces, hardly deconstructive paradoxes. But they suggest what the transcript of the discussion following the talk confirms, that the texts to be scrupulously reread are only those of what his questioner will call the "primary source," not those of the critics whose disputes are to be adjudicated. If what those critics have said cannot be "taken for granted," it may be that it does not have to be taken into account at all.[43]

Miller's remarks at this conference and my own reading of Miller's essay on "Westminster Bridge" add new force to the question William E. Cain asked of Miller's critical practice in 1979: "What is the responsibility of the critic towards a text, and *what kinds of judgments does he or she render on those who are also engaged in the interpretation of texts?*"[44] The premises on which I have constructed this symposium call into further question the answers Miller gives to this question. "Subjecting oneself to the words on the page" (Miller 1980, 613), as Miller proposes to do, does not take precedence over social relations to persons and institutions, for reading is a social act and both the language of the text and the capacities with which we respond to it are socially involved, whether we acknowledge it or not. Any text, as Bakhtin claims, is already "overlain with qualifications, open to dispute, charged with value, already enveloped in an obscuring mist—or, on the contrary, by the 'light' of alien words that have already been spoken about it" (1981, 276), and any reader reads such a text with linguistic expectations shaped at least in part by his or her experiences of languages in every social context with which they are familiar, from family to critical school.

Miller's idea of "a linguistic imperative which shapes what a critic or teacher says about a text" distinct from and prior to ethical responsibilities is a dangerous mystification that discourages critical self-consciousness about the linguistic resources one brings to the act of reading and about the social context in which the publication of that act takes place. To imagine that when one has submitted to that "linguistic imperative" then "the ethical operation will already necessarily have taken place" is to abdicate responsibility not only for one's relation to "students, colleagues, and the whole institution of literary studies" (Miller 1980, 613), but also, finally, for the social text itself.[45]

Critics who believe in this imperative will imagine the text "forcing" them to report readings that they have forgotten they learned from other sources, and they will take as necessary or beyond discussion readings to which significant alternatives already publicly exist. They will depend for their persuasiveness upon an audience ignorant of much that has been said and uninquisitive about much that might be said about the text. They will set themselves apart from the give-and-take of critical exchange, just as they set the texts with which they engage apart from public conversation in which amateur and professional readers reappropriate their meanings.

Like lyric speakers, literary critics shape their utterances in communities where available languages already assert their power, where much has already been said, and where others who have not yet spoken or not yet been heard have potential to concur or demur. Though these other languages and voices are sometimes represented as dispensable "experts" or intimidating precursors, as chaotic logomachies or discredited establishments, they are also the necessary provocations, enabling conditions, and formative influences of poetic and critical utterance alike. To ignore them is to be doomed to repeat them; to engage them in the fullness of their power and diversity is to articulate our topics and ourselves comprehensively and responsibly among the others who share our world and time.[46]

Notes

1. Chaviva Hosek and Patricia Parker, eds., *Lyric Poetry: Beyond New Criticism* (Ithaca, N.Y.: Cornell University Press, 1985), 346.

2. M. H. Abrams, "Structure and Style in the Greater Romantic Lyric," in *From Sensibility to Romanticism*, ed. Frederick W. Hilles and Harold Bloom (New York: Oxford University Press, 1965), 527–30.

3. National isolation as well as generic habit contribute to this problem of ignoring precedent work. Writing in London for publication in 1976, Harvey Peter Sucksmith naively declares that "Westminster Bridge" "has so far received almost no scrutiny at length" despite several substantial American readings of the sonnet, including Cleanth Brooks's in *The Well Wrought Urn* and J. Hillis Miller's lengthy 1971 reading (see note 9 below). Sucksmith's celebration of "spiritual illumination" and "affirmation" in the poem might have been sharpened or modulated had he answered the Americans' emphasis on its paradoxes. See Sucksmith's "Ultimate Affirmation: A Critical Analysis of Wordsworth's Sonnet 'Composed upon Westminster Bridge,' and the Image of the City in *The Prelude*," *Yearbook of English Studies* 6 (1976): 113–19.

4. See Arac's "Afterword" to *The Yale Critics: Deconstruction in America*, ed. Jonathan Arac, Wlad Godzich, and Wallace Martin (Minneapolis: University of Minnesota Press, 1983), 176–99.

5. J. Hillis Miller, *The Ethics of Reading* (New York: Columbia University Press, 1987), 15.

6. Mikhail Bakhtin, "Discourse in the Novel," in *The Dialogic Imagination*, ed. Michael Holquist, trans. Caryl Emerson and Michael Holquist (Austin: University of Texas Press, 1981), 276; hereafter cited parenthetically in the text.

7. Mikhail Bakhtin, *Problems of Dostoevsky's Poetics*, trans. and ed. Caryl Emerson (Minneapolis: University of Minnesota Press, 1984), 120; hereafter cited parenthetically in the text.

8. The sonnets are widely anthologized. I am using the texts of these sonnets as they appear in *The Poetical Works of William Wordsworth*, 5 vols., ed. Ernest de Selincourt, rev. ed., Helen Darbishire (Oxford: Clarendon Press, 1952–59).

9. Cleanth Brooks, *The Well Wrought Urn* (1947; reprint, New York: Harcourt Brace Jovanovich, 1975), 3–7; Norman Maclean, "An Analysis of a Lyric Poem," in *Discussions of William Wordsworth*, ed. Jack Davis (Boston: D. C. Heath, 1964), 130–38 (originally published in *University of Kansas City Review* 8 [Spring 1942]: 202–9); Kenneth Burke, *A Grammar of Motives* (1945; reprinted with *A Rhetoric of Motives*, Cleveland, Ohio: World Publishing, 1962), xvii–517; Charles Molesworth, "Wordsworth's 'Westminster Bridge' Sonnet: The Republican Structure of Time and Perception," *Clio* 6 (1977): 261–73; Michael Riffaterre, "Intertextual Representation: On Mimesis as Interpretive Discourse," *Critical Inquiry* 11 (September 1984): 141–62; J. Hillis Miller, "The Still Heart: Poetic Form in Wordsworth," *New Literary History* 2 (1971): 297–310 (Miller republished the essay with a few modifications as the second chapter of *The Linguistic Moment: From Wordsworth to Stevens* [Princeton, N.J.: Princeton University Press, 1985]; page references here are to the version in *NLH*); Judith W. Page, "'The weight of too much liberty': Genre and Gender in Wordsworth's Calais Sonnets," *Criticism* 30 (Spring 1988): 189–203.

10. The phrase is Bakhtin's, from "Discourse in Life and Discourse in Art," in his *Freudianism: A Marxist Critique*, ed. I. R. Titunik and Neal H. Bruss, trans. I. R. Titunik (New York: Harcourt Brace Jovanovich, 1976), 103. The volume was published under the name of Bakhtin's collaborator V. N. Voloshinov. All further references to this work will be given parenthetically in the text. I will also refer to a second translation of the essay, "Discourse in Life and Discourse in Poetry," trans. John Richmond, in *Bakhtin School Papers*, Russian Poetics in Translation no. 10, ed. Ann Shukman (Oxford: RPT Publications, 1983), 5–29; further references to this translation will also be given parenthetically in the text.

11. For an early response to Brooks that claims that he places "too much emphasis on the poetic force of the paradoxical situation" and argues that "harmony, not surprise, is the keynote of the Westminster Bridge sonnet," see Charles V. Hartung, "Wordsworth on Westminster Bridge: Paradox or Harmony?" *College English* 13 (1952): 201–3. For an effort to resolve the difference between Brooks's "surprise" and Hartung's "harmony" as a New Critical "tension," see Charles G. Davis, "The Structure of Wordsworth's Sonnet 'Composed upon Westminster Bridge,'" *English* 19 (1970): 18–21.

12. In looking for a theoretical position and a critical practice capable of challenging Riffaterre's, Paul de Man suggests that Bakhtin's theory and practice would pose a challenge of some magnitude, "for the reader/text relationship, in Riffaterre, is dialectical rather than dialogical"; see de Man, "Hypogram and Inscription: Michael Riffaterre's Poetics of Reading," *Diacritics* 11 (Winter 1981): 27. De Man does not develop the Bakhtinian challenge he anticipates but presents his own deconstructive critique of Riffaterre (27–35).

13. Though Riffaterre recognizes the "I" in the poem, he judges it as finally "superfluous" to what he calls the "parallelism of text and intertext" that suffice "to make representation into an interpretation" (159–60). The "I" of personal experience "must be general-

ized," he writes, so that "the beholder's 'I' is but the grammatical tool of the semiosis itself" (154). The speaker becomes a mere means to the reader's act of decoding signs. In an early and important essay from what de Man sees as the stylistic period that precedes Riffaterre's semiotic inquiries, Riffaterre asserts not just the precedence of reader over speaker but the complete dispensability of the speaker, whom Riffaterre identifies with the biographical poet. Riffaterre writes that the poetic "act of communication . . . is a very special act, however, for the speaker—the poet—is not present; any attempt to bring him back only produces interference, because what we know of him we know from history, it is knowledge external to the message, or else we have found it out by rationalizing and distorting the message. The message and the addressee—the reader—are indeed the only factors involved in this communication whose presence is necessary" ("Describing Poetic Structures: Two Approaches to Baudelaire's 'Les Chats,'" in *Structuralism*, ed. Jacques Ehrmann [1966; reprint, Garden City, N.Y.: Anchor Books, 1970], 202). Riffaterre goes on to reconstitute Jakobson's other factors in communication—code, context, and contact—"from the message" itself, but he does not reconstitute sender or speaker from within the message. He thus chooses not to make use of the classical rhetorical distinction between the speaker known outside the speech and his ethos as it is embodied in his utterance, a distinction probably most familiar to us in Wayne Booth's distinction between biographical author and implied author. The Bakhtinian speaker (like the listener and hero) to which I repeatedly refer is meant to be thus distinguished, as a constituent element of the work itself, from "all those definitions which the historian of literature and of society gives to the author and his heroes—the biography of the author, a more precise chronological and sociological qualification of the heroes, and so on" (Bakhtin 1983, 22). While Riffaterre imagines the text as a written message constraining the interpretations of actual readers who do not need to imagine its speaker, I follow Bakhtin in taking the text as a *"scenario"* of a verbal interaction among an implied speaker, listener, and hero whose mutual interrelations a reader must reproduce not just from the implied listener's position but from "the positions of the other participants too" (1983, 18).

14. Riffaterre seems far more sensitive to the sorts of emphatic features I here call attention to in his stylistic reading of "Les Chats" than in his semiotic reading of "Westminster Bridge." It may be that his current theme of intertextuality leads him to underplay the marked intratextual features his earlier essay highlighted. Or it may be that he has taken his reading of the poem too uncritically from the responses of his "informants" without himself taking on the task of re-creating its language. Though Riffaterre repeatedly asserts that poems objectively constrain readers' readings, I think there is an entropic tendency in his position that wears a poem down to its least common denominator of meaning, turns interesting features into conventional ones, and permits the reader to wait for the poem to work on him instead of going to work on it himself. Some of the power of Riffaterre's reading of "Les Chats" derives from the dialogic provocation of Jakobson's and Lévi-Strauss's reading; not all of it—I agree here with Stanley Fish—derives from Riffaterre's explicit method. See Fish, "Literature in the Reader: Affective Stylistics," in his *Is There a Text in This Class?* (Cambridge: Harvard University Press, 1980), 65.

15. Though I lump Riffaterre together with other linguistic formalists here, I must note that his early essay on "Describing Poetic Structures" to which I have already referred itself begins as a critique of the poetic application of the formal linguistics of Jakobson and Lévi-Strauss along lines similar to those Bakhtin follows in *Marxism and the Philosophy of Language*. He too sees the indeterminateness of purely grammatical elements in poetic usage, though he distinguishes poetic usage from everyday speech more radically than Bakhtin does. I include him nevertheless among the formalists he criticizes because his

account of what he, like Bakhtin, calls "the whole act of communication" (1970, 202) in a poem does not go beyond treating invariant linguistic structures or other cultural structures conceived on the model of invariant linguistic structures. He does not posit a variable unifying category like Bakhtin's "theme" as a dialectical counterpart to the invariant structures Bakhtin calls "meaning." De Man characterizes Riffaterre's persistent formalism succinctly with pertinence to the essay that immediately concerns us. Speaking of Riffaterre's shift in focus from stylistics to semiotics, he writes, "we in fact never left the field of formalist stylistics and the detour through semiotics has been an assimilation of semiotics to stylistics rather than the reverse" (1981, 26).

16. Mikhail Bakhtin, *Marxism and the Philosophy of Language*, trans. Ladislav Matejka and I. R. Titunik (New York: Seminar Press, 1973), 99–101. This book was also published under the name of V. N. Voloshinov. All further references to this work will be given parenthetically in the text.

17. Mikhail Bakhtin, *The Formal Method in Literary Scholarship: A Critical Introduction to Sociological Poetics*, trans. Albert J. Wehrle (Baltimore: Johns Hopkins University Press, 1978), 132. This work was published under the name of Bakhtin's collaborator P. N. Medvedev. All further references to it will be given parenthetically in the text.

18. R. S. Crane, "The Critical Monism of Cleanth Brooks," in *Critics and Criticism: Ancient and Modern*, ed. R. S. Crane (Chicago: University of Chicago Press, 1952), 92–93. Crane, to be sure, acknowledges occasional insights and even notes "promising" inconsistencies in Brooks's argument, but he needs a consistent opponent to place in his more comprehensive scheme and quickly finds the promise "dimmed" (94).

19. For an extended discussion of the difference between the Aristotelian poetics of plot and the Platonic poetics of speech to which Bakhtin adheres, see my "Narrative Diction in Wordsworth's Poetics of Speech," *Comparative Literature* 34 (Fall 1982): 305–29.

20. Maclean's essay appeared in an early Chicago school manifesto along with a theoretical essay by Crane and an essay by Elder Olson on Yeats's "Sailing to Byzantium." It was not reprinted in the definitive Chicago school volume *Critics and Criticism*.

21. It also happens, though Maclean does not rest his argument on these points, that this biographical reading both diminishes the dignity of the poet and the sublimity of his experience and turns on an "'imaginative disagreement'" between the poet and his daughter that spoils the harmonious portrayal of their relationship Maclean so values. For Emile Legouis, to whom Maclean is responding, it seems in the line "If thou appear untouched by solemn thought" that the child, like its mother, "'was ill-made for prolonged ecstasies before aspects of nature'" (131–32), but for Maclean the line has "none of the import Legouis suggests" when joined to the "subsequent lines, which affirm the child to be at least equal to the poet in sensitivity and divinity" (137). There is no hint in Maclean's reading that the affirmation could be a response to a felt deficiency in the child's response to the scene and no hint either that the poet's "Listen!" (treated by Maclean as an exalted apostrophe to an unspecified other) might be taken as an invitation to the child to share the speaker's response. The mother is a red herring from Bakhtin's perspective as well as from Maclean's, since Bakhtin argues that discourse in a poem, unlike discourse in life, must make some allusion in its language to elements of the situation necessary to its understanding, but the speaker's relation to the child is given verbal representation and, as I have argued, his concession of her lack of response to the scene makes most sense as itself a disappointed response to her apparent obliviousness to what he has called her to notice. The subsequent lines do not so much obliterate his disappointment in her as they answer it.

22. For Bakhtin's contrast of dialogic and dialectic, see 1984, 25–26.

23. A similar dialectic of genres, subject to a comparable collapse, appears in Bakhtin's

opposition of novelistic and poetic discourse in "Discourse in the Novel" (pp. 275–88). Just as Burke opposed the static lyric to the dynamic drama, so Bakhtin opposes monologic poetry to the heteroglossic novel. Poetry, in this opposition, aspires to a unitary distinctive poetic language, while the novel assimilates the widest range of social languages, including the poetic, and plays them off against each other. But it is clear that Bakhtin, like Burke, knows that his dialectical opposition is an exaggeration: "It goes without saying," he finds it necessary to say, "that we continually advance as typical the extreme to which poetic genres aspire; in concrete examples of poetic works it is possible to find features fundamental to prose, and numerous hybrids of various generic types exist" (1981, 287n). As the dramatic seems to include the lyric to which Burke dialectically opposes it, so the dialogic includes the monologic to which Bakhtin contrasts it. Action takes priority over the stasis with Burke, as verbal interaction takes priority over the monologue with Bakhtin. Burke's dialectical opposition of dramatic and lyric genres, like Bakhtin's dialectical opposition of novel and poetry, collapses into hyperbole.

24. For Bakhtin's contrast of dramatic and dialogic situations, see 1984, 17–18.

25. For an amplification of the city in the poem as a figure of "power in repose" and the details in the poem as "embodiments of London's majesty and power," see Patrick Holland, "The Two Contrasts of Wordsworth's 'Westminster Bridge' Sonnet," *Wordsworth Circle* 8 (1977): 32–34. Holland's New Critical discovery of a poem that "reconciles and unifies two visions" situates itself in response to W. J. B. Owen's prior contrast between *The Prelude* and "Westminster Bridge," "The Sublime and the Beautiful in *The Prelude*," *Wordsworth Circle* 4 (1973): 67–86.

26. The date in 1807 was mistakenly given as 1803 rather than September 1802.

27. The edition of these sonnets I am using is Wordsworth, *Poems in Two Volumes, and Other Poems, 1800–1802*, ed. Jared Curtis (Ithaca, N.Y.: Cornell University Press, 1983).

28. For further evidence of Wordsworth's nationalism, see James K. Chandler, *Wordsworth's Second Nature: A Study of the Poetry and the Politics* (Chicago: University of Chicago Press, 1984), 203–4.

29. See W. R. Johnson, *The Idea of Lyric: Lyric Modes in Ancient and Modern Poetry* (Berkeley and Los Angeles: University of California Press, 1982), for an interesting account of the rhetorical tradition of the lyric. Johnson, however, relying too much on such standard accounts of the romantic lyric as Abrams's "Structure and Style" essay, underestimates the continuation of that tradition into the romantic period.

30. On Bakhtin's pertinence for feminist criticism and his own neglect of the category of gender, see Wayne C. Booth, "Freedom of Interpretation: Bakhtin and the Challenge of Feminist Criticism," *Critical Inquiry* 9 (September 1982): 45–76; Laurie Finke, "The Rhetoric of Marginality: Why I Do Feminist Theory," *Tulsa Studies in Women's Literature* 5 (Fall 1986): 251–72; Dale M. Bauer, *Feminist Dialogics* (Albany: State University of New York Press, 1988); Myriam Diaz-Diocaretz, "Sieving the Matriheritage of the Sociotext," in her *The Difference Within: Feminism and Critical Theory* (Amsterdam: John Benjamins, 1988), 115–47; and Anne Herrmann, *The Dialogic and Difference* (New York: Columbia University Press, 1989).

31. Page does recognize the provenance of those terms, however, in the recent feminist work of Elaine Showalter, Anne K. Mellor, Margaret Homans, Gayatri Chakravorty Spivak, and Mary Jacobus.

32. J. Hillis Miller, "On Edge: The Crossways of Contemporary Criticism," *Bulletin of the American Academy of Arts and Sciences* 32 (November 1978): 18; reprinted in *Romanticism and Contemporary Criticism*, ed. Morris Eaves and Michael Fischer (Ithaca, N.Y.: Cornell University Press, 1986), 96–111.

33. J. Hillis Miller, "Ariachne's Broken Woof," *Georgia Review* 31 (1971): 58.

34. J. Hillis Miller, "Theory and Practice: Response to Vincent Leitch," *Critical Inquiry* 6 (Summer 1980): 610.

35. Miller's reading of "A Slumber" appears in "On Edge: The Crossways of Contemporary Criticism." Abrams's rejoinder appears along with Miller's response to it in Eaves and Fischer (1986). See also Karl Kroeber's remarks in his review of Eaves and Fischer, *Studies in Romanticism* 27 (Summer 1988): 341–42.

36. In his reading of "Upon Westminster Bridge" the only other voice Miller engages is Wordsworth's, as Miller constructs it from two of his sonnets that make their form their explicit theme. What gives this stage of Miller's argument special interest is the difference between the reading practice he follows when he construes these sonnets as reliable sources for Wordsworth's views and those he follows when he deconstructs "Westminster Bridge" as a poem that enacts the indeterminacies they only describe. Miller's readings of "Nuns fret not at their convent's narrow room" and "Scorn not the sonnet" are as centripetal or centering as his reading of "Westminster Bridge" is centrifugal or decentering.

Miller makes two characteristic kinds of constructive or centering moves in his readings of the thematic sonnets. First, he determines the meaning of Wordsworth's use and theory of the sonnet in these poems by asserting that they "must be understood in the context of [his] theme of poetic impotence" as it appears in the language and the history of composition of *The Prelude* (1971, 300). Though he elsewhere will assert that "the concept we so blithely name *context* for a given text . . . can nowhere be fully identified or fully controlled" ("Ariachne's Broken Woof," 58–59), he here asserts the compelling power of the context he suggests and cites corroborating evidence from Wordsworth's letters. Had Miller chosen a comparable strategy for his reading of "Westminster Bridge," some of its indeterminacies might have been determined.

Second, and more revealingly, Miller pulls the diverse metaphors of the two sonnets toward a center instead of probing them for the "radical ambiguity" (1971, 306) he discovers in "Westminster Bridge." He tries to make all the metaphors in "Nuns fret not" illustrate a unifying and impersonal Brooksian paradox—that small size allows for a kind of largeness—but his explication can make this point stick only to the figures of the first quatrain. He asserts of "Scorn not the sonnet" that "a coherent system of thought underlies [the] metaphors" in the image of "something small and enclosed which is nevertheless articulated or structured," but he must concede that Spenser's "glow-worm lamp" does not quite fit the pattern and he must imagine as "reticulated" a myrtle leaf that only glitters gaily in the poem (1971, 30).

Miller clips and adjusts the figures in these poems to fit a single determinate "system of thought" instead of highlighting their differences and celebrating the indeterminate oscillations they set up. He constructs these poems to bring out his theme of the "paradoxical relation of the sonnet to its origin" (1971, 302) in order to deconstruct "Westminster Bridge"; he reduces them to a determinate pattern, comprehends them as if their meaning were unambiguous the better to show how "Westminster Bridge" cannot be so reduced or comprehended.

37. "To the Poet, John Dyer," in de Selincourt, ed. (3:10).

38. David Ferry, *The Limits of Mortality* (Middletown, Conn.: Wesleyan University Press, 1959), 12–15.

39. Brooks, it should be noted, introduces the topos of the "city under the semblance of death," though he does not use the word "corpse" or discover the same paradox as Miller and Ferry; see *Well Wrought Urn*, 6–7. G. M. Harvey, in a reading later than Miller's but without reference to it or any other prior reading, follows a similar New Critical trajectory,

discovering a dialectic between a mimetic "rhetoric of sympathy" and a paradoxical "rhetoric of irony" in the poem and claiming that "the calm is, after all, in reality only the serene majesty of a corpse" ("The Design of Wordsworth's Sonnets," *Ariel E* 6 [1975]: 78–83).

40. See Paul de Man's account of the experience of sitting in on Reuben Brower's course "The Interpretation of Literature" at Harvard in the 1950s in "Return to Philology," *The Resistance to Theory* (Minneapolis: University of Minnesota Press, 1986), 23–25.

41. See, for example, Geoffrey H. Hartman, "The Unremarkable Poet," in *The Unremarkable Wordsworth*, ed. Donald G. Marshall (Minneapolis: University of Minnesota Press, 1987), 207–19. I discuss Alan Liu, "The Idea of the Memorial Tour: 'Composed upon Westminster Bridge,'" *Wordsworth: The Sense of History* (Stanford: Stanford University Press, 1989), 455–99, 633–43, in my *Wordsworth, Dialogics and the Practice of Criticism* (Cambridge: Cambridge University Press, 1992), 127–33.

42. The "Oklahoma Conference on Contemporary Genre Theory and the Yale School" was held in Norman, Oklahoma, 31 May–1 June 1984. Papers from the conference were published in a double issue of *Genre* 17 (Spring and Summer 1984). I make reference to J. Hillis Miller, "The Search for Grounds in Literary Study," 19–36, and "Marxism and Deconstruction: Symposium at the Conference on Contemporary Genre Theory and the Yale School 1 June 1984," 75–97; and to Robert Markley, "*Tristram Shandy* and 'Narrative Middles': Hillis Miller and the Style of Deconstructive Criticism," 179–90. The collection has been reprinted with the same pagination as *Rhetoric and Form: Deconstruction at Yale*, ed. Robert Con Davis and Ronald Schleifer (Norman: University of Oklahoma Press, 1985).

43. The questioner first suggests to Miller, "Criticism always adds to the primary text so that you have to rehabilitate the texts that you use as intertexts. But from what Professor Miller said this morning, any time you deal with, say, a Freudian critic who quotes Freud at you, what you ought to do is go pick up Freud. So what happens is you displace the criticism with another primary text." Asked if that is what he meant, Miller answers affirmatively, distinguishes between canonical and noncanonical readings, and cites the authority of both Derrida and de Man to the effect that most or all of the traditional or canonical readings are wrong. The questioner continues, "But it's almost impossible to write about a text without finding out what the canonical reading is and using it as a constructive motive through the material. It gives you a strong hand or some other kind of force to spring off of in the text." In reply to this reassertion of the role of "canonical" readings in provoking further readings of the "primary" text, Miller continues to emphasize the "bold" and "radical" hypothesis that informs de Man's practice (and presumably Miller's own): "What de Man is saying is, here's a professor, very distinguished, who has spent his whole life studying Arnold. He's one of the recognized experts on Arnold. I read him and then I read Arnold, and I find that there is no correspondence between the two. And he finds this as a kind of regular law. When people would ask Professor de Man on what basis he knew he was right and all the others were wrong he would just smile an enigmatic smile" ("Symposium," 92–93).

In Miller's account of it, de Man's law appears to be that the "noncanonical" critic is a law unto himself, responsible only to the text but not to another critic's reading of it or of him. This same law is formulated in slightly different terms in one other document from the conference, a paper on "The Style of Deconstructive Criticism" focused primarily on an essay by Miller about *Tristram Shandy*. Robert Markley writes, "Miller's article is, at once, a rewriting of both *Tristram Shandy* and the rules of critical discourse. It contains, for example, no citations to any other critics of Sterne or Schlegel (though Miller does acknowledge his debt to Ronald Paulson's reading of Hogarth). This lack of footnoting, of any reference to critical tradition, implies a hierarchical distinction between what we might call 'originary' repetitions (those of a deconstructive criticism) that 'continue' the text and parasitic repetitions (those of 'monological' criticism) that, it seems, are not work repeating" ("Style," 183).

44. William E. Cain, "Deconstruction in America: The Recent Literary Criticism of J. Hillis Miller," *College English* 41 (December 1979): 374–75; revised and reprinted in Cain, *The Crisis in Criticism* (Baltimore: Johns Hopkins University Press, 1984), 39.

45. Miller's account of "what deconstruction is about" in "Symposium" (92) continues to talk about the coercion of the reader by the text. Appealing again to de Man's authority, he says "that what takes place in any act of reading is what has to happen because of the words, not what one wishes to happen or expects will happen. When you read, in a way it's a no-lose situation; something's going to happen to you, the text is going to make a necessary occurrence take place even in the worst reading. That has nothing to do with subjectivity. It has to do with the language and your response to it."

46. See my "Dialogics as an Art of Discourse in Literary Criticism," *PMLA* 101 (October 1986): 788–97. I am grateful to Lynn Anderson, Bruce Bashford, Peter Elbow, Charles O. Hartman, Michael Macovski, Wendy Olmsted, and Michael Sprinker for their comments on various drafts of the present chapter.

Involvement as Dialogue

Linguistic Theory and the Relation between
Conversational and Literary Discourse

Since the rise of transformational grammar as the dominant paradigm in linguistics, literary theorists have tended to look to it as the primary if not only available model of linguistic theory.[1] At the same time there has developed among literary scholars, as it has among scholars in a range of other disciplines, a growing and spreading interest in the theoretical framework of Mikhail Bakhtin. The coincidence of these two strands of theoretical interest among literary theorists is in a sense ironic, since, as elucidated by Gary Saul Morson and Caryl Emerson in their book *Mikhail Bakhtin* (1990), Bakhtin positioned himself in opposition to linguistic theory, about which he was loudly skeptical. For Bakhtin, linguistic theory referred primarily to "the work of Saussure and those influenced by him: the Formalists, structuralists, and, later, the semioticians" (Morson and Emerson 1990, 123). Many of the Saussurian foundations of the linguistics of his time that Bakhtin challenges are also fundamental to contemporary structural and generative linguistics: the separation of language into an idealized *langue* and a vulgarized *parole* (in the Chomskyan paradigm, "competence" and "performance"), its reduction to rules, the formal representation of a monolithic conception of language, and focus on the speakers' production of language to the exclusion of interactive context and listeners' (or readers') inextricable influence and participation.

There are, however, vibrant strains of linguistic theory that are far more congenial to Bakhtinian theory, even parallel to it, but which have not, so far as I know, been taken up by literary scholars. In this chapter I offer a brief indication of some of these alternative linguistic theories, mention some ways they are similar to Bakhtin's view of language, and then turn to my own work in this linguistic tradition. Specifically, I investigate the relationship between conversational and literary discourse in terms of a theoretical framework I have been developing which I call "involvement in discourse." Involvement, I argue, is a reflection of the interactive nature of language, the aspect of language that is fundamental to Bakhtin's notion of dialogue. Indeed, the very concern with the relationship between conversational and literary discourse is central to Bakhtin's writing, especially "The Problem of Speech Genres" (1986). On the basis of analysis of conversational and fictional versions of the same material by the same author, I will argue for what I call the poetic nature of spontaneous conversational discourse. I will also claim that literary dialogue does not literally represent spoken dialogue, but rather gives the impression of representing it by a process of synecdoche.

Overview of the Chapter

In what follows, I begin by describing the work of a number of linguists whose theoretical approaches to language differ from those of practitioners of transformational grammar. I briefly indicate some ways that their work is congenial to Bakhtin's theoretical framework as it is summarized by Morson and Emerson (1990) and as Bakhtin (1986) presents it in "The Problem of Speech Genres." I then present a brief sketch of my own recent work in this linguistic tradition, in which I propose a theory of literary discourse as an artful reworking of strategies that are spontaneous in conversational discourse. In this regard, my argument is similar to what Morson and Emerson call Bakhtin's "prosaics": his claim that ordinary speech is not simply "practical" but contains within it the "speech genres" that are elaborated in literary discourse. The main analytical portion of this chapter is then devoted to a comparison of conversational and novelistic presentations of the same material by a modern Greek novelist, Lilika Nakos. I show that Nakos's conversational rendering of her experience is more "involving" (in a sense, I argue, more "poetic") than the fictional rendering of the same events in her novels; in contrast, the fictional representations may be considered more "literary." This analysis demonstrates the quality I call "involvement" in discourse at the same time that it elucidates the relationship between conversational and literary discourse.

Alternative Linguistic Theories

"Prosaics" is a term coined by Morson and Emerson (1990) to reflect two aspects of Bakhtin's linguistic philosophy. One sense in which they use this term is to reflect Bakhtin's belief in "the importance of the everyday, the ordinary" (15). In this, Bakhtin's philosophy parallels a developing interest in the language of everyday conversation, in contrast with the mainstream focus of linguistic theory on sentence-based transformational grammars. Prominent among these developments has been the rise of interest in interactional sociolinguistics and discourse analysis, branches of linguistics concerned with the language of everyday conversation.

Paul Friedrich (1986) claims that the poetic dimension of language is its most important dimension, and that all language is relatively poetic, if poetry is seen as "integrating or organically fusing the music of language with the nuance of myth" (3) and as "all parts of a language system that exemplify a figure" such as "metaphorlike relations in grammar" and structures or speech that "may evince analogical freshness or ambiguity" (24). Friedrich also observes that linguistics has been characterized by a rage for order and a consequent ignoring of the ways that language is not ordered but chaotic. "Many of us have overemphasized," he argues, "the discreteness of units, the depth of structures, the strictness of rule ordering, freedom from context, and the linearity of messages in single-track communication . . ." (147–48).[2] Compare this perspective to Bakhtin, as paraphrased by Morson and Emerson: "For Bakhtin, the attempt to explain away messiness by postulating still more systems and the higher order of a system of systems is at best like adding epicycles to a Ptolemaic astronomy and at worst a wholly unjustified leap of theoretist faith" (1990, 144).

A. L. Becker's (1984b) notion of "prior text" is analogous to Bakhtin's "speech genres." First, Bakhtin: "When we select words in the process of constructing an utterance, we by no means always take them from the system of language in their neutral, *dictionary* form. We usually take them from *other utterances*, and mainly from utterances that are kindred to ours in genre, that is, in theme, composition, or style" (1986, 87). Now Becker: "The actual a-priori of any language event—the real deep structure—is an accumulation of remembered prior texts" (1984b, 435). Consequently, "our real language competence is access, via memory, to this accumulation of prior text." Here and elsewhere (1982a, 1982b, 1984a, 1988a, 1988b, 1995) Becker argues for a linguistics of particularity, for a conception of language as languaging, that is, as active rather than static, and for a nonreductionist linguistics.

According to Bakhtin, "Nineteenth-century linguistics, beginning with Wilhelm von Humboldt, while not denying the communicative function of language, tried to place it in the background as something secondary. What it foregrounded was the function of thought emerging *independently of communication*" (1986b, 67). Bakhtin's own discussion of the importance of communicative context is reminiscent of the large body of work in the subfield of linguistics that is sometimes referred to as sociolinguistics. For example, Dell Hymes (1974, 1981) has argued repeatedly for a focus on communicative competence, as distinguished from Chomsky's notion of competence, which is strictly grammatical. Here belongs as well the lifelong work of John Gumperz (1982), who argues against the separation of language into "core" and "marginal" features. Quite the contrary, in his theory of conversational inference, a primary role is played by "contextualization cues," which are primarily prosodic and paralinguistic features that would have been relegated to "marginal" status by Saussurian linguistics. Finally, Shirley Brice Heath's (1983) long-term investigation of language use in three communities emphasizes the inextricable relationship between language use and other cultural patterns. Morson and Emerson note Bakhtin's conviction that "native speakers do not apply rules, they enter the stream of communication" (1990, 145). This could as easily be describing the work of numerous contemporary linguists who question the transformational grammarians' conception of language as generated according to rules. A linguist who resisted the transformational model from its inception and stalwartly continued to do so until his death,[3] Dwight Bolinger argued for a view of language as "an organism" rather than "an Erector set." He observed that "our language does not expect us to build everything starting with lumber, nails, and blueprint, but provides us with an incredibly large number of prefabs, which have the magical property of persisting even when we knock some of them apart and put them together in unpredictable ways" (1961, 1). How similar Bolinger's view of language is to Bakhtin's: "If speech genres did not exist and we had not mastered them, if we had to originate them during the speech process and construct each utterance at will for the first time, speech communication would be almost impossible" (1986, 79).

Bolinger's conception of linguistic "prefabs" is related to Bakhtin's notion of "speech genres," which he defines as "the typical forms of utterances" (1986, 79). Indeed, there is a small but significant and growing body of theoretical work on the linguistics of formulaicity, or the relative prepatternedness of language. In addition to Bolinger, Wallace Chafe (1968, 1970) and Adam Makkai (1972) were linguists who early explored the significance of idioms in linguistic theory. Paul Hopper (1988a, 1988b) argues for a conception of grammar as emergent, in order to take into account the prior history of collocations. My own work (Tannen 1987, 1989) surveys the prior literature and argues for the fundamental role of formulaicity in language use. I show that repetition, the basis for all linguistic structure and meaning, can be understood as a kind of spontaneous formulaicity.

Another facet of Bakhtin's objection to the linguistic theory of his time is that it regards language "from the speaker's standpoint as if there were only *one* speaker who does not have any *necessary* relation to *other* participants in speech communication" (1986, 67). This criticism calls to mind a group of anthropological linguists who have created a significant literature arguing for the inextricability of speaking and listening, for a conception of conversation as a "joint production" (Erickson 1982), for "audience participation in sensemaking" (Tannen 1989). A special issue of the journal *Text*, edited by Alessandro Duranti and Donald Brenneis (1986), is devoted to "the audience as co-author." (In the introduction to that volume Duranti provides an overview of the theoretical foundations of this perspective.) The lifelong work of Frederick Erickson (for example, Erickson and Shultz 1982) has been devoted to the study of listener behavior and its effect on speaking. In an article entitled "Listening and Speaking," Erickson (1986, 316) claims that speaking is like climbing a tree that climbs back. Kochman (1986) proposes the concept of "strategic ambiguity" by which speakers of vernacular black English intentionally leave it to hearers to determine the "meaning" of an utterance. Scollon and Scollon (1984) show that the structure of Athabaskan speakers' discourse is a reflection of the participation of their listeners (see also Scollon and Scollon 1981). Finally, the inextricability of interaction between speaker and hearer is fundamental to my own conception of involvement in discourse (Tannen 1989).

Involvement Strategies in Discourse

In this section I summarize the theoretical framework developed in my own recent work that grows directly out of the strains of linguistic theory described in the preceding section.

In *Talking Voices* (1989), I claim that ordinary conversation provides the source for linguistic strategies that are artfully developed in literary discourse.[4] This claim is analogous to Bakhtin's conception of ordinary conversation as made up of primary genres that are "absorbed" and "digested" by "secondary speech genres" such as novels and drama (1986, 62). More precisely, I argue that

> ordinary conversation is made up of linguistic strategies that have been thought quintessentially literary. These strategies, which are shaped and elaborated in literary discourse, are pervasive, spontaneous, and functional in ordinary conversation. I call them "involvement strategies" because, I argue, they reflect and simultaneously create interpersonal involvement. (1989, 1)

Involvement strategies drive both conversational and literary discourse by means of patterns of sound and sense. Sound patterns—the musical level of language, including rhythm and prosody—involve the audience with the speaker or writer and the discourse by sweeping them up in what Scollon (1982) calls rhythmic ensemble, much as one is swept up by music and finds oneself moving in its rhythm. At the same time, involvement is created through what I call audience participation in sensemaking: by doing some of the work of making meaning, hearers or readers become participants in the creation of the discourse.

I suggest, moreover, that these two types of involvement are necessary for communication, and that they work in part by creating emotional involvement. People understand information better—perhaps only—if they have discovered it for themselves rather than being told it. Listeners and readers not only understand information better but care more about it—understand it *because* they care about it—if they have worked to make its meaning.

The involvement strategies I identify in conversation are also those which literary analysts have independently identified as important in literary discourse. The three I have examined in depth are repetition, what I call "constructed dialogue," and details. *Repetition* establishes rhythm and also meaning by patterns of constants and contrasts. *Dialogue*, the representation of voices in discourse (what has been called, erroneously I argue, "reported speech"), creates rhythm and musical cadence as well as setting up a dramalike scene in which characters interact with each other and engage in culturally recognizable activities. *Details* provide seed from which listeners sprout characters, emotions, and meanings.

My notion of involvement is analogous to Bakhtin's notion of dialogue; it grows out of a view of language as fundamentally interactive and grounded in context; of meaning as the result of interplay between novelty and fixity; and of meaning as created by listeners as well as speakers in response to prior text. Furthermore, like Bakhtin, I have been concerned with the comparison of conversational and literary discourse. I have argued that listeners to and readers of discourse can "comprehend" what they hear or read only by reference to recognizable scenes composed of people engaged in meaningful activities. They create these scenes in their minds in response to the details, dialogue, and other clues provided by the discourse. This process of mutual participation in sensemaking gives rise to what I call involvement. In fictional dialogue, a similar process is at work. The fictional dialogue represents visually recognizable elements of conversation which provide the basis for the listener's re-creation of a complete conversation, standing in for a meaningful relationship. Fictional dialogue seems "real" by a process of synecdoche and involvement: the suggestion of remembered conversations. Put another way, Bakhtin claims that every conversation echoes other conversations, by the speakers and by others. In the same way, literary conversations echo both other literary conversations and remembered conversations from real life.

Conversational and Literary Discourse: Lilika Nakos

I turn now to analysis of conversational discourse, and a comparison of conversational and literary representations of the same events. I will show that there are more "involvement strategies" in the spontaneous conversational discourse than in the literary representation. I show, too, that the conversational discourse is more "poetic" in Friedrich's sense; that is, the involvement strategies result in discourse that is more "figured," more rhythmic, more elliptical, and, ultimately, more moving. In fact, my notion of involvement strategies constitutes a proposed account of what it means for a discourse to be "moving." On the basis of this analysis, I will conclude with a theory of the relationship between conversational and literary discourse.[5]

The discourse I analyze was produced by a modern Greek novelist, Lilika Nakos.[5] While researching a book about her work (Tannen 1983), I interviewed Nakos over a period of eight months in 1975 and 1976 at her winter and summer homes outside Athens. In the course of those interviews I asked her about the circumstances surrounding the creation of her novels. In her answers to my questions, Nakos recounted some events that she had also represented in the novels. Thus I had the opportunity to compare Nakos's literary and conversational re-creations of the same events.

Lilika Nakos (1899–1989) was a member of a group of Greek writers known as "The Generation of the Thirties" who forged the novel form in modern Greek. One of the first women to write prose fiction in Greek, Nakos was known for her lyrical use of the demotic, or spoken language.[6] A contemporary critic, commenting on Nakos's early writing, complained that she wrote "not literature, but conversation." He perceived her writing to be so conversational in tone that he could not see it as literature at all. This is precisely the view taken by the Russian Formalists in their approach to the language of the novel, and, according to Morson and Emerson, it is a basis for Bakhtin's opposition: "They [the Formalists] equate the 'artistic' with the 'poetic'; they consequently equate prose with nonliterary discourse; nonliterary discourse, in turn, is characterized as 'practical' or (in other cases) habitual . . ." (1990, 21). Morson and Emerson suggest that the term "prosaics" represents Bakhtin's insistence on the artistic nature of the language of the novel, in contrast to the Formalists' view that it merely apes the language of everyday speech, which they claimed was used automatically without attention to the language itself (attention to the language being the hallmark of poetry).

Comparing Nakos's conversation with her fiction provides the basis for making observations about the linguistic strategies used in these two forms of discourse. I will argue that the conversational versions of events are more "poetic" than the excerpts from the novel, if "poetic" is understood in terms of linguistic strategies that create involvement, such as ellipsis, rhythmic repetition, tropes, and figures of speech. The novel, however, is more "literary" in the sense of using elaborated metaphors and developed scenes. (Thus my claim that Nakos's conversation is more "poetic" in the sense of "more involving" does not undercut the literary inventiveness of the novel, and consequently in no way disagrees with Bakhtin's evaluation of the novel form as a kind of literary "hero," in Morson and Emerson's [1990, 308] terms.)

In the next section, I examine three examples of Nakos's discourse, then discuss the implications of my analysis for a theory of dialogue in literature.

Poetic Elements in Nakos's Conversational Discourse

I begin with an excerpt of Nakos's conversational discourse alone, in order to show what I am calling its "poetic" nature, that is, the workings of what I call involvement strategies. The first example is taken from a conversation in which Nakos is telling me about the circumstances that led her to write one of her novels.

EXAMPLE 1: "What, humorous?"

Lilika Nakos wrote her most commercially successful novel, *Mrs. Doremi* (*I Kyria Ntoremi*)[7] in 1947 for a French-language magazine in Switzerland. She subsequently rewrote it in Greek, and it was published in Athens in 1955 and serialized on television in the 1980s. These are the circumstances leading up to the writing of that novel.

During the devastating German occupation of Greece during World War II, Nakos starved, froze, was beaten, and lost most of the people she was close to; her mother died shortly after the war as a result of hardships she suffered during it. The death of her mother, who had been her only family and her main companion and responsibility, freed Nakos to leave Greece, which was then embroiled in a civil war as devastating as the world war upon whose heels it followed. In 1947 she returned to Switzerland, where she had grown up from the age of twelve, where she had written her first work in French, and where she had developed a reputation as a writer before she returned to her homeland, Greece, at the age of thirty-one.

The following excerpt is from a conversation in which Nakos was telling me about how she came to write the novel *Mrs. Doremi*, her only comic novel. As she described the setting, she had just arrived in Switzerland and was sitting in the train station, destitute and aimless. An acquaintance from her earlier time in Geneva approached and told her that a magazine editor had heard about her arrival and wanted to commission a humorous novella. She remarked, "What, humorous?"

She wasn't feeling humorous at all because, as she explained,

Den eicha tipota.	I didn't have anything.
Oute na koimitho,	Neither to sleep,
Oute na fao,	neither to eat,
oute domatio,	neither a room,
oute tipota.	neither anything.

I have laid out the transcription of Nakos's conversation in lines, not to suggest that it is poetry, but to reflect the rhythmic "chunking" that is created in speaking by intonation and prosody. It is hard to render a sense of the Greek in English translation because Greek, by virtue of its grammar as well as its conventional use, is far more elliptical than English. Structures that are natural and grammatical in Greek sound truncated and ungrammatical in English.[8]

The first line contains two negatives:

Den eicha   tipota.
Neg. (I) had nothing

One could render this in English as "I didn't have anything" or "I had nothing," but in either case the double negative is lost. (The more literal translation, "I didn't have nothing," sounds either ungrammatical or extremely colloquial in English.) This negative statement is then illustrated with three specific lacks, three things she did not have, also expressed in elliptical form:

Den eicha tipota—	I had nothing—
oute na koimitho	nowhere to sleep
oute na fao	nothing to eat
oute domatio	no room
oute tipota.	no nothing.

The first thing one may notice about this set of lines is that they are framed by the word *tipota*, "nothing," which ends both the first and the last intonation units. This is a figure that Quinn (1982) calls epanalepsis—the repetition of a beginning at the end. This figure is equally evident in the original Greek and the English translation.[9] Looking at the Greek in the left column, however, one can see that it contains more parallelism than the English in the right column: the word *oute* was spoken four times, each time beginning a new "intonation unit" or burst of speech bounded by a coherent intonational contour.[10] In addition, the negative particle *Den* that begins the first line patterns with the negative particle *oute* that begins the next four lines. In order to allow the reader to perceive more directly the rhythm of the Greek, I present a word-by-word gloss:

Oute   na koimitho
Neither to sleep

oute   na fao
neither to eat

oute   domatio
neither room

oute   tipota.
neither nothing.

Part of the impact of this segment in Greek derives from its iconicity. The elliptical grammatical expression in Greek reinforces the impression of scarcity that Nakos is describing. Furthermore, the rhythm established by the parallelism ("not to sleep, not to eat, no room, no nothing") creates a listing intonation that implies a longer, perhaps even an endless, series of which only three items are specified. At the same time, this rhythmic pattern involves the hearer in the world created by the discourse, with its sense of isolation and deprivation.

Against this background, Nakos describes why (and, elliptically, how) she complied with the request for a comic novel:

kai mou edose pentakosia fragka.	And he gave me five hundred francs.
Piga,	I went,
pira domatio,	took a room,
efaga,	ate,
kai archisa na to grafo.	and began to write it.

The three statements of what she did not have are now matched rhythmically by three statements of what she was able to get with the five-hundred-franc advance. Again, to give a sense of the elliptical nature of the Greek expressions, I present a word-by-word gloss:

Piga,
went

pira domatio,
took room

efaga
ate

kai archisa na to grapso.
and began to it write

I have omitted the grammatically requisite pronouns in English to represent the sparsity of the Greek; one must try to "hear" it, though, as perfectly grammatical, and to sense the first person as included in the verb.

One may wonder why Nakos included the first line, "Piga," since semantically the word does not add anything to the story. I suggest that this line is there mostly to supply a third element to balance the list of three items she lacked: "nowhere to sleep, nothing to eat, no room." One may also wonder why, in the first case, "nowhere to sleep" and "no room" were both present since they are essentially synonymous. Here, too, the rhythmic realization of three is crucial to create a listing intonation, where the list effect suggests that there are more items that could have been listed than are actually named. At least three items are needed to give the sense of a list. The parallel rhythm is completed with the final line, which varies from the preceding three: "and I started to write it," much as the last line of the preceding "verse" ends with a change in syntax ("No nothing") and intonation (the last item has falling rather than rising intonation).

This brief example shows what I am calling the "poetic" nature of ordinary conversation, by which I mean its creation of involvement through audience participation in sensemaking and rhythmic ensemble. In particular, I have focused on repetition and ellipsis. The work of the listener in filling in elided meaning is suggestive of what Bakhtin calls "actively responsive understanding" (1986, 68), the participation of the listener that is an inextricable element in any utterance.

The following two examples contrast Nakos's conversational presentation of a story with her fictional representation of the same material.

Comparison of Conversation and Fiction

The next two examples compare conversational and fictional accounts of the same events in order to show that the conversational discourse is more "involving" than the fictional.

EXAMPLE 2: "To the kitchen!"

Toward a New Life (Yia Mia Kainouryia Zoi) is another of Nakos's major novels. It was written before World War II but was first published in 1960. It too was serialized for Greek television in the 1980s. Partly autobiographical, the novel is about a young woman, Barbara, who lives with her mother in Athens during the period of the repressive Metaxas dictatorship immediately before the entry of Greece into World War II. During one of our many conversations, Nakos told me about her experiences in the 1930s as the first—and for a significant period of time the only—woman journalist in Greece:

> Ego egrafa stin *Akropoli*
> kai olo mou legan
> "Stin kouzina! Stin Kouzina!"
> Nai, mia mera thimosa k'ego
> sto diefthindi.
> "Ma i kouzina thelei fayi,
> a ma pios tha ergastei?"

> I was writing for the *Acropolis*
> and they kept saying to me,
> "To the kitchen! To the kitchen!"
> Yeah, one day I got mad
> at the director.
> "But the kitchen needs food,
> so who's going to work?"

In the novel, this interchange is expanded and elaborated. Barbara's director says:

> "De thelo ego ginekes mesa sta grafia," xefonize. "I gineka einai ftiagmeni yia tin kouzina kai to kravati."
> I Varvara tote den vastaxe ke apantise: "Ma i kouzines, stratige, chriazonte simera pola chrimata yia na yiomisoune trofima. Ego doulevo kai i mitera mou magirevi."

"I don't want women in the offices," he yelled. "A woman is made for the kitchen and the bed."

Barbara then couldn't take it anymore and answered, "But kitchens, general, require a lot of money nowadays to fill them with food. I work and my mother cooks."

I will explore now why I claim that the conversational version of the story is more "involving." Nakos told me she was taunted,

"Stin kouzina! Stin kouzina!"

"To the kitchen! To the kitchen!"

This taunt, which is ambiguously attributed ("they kept saying to me"), is, first of all, elliptical. "To the kitchen" is a short way of saying, "Go to the kitchen," which in itself is a figurative representation of, "You should be in the kitchen." That she should be there because she is a woman is implied. All these implications are lexicalized and elaborated in the novel and attributed to the director (the person who in our day might be called the managing editor) of the newspaper:

"I don't want women in the offices," he yelled.
"A woman is made for the kitchen and the bed."

Nakos's response, as she reported it to me, is similarly elliptical:

"But the kitchen needs food [*thelei fayi*],
so who's going to work?"

The rhetorical question "who's going to work?" is an elliptical way of saying that Nakos herself had to work; "the kitchen needs food" is figurative in that the kitchen is anthropomorphized (Kakava 1988). The assumptions underlying this statement are spelled out in the novel:

"But kitchens, general, require today a lot of money to fill them with food [*chriazontai trofima*]. I work and my mother cooks."

It is worth noting that Nakos employed a more formal register in the fictional version. In our conversation she used the demotic or vernacular term *fayi*, but in the novel she used the formal register, or puristic form, *trofima*. The verbs, too, are different: in speaking, she said *thelei* ("needs") food, whereas in the novel she wrote *chriazontai* ("requires") food. This is particularly noteworthy in light of the criticism that she wrote "conversation, not literature." Clearly, her literature is not the same as her conversation. Her conversation is, paradoxically, more "poetic," in the sense of creating involvement through the use of ellipses and repetition. In Bakhtin's framework, one might say it is more "dialogic" in making less meaning explicit and requiring more participation from the listener. But the novel is more elaborated and written in a more formal or literary register. Most important for Bakhtin's notion of speech genres is that the novel conforms to expectations established by other novels.

I am not suggesting that the conversational version is in any sense the real one, what really happened or what was actually said. Quite the contrary, I have argued in detail elsewhere (Tannen 1989) that any occurrence of discourse is a creation;

in other words, there is no such thing, literally, as reported speech: even if a speaker re-creates the exact words that were said, the fact of creating them in a new context constitutes an original utterance. As Bakhtin has shown and emphasized, every utterance is new, even as it is patterned on previous utterances, or prior text.

EXAMPLE 3: "I am a little ant"

In the next and last example I again juxtapose two versions of the same events, one as spoken by Nakos in conversation with me and the other as she wrote it in her novel *Toward a New Life*. The conversation took place as Nakos and I were sitting on the porch in front of her summer house in Ekali, a suburb of Athens. The house, which was later razed to make way for an apartment building, had been built by Nakos's father. (Nakos had hidden Communists there during the Metaxas dictatorship.) In telling me the circumstances surrounding her writing of this novel (she said she wanted it to stand as a protest against the repressive Metaxas regime), Nakos told me about a woman who became a character in the novel: a young Communist whose real name was also the name of the character in the book, Chrysa (literally, Gold.) Nakos told me that Chrysa, who had been her friend and a frequent visitor to her home, was arrested and imprisoned in Athens. When Nakos went to visit her in prison, she discovered that Chrysa had been tortured.[11] Following are juxtaposed excerpts from one conversation on the left and from the novel on the right, first in Greek and then in a free translation into English.

Conversation	*Fiction*
Piga sti filaki	"Ela pio konta," tis eipe.
m'ena mantili	Kai koitaxe yiro tis
etsi palia dimena os ergatria.	san na fovotan
	na min tin akousi kanenas.
Kai ti ferane.	"Den boro na milo dinata
Kai ti na do?	kai den kanei.
Ti ferane etsi dyo nosokomes.	Kai an sou po ti mou kanan
Kathise sta kagela	den einai yiati
kai mou leei,	zito tin symponia kanenos.
"Lilika	Mono tora kai si kratas mia pena
an se zitisa	kai prepei na xereis ti yinete
den einai na sou po	ston topo mas.
ti travixa ego,	Prepei na xereis tous dimious.
yia na matheis omos ti travaei	Ma de sta leo afta, Varvarva,
o Ellinikos laos.	yia na kles.
Ego 'me ena mirmigaki.	Ma yia na xereis
Afto to mirmigaki na foundosei	ti travaei o kosmakis
yia n'alaxei i zoi	kai poii einai oi stavriotides tou.
ton anthropon pou ergazontai.	Eisai nea...
Leei, "Min kles, min kles.	tha ziseis

Ego," leei, "eimai ena mirmigaki.
Kai esi," leei, "na se fonaxa
yiati, epei-epeidi grafeis.
Echete kathikon eseis oi grafiades."
Etsi milouse, "oi grafiades."
"Na xerete ti travaei
o Ellinikos laos."

kai prepei na xereis
ti felana oi diktatories...
Yia mena den beirazei...
Ti eimai allo para ena halikaki,
ston kosmo pou chtizetai,
ston kosmo pou erchete.

Conversation

I went to the prison
with a kerchief
like that, poorly dressed,
like a worker.

And they brought her.
And what do I see?
They brought her like this,
two nurses.
She sat by the bars
and she says to me:
"Lilika, if I asked for you
It's not to tell you
what I went through,
but for you to learn
what the Greek people go through.
I am a little ant.
This little ant will expand
to change the life of working people."
She says, "Don't cry, don't cry.
I," she says, "am a little ant.
And you," she says, "I called you
because, si-since you write.
You have a responsibility,
you scribblers.
(That's how she talked, "scribblers")
to know
what the Greek people go through.

Fiction

"Come closer," she said to her.
And she looked around her
as if she was afraid
someone might hear.
"I can't speak loudly,
and I shouldn't.
And if I tell you what they did to me,
it isn't because I'm looking for
anyone's sympathy.
It's only that now you hold a pen,
and you should know what's happening
in our country.
You should know the executioners.

But I don't tell you this, Barbara,
to make you cry.
But for you to know
what the people go through,
and who their crucifiers are.
You are young...
You will live,
and you should know what dictatorships
are good for.
For me, it doesn't matter.
What am I, but a little stone,
in the world that is being built,
in the world that is coming."

(*The image of Chrysa as a little ant appears
elsewhere in the novel:*)

Kai i Chrysa ystera skeftiki eipe:
"Ach! ki ego etsi thelo na eimai.
Ena anonimo mirmigaki
na kouvalao

petradaki me petradaki
yia na chtisti
enas kosmos kainouryios.

And then Chrysa, thoughtful, said:
"Ach! And I want to be like that.
An anonymous little ant
to drag
pebble after pebble
to build a new world.

I have been intrigued, in all the years since this conversation took place, and am constantly struck anew when reading the transcript, that the story as Nakos told it to me is more moving than the one that appears in the novel. I can hardly read the words "Don't cry, don't cry," without feeling the urge to cry. What is it about the spoken version that has this effect? Again, I think, it is the combination of musical rhythm created by the alternation of small bursts of speech and pauses plus the repetition that together create involvement. Furthermore, the elliptical expression makes the listener fill in meaning and therefore have strong feelings for what is filled in. Finally, visual details create images that lead the listener to reconstruct a scene. All these are ways that, as Bakhtin puts it, "the listener becomes the speaker" (1986, 68).

First is the detail that leads the hearer to create an image of how Nakos was dressed, "with a kerchief," "like a worker." Next, the scene is set with a repetition that is lost in the English translation:

Kai ti ferane.	And they brought her.
Kai ti na do?	And what do I see?
Ti ferane etsi dyo nosokomes.	They brought her like this, two nurses.

The repetition of *kai ti* (pronounced keh-tee) in the first two lines is lost in English because the Greek word *ti* is actually two different words, homonyms. In the first line,

kai ti   ferane
and her brought

"and they brought her"

ti means "her," spelled in Greek with the vowel η (*eta*). In the second line,

kai ti   na do.
and what to see.

"and what do I see?"

ti means "what," spelled in Greek with the vowel ι (*iota*). When the third line picks up the phrase *ti ferane* (they brought her), in Greek it is continuing a thread that has woven through the three lines, rather than resuming a thread that has been lost in the English.

In both languages, however, the interjection "What do I see?" creates a pause as the reader waits to see what Chrysa looks like, just as Nakos, or Barbara, waited to see her friend. This iconically creates suspense.

Part of the rhythm of the spoken Greek is created by the repetition of the word *leei* "(she) says," which is uttered four times, three of them in three consecutive lines during the part of the greatest emotional intensity, when Chrysa tells Nakos not to cry. Elliptically, by representing Chrysa as telling her not to cry, Nakos informed me that she was crying. The repetition, "Don't cry, don't cry," is similar to the repetition in the earlier example, "To the kitchen, to the kitchen." The repetition creates a sense of repeated action.

In this section, the word *leei* is used to introduce the dialogue and then is interjected between subject and verb, an unlikely but not ungrammatical placement in English. In the following, I present the English with the phrase "she says" rendered in Greek because the single word suggests the rhythm better than do the two words required in English. (*Leei* is a "falling diphthong," pronounced "lay-ee" with slight emphasis on the first syllable.)

> *Leei* "Don't cry, don't cry.
> I," *leei*, "am a little ant.
> And you," *leei*,
> "I called you because,
> si-since you write."

The repetition of *leei* creates a thread through the discourse that has a hypnotic rhythmic effect; it also reminds the hearer of Chrysa's presence and her voice at each repetition.

Contrast the direct address, "Don't cry, don't cry," with the wording of the novel:

> Ma de   sta leo afta, Varvara, yia na kles.
> But neg. you say these Barbara for to cry.
>
> "But I don't tell you this, Barbara, to make you cry."

The repetition in "Don't cry, don't cry" iconically creates the impression that Barbara was crying continually. Also, the line of dialogue prompts the hearer to imagine a scene in which Nakos is crying and Chrysa is comforting her. In other words, the very sparsity of the dialogue prompts the hearer to do more work and create a more complete scene. In contrast, the line of dialogue in the novel does not create the image of Barbara crying—at least not as surely or as dramatically. It does not prompt the reader to imagine as vivid a scene as does the spoken discourse.

We are reminded of Chrysa again when Nakos interjects,

> Etsi milouse,   "oi grafiades"
> Thus (she) spoke, the writers
>
> "That's how she talked, 'scribblers.'"

The Greek word *grafo*, "to write," yields the noun *grafiades* in the demotic vernacular. I use the term "scribblers" to suggest the vernacular tone. The more standard "puristic" term would be *syngrafeis*, a term that Nakos does not use in the novel either. There she uses metonymy instead: "You hold a pen" (Kakava 1988).

Repetition is also crucial in the central metaphor of the conversational version, which is also used in the novel but in another section: that Chrysa is a little ant who is doing her part to build a new world. From the conversation:

"Ego 'me ena mirmigaki.
I   am a   little-ant

Afto to mirmigaki na   foundosei
This   little-ant   will expand

yia   n'alaxi   i   zoi
in order to change the life

ton   anthropon pou ergazontai."
of the people   who work.

Leei,   "Min kles, min kles.
(She) says, Don't cry, don't cry.

Ego," leei,   "eimai ena mirmigaki."
I,   (she) says, am   a   little-ant.

The Greek word that must be represented in English by "little ant" is a single word, *mirmigaki*. It is a word that has an iconic effect in itself. The "i" sound (as in English "bee") is one of the few phonological linguistic universals: in all languages, it represents something small.[12] The onomatopoetic /i/ sound, which occurs three times in *mirmigaki* (meermeengakee), is echoed as well in the verb *eimai* (pronounced *ee*-may), "I am." The word *mirmigaki* is also semantically marked for smallness by virtue of the diminutive ending *-aki*. This is the sort of sound play whose pervasiveness in language leads Friedrich (1986) to regard all language as "poetic."

The relationship between the little ant and the new world is explicit in the novel; indeed, it is one of the novel's central metaphors and also lends it its optimistic title. In the conversation, Chrysa says simply that she is a little ant and the little ant will grow to change the life of working people. In the novel, in the section quoted first, the metaphor of a stone is used:

What am I but a little stone in the world that is being built, in the world that is coming.

In the later section the figure of the ant is elaborated, now as a simile rather than a metaphor:

I want to be like that. An anonymous little ant, to drag little-stone after little-stone, in order to build a new world.

In the novel there is also more elaborate condemnation of the dictators who have tortured Chrysa, in fancier terms:

Prepei na xereis tous dimious.

. . . .

Ma yia na xereis ti travaei o kosmakis
kai poii einai oi stavriotides tou.

. . . .

Kai prepei na xereis ti felana oi diktatories.

And you should know the executioners.

. . . .

But to know what the people go through
and who their crucifiers are.

. . . .

And you must know what dictatorships are good for.

Thus, the discourse of the conversations in which Nakos told me about her novels is more "poetic" than the fictional discourse in which she wrote about the same events. I am defining "poetic" as making use of what I have called "involvement strategies": rhythmic repetition, ellipsis, and figurative language that both sweep hearers along and require them to participate in sensemaking by imagining scenes suggested by the discourse. The fictional discourse, however, is artful as well, only in a more elaborated, "literary" way.

Summary: The Relation between Conversation and Fiction

In the first part of this chapter I briefly summarized the work of a number of linguists whose theories of language are more congenial, even parallel, to those of Bakhtin than are the theories of generative grammar that dominate the field and that have attracted the attention of literary theorists. I then summarized briefly my own theory of conversational involvement, which is in the tradition of these alternative linguistic theories. Finally, I devoted the major portion of this chapter to comparing conversational and literary versions of the same events, as told and written by the same author. I found that the conversational versions of events were more "involving," and in my experience more "moving," than the literary versions. I demonstrated that this resulted from a pattern of rhythmic repetition and ellipsis that worked together to sweep the hearer along and to force the hearer to fill in meaning. "Involvement," in my schema, is comparable to Bakhtin's notion of dialogism (although I developed my framework before reading Bakhtin), in that meaning is created jointly in conversation by hearers and readers along with speakers and writers. Finally, I suggested that literary discourse works by a similar process. That is, by a process of synecdoche, the representation of recognizable conversational parts triggers in the reader the re-creation of a conversation like those that have been experienced.

ACKNOWLEDGMENTS   My comparison of Lilika Nakos's conversation and fiction was originally conducted with the support of a grant from the National Endowment for the Humanities. I am grateful for this support. In this comparison I was immeasurably aided by my research assistant Christina Kakava. She helped transcribe my taped conversations with Nakos and identified the passages in the books that corresponded to them. She also provided her own commentary on the comparison in her master's research paper (Kakava 1988). The analysis presented here is mine, but I have drawn upon Kakava's observations about Nakos's lexical choices.

Notes

1. See, for example, Traugott and Pratt (1980). Another branch of the field, pragmatics, has led to some interest in speech-act theory as a resource for literary theory (Lanser 1981; Pratt 1977).

2. For further discussion of chaos in language, see Friedrich (1988).

3. Bolinger died in July 1992. See also Bolinger (1976) for discussion of what I am calling formulaicity: the relative fixity of language.

4. This section is based directly on *Talking Voices* (Tannen 1989). There, in addition to discussing this theoretical framework in detail, I explore in depth three involvement strategies: repetition, dialogue, and detail.

5. In writing the book, I confronted the dilemma of choosing a form for the subject's name. Her surname in Greek is *Nakou* (pronounced nah-koo), but her father's surname is *Nakos*. In Greek, a woman's last name is in the genitive case: literally, she is the Lilika belonging to Nakos. Greek women usually, but not always, adapt their names in English and European languages to reflect the same form as their husband's or father's. This is what Lilika Nakos did when publishing in French (though it was occasionally spelled "Nacos"), and her few works published in English in the United States (translated from French) were published under that name as well. That is why I opted for the name "Nakos," even though I knew her as "Lilika Nakou," and that is how she is known to Greek audiences.

6. The "language question" in Greece is a complex and highly politicized issue with a long and much-remarked history. After Greece achieved liberation from four hundred years of Turkish occupation, there was a movement to return to the use of classical Greek in order to purge the Greek language of Turkish influence just as Greeks had purged their land of Turkish rule. As a compromise between those who wished to revive classical Greek and those who wished to retain the form of Greek that had developed naturally over the years ("demotic"), an expatriate Greek scholar named Koraïs developed a synthetic form of the language that was purified of Turkish influence and reintroduced many grammatical aspects of classical Greek that had been lost to natural processes of linguistic change. This form of Greek, called "puristic" (*katharevousa*), was legally imposed as the official language of public discourse, with the result that fiction writers found themselves forbidden to represent the language of spoken discourse in print. For a brief summary of the influence of the language question on the development of modern Greek literature and Nakos's place in this history, see Tannen (1983). For a detailed discussion of the language question and Greek literature, see Bien (1972).

7. The title *Mrs. Doremi* refers to the first three notes of the musical scale, "do-re-mi." It comes from the nickname given to Nakos by the students to whom she taught music in a high school in Rethymnon, Crete, in 1933. Following her father's death, Nakos had been obliged to go to work to support herself and her mother, and to repay the debts her father had left. Having been raised in the upper-class Athenian district of Plaka and the cosmopolitan European city, Geneva, she spent a harrowing year as a high school teacher on the still-wild island of Crete before locating a position as a high school teacher in Athens.

Herzfeld (1991), in an ethnographic study of the Cretan town of Rethymnon, discusses older townspeople's recollections of Nakos's year spent in their midst as well as their responses to the serialization of her novel on television in the 1980s.

8. An example of the elliptical nature of Greek syntax and discourse is the expression that I have used to name Example 1: "What, humorous?" This is a direct translation of the Greek *Ti, asteia?* which Nakos told me she had responded with when someone informed her that a Swiss editor wanted her to write a humorous novel about her experiences on Crete (*Thelei ena- mia istoria yia tin Kriti asteia*). The expression, *Ti, X?* ("What, X?") is a recurrent Greek "figure" (Becker 1979) or sentence frame that is conventionalized in Greek discourse. To get a sense of the meaning, it would be necessary to say in English, "Humorous? What are you talking about?" or, "Humorous? Are you kidding?"

9. I owe this observation to Paul Fallon, who credits Christina Kakava with identifying the figure of speech and its source.

10. The term "intonation unit," like the term "chunking," was developed by Chafe (1980) and his collaborators (of whom I was one) in conjunction with a study of the verbalization of past experience.

11. As I recount elsewhere (Tannen 1983), Nakos said that Chrysa was suspended upside down and beaten, with her slip stuffed into her mouth to muffle her screams. Then a woman burned her genitalia with a match.

12. The universality of the association of what linguists call the high front vowel, /i/, with smallness is observed by Sapir (1929), Jespersen (1933), and Jakobson and Waugh (1979).

Works Cited

Bakhtin, M. M. "The Problem of Speech Genres." In *Speech Genres and Other Late Essays*, translated by Vern W. McGee and edited by Caryl Emerson and Michael Holquist. Austin: University of Texas Press, 1986.

Becker, A. L. "Attunement: An Essay in Philology and Logophilia." In *On the Ethnography of Communication: The Legacy of Sapir. Essays in Honor of Harry Hoijer 1984*, edited by Paul V. Kroskrity. Los Angeles: Department of Anthropology, University of California, Los Angeles, 1988a.

——. *Beyond Translation: Essays toward a Modern Philology*. Ann Arbor: University of Michigan Press, 1995.

——. "Beyond Translation: Esthetics and Language Description." In *Contemporary Perceptions of Language: Interdisciplinary Dimensions. Georgetown University Round Table on Languages and Linguistics 1982*, edited by Heidi Byrnes. Washington, D.C.: Georgetown University Press, 1982a.

——. "Biography of a Sentence: A Burmese Proverb." In *Text, Play, and Story: The Construction and Reconstruction of Self and Society*, edited by Edward M. Bruner. Washington, D.C.: American Ethnological Society, 1984a.

——. "On Emerson on Language." In *Analyzing Discourse: Text and Talk. Georgetown University Round Table on Languages and Linguistics 1981*, edited by Deborah Tannen. Washington, D.C.: Georgetown University Press, 1982b.

——. "The figure a sentence makes." In: Talmy Givon (ed.), *Discourse and Syntax*, pp. 243–259. New York: Academic Press, 1979.

——. "Language in Particular: A Lecture." In *Linguistics in Context: Connecting Observation and Understanding. Lectures from the 1985 LSA/TESOL Institute*, edited by Deborah Tannen. Norwood, N.J.: Ablex, 1988b.

————. "The Linguistics of Particularity: Interpreting Superordination in a Javanese Text." In *Proceedings of the Tenth Annual Meeting of the Berkeley Linguistics Society*. Berkeley, Calif.: Linguistics Department, University of California, Berkeley, 1984b.

Bien, Peter. *Kazantzakis and the Linguistic Revolution in Greek Literature*. Princeton, N.J.: Princeton University Press, 1972.

Bolinger, Dwight. "Meaning and Memory." *Forum Linguisticum* 1, no.1 (1976): 1–14.

————. "Syntactic Blends and Other Matters." *Language* 37, no.3 (1961): 366–81.

Chafe, Wallace L. "Idiomaticity as an Anomaly in the Chomskyan Paradigm." *Foundations of Language* 4 (1968): 109–25.

————. *Meaning and the Structure of Language*. Chicago: University of Chicago Press, 1970.

————, ed. *The Pear Stories: Cognitive, Cultural, and Linguistic Aspects of Narrative Production*. Norwood, N.J.: Ablex, 1980.

Duranti, Alessandro, and Donald Brenneis, eds. *The Audience as Co-Author*. Text 6, no.3 (1986). (Special issue)

Erickson, Frederick. "Listening and Speaking." In *Languages and Linguistics: The Interdependence of Theory, Data, and Application. Georgetown University Round Table on Languages and Linguistics 1985*, edited by Deborah Tannen and James E. Alatis. Washington, D.C.: Georgetown University Press, 1986.

————. "Money Tree, Lasagna Bush, Salt and Pepper: Social Construction of Topical Cohesion in a Conversation among Italian-Americans." In *Analyzing Discourse: Text and Talk. Georgetown University Round Table on Languages and Linguistics 1981*, edited by Deborah Tannen. Washington, D.C.: Georgetown University Press, 1982.

Erickson, Frederick, and Jeffrey Shultz. *The Counselor as Gatekeeper: Social Interaction in Interviews*. New York: Academic Press, 1982.

Friedrich Paul. "Eerie Chaos and Eerier Order." Review of James Gleick, *Chaos: Making a New Science. Journal of Anthropological Research* 44, no.4 (1988): 435–44.

————. *The Language Parallax: Linguistic Relativism and Poetic Indeterminacy*. Austin: University of Texas Press, 1986.

Gumperz, John J. *Discourse Strategies*. Cambridge: Cambridge University Press, 1982.

Heath, Shirley Brice. *Ways with Words*. Cambridge: Cambridge University Press, 1983.

Herzfeld, Michael. *A Place in History: Social and Monumental Time in a Cretan Town*. Princeton, N.J.: Princeton University Press, 1991.

Hopper, Paul J. "Discourse Analysis: Grammar and Critical Theory in the 1980's." *Profession 88* (1988): 18–23.

————. "Emergent Grammar and the A Priori Grammar Postulate." In *Linguistics in Context: Connecting Observation and Understanding. Lectures from the 1985 LSA/TESOL Institute*, edited by Deborah Tannen and James E. Alatis. Norwood, N.J.: Ablex, 1988.

Hymes, Dell. *Foundations in Sociolinguistics*. Philadelphia: University of Pennsylvania Press, 1974.

————. *"In vain I tried to tell you": Essays in Native American Ethnopoetics*. Philadelphia: University of Pennsylvania Press, 1981.

Jakobson, Roman, and Linda R. Waugh. *The Sound Shape of Language*. Bloomington: Indiana University Press, 1979.

Jespersen, Otto. "Symbolic Value of the Vowel *i*." In *Linguistica: Selected Papers in English, French, and German*. Copenhagen: Levin and Munksgaard, 1933.

Kakava, Christina. "Metaphor and Other Figures of Speech in the Discourse of Lilika Nakou." M.A. thesis, Georgetown University, 1988.

Kochman, Thomas. "Strategic Ambiguity in Black Speech Genres: Cross-Cultural Interference in Participant-Observation Research." *Text* 6, no.2 (1986): 153–70.

Lanser, Susan Sniader. *The Narrative Act: Point of View in Prose Fiction*. Princeton, N.J.: Princeton University Press, 1981.

Makkai, Adam. *Idiom Structure in English*. The Hague: Mouton, 1972.

Morson, Gary Saul, and Caryl Emerson. *Mikhail Bakhtin: Creation of a Prosaics*. Stanford, Calif.: Stanford University Press, 1990.

Pratt, Mary Louise. *Toward a Speech Act Theory of Literary Discourse*. Bloomington: Indiana University Press, 1977.

Quinn, Arthur. *Figures of Speech*. Salt Lake City: Gibbs M. Smith, 1982.

Sapir, Edward. "A Study in Phonetic Symbolism." *Journal of Experimental Psychology* 12 (1929): 225–39.

Scollon, Ron. "The Rhythmic Integration of Ordinary Talk." In *Analyzing Discourse: Text and Talk. Georgetown University Round Table on Languages and Linguistics 1981*, edited by Deborah Tannen. Washington, D.C.: Georgetown University Press, 1982.

Scollon, Ron, and Suzanne B. K. Scollon. "Cooking It Up and Boiling It Down: Abstracts in Athabaskan Children's Story Retellings." In *Coherence in Spoken and Written Discourse*, edited by Deborah Tannen. Norwood, N.J.: Ablex, 1984.

———. *Narrative, Literacy and Face in Interethnic Communication*. Norwood, N.J.: Ablex, 1981.

Tannen, Deborah. *Lilika Nakos*. Boston: G. K. Hall, 1983.

———. "Repetition in Conversation as Spontaneous Formulaicity." *Text* 7, no.3 (1987): 215–43.

———. *Talking Voices: Repetition, Dialogue, and Imagery in Conversational Discourse*. Cambridge: Cambridge University Press, 1989.

Traugott, Elizabeth Closs, and Mary Louise Pratt. *Linguistics for Students of Literature*. New York: Harcourt Brace Jovanovich, 1980.

"The Bard I Quote From"

Byron, Bakhtin, and the Appropriation of Voices

In one of the most celebrated accounts of Byron's political persona, Hazlitt inveighs against what he calls the poet's "preposterous *liberalism*." "[I]f he is a patrician in rank and feeling, he would fain be one of the people," writes Hazlitt in 1824. "He may affect the principles of equality, but he resumes his privilege of peerage. . . ." For Hazlitt, the "chief cause of most of Lord Byron's errors is that he is that anomaly in letters and in society, a Noble Poet" (*Spirit of the Age*, 178–79, 177). It is not surprising, then, that Hazlitt would type *Don Juan* as the "satire of a lord," a privileged lampoon founded upon "some circumstance of external situation" (172). What is more striking, however, is that Hazlitt modulates this sociopolitical critique into a sweeping indictment of Byron's style. Whereas Scott "shows us the crowd of living men and women, the endless groups," Byron "holds no communion with his kind" and "casts his descriptions . . . constantly in the mold of his own individual impressions." "Instead of taking his impressions from without," Hazlitt goes on, "he moulds them according to his own temperament, and heats the material of his imagination in the furnace of his passions." According to this view, the Byronic "I" remains "solitary," "proceeds from an internal source," such that he "invariably shuts himself up in the Bastile of his own ruling passions" (160, 161, 164).

This last image of the Bastile stands as a synecdoche for the political implications of Byron's style. Hazlitt's avowed Toryism notwithstanding, we are liable to characterize the Byronic narrator as "solitary," "internal," and ultimately solipsistic. In this context Byron's alleged reflexivity and self-oriented "spontaneity"[1] have become whipping boys for the charge of social "antipathy" and solipsism. Political self-exile thus becomes a metaphor for a kind of stylistic iconoclasm, severing both author and narrator from "communion with his kind." Like Aurora Raby, each persists "Apart from the surrounding world . . . —most strange in one so young!" (*Don Juan*, 15.47.375–76).

Yet even if Byron remains a "patrician in rank and feeling," it does not necessarily follow that the "privilege of peerage" skews his poetic range, his capacity to enact a diversity of viewpoints, characters, and voices. Peter Manning has demonstrated, for instance, that Byron seeks to "display the *multiple* functions of language itself," to suggest the "dynamic" "relationship between words."[2] We must consider, then, whether Byron's position as a "Noble Poet" does in fact limit his poetic portrayal of these "multiple" voices—whether it distorts the politics of representation. In what follows I suggest that while Byron may have severed his political moorings within British society, he nonetheless *reconstructs* and encounters this society by representing it in his discourse—in the manifold voices of a stochastic style. I argue that *Don Juan* deploys a multivoiced, polyphonic style in order to represent several discrete kinds or "levels" of discourse: first, the divergent and conflicted aspects of the Byronic self; second, the cacophonous voices of his literary contemporaries and rivals; and third, the broadest scope or echoes of what he refers to as Regency "Society," manifested in the casuistic voices of gossip and rumor.

Before delineating these stylistic voices or levels of discourse, however, we would do well to consider the critical background for such an argument. To approach *Don Juan* as an interchange of voices—as a model of what Byron calls "conversational facility" (*Don Juan*, 15.20.155)—one must recall the Pulcian oral tradition that informs the poem. Both George Ridenour (1960, 10.125–26, 165–66) and Jerome J. McGann (1976, 69–70), for instance, have traced *Don Juan* to the "chatty," "conversational manner of the *sermo*," the Horatian "plain style." This view of the poem as "conversational" in tone and form thus supports an approach that reads it as a compilation of voices. In a parallel manner, this tendency toward opposing voices and tonal diversity also becomes apparent in McGann's discussion of "Byron's use of series, one of the poem's staple devices" (1976, 95). For when Byron presents the multiple layers of figures, tropes, and viewpoints that characterize this "series" *techné*, his style reflects a stratification of voices that defines the societal conversations, literary interchanges, and multivocal selves I will consider.

My reading of Byron's style begins with the notion of a polyphonic text: a narrative form that uses both conversational diversity and multilayered series description to represent what Byron repeatedly refers to as a "world of words" (*Don Juan*, 2.162.1296; 5.104.825). The nature of this literary form has been most thoroughly formulated by Mikhail Bakhtin, who argues for the interpenetration of literary language (what he refers to as "secondary speech genres") and everyday, "primary" discourse. "In each epoch," he writes,

> certain speech genres set the tone for the development of literary language. And these speech genres are not only . . . literary . . . but also primary (certain types of oral dialogue—of the salon, of one's own circle, and other types as well, such as familiar, family-everyday, sociopolitical, philosophical, and so on). Any expansion of the lit-

erary language that results from drawing on various extraliterary strata of the national language inevitably entails some degree of penetration into all genres of written language. . . . (1986, 65–66).

For Bakhtin, "literary language" is thus imbued with "oral dialogue," with voices from the "various extraliterary strata of the national language." It is just such voices, moreover, that *Don Juan* incorporates into its conversational style: the "familiar, family-everyday, sociopolitical, philosophical, and so on." What distinguishes Byron's style from others, however, is the self-consciousness of his "oral" appropriation, the notion that these quotidian echoes can actually become a thematic locus of the poem.

To enumerate the various tones of the Byronic voice, then, is to suggest that Byron's style strives for heterogeneity—what Bakhtin refers to as "assimilation." It moves, in Bakhtin's words, toward the

> process of *assimilation*—more or less creative—of others' words (and not the words of a language). Our speech, that is, all our utterances (including creative works), is filled with others' words, varying degrees of otherness or varying degrees of "our-own-ness," varying degrees of awareness and detachment. These words of others carry with them their own expression, their own evaluative tone, which we assimilate, rework, and re-accentuate. (1986, 89)

For Byron, too, the assimilation of "others' words" enables him to "rework" their voices, to reevaluate them according to his own beliefs. His style thus empowers him to establish "varying degrees of otherness or varying degrees of 'our-own-ness.'" We might begin, then, with Byron's own representation of "our-own-ness"—the multiple aspects of his own psyche.

I

Byron's attempt to present a protean view of his own personality emerges early in his career. Trelawny, for one, observes that "he seemed to take an especial pleasure in making a clean breast to every newcomer, as if to mock their previous conceptions of him, and to give the lie to the portraits published of him." Trelawny later elaborates on one of these transitory "portraits," suggesting that "in his perverse and moody humours, Byron would give vent to his Satanic vein" (1858, 43). This self-presentation of changing "humours," "moods," "veins," and "portraits" thus begins to suggest Byron's literary attempts to present a diversity of voices. In his desire to offer a series of public portraits, to confound his external persona, we sense a need to rewrite his sundry versions of the self.

It is this protean sense of self-presentation, moreover, that suggests how Byron's compilation of multiple voices comes to represent the diverse facets of his own self. For Byron's style derives form a more divergent, conflicting, and even dissonant aggregation of voices than perhaps any of the other Romantics. It is Byron's desire to juxtapose these divergent aspects of the self, to locate each in direct relation to the others, that gives rise to what I call his polyphonic style. What is more, this stylistic juxtaposition of conflicting voices is, for Byron, actually self-constitutive: it not only encompasses the various parts of the self, but orients them in relation to one another. The resulting expression of self is not so much organically developed as it is incrementally aligned: it puts forth not a central, core self, but an association of composite selves. It follows not the growth of a poet's mind, but its elaborated construction: the lamination of voice upon voice. We hear not what Coleridge calls "multeity in unity," not a unitary voice, but an often dissonant chord.[3]

Byron accordingly begins *Don Juan* with the consciousness that self is constituted by a multitude of voices—opinions, valuations, and internal self-judgments:

> He that reserves his laurels for posterity
>   (who does not often claim the bright reversion?)
> Has generally no great crop to spare it . . .
>
> . . . .
>
> The major part of such appellants go
> To—God knows where—for no one else can know.
>   (Dedication, 9. 65–67, 71–72)

Without the repeated praise of "laurels"of fame, then, we are "fallen in evil days on evil tongues" (Dedication, 10.73). However ephemeral such fame is, selfhood nevertheless develops from an aggregation of voices, reports, or "tongues." In canto 1, when the "age" " wants a hero," it can thus create one with the "cant" and verbal "pantomime" afforded Don Juan (1.1). There is a sense, too, that Juan is no more than the sum of the voices around him, an aggregate of reported stories—so that as the poem ends he has been constituted by the vocal "fame" that has accrued about him:

> His fame too, — for he had that kind of fame
>   Which sometimes plays the deuce with womankind,
> A heterogeneous mass of glorious blame,
>   Half virtues and whole vices being combined
>   (15.57.449–52)

Juan's selfhood thus consists of a "heterogeneous mass" of "fame," pronouncements, and other vocal legends. He becomes the totality of others' retellings, a creation of repeated versions of the "Don Juan" scandal. At the same time, however, this distinction between diverse versions or aspects of the self enables him to delineate the parts of his being, to make sense of the "heterogeneous mass of glorious blame." According to this view, dialogic narration actually becomes a way of encountering and understanding the divergent aspects of the Byronic self, within the context of ontological dialogue.[4]

II

Byron's juxtaposition of discrete voices orients him not only in relation to various aspects of the self, but also in relation to his contemporary poets. He plays out the foregoing psychomachia not only on a personal level but also on a national one—on the level of what he refers to as "literary England." Writing from Italy, for instance, he forbids John Murray to send him any "*English* works," reviews, or *"periodical works"* that might remind him of English letters. "The same applies," he goes on,

> to opinions—*good, bad,* or *indifferent*—of persons in conversation or correspondence; these do not *interrupt* but they *soil* the *current* of my *Mind*;—I am sensitive enough— but *not* till I am *touched & here* I am beyond the touch of the short arms of literary England—. . . .

> All these precautions *in* England would be useless—the libeller or the flatterer would there reach me in spite of all—but in Italy we know little of literary England & think less except what reaches us through some garbled & brief extract in some miserable Gazette. (*BLJ* 8.219–20)

Despite these protests, Byron of course heard and remembered much about "literary England" during his Italian self-exile. Indeed, his frequent citations of, and commentary on, such figures as Wordsworth, Coleridge, Keats, and Southey suggest that he may have preferred to debunk them in absentia than to debate them on their own turf. Yet I would also stress that the style we have been considering enables Byron to effect a more subtle engagement with his literary rivals. For by quoting and recontextualizing the poetic voices of his contemporaries, Byron essentially rewrites "literary England"—reconstitutes it as a fictive discourse. By imitating the diction of "literary matters," he can encounter his contemporaries in his own terms— actually appropriate their language into his own poetic voice (*BLJ* 1.216).

What Byron establishes in *Don Juan*, then, is essentially a transhistorical encounter with his literary compeers, a poetic dialogue. In the well-known conclusion to canto 1, for instance, he incorporates Southey's discourse in order to force a comparison:

> "Go, little book, from this my solitude!
>   I cast thee on the waters—go thy ways!
> And if, as I believe, thy vein be good,
>   The world will find thee after many days."
> When Southey's read, and Wordsworth understood,
>   I can't help putting in my claim to praise—
> The four first rhymes are Southey's, every line:
> For God's sake, reader! take them not for mine!
>   (1.222.1769–76)[5]

Here Byron manages to appropriate Southey's language by incorporating it within both his own stanzaic form and the worldview it represents. What is more, the rhetorical juxtaposition of Southey's verse and his own allows Byron to assert an external and by implication transcendent position. Although Southey can never respond to such a charge, the fiction of dialogue ensures Byron's self-engendered "claim to praise."

In the following passage, Byron's position in relation to the Lake Poets becomes less a dialogue than an encounter. By assimilating the voices of several anonymous critics, he is again able to instantiate an omnipotent position over both them and their objects of judgment:

Some persons think that Coleridge hath the sway;
　And Wordsworth has supporters, two or three;
And that deep-mouth'd Boeotian "Savage Landor"
　Has taken for a swan rogue Southey's gander.

John Keats, who was kill'd off by one critique,
　Just as he really promised something great,
If not intelligible, without Greek,
　Contrived to talk about the Gods of late,
Much as they might have been supposed to speak.
　Poor fellow! His was an untoward fate;
'Tis strange the mind, that fiery particle,
Should let itself be snuff'd out by an article.
(11.59–60.469–80)

Byron thus avoids Keats's "untoward fate" by assimilating the same voice of "critique" that allegedly "snuff'd" the younger poet.

Byron's multivocal style thus represents a kind of poetic control or encapsulation. In subsuming a series of literary voices, he violates the notion of an artistic hierarchy. In the following passage we witness a satiric leveling in which poetic competition becomes meaningless:

He saw ten thousand living authors pass,
　That being about their average numeral;
Also the eighty "greatest living poets,"
As every paltry magazine can show *it's*.

In twice five years the "greatest living poet,"
　Like to the champion in the fisty ring,
Is call'd on to support his claim, or show it,
　Although 'tis an imaginary thing.
(11.54–55.429–36)

Laureate pretensions thus come to resemble a series of capricious, unfounded "claims"; fame is an "imaginary thing." As Byron writes elsewhere,

What is the end of fame? 't is but to fill
　A certain portion of uncertain paper:
Some liken it to climbing up a hill,
　Whose summit, like all hills, is lost in vapor;
For this men write, speak, preach, and heroes kill,
　And bards burn what they call their "midnight taper,"
To have, when the original is dust,
A name, a wretched picture, and worse bust.
(1.218.1737–44)[6]

By incorporating the complementary voices of both poets and judges, Byron strikes at the very language, the very "name" of "fame." Paradoxically, it is his own ability to "write, speak, [and] preach" with the voice of others that renders his own name "certain."[7]

III

Yet the broadest level of interchange represented by Byron's polyphonic style is societal discourse. Byron invokes the conflicting voices of Regency society in order to demonstrate how the individual's reach is delimited by societal expectations. As Karl Kroeber has demonstrated, "Typical . . . was his interest in the subjective, emotional aspects of human life in conjunction with his perception of society as mobile, shifting, alive, and his concern with the problems of individual personality functioning as part of such an organic society" (1975, 167). Kroeber goes on to "stress that Romantic realistic narrative appears in conjunction with an assertion that the relationship of the individual to his social group is uncertain, unstable, fluid—is not absolutely fixed and defined by tradition." In this context, "Byron's flashy Oriental adventures . . . are based on a melodramatic, if not tragic conception of the individual spirit in conflict with its society, a society which the individual may reject but cannot escape, for upon it depends his very existence as a human being" (1975, 190–91).

Byron accordingly evokes societal discourse in order to represent the predicament of the lyrical voice amid a plural society—amid the plural, polyphonic discourse spoken by the body politic. In his private language, moreover, the poet also impersonated this multiphasic contrast. Trelawny notes, for instance, that even Byron's conversational style was marked by an unusual diversity of voices, dialects, and personas: "[H]is talk was seasoned with anecdotes of the great actors on and off the stage, boxers, gamblers, duellists, drunkards, &c., &c., appropriately garnished with the slang and scandal of that day" (1858, 41). It is this linguistic diversity of character and "slang" which, transferred to *Don Juan*, becomes an emblem of communal voices, an echo of "public feeling"—what Byron himself refers to as "Society" (1.34.263,266; *BLJ* 7.43).

For Byron, this "Society" represents that moralistic cacophony that threatens to drown out the individual voice. "[Y]ou live near the *stove* of society," he writes to Thomas Moore, "where you are unavoidably influenced by its heat and its vapours. I did so once—and too much—and enough to give a colour to my whole future existence. As my success in society was *not* inconsiderable, I am surely not a prejudiced judge upon the subject, unless in its favour; but I think it, as now constituted, *fatal* to all great original undertakings of every kind" (*BLJ* 9.119). It is Byron's desire to sustain his "original undertakings," to eschew the "*stove* of society," that also in part explains his self-exile to Italy. For him, Italy manages to sustain social voices without privileging the authoritarian discourse of a separate "Society." In place of societal gossip, judgment, and rumor, Italy offers the privacy of what Byron refers to as "talk." In characterizing his love for Italian "manners," for instance, he writes to John Murray, "I know not how to make you comprehend a people—who . . . *actually* have *no society* (what we would call so). . . . [¶] Their Conversazioni are not Society at *all*.—They go to the theatre to talk—and into company to hold their tongues" (*BLJ* 7.42–43).

Byron refers to the linguistic currency of Regency society as "cant"—a cacophony of "rumor" and "fame" in a community that can only echo its own pronouncements, condemnations, interdictions, and gossip. "I had such projects for the Don," he writes to Douglas Kinnaird, "but the *Cant* is so much stronger than *Cunt*—now a days,—that the benefit of experience in a man who had well weighed the worth of both monosyllables—must be lost to despairing posterity.— After all what stuff this outcry is" (*BLJ* 6.232). For Byron, cant is the attempt to transmute narrative into gossip, to fix "experience" within language—to domesticate history for "posterity." Paradoxically, however, this same language is also an inspiration for Byron, a kind of poetic goad for satiric writing. Trelawny quotes him as saying, "I opined gin was inspiration, but cant is stronger. To-day I had another letter warning me against the Snake (Shelley). He, alone, in this age of humbug, dares stem the current, as he did to-day the flooded Arno in his skiff, although I could not observe he made any progress. The attempt is better than being swept along as all the rest are, with the filthy garbage scoured from its banks" (1858, 43–44). Here "cant" signifies the casuistic "humbug" of society, the moral "current" that both Shelley and Byron seek to "stem." When Byron brings such cant into *Don Juan*, then, it becomes the linguistic equivalent of this societal "humbug"; at this point the poem itself becomes a rhetorical arena for both the reproduction and the parody of "Society's" discourse.

IV

Byron depicts this cant or discourse of "Society" in terms of petty gossip, whispered condemnations, and resonating rumors. In a crucial sense the many dialogic voices of his poetry echo the voices of society at large. What these voices represent, however, is the plurality that constitutes collective judgment—that voice-to-voice movement of reputation in the form of what Byron variously refers to as "circulating scandals" (1.190.1514), "public feeling" (1.34.263,266), and, more generally, dialogic "fame" (1.146.1166; 1.218.1737). In this sense, then, Byron's use of polyphonic viewpoints reflects the multiplicity of voices that goes to make up rumor, hearsay, and Byronic notoriety. His style is a rhetorical trope of cultural judgment. In the following passage, for instance, Byron stresses societal responses to the death of Juan's father, Don Jose:

> His death contrived to spoil a charming cause;
> A thousand pities also with respect
> To public feeling, which on this occasion
> Was manifested in a great sensation.
> (1.33.261–64)

Here, the vanity of "public" consensus emerges not only in the futile quest for "sensation," but in the very multiplication of censorious "feeling," the "thousand" voices of concern. Byron then goes on to parody this "public" commentary; yet he does so by giving each commentator a voice. Much as Jose's "doctors" circulate his bogus diagnosis, for example, Julia's muckraking relatives and lawyers pass his reputation from mouth to mouth:

> Besides her good old grandmother (who doted);
> The hearers of her case became repeaters,
> Then advocates, inquisitors, and judges,
> Some for amusement, others for old grudges.
> (1.28.221–24)

Such "repeaters" of local rumor appear throughout the poem; they stand as the poetic equivalent of scandal. Byron's portrayal of diverse, concurrent viewpoints demonstrates the notion of a "circulating" reputation or transgression.

Yet by repeating (or "re-envoicing") these viewpoints himself, Byron actually demonstrates that such scandals are nothing more than that: a reiteration of voices. The numerous public outcries in the poem thus become innocuous, as if repetition renders them predictable, habitual, and ultimately unremarkable:

> The pleasant scandal which arose next day,
> The nine days' wonder which was brought to light,
> And how Alfonso sued for a divorce,
> Were in the English newspapers, of course.
> (1.188.1501–4)

Because such scandals are a matter "of course" — of vocal repetition and echoing — we come to see them as trumped up, inconsequential. Byron then goes on:

> If you would like to see the whole proceedings,
>   The depositions, and the cause at full,
> The names of all the witnesses, the pleadings
>   Of counsel to nonsuit, or to annul,
> There's more than one edition, and the readings
>   Are various, but they none of them are dull,
> The best is that in short-hand ta'en by Gurney,
> Who to Madrid on purpose made a journey.
> (1.189.1505–12)

The "English newspapers" are of no greater moment than "literary England": both seek to enshrine a set of normative "readings" and "editions," multiple perspectives that ultimately neutralize one another. In re-creating a series of these "readings" or perspectives, then, Byron ironizes the "whole proceedings," exposes it as a bogus process of listing, repeating, and implicating "names."

According to this view, Byron's frequent references to "newspapers," "editions," and variant "readings" can be seen as written emblems of societal discourse, records of those conflicting voices that go to make up "scandal." In the following passage, for instance, Donna Inez keeps a record of her husband's infidelities:

> She kept a journal, where his faults were noted,
> And open'd certain trunks of books and letters,
> All which might, if occasion served, be quoted;
> And then she had all Seville for abettors . . .
> (1.28.217–20)

Here again, the inscribed word stands as the written equivalent of societal voices — of collective rumor and published invective. The "trunks of books and letters" are a compilation of "Society's" condemnations. What is more, the proliferation of Seville's "abettors" underscores Byron's parodic intention. The eagerness of Jose's accusers to perpetuate "scandal" and report, to overstuff "trunks" of hearsay, suggests the hollowness of the charges. It is the propagation of Jose's alleged "faults," multiplied by rumor and reputation, that belies the very discourse of accusation.

V

No matter how heterogeneous these voices appear, though, it would be misguided to see them as unrelated. For what appear to be isolated oppositions and discrete voices can in fact be viewed as parts of a single process, a process of interchange between conflicting aspects of Byron's society. These agonistic interchanges or "dialogues" within Byron's style accordingly reflect more than just his personal conflicts and psychological vicissitudes. For in *Don Juan* such dialogic narration actually becomes an interpretive process—a means of mediating between such antagonistic forces as private and public, lyric and narrative, Horatian and Juvenalian. In canto 15, for instance, Lady Adeline's method of choosing a wife for Juan becomes a communal process, giving voice to a wide range of opinions:

> But Adeline determined Juan's wedding
>   In her own mind, and that's enough for woman.
> But then, with whom? There was the sage Miss Reading,
>   Miss Raw, Miss Flaw, Miss Showman, and Miss Knowman,
> And the two fair co-heiresses Giltbedding.
>
>   (15.40.313–17)

Byron further determines to give each of Juan's matchmakers a voice, replete with particular reasons for her past selections:

> But never yet . . .
>   Was there chaste dame who had not in her head
> Some drama of the marriage unities,
>   Observed as strictly both at board and bed
> As those of Aristotle, though sometimes
> They turn out melodramas or pantomimes.
> . . . .
> From these they will be careful to select,
>   For this an heiress, and for that a beauty;
> For one a songstress who hath no defect,
>   For t'other one who promises much duty;
> For this a lady no one can reject,
>   Whose sole accomplishments were quite a booty;
> A second for her excellent connexions;
> A third, because there can be no objections.
>
>   (15.32.249,252–56; 15.34.265–72)

It is the range of reasons in this latter passage that gives the rhetorical illusion of distinct approaches, of discrete voices. What is arresting about this multivoiced portrayal, however, is that it enables Byron to enact and examine a communal decision, a process of interpretation. In representing this process, Byron not only replicates the casuistic judgments of Regency society, but also exposes them as capricious and arbitrary—as staged "melodramas" or re-created "pantomimes."

This interpretive or analytic intention is further confirmed by the stylistic models that Byron chooses. As Jerome McGann has noted, Byron envisions *Don Juan* within the style of Horatian satire—that historical mode known as the "stylistic embodiment of dialectic or reasoned discourse," as a specifically "analytic" rhetoric (1976, 75). Byron's dialogic narrative thus partakes of a historical style that is inherently hermeneutic. We should recognize, moreover, that this analytic quality derives as much from formal as from stylistic models, for the Horatian style is specifically conversational, and thereby formally linked to both Socratic dialogue and its analytic intention. It re-creates an essentially epistemological dialogue.

VI

The dialogic dimension of *Don Juan* also has vital implications for the affective force of the poem, for its rhetorical capacity to engage a reader. For despite Byron's defilement of "fame" and "rumor," he nevertheless strives for a didactic relation with his audience: "The public approbation I expect," he writes, "And beg they'll take my word about the moral, / Which I with their amusement will connect" (1.209.1665–67). Jerome McGann has further stressed this Horatian didacticism, this belief that men "have to be taught the nature and importance of correct poetic and civil behavior" (1976, 70). He notes that Byron's predilection for the Horatian mode leads him to seek a common ground with his audience, to persuade rather than overwhelm (1976, 74, 79). Yet it is the dialogic aspect of Byron's style that engenders this common ground—this rhetorical inclusiveness—in that it specifically engages other voices, other witnesses, and incorporates them into the text. In many stanzas Byron's apostrophes pointedly assure his reader, as in "Start not; still chaster reader" (1.120.954), and the well-known "For God's sake, reader! Take them not for mine" (1.222.1776; compare 1.22.175–76). Despite the internal ironies of such lines, Byron has nonetheless dialogized his reader within his poem's rhetoric. It is his ability to expropriate his audience that ensures that they will listen.

In other passages such apostrophes take the form of ironic testimonials for a reader's benefit. The following stanza, for instance, stands as a satiric emblem of the poem's rhetorical appeals to authority, where the assimilation of authorial voices supports a process of persuasion:

> If any person doubt it, I appeal
>   To history, tradition, and to facts,
> To newspapers, whose truth all know and feel,
>   To plays in five, and operas in three acts;
> All these confirm my statement a good deal,
>   But that which more completely faith exacts
> Is, that myself, and several now in Seville,
> *Saw* Juan's last elopement with the devil.
>   (1.203.1617–24)

Again, notwithstanding Byron's irony here, the rhetorical intention is Horatian argument. But it is an argument both for and even by Byron's readers. Indeed, one effect of portraying his narrator as a naif is to underscore the universality of this persuasive process, as in the following lines:

I think I picked up too, as well as most,
   Knowledge of matters—but no matter *what*—
I never married—but, I think, I know
That sons should not be educated so.
(1.53.421–24)

Here Byron pays homage to persuading an audience by essentially reenacting the process within the text. His appropriation of diverse voices enables him to depict this process in a plethora of characters—many of whom stand for his diverse readership. In this context the multivoiced exchanges between Byron's characters often reenact his own relations with his audience. Put another way, we can say that Byron's polyphonic style both anticipates and "envoices" its own response, that he essentially conjures his own readers.

VII

In one sense, then, Byron peoples a world that serves as his agon. He gives voice to both his precursors and detractors in order to contend with them in his own terms. By re-creating and parodying the discourse of what he calls "Society," Byron can appropriate it, delimit it, and even begin to rise above it. In another sense, however, Byron has also joined the discourse of "Society": he has fashioned this agonistic world in his own image. For by voicing the mockeries and complaints of his detractors, he necessarily introduces his own retort, juxtaposes both critique and rejoinder—and thereby places himself in *dialogue* with his critics. In re-creating the discourse of the "Society" he has abandoned, he paradoxically reenters it on his own terms. Although the act of ventriloquism displaces his views of this society, it nevertheless locates him within the "public" discourse. In place of the silenced exile—with "no tongue to say, / What was"—Byron instantiates a vocal interchange—that polyphonic "world of words" (2.162.1296; 5.104.825).

We have also considered this reframing of social discourse as a function of Byron's conversational style. Yet this "conversational" or familiarizing mode has crucial implications for Byron's rhetoric of appropriation, his attempt to come to terms with the language of moral condemnation. For when he assimilates the voices of his rivals and detractors, Byron necessarily brings them into his own world, makes them his immediate addressees, his *conversational familiars*. He thereby subverts the voices of "Society" by recontextualizing them within his own familiar style. Deprived of social formality, they lack the sanctioned, official discourse that underlies social ostracization—the conventional language of social stratification. In this sense, the conversational incorporation of an addressee's voice constitutes a kind of social leveling. As Bakhtin puts it, such authors

> perceive their addressees . . . more or less outside the framework of the social hierarchy and social conventions, "without rank," as it were. This gives rise to a certain *candor* of speech (which in familiar styles sometimes approaches cynicism). In familiar speech, since speech constraints and conventions have fallen away, one can take a special unofficial, volitional approach to reality. This is why during the Re-

naissance familiar genres and styles could play such a large and positive role in destroying the official medieval picture of the world. In other periods as well, when the task was to destroy traditional official styles and world views that had faded and become conventional, familiar styles became very significant in literature. (1986, 97)

In Bakhtin's terms, stylistic familiarity and candor can act "to destroy traditional official styles and world views that had faded and become conventional." In this context, Byron's desire to impugn "social conventions" leads him to locate his fictional "addressees . . . outside the framework of the social hierarchy"—to place them within the "familiar styles" of conversational rhetoric. By recontextualizing the language of his critics, he establishes an alternative frame of reference: he "can take a special unofficial, volitional approach to reality."

WE CAN NOW RETURN to Hazlitt's characterization of Byron's style as "solitary," "internal," and ultimately solipsistic, and reconsider it in light of his polyphonic re-creation of societal discourse. For what Hazlitt calls Byron's refusal to depict the "crowd of living men and women, the endless groups" is in fact countered by his capacity for speaking with the voice of others, for engendering dialogue—for reclaiming "fame" and "rumor." If Byron does (in Hazlitt's words) "think that there is nothing in the world out of a man's self," he also extrapolates beyond this self by recovering a dialogic "world of words." Indeed, it is Hazlitt who captures the essence of Byronic style when he suggests in 1824 that "Sir Walter Scott is the most *dramatic* writer now living; and Lord Byron is the least so" (*Spirit of the Age*, 165, 166). For Byron's dialogic style of reconstituted voices seeks to create not drama but ventriloquism: the representation of societal discourse *through the medium of his own voice*. He seeks not to dramatize *others*' voices mimetically, but to locate his *own* voice in relation to those around him;[8] as Bakhtin puts it, his task is "to find one's own voice and to orient it among other voices, to combine it with some and to oppose it to others, to separate one's voice from another voice with which it has inseparably merged. . . . It must find itself, reveal itself among other words . . ." (1984, 239).

Notes

1. Byron's alleged "spontaneity" has by now become a critical commonplace; see, for instance, Cooke (1975) and Ridenour (1960).

2. Peter J. Manning, "*Don Juan* and Byron's Imperceptiveness to the English Word," 208; emphasis added. Manning further illustrates how *Don Juan* evokes a "poetics based not on the word but on words" (208).

3. See Coleridge, *Shorter Works and Fragments*, 11.1:369.

4. Byron's multiphasic narrative thus enacts a process of self-creation: it juxtaposes aspects of the psyche in order to reveal them, to develop their implications. Here again the critic who has most thoroughly explained this ontological connection between opposing voices is Bakhtin. In his formulation, the opposing voice is an "other"—a voice that enables a speaker to establish selfhood or what Bakhtin calls "consciousness." He writes, "I

am conscious through another, and with the help of another. The most important acts constituting self-consciousness are determined by a relationship toward another consciousness (toward a *thou*)" (1984, 287). For Bakhtin, this "*thou*" hypostatizes self-consciousness— which is to say that only such interchange (what he refers to as "dialogue") can make the self aware of its own distinctness, can actually unveil the self to itself. He goes on to say that "in dialogue a person not only shows himself outwardly, but *he becomes for the first time that which he is*—and, we repeat, not only for others but for himself as well. To be means to communicate dialogically" (1984, 252; emphasis added). In the case of *Don Juan*, then, dialogue with the many voices in the poem enacts the ego. As Bakhtin says later,

> The hero's attitude toward himself is inseparably bound up with his attitude toward another, and with the attitude of another toward him. His consciousness of self is constantly perceived against the background of the other's consciousness of him— "I for myself" against the background of "I for another." Thus the hero's words about himself are structured under the continuous influence of someone else's words about him. (1984, 207)

Consciousness thus dissolves unless projected against the "background" of the other. The limits of the "I" emerge only amid contrasts with the "thou," much as the Freudian ego glows only within the shadow of the superego. We can say that when Byron writes in a diverse array of voices, he recognizes that "consciousness of self is constantly perceived against the background of the other's consciousness of him." When he includes the voices of Pope and Dryden, he acknowledges that only in engaging the other does he "become for the first time that which he is." In either case, establishing the ego is a contrastive act, a matter of envisioning the other as "background" for identity. It is not extraordinary, then, that Byron would abhor Wordsworthian egotism since, again, "to be means to communicate dialogically"—and only this dialogic presence can sustain his "consciousness of self." In the end, these conflicting voices are "*life . . . the thing*" to Byron.

Indeed, throughout *Don Juan* the self-affirming other is *necessarily* a separate voice— and the foregoing social "interorientations" are necessarily spoken, what Bakhtin refers to as "dialogues." "Life," he writes, "by its very nature is dialogic. To live means to *participate* in dialogue: to ask questions, to heed, to respond, to agree, and so forth" (1984, 293; emphasis added). Later, he goes on to explain this desire to envoice the self through dialogue, to hypostatize one's ego: "To find one's own voice and to orient it among other voices, to combine it with some and to oppose it to others, to separate one's voice from another voice with which it has inseparably merged—these are the tasks that the heroes solve in the course of the novel. And this determines the hero's discourse. It must find itself, reveal itself among other words" (1984, 239). Here again, the process of defining the self is both contrastive and verbal: one must "oppose" one's "voice" to another. In *Don Juan*, too, the central, most common narrative voice must "orient [themselves] among other voices"; each must "find itself, reveal itself among" the spoken responses of inadequate listeners. Only such interchanges can resonate the social self.

If we reconsider Byron in light of Bakhtin, moreover, the foregoing exchange between "I" and "other" comes to reflect on Byron's own interchanges between narrative voices. In both cases, multivocal narrative enables an author to fathom the self—"to become for the first time that which he is." "To find one's own voice," he writes, one must "oppose it to others." The purpose of depicting these voices is not mimetic, but developmental: they serve not merely to duplicate vocal interchange, but to enact an ontological process of "finding one's voice."

5. Compare 3.98.100.

6. Compare 11.53.419.

7. Byron's ambivalence concerning the politics of literary reputation manifests itself in his paradoxical treatments of both transient and historical fame. On the one hand, such fame sounds the hollow echo of false reputation, the present repetition of rumors, scandal, and gossip. Yet, on the other hand, the creation of a literary reputation can also instantiate a poet's temporal connection within literary history—that historical continuum or lineage in which authors both ventriloquize the past and project their private voices into the future. By locating himself within this continuum, Byron effectively invokes both his literary predecessors and his proleptic successors. Indeed, it is this historicized linkage with both past and future voices that is represented by what I have termed Byron's dialogic language.

Thus the dual potential for fame both to scandalize and to historicize the poet underlies Byron's entire conception of literary reputation. It is this same ambivalence, moreover, that Hazlitt recognizes in the following passage—though he finally comes to misapprehend its meaning:

> [Byron] takes the highest points in the history of the world, and comments on them from a more commanding eminence: he shews us the crumbling monuments of time, he invokes the great names, the mighty spirit of antiquity. The universe is changed into a stately mausoleum:—in solemn measures he chaunts a hymn to fame. Lord Byron has strength and elevation enough to fill up the moulds of our classical and time-hallowed recollections, and to rekindle the earliest aspirations of the mind after greatness and true glory with a pen of fire. . . . Lord Byron seems to cast himself indignantly from "this bank and shoal of time," or the frail tottering bark that bears up modern reputation, into the huge sea of ancient renown, and to revel there with untired, outspread plume. Even this in him is spleen—his contempt of his contemporaries makes him turn back to the lustrous past, or project himself forward to the dim future! (1825, 169–70)

For more on Byron's ambivalence concerning literary fame and history, see McGann (1985).

8. Hazlitt's view is again revealing on this point. He writes, "Instead of taking his impressions from without, in entire and almost unimpaired masses, he moulds them according to his own temperament, and heats the materials of his imagination in the furnace of his passions" (1825, 161).

Works Cited

Bakhtin, Mikhail. *Problems of Dostoevsky's Poetics*. Translated and edited by Caryl Emerson. Minneapolis: University of Minnesota Press, 1984.

———. *Speech Genres and Other Late Essays*. Translated by Vern W. McGee. Edited by Caryl Emerson and Michael Holquist. Austin: University of Texas Press, 1986.

Byron, George Gordon. *Byron's Letters and Journals*. 12 vols. Edited by Leslie Marchand. Cambridge: Harvard University Press, 1973–82.

———. *The Complete Poetical Works*. 5 vols. Edited by Jerome J. McGann. Oxford: Oxford University Press, 1986.

Coleridge, Samuel Taylor. *Shorter Works and Fragments*. Vol. 11.1 of *The Collected Works of Samuel Taylor Coleridge*. Edited by H. J. Jackson and J. R. de J. Jackson. Princeton, N.J.: Princeton University Press, 1995.

Cooke, Michael G. "Byron's *Don Juan*: The Obsession and Self-Discipline of Spontaneity." *Studies in Romanticism* 14, no.3 (Summer 1975): 285–302.

Hazlitt, William. *The Spirit of the Age: or Contemporary Portraits.* London: Henry Colburn, 1825.

Kroeber, Karl. *British Romantic Narrative.* Ithaca, N.Y.: Cornell University Press, 1975.

McGann, Jerome J. "Byron, Mobility, and the Poetics of Historical Ventriloquism." *Romanticism Past and Present* 9, no.1 (1985): 67–82.

———. *Don Juan in Context.* Chicago: University of Chicago Press, 1976.

Manning, Peter J. "*Don Juan* and Byron's Imperceptiveness to the English Word." *Studies in Romanticism* 18, no.2 (Summer 1979): 207–33.

Ridenour, George M. *The Style of Don Juan.* New Haven, Conn.: Yale University Press, 1960.

Trelawny, Edward John. *Recollections of the Last Days of Shelley and Byron.* Boston: Ticknor and Fields, 1858.

Marxism, Romanticism, and Postmodernism

An American Case History

Prof. J.: Then what can it mean, to practice a Marxist literary criticism?

Prof. M.: In 1988?[1] Simply this: the appropriation of a set of sociological and historical tools, and an emphasis on materialist analyses of culture and society.

To the degree that Marxist thought has (historically) also invested itself in a philosophy of historical determinism, its studies of cultural work have tended to be coherently, sometimes even rigidly, organized. Marxist thought has always been closely tied to teleologal, holist, and organic conceptions—a feature of Marxism that has proved extremely significant so far as the American appropriation of Marxist criticism is concerned. Its holism marries nicely with some essential commonplaces of mid- and late-twentieth-century American critical theory, most obviously with the synthetic emphases of the New Criticism and its various structuralist inheritors.

Prof. J.: But in a Marxist view synthetic processes are organized through collisions and contradictions. Classical Marxist theory would therefore incline to display a poem or a novel as a reflection, perhaps even an instance, of significant social instabilities or dislocations. There is a liberal American equivalent of those kinds of contradiction that the New Criticism called "ambiguity." And while a clear analogy may be seen between these two ideas ("contradiction" and "ambiguity"), in the end they are quite different. Where the one—ambiguity—funds stabilities and continuities, the other—contradiction—has in view instabilities and more-or-less radical change. Marxist contradiction reflects dangerous social emergencies; to the degree that New Criticism concerns itself with anything extratextual, its tensions and ambiguities would reflect positive social dynamisms.

Prof. A.: So?

Prof. M.: These differences describe certain institutional behaviors in the American academy, particularly during the past twenty years or so when we saw the emergence of "Deconstruction in America." For the conceptual self-representations of deconstruction show remarkable symmetries with certain aspects of Marxist thought, as the influential journal *Glyph* indicates so clearly. With deconstruction, the hermeneutics of "ambiguity" and "tension" give way to the hermeneutics of suspicion, of "repressed contents," of "instabilities," of contradiction. Indeed, it is in this period that Marxist ideas and literary strategies flooded the American academic market. This is not to say that Marxist thought and deconstruction represent, or imagine themselves to be, congruent movements in recent American literary studies. On the contrary, in fact: for the social and historical orientation of Marxism has generally been despised by the subject-oriented procedures of deconstruction, while the latter has often been judged simply a set of textual technologies, more-or-less useful *as technologies*, but utterly void of an activist social and educational agenda by Marxist theorists.

This schematic history is familiar to all of us, I daresay. I give it here only to draw your attention to a crucial element in Marxism that I have not yet emphasized, but that your initial question clearly reflected: Marxism's commitment to fundamental (as opposed to reformist) social change. This commitment is foundational in the precise historical sense that Marxism reflects upon capitalist society as an engine for generating exploitation and social inequities. The Marxist view is that these oppressions are class-based, that they are systemic, and that they will be overcome only with a radical transformation of political, social, and economic relations. In simple but not (therefore) inaccurate terms, capitalist society is structured to privilege the rich and to exploit the poor.

These ideas have taken a singular form since the period of the Russian Revolution. Oddly, the continuity of important and influential Marxist thought after the revolution was not maintained by the originary "Marxist" and socialist society, the Soviet Union. For the past seventy years Marxist thought has flourished, as it did from the first, in various pre- or parasocialist societies: the Western societies of Europe still dominated by capitalism or even by fascism, the third world, China. The exceptions to this rule—most spectacularly, the work of Mikhail Bakhtin and his circle—operated at the periphery of Soviet cultural life.

Reactionary commentators who have observed this situation have tended to regard it as the sign of a god that failed, as definitive proof of the poverty of Marxist theory and practice. But a "Marxist"—as opposed to a "Soviet"—view of the matter would be, has been, very different. For it is arguable, and it has been argued (by Marxists), that to the extent the Soviet Union organized itself—bureaucratized itself—*against* change and its own social contradictions, it had abandoned its revolutionary programs. Trotsky and Luxemburg merely stand at the head of a long and sometimes tragic red line.

The recent emergence of a significant body of Marxist thought in America there-fore calls attention to the critical imperative driving Marxist reflection. In such a context, an important question arises and must be faced: How does Marxism oper-ate in the theater of American pluralism? Have Marxist ideas been appropriated as a set of research tools and protocols for literary scholars, or do they involve a radi-cal critique of the American theater of pluralism? Do they make a call for funda-mental social and institutional change? Are they programmatic in this respect?

Prof. J.: Exactly my question. And the problem strikes close to the work of cer-tain Marxist-influenced critics and scholars of the modern period (that is, the pe-riod that saw the rise of the novel, the institutionalization of Kantian-based aesthet-ics, and the emergence of American culture). This is of course the period of capitalist development, early to late (so-called). For Marxist criticism, in that context, neces-sarily finds itself in an acutely problematic relation to its own materials, subject matter, and procedures.

I can explain this best by giving an example. In recent years a "new historicism" has been said to have arisen in literary studies. This general rubric has been used to characterize a diverse group of academics who operate in sociohistorical frames of reference. Marxist-influenced critics and scholars have sometimes been associated with this phenomenon, but to the degree that they embrace Marxian ideas and procedures, to that extent they have generally refused the designation. Marjorie Levinson explains this refusal by observing that "historicism," whether of the "old" nineteenth-century kind or of the "new" types associated with the journal *Repre-sentations*, does not characteristically make a problem of its own subject matter and critical procedures.[2] Historicism, new or old, is fundamentally a structural and formal set of operations; Marxist criticism, by contrast, is not Marxist if it is not dialectical.

Marxism is a set of tools and ideas that emerged in a critical relation to its own immediate context: capitalism. Its founding years mark out the period of its so-to-speak "happy consciousness," the period when Marxist studies underwrote them-selves with the systematic formalisms appropriated from the Hegelian absolutes. But Marxism, the critical method that included history in its procedures, would eventually find itself included in history in ways it had not been able to imagine, and least of all foresee. As a consequence, Marxist thought from approximately 1930 to the present was driven to operate at a metacritical level. As a set of descriptive and analytical tools for studying human beings and societies in their historical re-lations, Marxist thought was ultimately led to conclude that it had to factor its own activities into its critical equations. Marxism was a variable value as much as any other.

Prof. M.: Yes, and this understanding was forced upon Marxist thought by its own most privileged category, the experience of history. Yet the event, which came as a profound theoretical crisis in Marxism, proved a theoretical boon to its subse-quent development. From the heterologies of Bakhtin and the Frankfurt school to the post-Marxism of Bourdieu and Baudrillard, Marxist thought has developed an astonishing range of critical skills for the study of cultural phenomena. These tools and skills have been widely appropriated in American literary studies over the past fifteen years or so. Nonetheless, in America the question remains: Has the implementation of Marxist critical strategies become a new kind of formalism, simply another "method" or "critical structure" in the market of literary studies?

Prof. J.: Clearly, in some sense, the answer must be yes. Indeed, one will find that representation of the situation quite common now: in the way departments display themselves to prospective students and faculty, in the organization of courses in criticism and theory, in the eclectic (one might even say balkanized, or pragmatic) conceptualization of critical activities generally. Like "feminism," "intertextuality," "deconstruction," "new historicism," and so forth, Marxist studies can be offered as and taken for an optional procedure one may choose to identify with (as a move in one's personal goals within the educational institution), or as a set of critical strategies one may decide to employ or not, depending on the circumstances. Indeed, as modern Marxism has deliberately underprivileged itself, as it has laid itself under its own historical critique, it has opened itself to democratizing processes.

Prof. M.: And in that event, as I have said, Marxist work in America has raised a difficult problem for itself. For it must be a serious question now whether the pluralization of Marxist thought is part of a self-critical investigative procedure, an opening of its own doors of perception, or whether such pluralization entails rather an abandonment of critical reflection altogether, a turning away from—even a tacit acceptance of—the real contradictions and disfigurements in American society, and a concentration upon merely formal and subjective matters (for example, the development of various technical skills and methods, or what we call literary criticism, and the pursuit of the theology of the text, or what we call literary theory).

Prof. A.: A particularly acute form of this problem emerges in the work of Professor Jerome McGann, an American scholar whose work centers in this pivotal modernist moment, the romantic period. Unlike Frederic Jameson and Frank Lentricchia—the one primarily a theoretician, the other primarily a critic of culture—McGann has never been anything but a *literary* critic in the narrowest sense. His interpretive work characteristically gravitates around "readings" of particular texts, "interpretations" whose originary models are clearly those produced in the period of the New Criticism. These interpretations, moreover, are grounded in sets of detailed and often highly technical matters, scholarly and archival materials that are drawn forth in order to highlight those sociohistorical aspects of a text which are occluded at the surface of its various illusions. Jameson and Lentricchia generate literary interpretations, but they do not interrogate their texts with the often-microscopic attention upon which McGann insists. That McGann is also a scholarly editor, an editorial theorist, and a textual scholar (in the technical sense of that technical term) is not surprising. Besides, if his work shows the marked influence of Bakhtin, Benjamin, and Habermas—seminal figures for all current Marxist studies—his scholarly, not to say pedantic, face is revealed in two other unusual but equally important influences. The Italian Marxists Galvano della Volpe and

Sebastiano Timpanaro are invoked at crucial moments in his work, and both of these critics are themselves, like McGann, distinctly scholastic figures, persons who used to be called, and who are still often called, philologians (at least in the traditional European university system, both Eastern and Western).

McGann's work is therefore often highly technical and specialized. Adorno might have scorned it as positivist. Yet because he himself unequivocally situates his work in Marxian terms, it is fair to ask in what its Marxism could consist.

This problem can be illuminated, I think, by beginning with one of his foundational ideas: his social theory of "the text." McGann's view here cuts sharply across and against the theory of the text that stretches from the New Criticism, on one hand, and the Barthesian and deconstructive theory of the text, on the other. McGann does not move into an interpretive operation without having first analyzed the so-called text into three distinct phases or aspects. As he puts it, one must "distinguish 'the text' (or the poem as a purely linguistic event) from the 'version' (or the immediate and integral physical object 'through which' the 'text' is being executed), and make yet a further distinction of 'text' and 'version' from the 'work' (this term to stand for some more global constitution of the poem."[3] These distinctions will arise, clearly, only if one has made a series of microstudies of the text, studies that depend for their execution upon the existence of research archives. The critical and interpretive exposure of literature is in this sense fundamentally sociohistorical, or as scholars used to say, philological.

Correlative with this "theory of the text" is a set of investigative protocols designed to clarify the literary event even further. According to McGann, literary works are best conceived as events rather than as objects, as acts of representation rather than as representations. I shall return to this important idea later. For the moment we should observe that this eventual conception of literary works entails certain specific investigative procedures. Criticism is thereby structured as a kind of double helix, an interconnected investigation of the textual history of the work, on one hand, and the reception history on the other. Interpretation begins as a set of extremely detailed (and they would be, if they could be, exhaustive) descriptions of the literary work at every level of its structure and every phase of its development. For McGann, to display the operations of the double helix—to observe the historical interaction of its two strands (textual history and reception history)—is to raise the literary work out of a historical amnesia.

These operations, according to McGann, always and inevitably reveal a Bakhtinian heteroglossia. The textual history imbeds different and often conflicting voices even at its most primitive levels (at the linguistic level, for example, and at the level of the work's originary, "authorial" constitution). These "textual" voices only multiply further as the work moves through its later developments, through its many subsequent material constitutions, its many "versions" (as McGann calls them). A congruent and interactive situation prevails in the work's reception history, which is marked by a similar multiplicity of voices. For McGann, to expose these complex and interacting sociohistories is in itself a critical act, an act of re-membering.

One last detail of this general project must be clarified. For McGann, the complex dialectic of social subjects living and dead is ideological at every point, with "ideology" here understood in the classical Marxist sense of "false consciousness." As he puts it in a recent formulation, "the body of literature is a body of falsehood" whose function is Blakean: to "Give a Body to Falshood that it may be cast off for ever."[4] The phrase "for ever" is there understood as a process that goes on "for ever," *in perpetuum* rather than *in eternum.* Thus if McGann says, after Arnold, that literature embodies "the best that has been known and thought in the world," he also says, after Benjamin, that "every document of civilization is at the same time a document of barbarism."

Now, to the degree that this structure of thought confronts Kantian-based conceptions of art and literature, it clearly represents a radical departure. In this view literary work (including those specific events we call "literary works") is not disinterested, is not aesthetic, is not subjective. Furthermore, it is not even integral and self-consistent. All such work is in every case, in all such works, marked not merely by the classic Marxist "contradiction," it also displays random elements, as well as patterns of congruence and incongruence, consequence and inconsequence. The structure is much closer to what mathematicians call "fractal," a form of "chaos" in the technical sense of that term.

This imagination of works of imagination as "chaotic"—as eventual forms marked equally, and contradictorily, by order and randomness—institutes a radical critique of the dominant Western and capitalist ideas about art and literature over the past two hundred years. It is a theory of literature, moreover, as we have seen, deeply in debt to the entire history of Marxist thought. But is it *Marxist?* The problem is not so much a theoretical one, that McGann's thought contravenes certain (apparently essential) Marxist ideas about the organic and dialectical structure of literary works, and about the historically determinate character of every social event, including that social event we call poetry or literature. These ideas are certainly contravened by McGann, whose subjects of study display at every point both determinacy and indeterminacy, organic form and arbitrary ornament, consciousness and nonconsciousness. Rather, the problem arises as a kind of metadeterminacy that appears to govern the immediate social subject, the specific current acts of critical reflection. This is not the Hegelian determinacy of the progress of the history of consciousness, so cherished by classical Marxist thought. It is rather the determinacy of atomization and randomness, the immobilization of the social subject in the face of an indeterminacy (the multiply voiced social text) that will never yield to consciousness. In the words of a recent lecture, "experience always outruns conception."[5] But the question then arises, Why does this remark not simply translate into that mordant Yeatsian observation that Yeats stole from Shelley and then deradicalized: "The best lack all conviction while the worst / Are full of passionate intensity"?

McGann argues frequently against that passivist theory of literature which, in Auden's famous revisionist (and inaccurate) formulation, declares that "poetry makes nothing happen." On the contrary, for McGann, "poetry is a deed of language," or—in an alternative formulation—"poems are acts of communication." Consequently, critical reflection on poetry is an effort to declare not what poems *mean*, but "what they are doing in saying what they say."[6] But such a view surely contradicts McGann's correlative ideas about "art as experience," for poetic acts (including the acts of criticism) cannot possibly know what they are doing in saying what they say. They cannot because "experience always outruns conception," which is itself a condition predicated by the originary Bakhtinian insights into the multiplied voices and histories speaking through and occupying "the texts."

Prof. J.: Well, if "contradiction" is to be the criterion by which we judge the adequacy of thought, then we will have to give up thinking.

Prof. A.: It is not the "contradictions" of McGann's work that present a problem: it is the atomized and indeterminate—the "chaotic"—situation that his kind of "contradictions" foster. In classical Marxist thought, "contradiction" is a field of dynamic instabilities that develop linearly and progressively. In McGann, however, contradiction appears as a set of nonlinear equations that cannot be solved, for which there are no integrals. McGann's theory therefore maps a field of dynamic change that exhibits determinateness but not determinability.

Prof. J.: I don't understand mathematics. Can you change your metaphor; can you speak in English?

Prof. A.: Within certain limits defined by the initial materials, literary works can mean—can be made to mean—anything. In more practical terms, the uses to which they are put, the tasks they perform in society, cannot be determined, for good or for ill. As they tell the truth, it is a truth that may or may not set you free.

Prof. J.: What is this, neo-Kantianism? The work of art as "disinterested," as "the still point in the turning world"? The view that poetry and art are nonideological hardly seems to me a Marxist idea, and it is certainly not McGann's idea. The view that literary work is a praxis, a "deed of language," clearly entails an ideological function.

Prof. M.: Could I induce you both to make a Lucretian swerve from this topic you are embroiled in? It seems a bit theological to me anyhow, and has us drifting from the key issues—well, has me drifting at any rate. But as I drifted I was thinking back to something Ms. A. was saying about poetry as an act of re-membering multiple voices. The great American scholar Milman Parry once described such a process in the following graphic metaphor: "I make for myself a picture of great detail." And I recall McGann appropriating that very description from Parry several times in his work. But he makes an important alteration to it: he removes the first-person syntax. His formulation thus keeps the concept of the "picture of great detail," but refuses to see the picture as a purely subjective creation.[7] This refusal seems to define for him the objective status of literary activity. The literary work comes to appear not merely as an object, the thing "fixed and dead," as Coleridge once described the "object as object." It appears rather a complex, multiply voiced subject of study interacting dialectically with immediate criticism, that other multiply voiced subject engaged in the critical process of literary work. These two subjects perpetually interrogate each other. They are both social subjects, and their interaction is together *the* social subject of literary study.

This seems to me the *object* of McGann's criticism: to re-present, or re-member, that social subject, to perpetuate its activity. His literary criticism, in particular the set-piece acts of interpretation focusing on specific works, seem to me allegories — extended figures — of his social subject, the social text. And I set before you here, by way of illustration, one of his recent interpretive allegories. We should probably have to call them not "Allegories of Reading," after De Man, but "Allegories of Communicative Exchange."

Byron's "Fare Thee Well!"

As we know, Byron addressed this notorious poem to his wife at a volatile time, during the marriage separation controversies which stretched over the first five months of 1816.[8] It descends to us largely through one line of interpretation, where it is read as a *cri de coeur* from a heartbroken husband.[9] This is the way the poem was read by many people in 1816. Madame de Stael, for instance, and Sir Francis Burdett, and various reviewers all read it this way and praised it extravagantly.[10] And Wordsworth read it this way as well, only he anticipated the common later judgment that the poem is hopelessly mawkish: "disgusting in sentiment, and in execution contemptible. . . . Can worse doggrel be written?"[11]

But another, very different reading sprang up when the poem began circulating in 1816, like tares among the wheat of that first reading. Byron's friend Moore — who was later to endorse the sentimental theory of the poem — was at first deeply suspicious of "the sentiment that could, at such a moment, indulge in such verses."[12] Moore did not elaborate on his suspicions, but others did. The reviewer of *The Prisoner of Chillon and Other Poems* in the *Critical Review* of November 1816 paused to reflect on the earlier "domestic" poem:

> for many who disapproved most of his lordship's . . . publication of his "Farewell" address, as inflicting a parting and lasting pang upon his lady, thought that the lines were most delightfully pathetic, and wondered how a man, who shewed he had so little heart, could evince such feeling. They did not know how easy it was for a person of his lordship's skill to fabricate neatly-turned phraseology, and for a person of his lordship's ingenuity to introduce to advantage all the common-places of affection: the very excellence of that poem in these particulars, to us and to others, was a convincing proof that its author had much more talent than tenderness.[13]

As it happens, Anabella herself, the person to whom "Fare Thee Well!" was most directly addressed, read the poem in just this insidious way. It seemed to her yet another instance of Byron's "talent for equivocation . . . of [which] I have had many proofs in his letters."[14] On 13 Feb., a month before Byron wrote his poem, she explained this "talent" further and pointed out that she learned about it from Byron himself:

> I should not have been *more* deceived than I was by his letters, if he had not pointed out to me in similar ones addressed to others, the deepest design in

words that appeared to have none. On this he piques himself—and also on being able to write such letters as will convey different, or even opposite sentiments to the person who receives them & to a stranger.[15]

"Every day," she added, "proves deeper art" in her husband. What she most feared was "this ambiguity of Language in the Law," that it would give Byron an advantage over her in the Separation proceedings.

Anabella went on to add two observations which are equally interesting and shrewd. Byron's skill in manipulating language reminded her of a passage in *Lara* (I.504–9) in which the deportment of that Byronic hero is exposed as a text of such ambiguity that, reading it, one cannot be certain if it signals a heart filled with "the calmness of the good" or with a "Guilt grown old in desperate hardihood." And she added that this skill with words was one "he is *afraid* of" himself.

In a good essay W. Paul Elledge has revived a variant of this insidious reading of "Fare Thee Well!" The poem, he argues, is "a portrait of indecision, taut with antithetical tensions"; it "charts . . . the depth and configurations of the poet's ambivalence . . . toward reconciliation with his wife."[16] Although Elledge is, I believe, certainly correct in this reading of the poem, he does not go nearly far enough, either substantively or methodologically. In this respect the readings of both the *Critical* reviewer and Lady Byron seem to me more weighty and profound.

What Anabella and the *Critical* reviewer call attention to are the social contexts in which the poem was executed. Anabella was peculiarly alive to such matters because they touched upon her life in the most important ways. "Fare Thee Well!" was not simply a thing of beauty, an aesthetic object spinning in the disinterested space of a Kantian (or Coleridgean) theoretical world. It was an event in the language of art, specifically located, and she registered that event in particular ways. To her the Separation controversy came to involve two primary matters. There was first the matter of the law, and who, in the complex legal maneuverings, would have power over the other to influence various decisions (Lady Byron feared, for example, that Byron would seek to deprive her of custody of their daughter Ada). And second there was the (closely related) matter of public opinion, and who would enter into and finally emerge from the Separation proceedings with what sort of public image.

When Byron sent her a copy of "Fare Thee Well!" soon after he wrote it, Lady Byron was quick to read it as a shrewd ploy to gain power over her in the context of those two areas of interest which most concerned her. At first she emphasized the "legal" reading, for she felt, as we have already seen, that Byron's various communications were designed to construct a sympathetic self-image in order to improve his bargaining position. "He has been assuming the character of an injured & affectionate husband with great success to some," she remarked in mid-February.[17] When Byron sent her a MS copy of the poem late in March, she wrote ironically to her mother of its apparent tenderness, "and so he talks of me to Every one."[18] But the poem did not disturb her greatly until she learned that Byron intended to print and distribute it privately in London society. This act, she feared, would turn "the Tide of feeling . . . against" her,[19] but she was dissuaded from her first impulse—to publish a rejoinder—by the counsel of Dr. Stephen Lushington.

The significance of all this becomes more clear, I think, if we recall that "Fare Thee Well!" was initially constituted as three very different texts, only two of which were manipulated by Byron, while the other fell under the co-authority of persons and powers who were hostile to him. The first of these texts is the one which originates in the MS poem addressed to Lady Byron, and which Byron caused to have circulated in London in late March and early April. The second is the text privately printed and distributed in fifty copies on 8 April, at Byron's insistence and over the objections of his publisher Murray. Byron's activities here are important to remember because they show that he was manipulating the poem, was literally fashioning an audience for it of a very specific kind. The original MS may have been addressed to his wife, but when copies of that poem began to be made and circulated, a new text started to emerge. The printed text in fifty copies represents the definitive emergence of that text, which was addressed past and through Lady Byron to a circle of people—friends, acquaintances, and other interested parties—whose "reading" and "interpretation" of the poem Byron wanted to generate, and of course influence.

In the most limited sense, Byron wanted his poem to be read as the effusion of an "injured and affectionate husband." Moore's later report in his *Life*, that the MS text he saw was covered with Byron's tears, represents in effect such an interpretation of the poem. But the fact that Byron was also managing a certain kind of circulation for the poem set in motion other forces, and other readings, which were only latent (so to speak) in the verbal MS text. The poem, that is to say, came to be widely seen—and read—as another event in Byron's troubled "domestic circumstances." It is this circulation of the verses which begins to change the meaning of the poem— indeed, which begins to change the poem itself. The words of the original MS do not significantly differ from the privately printed text; nonetheless, that first printed text has become another poem, and one which sets in motion an urgency toward the production of yet another textual change.

This new change is definitive when the privately printed text finally makes its appearance in *The Champion* on 14 April and thence throughout the periodical press. This is a new poem altogether. In the first place, it does not appear alone but alongside "A Sketch," Byron's cutting satire on Mrs. Clermont which he had also put into private circulation in fifty copies several days before he began circulating "Fare Thee Well!" The editors of *The Champion* text so print and position "A Sketch" as to make it an exponent of the "real meaning" of "Fare Thee Well!," that is to say, it is used partly for the light it sheds on "Fare Thee Well!" and as a way of exposing Byron's hypocritical malignancy. In the second place, the farewell poem is accompanied, in *The Champion*, by a long editorial commentary denouncing Byron's character as well as his politics, and explicitly "reading" the two poems as evidence of his wickedness.

The Champion's text of "Fare Thee Well!" is, I would say, the definitive version of the (so to speak) *hypocritical* poem, just as the MS version sent to Lady Byron— which, interestingly, seems not to have survived—would be the definitive version of the *sentimental* poem. The "texts" which extend between these two versions dramatize this first, crucial stage in the poem's processes of transformation. But they do not conclude those processes. Even as *The Champion* text is completing that first stage of the poem's transformations, it has initiated a new stage, the one in which the two faces of this poem are forced to confront one another. And it is in this next stage of its textual development that "Fare Thee Well!" becomes most rich and interesting. This is the poem whose meaning focusses and culminates the controversies among the readers in Byron's day. The question is gone over again and again: is this a poem of love ("sentimental") or a poem of hate ("hypocritical")? The final contemporary text declares that in some important sense it is both. Byron himself produced the materialized version of this culminant text when he published the poem, with the telling epigraph from "Christabel," in his *Poems* (1816).

This is the text which Elledge has recently revived, a work full of painful and even frightening tensions and contradictions. And while I want to salute Elledge's success in rescuing Byron's poem from its impoverished sentimental readings, I must also point out Elledge's insistence—it stems from his New Critical background— that his is not a reading of a work of poetry so much as an exploration of a set of tense personal circumstances: "my concern is less with the poem as poem than with the dynamics of the relationship between poet-husband and audience-wife as Byron represents them."[20] He makes this statement because his notion is that "the poem as poem" is an abstract verbal construct, a "text" that not only can be, but must be, divorced from the social and material formations within which the work was instituted and carried out.

Such an idea commits one to a certain way of reading poetry which seems to me intolerable. But it is a way which is particularly destructive for a poet like Byron, whose poetical language is characteristically executed by invoking and utilizing its available social and institutional resources. More, Byron's work insists that this is the way of all poetry, though some poets and apologists for poetry argue that it is otherwise, that poetry operates in a space of disinterestedness and autonomy. "Fare Thee Well!" is therefore, in this respect, a kind of metapoem, a work which fore-grounds Byron's ideas about what poetry actually is and how it works.

Byron himself seems to have recognized very clearly—that is to say, with pain and reluctance—the full significance of his poetic practice. In writing and circulat-ing "Fare Thee Well!" he was the author and agent of the completed work, the one who finally would be responsible for all of the texts. Yet while Byron authored those texts, he could not fully control them—this, the fate of all poets, is sometimes called their "inspiration"—so that in the end he found that he too, like everyone else who would involve themselves with the poem, would have to trust the tale and not the teller. His discovery of this, a bitter revelation, would soon find expression in an-other of the "Poems on his Domestic Circumstances": the "[Epistle to Augusta]" which he wrote in the summer of 1816. Reflecting on that "talent for equivocation" which he flaunted before his wife, Byron would expose its equivocal character.

> The fault is mine—nor do I seek to screen
>   My errors with defensive paradox—
> I have been cunning in mine overthrow
>   The careful pilot of my proper woe.
>   (21–24)

Which is as much to say of that most "cunning" of his poems to date, "Fare Thee Well!," that it tells more than one would have imagined possible, tells more than its own author wanted told.

I shall shortly return to indicate what I believe this kind of analysis signifies for any concrete "reading" of "Fare Thee Well!" But first I would ask you to reflect upon certain matters of general relevance for Byron's poetry. When we say that Byron's is a highly rhetorical poetry we mean—we should mean—not that it is loud or over-blown, but that it is always, at whatever register, elaborating reciprocities with its audience. These reciprocities, like all social relations, accumulate their own histo-ries as time passes and more interchanges occur—and we then call these, as Donald Reiman has called them, "the cumulative effect" of the work.[21] New poetry is writ-ten—and read—within the context of those accumulations. The development of the

various texts of "Fare Thee Well!" between March and November 1816 is a minia-
ture example of how these reciprocities can get played out.

I want to emphasize that Byron wrote this way throughout his life. The masterpiece
of *Don Juan* is a work of, quite literally, *consummate* skill, because the whole of his life
and career is gathered into it. Without an awareness of, an involvement in, that poem's
"cumulative effect" one will be reduced simply to reading its words: as Eliot in this
connection *might* have said, *not* to have the experience *and* to miss the meaning.

Related to this rhetorical framework of the poetry is Byron's habit of manipulating
his texts. To present a work through a "cumulative" context is to open it to changes
and modifications, in fact, to new opportunities of meaning: not so much, as Coleridge
would have had it, the "reconciliation" of "opposite and discordant qualities" as their
artistic exploitation. "Fare Thee Well!" did not bring about any reconciliations, poetic
or otherwise, it raised a tumult of new discords and conflicts. Yet it is those very tumults,
and their artistic significance, which turned the period of Byron's separation—from
his wife, from England—to a watershed in his career, and in his understanding of what
was involved, for him, in his methods of poetic production.

To understand this better we have to retreat in time, to Byron's years at Harrow
and especially Cambridge, when he took his first lessons in the art of literary equivocation. Byron told his wife that he had a talent for that sort of thing, and Louis
Crompton's recent book *Byron and Greek Love* has shown that it was a mode of writing
practised by Byron's circle of Cambridge friends—a deliberate and quite literally a
methodical set of procedures for saying one thing and meaning something else.
Briefly, they cultivated a mode of homosexual doubletalk.

One of Byron's first epistolary exercises in this equivocal style was in his letter to
Charles Skinner Matthews of 22 June 1809; Matthews' answer to this letter is important because of its explicit discussion:

> In transmitting my dispatches to Hobhouse, my carissime Buron I cannot
> refrain from addressing a few lines to yourself: chiefly to congratulate you on
> the splendid success of your first efforts in *the mysterious*, that style in which
> more is meant than meets the eye. . . . [B]ut I must recommend that
> [Hobhouse] do not in future put a *dash* under his mysterious significances,
> such a practise would go near to letting the cat out of the bag. . . . And I posi-
> tively decree that every one who professes *ma methode* do spell the term wch
> designates his calling with an e at the end of it—*methodiste*, not method*ist*,
> and pronounce the word in the french fashion. Every one's taste must revolt
> at confounding ourselves with that sect of . . . fanatics.[22]

Byron's letter may in fact have been his "first effort" at writing in Matthews' particular dialect of "the *mysterious*," but it was a language he was already practised in, and
one which would receive its apotheosis in the incredible display of puns and coded
talk that constitute *Don Juan*.

Matthews' letter is also interesting because it suggests that the use of this kind of
style is a game that can be played with, and that its practitioners should think of
themselves as a kind of *elite* group with special gifts and powers. But it was also a
style that ran grave risks for the user. Byron told his wife that he was afraid of his own
skill with this method of writing. And well he might be, for it entailed the conscious
deployment of duplicitous and hypocritical postures.

All of Byron's early tales are written in this equivocal style—which has become, in Byron's hands, a vehicle of immensely greater range and complexity than Charles Skinner Matthews would have imagined possible, had he lived to see Byron's displays. But the more Byron developed his talent for equivocation, the more he built a store of explosive and dangerous contradictions into his work. Those contradictions came to a head during the Separation controversy, and in "Fare Thee Well!" they finally reached their flash point.

That the poem is not what the commonplace "sentimental" reading has taken it to be is exposed unmistakably for us in the initial period of its production and reception. Many readers were alive to its duplicities. The opening four lines, in fact, signal the poem's method by installing a grammatical pun of fundamental importance:

> Fare thee well! and if for ever—
>> Still for ever, fare *thee* well—
> Even though unforgiving, never
>> 'Gainst thee shall my heart rebel.

The sense here urges us to take Lady Byron's as the "unforgiving" heart, but the grammar tells us that heart is Byron's own. The poem will operate under this sign of contradiction to the end. Noteworthy too is Byron's assertion that, though his heart is unforgiving, it will never "rebel" against hers: as if he were imagining their separation and mutual antagonisms succeeding to a second, darker marriage which would "never" be dissolved or put asunder.

In fact, the poem is replete with this kind of complex double-speaking. Ponder, for example, these four lines:

> Would that breast by thee glanc'd over,
>> Every inmost thought could show!
> Then thou would'st at last discover
>> 'Twas not well to spurn it so—
>> (9–12)

It is a nice question what the inmost thoughts of an unforgiving and yet *un*rebellious heart would look like. Blake wrote a great deal of poetry about just such a heart, and he always imagined it as dangerous and fearful. And if we merely "glance over" Byron's lines here we may easily fail to "discover" their full truth: that the passage does not merely tell about the dark truths of unforgiving hearts, it is itself executing them. "'Twas not well to spurn it so" is a warning of possible danger, but as coming from *this* speaker it carries as well a threatening message and rhetoric.

Of course the poem delivers these kinds of messages obliquely, but in doing so it only increases the volatile character of the text. Because more is meant here than meets the eye directly, the censored materials exert enormous pressure for their freedom of complete expression. The parallel text in Canto III of *Childe Harold's Pilgrimage* meditates the situation by comparing it to the fury of a storm breaking over the Alps: "Could I embody and unbosom now / That which is most within me,— could I wreak / My thoughts upon expression. . . ." (st. 97). And so forth: he longs for "one word [of] Lightening," one word of comfort that would "lighten" his heart of its weight of sorrow, one word of insight that would "enlighten" his understanding of his situation, and one word of power that would, like a bolt of lightening, "blast" and purify those places "where desolation lurk[s]" (st. 95).

Like Manfred—another creature of Separation—who begs from Astarte "one word for mercy" (II.iv.155), Childe Harold's longings remain incompletely satisfied. In all these cases the very effort to achieve some kind of completion, to reconcile the various contradictions, only seems to install them more deeply and more firmly.

Charles Skinner Matthews wrote gaily of his "mysterious" style of discourse, but it was a style which Byron, its supreme master, came to fear as he developed it through his Years of Fame. And well he might have feared it since it was a style which forced into the open the hypocrisies of those who read and write poetry as if it were a beauty or a truth, as if it were something that could be controlled—enlisted to the purposes of either those who produce it or those who receive it. "Fare Thee Well!" is Byron's farewell to the illusion that he could be the master of the artistic powers which were given to him. Written in hopes that it would allow him to control the dangerous cross-currents of his circumstances in 1816, the poem's bad faith—which is its genius—worked to undermine the actual despair latent in such petty hopes.

This interpretation of Byron's "Fare Thee Well!" involves an implicit critique of intrinsic, thematic, and text-centered hermeneutic methods that I want to make explicit. In the first place, important deficiencies follow when circumstances of production are not factored into the interpretive operation. At the most elementary level—at what Blake called "the doors of perception"—readers will be inclined to see, and hence to deal with, only the linguistic text. But the poetic event always comprehends a larger scriptural territory, one which is bibliographically (as well as linguistically) encoded.[23] The physical forms within which poetry is incarnated are abstracted from an interpretive activity only at the price of a serious critical blindness, and a blindness that brings with it little corresponding insight.

The problem emerges dramatically in the work of Blake, whose illuminated texts do not lend themselves to the kind of physical variabilities which are common in the case of typographical texts. I am speaking here of the variabilities which develop when texts are transmitted over time to later readers. That transmission history tends to erase not merely the bibliographical terms in which the texts—the meanings of the texts—were initially encoded, it tends to make us unaware of the presence and significance of bibliographical coding in general. People tend not to realize that a certain way of reading is privileged when "Ode on a Grecian Urn" is read in *The Norton Anthology of English Literature*, and that it is a way of reading which differs sharply from what is privileged in Palgrave's *Golden Treasury* or in the *Oxford Book of Romantic Verse*; and when the poem is (or was) read in other kinds of formats—for example, in its first printing in the *Annals of the Fine Arts*—an entirely different field of reading is once again deployed. Furthermore, the work that descends to us descends through particular forms of transmission, and the work does not pass through those incarnations without having its meaning affected by them. We are able to discern patterns in a work's reception history precisely because those historical influences have inscribed themselves in the works we receive.

The example from Byron, however, underscores yet another important matter. Poetic works are not autonomous in either of the senses that the academy has come, mistakenly, to believe. That is to say, poems are neither linguistically self-contained, nor are they simply the expressed forms of a single—an authorizing and integral—imagination. The actual production of poems is one part of that social dialectic by which they live and move and have their being, one part of the communicative interchange which they always solicit.

The Byron example is especially instructive, I think, because it shows how those interchanges can never be brought under the control of the author. Poems are produced, used, and read in heterogeneous ways; unlike other forms of discourse, in fact, they require—they thrive upon—those diverse forms of life. Crucial parts of those interchanges are encoded in the bibliographical, productive, and reception histories of the poems we read. When we neglect those histories we simply condemn our readings to a culpable—because an unnecessary—ignorance.

Prof. A.: Surely whatever residual "Marxism" one may discover in that unpublished document has been so academicized as to have become a pure formality. An "Allegory of Communicative Exchange" indeed! What pretentiousness and hypocrisy! The problem with such criticism reappears in all his work: they don't *change* anything essential in the way the academy goes about its business.

Prof. M.: But they do make change possible. They postulate, and deploy, a critical procedure where scholarly exchanges reflect each other in distorting, differential mirrors.

Prof. A.: That is simply what you *say*! Such a view would begin to be meaningful only if you could show that McGann's criticism is both true and false. In rhetorical terms, it would have to be a criticism we would want to accept and dismiss at the same time.

Prof. J.: Well, here is another piece of unpublished criticism. McGann has headed it "A Commentary on the Opening Passage of 'Stopping by Woods on a Snowy Evening.'" It seems a finished piece of work, though of course it has to be regarded as in some sense a fragment, given the arbitrary limit it has set to its "commentary." There can be no question, I think, that the piece is authentic. The computer disk is clearly labeled and has many of his other works coded on it, some in working forms. Furthermore, though the piece may appear in certain respects incongruent with his published work, its bibliographical preoccupations have a distinctively McGannian quality. Whatever, I think you will find it scandalous enough, both in itself and in relation to McGann's work in general.

A Commentary on the Opening Passage
of "Stopping by Woods on a Snowy Evening"

What comes to us as the title, the prefatory "Stopping by Woods on a Snowy Evening," is a set of words which, even if we regard them as a single word string, are by no means self-identical. An initial reading may legitimately ask, for example, whether the third word is a common or a proper noun, and hence whether the "stopping" referred to is a casual "stopping by" at the Woods' house, or whether it is a "stopping alongside" a stand of trees. To say that the former reading is eliminated by the first line of the poem is merely to say that one has assented to the traditional formatting imposed upon the words of the poem. As we shall see in a moment, those words carry—fatally, as it were—many more signifying possibilities than the narrow range of significations so cunningly, and deceptively, specified by the received formatting.

But to return for a moment to the "title," or prefatory material. If we put a period after "Stopping by" the title changes; if we put "Stopping" on a line by itself, then place immediately below it, centered, "by Woods," and then on a third line, centered, put "On a Snowy Evening" another set of possible signifiers opens up for us (one much closer, perhaps, to what one could find in verse published in certain periodical formats).

Finally, of course, the words may be imagined to have been so arranged as to set all these (and perhaps other) signifying chains in motion, along with the corresponding diversity of signifiers as well as the contexted referents that they evoke. A multiplied text is latently present in these words, a text which reaches out to the equally multiplied textual codes that are socially dispersed in the audience of readers.

But let us move into the body of the poem's text, specifically, into what the traditional poem sets down as the first two lines, which thus appear thus:

> Whose woods these are I think I know,
> His house is in the village, though;

If we ask, once again, whether the final word of this couplet is a common or a proper noun, we begin to see how arbitrary is the traditional text of these words. Furthermore, if we take "Though" to be the name of the village where "His house" is located, we may find ourselves inclined to construct a wholly different poem here, a wholly different set of signifiers. If a village may be called "Though" we may have found ourselves pitched into a world where "concrete realities" are to be imagined as parts or operations of language. If "Though" is imagined as a village in a purely linguistic "world," that fact may be taken to signify that subordinate clauses are to stand metaphorically for certain types of subordinate political entities, like villages (with the corresponding analogy to be understood as operative—that sentences are "cities," and so on up [and down] the grammatical hierarchy).

This metaphorical structure will incline one to "read" the text very differently from the reading under which the couplet has traditionally functioned as a couplet. These other readings emerge if, following the lead of the work's traditional arbitrary formulae, we arbitrarily shift the punctuation—for instance:

> Whose woods? These are, I think. "I know!
> His house is in the village Though!"

or:

> Whose woods? These are "I think," "I know,"
> "His house" is in the village Though.

In the latter case, the text calls attention to the fact that certain words that are arbitrarily arranged to act as points of reference to an extra-linguistic field (the place of forests and villages, the place where a man named Woods may be imagined to be living) may equally and at the same time function as parts of a system of pure signifiers. In such a case, what has been set in motion is an allegorical work entirely analogous, for example, to the opening of Charles Olson's "In Cold Hell, In Thicket," or to the opening of Olson's more famous precursor text, the *Inferno*:

> Nel mezzo del cammin di nostra vita
> mi ritrovai per una selva oscura

This resonant text calls out to the "woods" in Frost's work, an equally "dark and deep" woods of a self obscured from itself. (And how appropriate it now seems that the text of "Stopping by Woods" should be attached to an author named Frost!) We may

name the woods of the modern poem "I think" and "I know" on the Dantean allegorical analogy, and we add the distinctively postmodern touch by noting that this
woods exists in purely linguistic space, near a village here named "Though."

The immediate conventional power impinging on Frost's work is probably
not Dante, however, but the late Romantic Dante Gabriel Rossetti, whose great
and nightmarish work *The House of Life* seems to be glanced at in Frost's word
"house." The house of Frost's text is partly Rossetti's poetical house, where one frequently encounters a discourse analogous to one that would name a stand of trees "I
think" and, alternatively, "I know." One recalls, for instance, Rossetti's sonnet
"Superscription":

> Look on my face; my name is Might-have-been;
>   I am also called No-more, Too-late, Farewell;

The Rossetti text, where the "house of life" is at all points the house of language, a
house of pure (and impure) signifiers, allows us to appreciate the signifying laby-
rinth into which the Frost text has led us. So bound are we to positivist structures of
reading that we initially overlook the strength of the word-play being carried, and
carried out, in those key terms in the poem's title and first line, "Woods" and "woods."
The words are metaphors, of course, but they are metaphors embedded in a metonymic word-play concealing the correspondent (and purely linguistic) signifier,
"Woulds" and "woulds." "Stopping by Woulds" is a poem about subjunctive states
of desire, and of the darkness and cold with which they seduce and threaten us. To
stop by this "selva oscura" is to confront the promise and the threat of all that we
"would," or "would not," encounter and understand.

More than that, however, the text is about how texts signify in the first place. Poetry
is the discourse that lays bare those signifying mechanisms. Thematizing the work's
textual operations (for example, saying that the poem is about desire and subjunctive states) tends to conceal the more important and powerful communicative exchange executed through the poem. "Stopping by Woods on a Snowy Evening"
displays the heteronomy that Bakhtin, for example, postulated of fictional discourse.

Prof. M.: This cannot be an authentic text. It is a travesty of scholarship and
criticism.

Prof. A.: Perhaps it is authentic. Its absurd frivolity unmasks the hidden face of
McGann's spurious Marxism. The whole thing is a game, a game of academic scholarship whose correspondent breeze is this shameless personal *jeu.*

Prof. J.: Perhaps it is a serious travesty, or even a travesty of seriousness, or both.
The piece reminds me that McGann extolled, in *The Romantic Ideology*, the
deconstructive ironies of Heinrich Heine. In fact, that book seems to me plainly
set on a strange series of self-contradictions. Most apparent, I suppose, is the colli-
sion between the book's authoritative—not to say arrogant—prose style, and its
commitment to the program (dare one say the ideology?) of the romantic ironist.

Prof. A.: I recall that several reviewers have associated McGann's last ten years
of work with postmodern and even De Manian positions. McGann's most recent
books produce studied critiques of De Man, but they seem to me carried out from
a position of sympathy. How could it be otherwise? McGann is after all an open

supporter of that body of flagrantly postmodern work known commonly as "Language Writing."

Prof. M.: But his allegiances emphasize the socially activist orientation of that writing. Language Writing for McGann seems nothing more or less than a contemporary instance of Marxist expression.

Prof. A.: It doesn't matter what he *thinks*. That is not the point. The point is that these kinds of contradiction undermine the seriousness of the work—as if it were all finally inconsequent.

Prof. J.: Contradictions seem of great consequence, as all Marxists think and have always thought. Only when they are not *real* contradictions, even shameful ones, are they inconsequent. Isn't that one of the implicit points of the discussion of Byron's "Fare Thee Well!"? Perhaps the short piece on Frost comes to underscore the point, perhaps its meaning rests in the way it scandalizes the ground of meaning—as if meaning had to seek its renewal through paths of falsification. The pretentiousness and shamelessness within. . . .

[Here the document breaks off, leaving its readers with various problems, and with what seems to us one overriding question, Is this a case of multiple personality disorder, or is it a social text? If so, is it a "Marxist" text? And what is "this" anyway?]

Notes

1. This piece was originally published in the summer 1989 issue of *South Atlantic Quarterly*. It has been revised for this printing.

2. See Marjorie Levinson's introduction to her *Rethinking Historicism: Critical Readings in Romantic History* (Oxford: Basil Blackwell, 1989).

3. Jerome J. McGann, "Theory of Texts," *London Review of Books*, 18 February 1988, p. 21. For an earlier, and slightly different, formulation, see "The Text, the Poem, and the Problem of Historical Method," in his *The Beauty of Inflections: Literary Investigations in Historical Theory and Method* (Oxford: Clarendon Press, 1985), 114–15n., 121.

4. Jerome J. McGann, *Towards a Literature of Knowledge* (Oxford: Clarendon Press, 1989), 32.

5. *Ibid.*, 7. The book *Towards a Literature of Knowledge* comprises McGann's Clark Lectures, delivered at Trinity College, Cambridge, in February 1988.

6. See Jerome J. McGann, *Social Values and Poetic Acts* (Cambridge: Harvard University Press, 1987).

7. *Ibid.*

8. This Jerome J. McGann piece is excerpted from a longer essay, originally given as a lecture in London in 1987, titled "Lord Byron and the Truth in Masquerade."

9. The essential critical discussions of the poem are the following: *The Works of Lord Byron: Poetry*, ed. E. H. Coleridge (London: John Murray, 1898–1904), 3:531–35; David V. Erdman, "'Fare Thee Well!'—Byron's Last Days in England," *Shelley and His Circle: 1773–1832*, ed. Kenneth Neill Cameron (Cambridge: Harvard University Press, 1970), 4:638–65; W. Paul Elledge, "Talented Equivocation: Byron's 'Fare Thee Well!,'" *Keats-*

Shelley Journal 35 (1986): 42–61; and *Lord Byron: The Complete Poetical Works*, ed. Jerome J. McGann (Oxford: Clarendon Press, 1980–   ), 3:493–94.

10. See Ethyl Colburn Mayne, *Byron*, 2d ed., rev. (London: Methuen, 1924), 256, and Erdman, "'Fare Thee Well!,'" 642 and n.

11. See *The Letters of William and Dorothy Wordsworth*, ed. Ernest de Selincourt, 2d ed., rev. by Mary Moorman and Alan G. Hill (Oxford: Clarendon Press, 1970), 3: pt.2:304. Wordsworth's reading is given in a letter to John Scott, who put out the unauthorized printing of Byron's poem (see below).

12. Quoted in Mayne, *Byron*, 256.

13. *Critical Review*, 5th series (December 1816), 577–78.

14. Quoted in Malcolm Elwin, *Lord Byron's Wife* (New York: Harcourt, Brace and World, 1962), 394.

15. *Ibid.*, 400.

16. Elledge, "Talented Equivocation," 43.

17. Elwin, *Lord Byron's Wife*, 409.

18. *Ibid.*, 448.

19. Doris Langley Moore, *The Late Lord Byron* (London: John Murray, 1961), 164.

20. Elledge, "Talented Equivocation," 44n.

21. Donald Reiman, ed., *The Romantics Reviewed, 1793–1830: Contemporary Reviews of British Romantic Writers* (New York: Garland, 1972), Part B (Byron), 4:1779.

22. Quoted in Louis Crompton, *Byron and Greek Love* (Berkeley and Los Angeles: University of California Press, 1985), 128–29.

23. For further discussion of this matter, see McGann, *Social Values and Poetic Acts*, esp. 74–85, and "Theory of Texts."

PART III

DIALOGUE BETWEEN SPEAKERS, READERS, AND AUTHORS

The Essay in English

Readers and Writers in Dialogue

Canons—for conversation.
That their obviousness should procure for them the go-by of some, would
not be surprising. That, however, they find their application in those
everyday scenes of human existence . . . is reason enough for securing for
them a kind reception.

Knickerbocker magazine, September 1836

In a brief piece on "Talking vs. Conversation" published in a New York periodical
of the early nineteenth century, an unknown writer linked facility in conversation
with adeptness in writing essays. He reached back to Cicero for support of his claim
and quoted the Roman orator's "canons for conversation":

—adapt one's manner to the nature of the topic of conversation

—pay close attention to evidence of the state of pleasure and satisfaction of others
within the conversation

—be sincere and show respect for those with whom one converses.

Almost apologetically, the *Knickerbocker* writer prefaced his summary of Cicero's
recommendations with the epigraph above that calls attention to both the "obviousness" of these rules and their ready applicability to everyday experiences.

This unknown writer had no way of knowing that he stood in a long line of commentators—before and after him—who have passed on both rules for conversation
and comments about the close ties between conversations and essays. Since the
sixteenth century essayists and editors of collections of essays alike have called attention to the dialogic nature of the essay and to the plurality of voices within the
form; these commentators have also consistently compared both its form and the
conditions of its reception to those of letters, journals, and conversation.

This chapter takes a look at some of these observations and compares them with
what we have learned about spoken and written genres from some twentieth-

195

century literary theorists. Mikhail M. Bakhtin, V. Voloshinov, and members of the Prague school of linguistics, as well as the philosophers H. Paul Grice and John Searle, and the numerous conversational analysts that have followed them, repeatedly link utterances or texts with their contexts—from the immediate interactive situation of a single exchange to the social and economic conditions that permit certain spoken and written genres to be produced.

Through the writings of these scholars of language run many obvious and everyday observations that might "procure for them the go-by of some." They repeat in various ways the "canons" given by Cicero, and they elaborate the contexts that support them as well as the types of texts that emerge from them. Bakhtin, in discussing the problem of speech genres, tells us that the oral dialogue of the salon and of one's primary circle influences literary language, that the complex process of active speech communication extends well beyond speaker and listener and the speech flow, and that responsiveness means more than merely listening and replying to another's talk.[1] Both Voloshinov and Bakhtin remind us repeatedly that we must attend to the "situation" that gives rise to particular varieties of social communication and ensures the conversational character of even those forms (such as diaries and journals) that we think of as inner speech (Voloshinov 1983, 118–19). Prague school linguists and the Russian Formalists acknowledge that the appropriate study of conversation should be sociological and should take into account possibilities for the use of leisure time and the readiness of a capable audience (Tarde, quoted in Mukarovsky 1977, 83–84). Grice (1989) gives us "conversational postulates" that hold conversationalists to being brief, relevant, and sincere. Searle points out that we have both regulative rules, such as those of etiquette, that regulate preexisting activities, such as the salon, table talk, or the conversation. We also have constitutive rules that create certain types of exchanges, such as chess games, and thus allow us to monitor ongoing behaviors within such occasions (1969, 33–38). A host of linguists, discourse analysts, ethnomethodologists, and ethnographers of communication have elaborated on the constitutive order within single occasions of interaction, both spoken and written. They also have laid out the processes within these by which we manage to establish rapport with others, become involved with them and their messages, and make communication a social activity.

To those outside the world of the specialized study of language, much that is within the "findings" of these language scholars is already known by common sense and may therefore meet a "So what's new?" response. The *Knickerbocker* writer expected Cicero's canons to secure "a kind reception" precisely because they were familiar, agreeable, and obvious. And yet the writer lamented that society all-too-often ignored these "simple principles" and indeed that certain types of individuals could be predicted to ignore them and to display "prominent imperfections of the conversational habits." Here, then, is the reality: the rules *are* obvious and lie within everyday experience, yet we *do not* consistently adhere to them. It matters not whether these rules come to us from experience with nonacademic writers and speakers or from those whose professional commitment is to the study of language; that which is obvious about language, because it both does happen and is expected to happen, slips away from our willingness always to hear these rules or to adhere to those we consistently hold out as ideals. We hasten this slippage when we uproot genres from the situations or relationships upon which they depend.

Two common forms of language reflect this condition. Though both English conversationalists and essayists have repeatedly pointed out the contexts, social conventions, and linguistic features of these two forms, few who have wished to promote or teach these forms in English since the late nineteenth century have acknowledged or adhered to the experts' observations. Social critics, educational reformers, and pedagogues, while calling for ease and excellence in conversation and the essay, have ignored their interdependence, as well as the situations and conventions peculiar to each. Conversation is fundamentally a social process of oral exchange between two or more individuals who share sufficient background knowledge for turn exchanges to take place within a dialogism that takes it for granted that we perceive our own ideas best when set against the perspective of others. It is conversation of this sort that supported the essay into the contemporary era.

Since the late nineteenth century, however, formal education and the journalistic and literary worlds have split in their views of the essay. In both Great Britain and the United States "essay" came to be the term that schoolteachers and professors used to characterize the type of writing students must display before they can pass secondary-school requirements or enter college. The first course that most students take in college is one in which they learn to write "essays" that reflect the orderliness of their thinking and their ability to move from a thesis statement through its support by facts to a summative conclusion. Until students can display their knowledge in such forms, they are excluded from further academic work.

Within journalism, the form is used most often as an editorial frame to reflect the particular political stance of a periodical or the personal revelations of a well-known individual. In numerous literary periodicals, writers, often well-known for their artistry with other literary genres such as novels or poetry, use essays to take up any number of diverse subjects, but most often literary topics.[2]

History

The literary essay in English is a highly vocative text. Essayists themselves, as well as those who recount the history of the form in English, consistently agree that the form has evolved from conversation through letter writing and journal writing to become a highly interactive form that assumes multiple voices including not only the author's personae, but those of the readers as well.

Letters as Friendly Dialogues

During the Renaissance, resurrection of the classical genre of the letter helped prepare the way for the later widespread enthusiasm for the essay (sometimes called the letter-essay). Across Europe it became common to interject letters into long written narratives and occasionally to include within collections of letters classical theoretical writings on the nature and purposes of letters. Renaissance writers recalled the admonitions of Pliny, Cicero, and Quintilian to letter writers regarding the need for brevity, clarity, familiarity of style, and attention to topic as well as to audience. The editor of Aristotle's letters proposed the letter as "a halved dialogue, or part of a conversation with an absent friend" (Guillen 1986, 77). Classical writers emphasized the dialogue of the letter as a gift of friendship in "loose" writing. Epistolary dialogues avoided didacticism, admitted direct acknowledgment of the personae of both writer and reader, and were both plain and elegant in choice of language. In the Hellenistic world letters on astrology, science, and philosophy developed a strong intertextual quality that gave the writer the opportunity to explore a topic and to test ideas by bringing in multiple texts as supporting voices (Doty 1973, 8). Related to dialogue primarily as an expression of friendship, of "presence," letters were intended to be plain, honest, and revealing of the "soul" of the writer. Those letters of this era that debated ethical and moral questions—always without formalized presentation—came to be called "letter-essays" (Doty 1973, 8, 15).[3]

Through the increased use of letter-essays Renaissance writers and readers gained awareness not only of the open interactive nature of letters, but also of a sense of audience that could be characterized such that "the mental relationship with the person in question is indivisible from the conscious process of writing" (Guillen 1986, 81–82). This sense of connection to a listener-reader also fostered stylistic devices overtly imitative of oral language or conversation. Such attempts to recapture the oral had not received approval by classical or Hellenistic writers who feared the intrusion of either mannerisms or extended and broken sentences. During the Renaissance, however, writers came to embrace the goal of exhibiting voice in narrative, adapting language to both addressee and subject. Letters of all types, including those directed to scientific topics, came to interrogate ideas for their relevance to daily existence and varying contexts. Networks of scientists wrote letters to keep the exchange of ideas current and enlivened through questioning and argument. When, in the late seventeenth century, royal academies and societies became established in Great Britain, the form of the scientific essay grew out of earlier letters of those correspondents who had used letters for debates, comparative observations, and reports on experiments (Pearl 1984, 108).

During the fifteenth and sixteenth centuries, writers of other genres also began to take advantage of the literary value of the indiscretionary potential of letters— either when intercepted or preserved beyond writer and originally intended reader. Renaissance writers (especially those of Spain) noted the three-way nature of dialogue: that among the writer's inner voices, that between the writer and assumed reader, and that between the written text and unintended audiences (including even those readers of other literary texts into which letters might find their way).[4] The uncertainty about whether one's letters would remain inclusive only of writer and intended single reader made such writings trilogic, with the third party a potentially prying observer unknown to either member of the original communicative pair.

> The equivocal triangle, the latent voyeurism . . .—the only innocent participant being the original addressee of the letter—exists or increases in the exact degree in which the moral or newsworthy epistle becomes so familiar and private as to be lacking apparently in general interest and only be of concern to immediate friends and near

relatives. What was intended to be read, in principle, is actually reread; and, most important, reread by others. Literary letter reading has to be the rereading of curious minds. *Hence the proximity, when intimacy is shared, not of dialogue but of autobiography and of the forerunners of the essay.* (Guillen 1986, 100–101; my italics)

Among the growing literate class of the late-seventeenth and eighteenth centuries, letters and journals (often described as letters to the self though written with a keen sense of an audience) came increasingly to be public forms.

The intertwined trail of inner individual experience, conversation, letter, long narrative, essay, and literary letter reading received comment repeatedly from editors of collections of letters (either commonplace books or practical manuals for letter writing) and later also from both writers and editors of essay collections. Early letters were dictated or *indited*; even educated writers dictated their letters to a professional scribe and thus the literal voice figured largely in the construction of these forms.[5]

English letter writing evolved into epistolary novels, academic and scientific articles, and letters of highly institutionalized form to accomplish particular speech acts (such as requesting, pleading, and accusing—used in trials). Manuals for letter writing—and the continuing spread of literacy—made it possible for individuals to write their own letters. This evolution of a sense of voice led to "a talking mode (shall we say?) of writing, as natural, almost as easy as speech itself; one that was bound to settle itself at length, and take on a propitious fashion of its own" (Rhys and Vaughan 1913, viii). This talking mode from letter to essay depended on "self-revelation"—the clear indication of the writer as "a self worthy to be spoken of, and a self capable of real speech" (Gass 1985, 25)—in response to the "irritation of the idea" (Dawson and Dawson 1908, 9, 12) needling at the soul and mind of the writer.

The Essay and Conversation

These features of both the context and the text of letters bear close resemblance to those outlined by Michel de Montaigne, the French writer usually credited with establishing the essay as a literary form in the late 1500s. Those who trace the modern history of the essay—whether in English or another language—inevitably point to Montaigne and to the fact that those who brought the essay to English did so with full awareness of his views regarding both text and context: leisurely, serene, and comfortable surroundings should bring forth essays that needed intimate readers willing to inquire into diverse and diverting topics. But such inquiries must be based on reflective observations, contemplated in leisure, and shared as though the audience were friends and relatives.

Though English essayists from Sir Francis Bacon forward contributed their own features to lists of attributes of the essay, all seemed to hold the view that both the letter and the essay said much about both writer and context. Bacon, though far more philosophical in his essay topics than Montaigne had been, also endorsed the conditions that his French predecessor had laid out: "To write just treatises requireth leisure in the writer and leisure in the reader . . ." (1612 preface, n. p.). Bacon called his essays "brief notes" and developed an aphoristic style, aristocratic in its assertive intelligent force. He also added philosophical essays that focused the reader more on the ideas of the writing than on the character and personality of the writer. But throughout the seventeenth century lesser-known English writers continued to help promote the popularity of the personal essay and to sustain the letter-essay responding to curiosity about ideas and depending on keen observations of both the self and the surrounding environment. The casual air that Montaigne had given the essay ensured that personal or familiar essays remained dominant, though they were supplemented occasionally by philosophical and critical essays.

In Great Britain in the eighteenth century, the rise of journalism, and with it the rise of the periodical essay, put essays in the hands and on the lips of the reading public. Richard Steele published the *Tatler*, and later he and Joseph Addison established the *Spectator*. Essays in these works resembled modern editorials and treated topics ranging from the personal to the philosophical and scientific; social and political phenomena were favorite subjects. Addison's essays were often extended letters; Alexander Pope reestablished the letter as a prominent public form when he felt the essay had become too homilectic for his taste (Dawson and Dawson 1908, 10–11). The primary writers for the *Tatler* and the *Spectator*, and writers such as John Dryden, Daniel Defoe, and Samuel Johnson, helped establish the essay in prefaces to literary works, as commentary on other literary forms, and as travel pieces. The essay and the written forms in which it appeared benefited from literary influences that came not only from the rise of journalism, but also from the growing influence in England of the coffeehouse, a center for conversation and newspaper reading.

Here the habit of moving from periodical essay to direct conversation and debate about the topics discussed in pamphlets and periodicals installed some of the most prominent "oral" features of the essay. The first issue of the *Tatler* (run on 12 April 1709) made clear the connections between the periodical and the coffeehouse and the desire to achieve directness and simplicity and to cover a wide range of topics. The *Spectator* created the famous "Spectator Club" and gave greater attention to learning than had the *Tatler*, but remained clear in its dependence on being a major source for lively conversation not only at coffeehouses and tea-tables, but also at assemblies and clubs. Those who took part in the spread of the essay through these early periodicals and the clubs upon which they depended characterized the essay as thoughts written down simply as they occurred, without the need to make the method or aim of thinking evident. Samuel Johnson, whose essays played an important role in periodicals of the late eighteenth century, defined the essay as "a loose sally of the mind; an irregular undigested piece; not a regular and orderly performance."

The spread of newspapers in the nineteenth century ensured a reading public for essays, especially personal and critical essays. In Great Britain Charles Lamb followed Montaigne in centering the essay in his personality and in adding "whimsical," "familiar," and "intimate" to terms describing types of essays. Lamb characterized the essay as the form best suited to fragments and scattered pieces of truth, to hints and glimpses, and even to half-intuitions, semiconsciousnesses, partial illuminations, and dim instincts. William Hazlitt, on the other hand, used the essay primarily as an instrument of criticism, especially on literary topics. Matthew Arnold added political and historical essays.

The American Scene

Within the United States, Benjamin Franklin, instrumental in the establishment of periodicals and learned societies in the eighteenth century, used the essay form to encapsulate practical playful wisdom, primarily in *Poor Richard's Almanac*, published from 1733 for many years. These essays are playful in their wisdom. But Franklin also helped establish the American Philosophical Society, a center for debate and serious conversation about essays received from abroad on scientific, political, and linguistic topics. By the late eighteenth century, American periodicals both reprinted many political essays from European and British sources and provided their own. John de Crevecoeur, Thomas Paine, John Dickinson, Charles Brockden Brown, and Joseph Dennie wrote for a variety of American newspapers. Meanwhile, American statesmen, such as Thomas Jefferson, James Madison, and Alexander Hamilton, created an interest in the political essay, discussing various national issues and analyzing the role of particular documents such as the Constitution.

Literary figures, such as Washington Irving, Ralph Waldo Emerson, and Henry David Thoreau, linked their letters and journals to essay writing in the early nineteenth century. They used their journals as reminders to themselves to return to thoughts worth pursuing. Irving's *Sketch Book* paralleled in many ways Addison's *Spectator*. Emerson, in particular, used his journal to record his changing views on the essay, and its relation to other forms written and oral, such as the sermon, the lecture, and conversation. He saw a fundamental contradiction between the desire for "the natural" in writing and the recognition that to create such writing the artist must strive to work it to a state of perfection. Conversation, sometimes for Emerson but most often for other transcendentalists such as Bronson Alcott and Margaret Fuller, seemed the closest oral language form to natural perfection, and yet, transferred to the page, it fell far short of expectations. Thus written forms emulating conversation had to incorporate the best features of talk while honing these into a form appropriate for written texts.[6]

In his essay on Montaigne Emerson indicates the extent to which he viewed conversation as a model for written work. He wanted a written form that would admit all topics and a wide variety of genres: "[P]hilosophy, ethics, divinity, criticism, poetry, humor, fun, mimicry, anecdotes, jokes, ventriloquism. All the breadth & versatility of the most liberal conversation, highest lowest personal local topics, all are permitted, and all may be combined in one speech" (Gilman 1960–77, 7:224). In this July 1839 journal entry he speaks of his expectations for the lecture, a form he was soon to find disappointing and would replace with the essay. In the essay, Emerson found a way to provide personal communication—a revelation of himself debating and weighing serious intellectual topics with an openness that allowed others to enter the dialogue. Spaces for readers to enter came through the essayist's uses of suggestion, unexpected projection, and wit—all rendered in highly conversational subgenres of plain speech, such as aphorisms, anecdotes, and brief rhapsodic diversions (Buell 1973, 96–97). Such freedom meant for Emerson abandoning formal patterns or predictable order. As Atwan notes,

> To immerse ourselves in the essays [of Emerson] is to experience a constant shattering of rhetorical organization: definitions seem to alter or dissolve with the movement of syntax; systems of classification are outright ridiculed; logical transitions and connections are erased; examples, illustrations, and quotations sometimes undermine the points they are meant to support; chains of cause and effect are consistently interrupted. Emerson rarely narrates; seldom offers lengthy descriptions; almost never explains; does not care to build a tightly argued case for anything. (1986, 113)

It is important to note that Emerson's "shattering" of form received considerable attention only at the end of the nineteenth century (which coincided with a strong trend toward equating essays with rigidly formed and preplanned *school compositions*). He was then criticized both by British writers and by his American heirs (such as Henry James) for the formlessness of his essays. Numerous historians of the genre who have tried to explain why the form never flowered in the United States point to several puzzles. First, to follow in the tradition of Montaigne, the essay must be about the "naked self," the natural individual. Yet in a nation that has prided itself on individualism, a genre that celebrates individuals in conversation has never received the prominence of other genres. Second, though Montaigne, Lamb, Hazlitt, and Emerson were read by influential American thinkers and writers who applauded the essay form and could potentially have taken it up themselves, few chose the essay as their major literary presentation. Even "the dean of American essayists," E. B. White, complained that an essayist was a "second-class citizen" (1977, vii). Thus the major models of the form remained British well into the twentieth century, and Americans, while setting the form up as the preferred display of knowledge in educational institutions and persuasion in periodicals, never themselves opted to contribute substantially to the model. Those American writers who devoted themselves primarily to writing essays tended to rely on specific vehicles of journalism, and thus their rise and fall often paralleled that of the periodicals or editors with whom they associated themselves.[7]

The essay in the United States evolved with and through familiar letters and personal journals into a wide variety of styles and shapes as institutions (such as newspapers and periodicals) and contexts (for example, travel, political debates) provided outlets and fashionable topics. By the end of the nineteenth century, numerous commentators lamented the passing of conversation, the essay's major oral support. Altered work patterns and varying expectations for the use of leisure time pushed conversation aside in favor of discussions, debates, and other more singularly purposeful oral forms.[8]

The Essay and Pedagogical Display

During the second half of the nineteenth century, when schooling in both England and the United States began to depend almost exclusively on learners displaying their knowledge in written form, the essay emerged as the preferred genre of educational institutions. Along with the move from oral performance in active, informed conversational debate as the major mark of learning, came a shift from a reliance on direct sensory experience to a reliance on the written words of authorities: "[T]he interpretation rather than the bare observation of the universe seems the most essential thing in education," declared a 1908 critic of British education (quoted in Binn 1940, 168). Similarly, a British educator who visited the United States several times at the turn of the century noted the growth there "of the authority of methodical and specially instructed thought on social and political questions, as against average unspecialized opinion" (Wallas 1914, 175). Agnes Repplier, perhaps the most prominent essayist of the early twentieth century, noted with regret that the educator's hand had come to "lay heavy on schoolroom and nursery" (1908, 156). Since essays and conversations had centered for several centuries on topics in the political and social (including literary) realms, the replacement of opinion with specialized and methodical authority brought increasing attempts both to regiment the form and to replace the conversational or back-and-forth quality of the essay with the assertion of individual authority. Along with these changes in the United States came the march toward standardization of curricula and tests and bureaucratization of decision making that helped install this new "essay" form as the mark of "clear thinking" and "good writing" in schools.

But, curiously enough, these shifts of context and of form did not go unnoticed by compilers of texts of essays that could help teachers understand how they might lead their students to "clear, concise" writing of essays. These editors often acknowledged the contexts that had generated the models—leisure richly textured by human relationships and books as friendly sources of knowledge—and noted that the classroom promised little of either of these conditions. Instead, classrooms had become public places in which one could find individuals writing in silence to display their passive acceptance of books as authorities. These compilers of textbooks of essays admitted their insecurity about attempting to squeeze the essay not only into an unfriendly setting, but also into a form firmly fixed through a simple list of generic conventions.

Thus prefaces to these collections of essays echo many ideas about the essay expressed through the centuries by the writers whose essays were collected in textbooks for classroom use. No doubt, the close study of essays necessary before compiling and editing volumes for use in secondary schools or colleges resulted in the compilers' understanding of the essay's resistance to the usual types of conventions that characterized lyric poetry, tragedy, or comedy. Moreover, they had to be aware of the essay's close ties to leisurely conversation fed by observation and reading. However, these understandings of the essay did not reach school-board members, curriculum designers, teacher educators, and teachers, who forced the form for knowledge display. Collections of essays and the occasional single book on the form written for use in schools repeatedly set out reasons why the essay did not adhere to the expected format of a genre with conventions and components of predictability.[9]

Features of the essay that received the most frequent attention by compilers and editors highlight its dependence on a thinking writer, willing to let ideas flow, and to base ideas on observations. These observations relate not only to the world beyond the self, but to the self as reader in the process of preparing to write an essay. That the form offers no ready order or listing of components does not mean that it can result from a careless approach. A striking puzzle and one that receives notice with great frequency, especially after 1920, is that which also concerned Emerson: the apparent ease and even carelessness with which essays seem to be offered, while they are in reality carefully executed. Many who commented on the essay note an idea similar to the following point made by a compiler of a 1930 collection of essays: "The essay at its best . . . is marked by the appearance, but not the reality, of carelessness and ease" (Robertson 1930, 4). Writers must give attention to crafting the order of sentences, refining their shape, and cutting away repetitious portions (one compiler recommended to novice essayists: "The true worth of your first essay is going to depend very largely on what you cut out of it" [Johnson 1932, 41]). The essay's brevity and informality seemingly erupt from a clarity of vision and a stored simplicity of summative wit of a vibrant personality ideally pictured in the richest of webs connecting ready and intimate conversationalists and books and their readers.

Here, then, is the paradox that draws essays closest to conversation. The success of both depends on attentiveness to the voices in the head, to the potential listeners and audience, with a follow-up in the writing that indicates that these voices have been listened to. These signals come, however, as a result of its "polished form" and "*artful* disorder"; some have described it "as near an approach to simultaneity as the nature of literary art will allow." Those qualities of ease, naturalness, and flow—based on close observations of conversationalists and attention to voices in the head—depend, however, on the expertise and practice gained through taking advantage of such experiences in leisure time. The greater the available time for conversation with others, self-reflection, and rereadings, the greater the evidence of polish and art.

By the second decade of the twentieth century, the essay as the form through which students should display their ability to write was well established. But reconciliation between this use of the essay and the reading of the essay as a literary form did not come easily. The editors of essay collections for high school and college students addressed this issue repeatedly and with agreement that they and their students faced three dilemmas. First, the essay form demanded "more maturity in taste" than other forms, such as the novel or the short story (Chamberlain 1926, xiii). Second, the essay, while treating everyday subjects and the familiar, also treated life's complexities, and thus its interpretation often depended on a depth of knowledge and experience with the expression of beliefs, doubts, whims, and so on, that young people were not likely to have. Third, essays had their origins in the ordinary language of letters and conversations and in their expressions of the personality of the writer, and yet they gave their pleasure most directly through their unexpected ways of using language. Young people were highly unlikely to be sufficiently attuned to the nuances of language, generally acknowledged to come through immersion in literature, to be able to reconcile this delicate balance between the use of everyday language and the use of carefully crafted "talk-writing."

In addition, essays had to be written with some degree of consciousness about the making of ideas in the mind of the individual: "[T]he essay as it has gone on has not lost by being a little self-conscious of its function . . ." (Rhys and Vaughan

1913, ix). Such self-confidence, derived from experience in observation, familiarity with literary texts, and frequent talk with others so experienced, was unlikely to be characteristic of young writers, especially those in public schools now committed to mass education. The metaknowledge of both language and of self as maker of meaning had to come from what the essayist E. B. White once described as the "self-liberated man, sustained by the childish belief that everything he thinks about, everything that happens to him, is of general interest. . . . Only a person who is congenitally self-centered has the effrontery and the stamina to write essays" (quoted in Pack and Perrini 1991, v). This kind of self-confidence, as well as an awareness of language as both self-expression and social expression, had, from Montaigne forward, been the "natural" product of the leisure of the higher social classes and of a cultural confidence engendered by power based on society's institutions of governance and finance. In the twentieth century, American classrooms and their students and teachers—at both the precollege and higher educational levels—came less and less to reflect such class and cultural characteristics. Moreover, the well-established bond of shared backgrounds between reader and writer could no longer be expected. Almost apologetically, those who wrote prefaces to textbooks of essays gave teachers and students advice such as this: "[I]n a true essay the writer assumes a degree of acquaintanceship with his reader, and a consequent willingness to reveal *himself*, . . . [A] thoughtfully written letter is likely to be as perfect an essay as one may accomplish. . . . I would urge the beginner who finds essay writing especially difficult to put his first attempts into the form of an open letter to an intimate friend" (Johnson 1932, 11).

Observers of essays and recommenders of pedagogical strategies for bringing new writers to the form with the right mindset repeatedly talked of possible ways to recreate the conditions for the essay in classrooms. They urged that reading and conversing precede the writing of the essay, for its essence was "talk on paper" that should carry the same pleasure as that to be derived from conversation—both with the self and with others "to please the self." Neither coercion nor conformity could nurture the essay.

By the middle of the twentieth century, most textbook compilers and those familiar with the historical evolution of the context and forms of the English essay simply stopped mentioning the contradictions between current goals for the essay in schools and the central trends of its development. Moreover, numerous observers of the patterns of leisure and habits of social interaction noted the decline of conversation, the oral prototype of the essay.[10]

Modern Literary Theory and Conversation

Since the Anglo-American discovery near the end of the twentieth century of Mikhail Bakhtin and acknowledgment of his contributions to an "anthropology of literature," the genre of primary focus in discussions of the dialogic quality of literature has been the novel. Considerable attention has been devoted to the role of conversation in the novel and to Bakhtin's observations about speech genres, including conversation. Certain ironies exist in the considerable attention given to this work, however. The first is the failure to take up the recommendations of Bakhtin for an

"anthropology of literature" and to attend to the actual reports of contexts, definition, and forms of both producers and consumers of literature. The second is the
failure to link Bakhtin's ideas with those of linguists, especially those of the Prague
school (whose work was, so far as we know, unknown to Bakhtin[11]) and discourse
analysts, who have detailed "the living utterance" and its transfer to, as well as transformations in, literature.

The history of the essay illustrates the extent to which ordinary speakers, readers, and writers have noted many of its features that literary theorists appear to believe are unique to their field. The brief overview given here of what essayists have
said about letters, conversations, and essays demonstrates a strong similarity to points
made by Bakhtin and other literary theorists about speech genres and their uses in
written forms, as well as the dialogic nature of literature. Bakhtin noted the importance in Cicero's day, as public life increased for a greater portion of people, of
genres that allowed the expression of private life and thoughts. Conversation and
the familiar letter offered an "intimate and familiar atmosphere (one that was, of
course, semiconventionalized), a new private sense of self, suited to the drawing
room" (1981, 143).

In his insistence upon considering speech genres in their contexts, Bakhtin also
noted the difficulty of having society force an authoritative voice onto literature.
He argued that authoritative discourse could not be represented (interpreted), but
instead could only be transmitted. Without a receptive climate of interaction, such
transmission removed the discourse from "zones of contact"—of presumed relations between text and listener-reader. His description of authoritative discourse
parallels that of compilers of essays who argued the impossibility of the essay's reception and production under formal education's reshaping of it as an authoritative fixed form: "Its inertia, its semantic finiteness and calcification, the degree to
which it is hard-edged, a thing in its own right, the impermissibility of any free stylistic development in relation to it—all this renders the artistic representation of
authoritative discourse impossible" (1981, 344). Bakhtin further warned that internally persuasive discourses must be tightly interwoven with "one's own word," which
was in turn "wrought out of others' works that have been acknowledged and assimilated . . ." (1981, 345). That discourse cannot stand apart from the social situation
that engendered it or the expectation of response reverberates through the writings
of both Bakhtin and Voloshinov as well as those of members of the Prague school.
The dialogic depends not only on the current context of generation but also on the
anticipated situation of application. The dialogic is therefore "most apparent when
we have to take some decision. We hesitate. We do not know what is the best course
of action. We argue with ourselves, we try to convince ourselves of the rightness of
one decision. Our consciousness seems to be divided into two independent and
contradictory voices" (Voloshinov 1983, 119). Language's active relation to potential action, such as that which often lies not far below the surface in social and
political discourse, impels the dialogic form.

In summary, these links of the essay to social context and expectation, as well as
to forms such as the letter and conversation that share similar situational features,
have persisted since Montaigne. Major essayists in English have never lost sight of

the fact that, like conversations, essays are open-ended in their paths of development. Their major constraint is length; they, like conversations, do not lack for appropriate topics; they take up vast and significant topics in the barest of treatments; and they express the personality, opinions, and beliefs of the writer-talker. Similarly, both essayists and conversationalists exhibit strong tendencies to generalize, to take only a few of numerous possible vantage points, and to leave open any possibility of absolute closure on a topic. Both essays and conversations may toss a topic into the ring for discussion and then walk around the topic, ramble, and digress to unrelated matters. Neither essays nor conversations must have highly specific purposes or goals; they happen, more often than not, for the pleasure of speaker-writer and listener-reader and expect the latter to carry away memorable quotations. Both depend heavily on leisure time, and the separation of the activity of reading or conversing from distracting labor.

Americans, in particular, have struggled with their definitions and exhortations for conversation. Through the late eighteenth and first half of the nineteenth centuries, writers of every sort extolled the virtues of conversation and tried to delineate its major features. On one point, commentators on conversation agreed: in every community, it was then the most common form of intellectual activity. Its highly interactive nature made it something of a contest and called for agility, alertness, and sensitivity; at the same time it demanded mental acumen, wit, and adherence to certain social conventions.

In both Great Britain and the United States, major writers of the essay also received considerable praise for their conversational powers. Within the United States, periodical writers often pointed out that Samuel Johnson's conversational skills displayed even more of the powers of his mind than did his most-celebrated written performances. Similarly, Emerson, Margaret Fuller, and Bronson Alcott received acclaim as conversationalists as well as writers. Most recommenders of conversation agreed that those who would succeed in conversation must do so through keen attention to the world about them, and persistence in observing and mentally recording (or jotting down) their observations.

But by the late nineteenth century and consistently through the twentieth century, both essayists and editors of essay collections tried to link essay and conversation and often seemed to put forth their collections with an air of resignation that the presumed pedagogical and literary objectives for the essay were unlikely to be achieved in the classroom. Leisure, opportunity to practice conversation with close associates, and time for reflective reading were the prerequisites for success in the essay; both thoughts "in the head" and in conversation had to leak through into essays. In turn, essays had to be read against and with conversation. They had to be written after adequate time for observation and listening. These qualities—plus those of honing thoughts into witty language—came most readily through conversation, the prototypical form to sustain an active relationship between speaker-writer and listeners-readers and also among the various voices *within* the speaker-writer. As Bakhtin reminds us, in this latter polyphonic condition, writers work through an internalized dialogue or conversation in which they change course through the shifts of voices.

Such shifts may be of different durations, so that, for an extended period within an essay, the writer may assume a monologic stance that prevails over audienced voices. In other words, though seemingly monologic, certain portions of essays reveal the internal dialogue, or the play of ideas in the mind of the writer. Some essayists use different registers or styles to reflect such internalized roles and voices — sometimes making a point in elevated speech and then undercutting it by colloquial objection or counterpoint. Similarly, the intellectual, tightly reasoned point may be paralleled by the emotional argument or plea.[12]

Several members of the Prague school, in their quest to develop a theory of poetics and to differentiate "poetic" language from "workaday technical" language debated the nature of dialogue, placing considerable emphasis on the "natural" human tendency to establish a "tension" between the "I" and "you" of dialogue and arguing that both internal and external dialogues held such tensions. Those most informal or open would include "every dialogue without direct and immediate usefulness in which one talks primarily in order to talk, for pleasure, for play, out of politeness. This definition excludes from our concern both judicial inquiries and diplomatic or commercial negotiations, councils and even scholarly conferences even though they abound in superfluous talk" (Tarde, cited in Mukarovsky, 109). This focus on the "self-oriented" nature of conversation highlights the self-conscious ways in which both conversationalists and essayists *play* with language, often displaying a sense of "polite" admission of other voices: "The interrelation of the participants in a dialogue is therefore felt as a tension not bound to either of the two speaking persons but actually existing 'between' them; it is thus objectified as the 'psychological situation' of the dialogue" (Mukarovsky 1977, 86).

The range and frequency of such internal and external shifts will depend, of course, on circumstances. Just as an oral dialogue among several participants may be bound by spatial and ritual design (as in a doctoral examination, for example), so the internal dialogue of some essays may be much more confined to a particular theme and not as subject to extraneous thoughts or "side voices." The marking of these side voices makes clear the need to sustain the semantic unity of dialogic discourse — even that of the essay — which reveals the dialogic of the writer's voices and the active participation of the reader(s)' with the writer(s)' voices. The theme or subject of the essay that gives it semantic unity provides the boundedness of the essay. Voices that may seem to be contradictory or sharply divergent mark the transition of individual replies. Semantic reversals, changes of key (to irony, for example), or shifts of tempo, or devices that set up I-you oppositions (or within political essays, we-they polarities) may be marked by attribution through personal pronouns of the first and second or third persons, but more often this tension is revealed by other means. These include affirmation/negation, and the use of adversatives (*however, but, nevertheless*, and so on) and concessives (*despite, even if*, and the like).

These and other means demarcate the speaking-thinking subjects in dialogue and stress the working out of diverse paths to and through themes. Varying opinions, facts, interpretations, contexts, volitions, and intentions shape approaches to topics. Similarly, the spatial or intellectual closeness or distance of the speaker to a topic may mark the voices of dialogue — internal and external.

The usual deictic markers of space and time, as well as tense markers, also carry these distinctions.

The Future of the Essay

To call attention to the fact that both essayists and collectors of essays have long described the dialogic nature of the essay, as well as its interdependence with the letter and conversation, should not diminish the fact that some literary theorists have similarly characterized the form. Though several European theorists address the dialogic nature of the form and bring epistemology and social theory to their observations on the form, T. W. Adorno (1984) particularly acknowledges its possibly inevitable incompatibility with societal conditions of the late twentieth century.[13]

Adorno's comments take us back to where we began, with the lament of the anonymous nineteenth-century American observer of the canons of conversation. Adorno reminds us that the essay cuts through the self-preservative semblance of hierarchical ordering of thought transformed into visible language. He notes that the essay form undercuts current academic reifications of well-ordered and consistently reasoned discourse based on Cartesian principles. Adorno describes the essay in numerous ways that indicate its defiance of tradition, of hierarchy, of fixed form. In a personification of the essay form itself—that appears to take agency away from the writer and to place it in the very genre produced—Adorno notes that the essay simultaneously suspends the traditional concept of method: the essay "denies any primeval givens," "refuses any definition of its concepts," "takes the antisystematic impulse into its own procedure," and introduces concepts directly, "immediately," as it receives them (1984, 159–60).

Adorno notes the fetishizing of language that comes through academics' demand for strict and precise use of terms and fixed definitions. He tells us that within essays, this precision of both meaning and method must slip away because the essay "urges the reciprocal interaction of its concepts in the process of intellectual experience" (160). The essay defies Descartes's rules to establish certainty and refinement in method and presentation, for it neither urges the decomposition of objects or ideas into their parts, nor proceeds from the simplest to the most complex, nor attempts to be comprehensive. It is brief, moves in response to the irritation of an idea, has a mosaiclike connection to other essays, and usually shakes off any illusion that the world is simple and its forces clear-cut. In short,

> The essay is both more open and more closed than traditional thought would like. It is more open insofar as, through its inner nature, it negates anything systematic, and satisfies itself all the better the more strictly it excludes the systematic. . . . On the other hand, the essay is more closed in that it labors emphatically on the form of its presentation. (Adorno 1984, 165)

As a commentator on Adorno's essays has noted, "the more antagonistic and opaque society becomes, the more the attempt to name it [the essay] will incline the essay towards metabasis" (Hullot-Kentor 1984, 150).

Yet Adorno writes optimistically that current efforts both to fix the form and to theorize about its shapes and shapings will not erase its essential dialogic nature.

He notes the hour now "more unfavorable than ever" for the essay, as societal trends and academic rules provide no fertile ground for the types of human relationships and ways of knowing upon which the essay has traditionally depended. But he remains hopeful that its very defiance of convention and hierarchy—inextricably bound into its very being—will prevail over all efforts to redefine it away from its conversational and epistolary roots and connections. Thus the "obviousness" and application to "everyday scenes of human existence" may in the end be reason enough for securing its continuation.

Notes

1. In "The Problem of Speech Genres" (reprinted in 1986), Bakhtin includes the "genres of salon conversations" as well as those of "table conversation, intimate conversations among friends, intimate conversations within the family, and so on" among those genres subject to "free creative reformulation" (80). He goes on to address the importance of context—atmosphere and social relations—that supports the structures and expressive reception of such talk. Both readers and writers assimilate these genres and their contexts and carry them into their interpretations and creations of utterances. Several of the members of the Linguistic Circle of Prague address similar issues with regard to the language of the salon and the extensive power of conversational language there (see especially G. Tarde in Mukarovsky [1977]).

2. Since the 1920s the "five-paragraph essay" has been the best example of formal education's redefinition of the essay into a highly conventionalized purpose and format that has nothing in common with the literary genre. The "college essay" has become a repeated routine for students in English and social studies classes, a critical part of college applications and entrance examinations, and the staple of freshman English courses. Though commonly equated, the *essay* and the *article* have little in common; while the essay has many features found in the friendly informal letter and has the appearance of openness and spontaneity, the article is more consciously shaped, thorough, and final. While the essay is closely akin to conversation, the article has an affinity with discussion that must "set the problem in its significant terms" and "must end in agreement" (Bourne 1924, 6). The editors of *The Bread Loaf Anthology of Contemporary American Essays* caution: "An essay is *not* an article; it is not a thorough, scholarly treatment of an isolated subject. By definition it is an exploration, a journey out that frequently becomes, in the best examples, an inward journey too, a picking at the thread which finally unravels the garment of the writer's particular concern and scrutiny" (Pack and Parini 1991, v). Essayist William H. Gass characterizes the essay as "obviously the opposite of that awful object, 'the article' . . . [which must] appear complete and straightforward and footnoted and useful and certain . . ." (1985, 25).

3. Sir Francis Bacon, in the "Dedicatory Epistle" to the first book published in English that used the term *essay*, his *Essays or Counsells, Civill and Morall* (first published in 1597 and again in 1612 and 1625), tells his readers of the historic link of letters to essays. Of *essay*, Bacon writes "The word is late, but the thing is ancient; for Seneca's Epistles to Lucilius, if you mark them well, are but essays, that is, dispersed meditations, though conveyed in the form of epistles" (1612 edition, n.p.).

4. Throughout the history of the Christian church, letters, such as the Epistles of St. Paul, were written to be read aloud to churches consisting of individuals not directly known to the author.

5. This observation appears frequently in collections of letters from the seventeenth and eighteenth centuries. For example, Braumuller, editor of a facsimile edition of a Folger manuscript letter book of the seventeenth century, notes that "the form that was soon to be recognized as the essay owes a great deal to the letter" (1983, 10). A collector of "great English letter writers" notes, "[A]mong the earliest letter-writers of English literature the distinction between the essay and the letter was not very carefully preserved" (Dawson and Dawson 1908, 12). Though it is impossible to identify precise features of similarity that drew such notices, it is useful to note that writers often observed that letters and essays held certain acts or ways of thinking out as their desired outcomes. Samuel Richardson, in a collection of "familiar letters" he edited before he published his novel *Clarissa*, noted the extent to which letters had become public rather than private, and that letters both demonstrated ways of thinking and also illustrated particular types of acts (excusing, chiding, requesting, and so on) accomplished through these written forms of language (1974, xvi, xxvii). For a discussion of modern epistolary essays, see Hermann (1986) on those of Virginia Woolf.

6. The most comprehensive account of the links between conversation and essays for transcendentalist writers is Buell (1973), but see also Deese (1988) for the views of key figures on the difficulties of transferring conversation to the page.

7. The writings of Americans debating why Americans have never excelled in the essay form are abundant and include not only those who have tried to make their reputation through the form (for example, E. B. White), but also literary critics such as Alfred Kazin. When in 1986 the publishing company Ticknor and Fields began producing an annual volume called *The Best American Essays*, Robert Atwan, the editor of the series and a devotee of the essay, ironically based the expectation of success for the venture on the very versatility in coverage and sources that pieces of writing called essays had achieved by the end of the twentieth century (Hardwick 1986). Atwan acknowledged the essay's slippery definition and wide-ranging publication outlets and admitted that any essay was likely to be short lived in acceptance or popularity because essayists' topics were often of only passing interest and also highly dependent on knowledge of specific societal contexts. Two collections of scholarly studies of the essay (Butrym 1989; Good 1988) take up many of these same issues, and several authors continue the debate about the place of the essay in the literary history of the United States.

8. See, for example, several essays by Agnes Repplier (1908), prominent essayist of the late-nineteenth and early twentieth centuries, for an overview of the shifting contexts and evaluations of conversation in American life; also see Heath 1990.

9. This summary is based on a review of over 1,500 collections of essays published for use in secondary schools and colleges in the United States between 1800 and 1950. The bulk of materials for the eighteenth and early nineteenth centuries were consulted in the Library of Congress and the Library of the American Antiquarian Society. Those from the late nineteenth and early twentieth centuries were drawn from the libraries of Teachers College at Columbia University, Dartmouth College, Harvard University, the University of North Carolina, the University of Michigan, and the John A. Nietz Textbook Collection of the University of Pittsburgh. Single words or phrases that occur repeatedly in essay collections across the decades will be used here without bibliographic reference; complete citations will be given only for longer quotations.

10. It is curious to note that though by the late twentieth century many educational reformers promoted collaboration, "whole language," and the role of oral language in academic learning, few called attention to the ways in which these conditions might either lead educators to give up their long-held faith in the essay as the favored academic genre

or to acknowledge that only massive redefinitions of schooling could re-create earlier favorable conditions for essay writing; see Willinsky (1990) for an overview of these issues.

11. In an article that traces the influence of Mikhail Bakhtin on the Prague Linguistic Circle and the impact of Prague-school theory on Nicholai Bakhtin (brother of Mikhail), Galan (1987) argues that Mikhail Bakhtin remained unaware of the Prague school. Galan also posits that Bakhtin's work appeared in Prague only as being by Voloshinov.

12. Though all essayists shift voices, internal and external, in their writing, some make the turn-taking of alternative points of view more obvious than others. Virginia Woolf, always both playful and polite, indicates her shifts by phrases such as "On the other side, of course . . . ," "And yet . . . ," "How, we are made to wonder . . . ," and "But the gossip says . . ." To present views opposing her own, Woolf often created unknown characters whose nature becomes obvious through the voice she gives them: "At this very moment some Lady Bertram finds it almost too trying . . ." (Woolf 1984, 227). Some of her most playful and polite language comes in those essays highly critical of other literary critics; see, for example "Mr. Bennett and Mrs. Brown," a sharp rebuttal to an essay that critic Arnold Bennett had written on the topic of character in fiction. The essayist William H. Gass makes his turn-taking among different voices most evident in the opening pages of his essay "Emerson and the Essay" (1985).

13. Several studies of European speculative essayists portray their self-consciousness about the form and their awareness of its insistence on plural voices; see especially Kauffmann (1981), Beaujour (1981), and Bensmaia (1987).

Works Cited

Adorno, T. W. "The Essay as Form." Translated by Bob Hullot-Kentor and Frederick Will. *New German Critique* 32 (Spring–Summer 1984): 151–71.

Anonymous [W.H.] "Talking vs. Conversation." *Knickerbocker: N.Y. Magazine*, September 1836, pp. 331–37.

Atwan, Robert. "Ecstasy & Eloquence: The Method of Emerson's Essays." In *Essays on the Essay: Redefining the Genre*, edited by Alexander J. Butrym. Athens: University of Georgia Press, 1989.

———. "Foreword." In *The Best American Essays 1986*, edited by Elizabeth Hardwick. New York: Ticknor and Fields, 1986.

Bacon, Francis. *Essays or Counsells, Civill and Morall*. London: John Beale, 1612. [University microfilms no. 3209.]

Bakhtin, Mikhail. *The Dialogic Imagination*. Translated by Michael Holquist. Edited by Caryl Emerson and Michael Holquist. Austin: University of Texas Press, 1981.

———. "The Problem of Speech Genres." In *Speech Genres and Other Late Essays*, translated by Vern W. McGee; edited by Caryl Emerson and Michael Holquist. Austin: University of Texas Press, 1986.

Beaujour, Michel. "Genus Universum." *Glyph* 7 (1981): 15–31.

Bensmaia, Beda. *The Barthes Effect: The Essay as Reflective Text*. Vol. 54, *Theory and History of Literature*. Minneapolis: University of Minnesota Press, 1987.

Binn, Howard. "The Future of English Education in the Light of the Past." In *Men and Ideas: Essays by Graham Walls*. London: George Allen and Unwin, 1940.

Bourne, Randolph. "Discussion." In *Essays toward Truth*, edited by Kenneth Allan Robinson and William Benfield Pressey. New York: Henry Holt, 1924.

Braunmuller, A. R., ed. *A Seventeenth-Century Letter-Book*. Newark: University of Delaware Press, 1983.

Buell, Lawrence. *Literary Transcendentalism: Style and Vision in the American Renaissance*. Ithaca, N.Y.: Cornell University Press, 1973.

Butrym, Alexander J., ed. *Essays on the Essay: Redefining the Genre*. Athens: University of Georgia Press, 1989.

Chamberlain, Essie. *Essays Old and New*. New York: Harcourt, Brace and Company, 1926.

Dawson, William J., and Congsby W. Dawson. *The Great English Letter Writers*. New York: Harper and Bros., 1908.

Deese, Helen R. "Alcott's Conversations on the Transcendentalists: The Record of Caroline Dall." *American Literature* 60 (1988): 17–25.

Doty, William G. *Letters in Primitive Christianity*. Philadelphia: Fortress, 1973.

Galan, F. W. "Bakhtiniada, Part 2: The Corsican Brothers in the Prague School or the Reciprocity of Reception." *Poetics Today* 8 (1987): 565–77.

Gass, William H. "Emerson and the Essay." In *Habitations of the Word*. New York: Simon and Schuster, 1985.

Gilman, William, ed. *The Journals and Miscellaneous Notebooks of Ralph Waldo Emerson*. 16 vols. Cambridge: Harvard University Press, 1960–82.

Good, Graham. *The Observing Self: Rediscovering the Essay*. London: Routledge, 1988.

Grice, Paul. "Logic and Conversation (1967, 1987). Part I." In *Studies in the Way of Words*. Cambridge: Cambridge University Press, 1989.

Guillen, Claudio. "Notes toward the Study of the Renaissance Letter." In *Renaissance Genres: Essays on Theory, History, and Interpretation, Harvard English Studies*, no. 14, edited by Barbara Kiefer Lewalski. Cambridge: Harvard University Press, 1986.

Hardwick, Elizabeth, ed. *The Best American Essays 1986*. New York: Ticknor and Fields, 1986.

Heath, Shirley Brice. "Women in Conversation: Covert Models in American Language Ideology." In *Language, Society, and Thought*, edited by Robert Cooper and Bernard Spolsky. Berlin: Walter de Gruyter, 1990.

Hermann, Anne. "Intimate, Irreticent and Indiscreet in the Extreme: Epistolary Essays by Virginia Woolf and Christa Wolf." *New German Critique* 38 (1986): 161–80.

Hullott-Kentor, Bob. "Title Essay." *New German Critique* 32 (1984): 141–50.

Johnson, Burges. *Essaying the Essay*. Boston: Little, Brown, 1932.

Kauffmann, Robert Lane. "The Theory of the Essay: Lukas, Adorno, and Benjamin." Ph.D. diss., University of California at San Diego, 1981.

Lukacs, Georg. *Soul and Form*. Cambridge: MIT Press, 1974.

Mukarovsky, Jan. "Two Studies of Dialogue." In *The Word and Verbal Art*, translated and edited by John Burbank and Peter Steiner. New Haven, Conn.: Yale University Press, 1977.

Pack, Robert, and Jay Parini, eds. *The Bread Loaf Anthology of Contemporary American Essays*. Hanover, N.H.: University Press of New England, 1991.

Pearl, J. L. "The Role of Personal Correspondence in the Exchange of Scientific Information in Early Modern France." *Renaissance et Reforme*, n. s., 8 (1984): 106–13.

Repplier, Agnes. "The Educator." In *A Happy Half-Century*. New York: Houghton Mifflin, 1908.

Rhys, Ernest, and Lloyd Vaughan, eds. *A Century of English Essays*. London: J. M. Dent and Son, 1913.

Robertson, Stuart, ed. *Familiar Essays*. New York: Prentice Hall, 1930.

Searle, John R. *Speech Acts: An Essay in the Philosophy of Language.* Cambridge: Cambridge University Press, 1969.

Richardson, Samuel. *Familiar Letters on Important Occasions.* London: George Routledge and Sons, 1974.

Voloshinov, Valentin. "Literary Stylistics." In *Bakhtin School Papers,* Russian Poetics in Translation, no. 10, edited by Ann Shukman. Oxford: RPT, 1983.

Voloshinov, V. N., and M. M. Bakhtin. "The Latest Trends (1928) in Linguistic Thought in the West." In *Bakhtin School Papers,* Russian Poetics in Translation, no. 10, edited by Ann Shukman. Oxford: RPT, 1983.

Wallas, Graham. "The Universities and the Nation in America and England." In *Men and Ideas: Essays by Graham Wallas.* London: George Allen & Unwin, 1940.

White, Elwyn Brooks. *Essays of E. B. White.* New York: Harper and Row, 1977.

Willinsky, John. *The New Literacy: Redefining Reading and Writing in the Schools.* New York: Routledge, 1990.

Woolf, Virginia. "Jane Austen." In *The Common Reader. First Series,* edited by Andrew McNeillie. New York: Harcourt Brace Jovanovich, 1984.

Bakhtin and Beautiful Science

The Paradox of Cultural Relativity Revisited

I

At least some of the enormous success dialogism has experienced in the last few years can be explained by a coincidental surge of interest in cultural studies. The academic study of literature seems to go through periodic swings from inwardly looking formalisms of various kinds to different versions of outer-oriented studies of context, and back again. A rising tide of interest in ethnic studies, feminism, and neo-Marxism has been evident in key books and journals published during the last decade. And in the pages of such works few names are encountered as frequently as that of Mikhail Bakhtin. This development is hardly surprising, of course. Bakhtin spent his whole career seeking to articulate a philosophical anthropology, the outlines of which are in remarkable agreement with the parameters of most current work claiming the name of cultural criticism. And when given the opportunity to single out theorists in Russian criticism whom he considered most valuable, he named precisely those critics who made cultural setting an integral component of their work, scholars such as Nikolai Konrad (author of a huge book on relations between European and Oriental culture), Dmitry Likhachev (specialist on the cultural specificity of medieval Europe influenced by the French *annalistes*), and Jurij Lotman (founder of the Tartu school of cultural semiotics). Underscoring the point, Bakhtin in 1972 added, "The outstanding works of recent literary scholarship that I have mentioned—Konrad, Likhachev, Lotman and his school—with all the diversity of their methodology are alike in that *they do not separate literature from culture*. . . ."[1]

It is easy to accede to the proposition that Bakhtin provides a number of useful concepts for the fledgling field of cultural studies. But can dialogism aid in the area of that emerging discipline's greatest conflict? In other words, does Bakhtin's thought have a contribution to make to the thorny problem of cultural relativism?

This chapter will urge that it does, but before engaging the argument in greater detail, let me very quickly (and tentatively) lay out what I see as the problem. Cultural criticism is very much a postmodernist undertaking as it is currently practiced (in the anglophone world, at any rate): a basic assumption, crudely stated, is that there is no objective truth as such; each society produces its own version of reality by mapping cultural values onto the natural world. A constructionist impulse is at work in most cultural criticism, one of whose corollaries is that it is impossible, or at least very difficult, to choose between the world as it is perceived in one society, and the worldview of another society. Members of Papuan cargo cults may build bamboo sculptures based on airplanes, and Australians may fly through the air in planes (indeed, in cargo planes), but it is now widely felt that we must be very cautious in evaluating these differences.

What seems increasingly to be missing in certain versions of cultural criticism is a third term that would let the outside observer of any two versions of socially constructed reality judge between them. There are complex reasons why we find ourselves at such a pass, reasons that go back to the roots of modern ethnography in pragmatism and functionalism, guilt occasioned by the past excesses of colonialism, and a widespread suspicion of all claims to external authority, to name but a few. I am sympathetic to all these reasons for objecting to outside, transcultural valorizing. But I am even more persuaded by Bakhtin's objection to such objections.

> There exists a very strong, but one-sided and thus untrustworthy, idea that in order better to understand a foreign culture, one must enter into it, forgetting one's own, and view the world through the eyes of this foreign culture. . . . Of course, a certain entry as a living being into a foreign culture, the possibility of seeing the world through its eyes, is a necessary part of the process of understanding it; but if this were the only aspect of this understanding, it would merely be duplication and would not entail anything new or enriching. . . . In order to understand, it is immensely important for the person who understands to be *located outside* the object of his or her creative understanding—in time, in space, in culture.[2]

Can we reconcile the suspicion of claims to transcultural authority with Bakhtin's insistence on the necessary role of outsideness (vnenaxodimost') in any creative act of understanding? The argument of this chapter will be that such an accommodation can indeed be made if we keep in mind that all culture is humanly produced, and that all humans have certain physiological features in common. Most important of these is the somatic organization of perception in human beings. The physiology of human perception mandates that the world, no matter how it is constructed, be experienced from a body. Thus all experience is situated. On the basis of situatedness so understood, and the relations that must exist between organisms made as we are made, I believe we may open up the paradox of cultural relativity.

II

It was inevitable that the growing interest in cultural studies should soon claim Mikhail Bakhtin as one of its major theorists. From his earliest work to his last, Bakhtin tirelessly insisted on the importance of social and historical context. His first philosophical works of the 1920s are grounded in the master distinction between self and other, an ecological model of the world that defines the subject as ineluctably bound up with (and in large measure defined by) his or her surrounding environment. In the several genealogies of genres he wrote, such as "Epic and Novel," or in the monograph on the chronotope, he pays great attention to the development of formal details as they are shaped by differing historical details and cultural peculiarities. The study of Dostoyevsky's achievement is grounded in the discursive tensions growing out of nineteenth-century economic and social life; the Rabelais book insists on the relation between particular kinds of texts and specific institutional forms, most notably (but not exclusively) the carnival. In polemics directed against other literary scholars and theorists, such as the Russian formalists, Bakhtin is especially critical of those who ignore the contextualizing force of culture. *Marxism and the Philosophy of Language* is a long disquisition on the power of social factors to shape our very words. In his late essays he expresses uneasiness in the face of structuralism and semiotics[3] because of their single-minded emphasis on mechanical codes. In his final published testament to other Russian critics, Bakhtin implored them to "use opportunities more boldly" in general, but specifically to "establish closer links with the history of culture," repeating several times that "literature is an inseparable part of culture," and that it "must not be severed from the rest of culture."[4]

Culture is an important concept for Bakhtin because it provides him with the armature he needs to support his constitutional enthusiasm for variety. He reveled in the diversity of human expression, a heteroglossia nowhere more obvious than in the differences between culture systems, the most comprehensive form, as it were, of the utterance. But such emphasis on multiplicity always contains within it the seeds of chaos. If you begin by assuming that "no single sentence [as an utterance] . . . can ever be repeated," then the question must arise "as to whether science can deal with such absolutely unrepeatable individualities . . . or whether they are beyond the bounds of generalizing scientific cognition."

Bakhtin's answer to this question is that such variety can "of course" be studied, but only if the greatest attention is paid to the *specificity* of the utterance and its context: "[S]cience, and above all, philosophy, can and should study the specific form and function of this individuality."[5]

The great stress laid on particularity in Bakhtin's work results in a version of the subject that is remarkable for the degree to which it is localized, situated. The hallmark of those problems, genres, or authors Bakhtin singles out for study is that each is an especially sensitive indicator of specificity, and thus a key to the uniqueness of being located in a given situation. It is this quality of being able to display uniqueness that impels Bakhtin to choose such topics as intonation or phraseology in linguistics, the novel's attention to social nuance, or Rabelais's delight in the details of material and verbal culture in early modern European culture.

It is not only in such early texts as "Philosophy of the Act" that Bakhtin obsesses about the implications of situatedness: in key works of his middle period the materiality that inevitably accompanies such a radical emphasis on location is read into the possibility of consciousness itself. In the Voloshinov book, *Marxism and the Philosophy of Language*, for instance, the argument that "understanding itself can come about only within some kind of semiotic material," leads to the conclusion that "signs . . . are particular, material things," and therefore *consciousness itself can arise and become a viable fact only in the material embodiment of signs.*"[6] I believe that Ken Hirschkop, in a volume of essays called *Bakhtin and Cultural Theory*,[7] put his finger on an important aspect of dialogism: there is indeed a radical materialism at the heart of the Bakhtinian enterprise, and it is, perhaps in a sense unintended by Hirschkop and which remains yet to be investigated, also vulgar.

Hirschkop, along with a growing number of critics, has begun to wrestle with the question of the status of the natural sciences in dialogism. There is ample evidence in Bakhtin's allusions to relativity and quantum theory for concluding, as have Hirschkop and other critics, such as D. S. Neff in an important essay,[8] that he was indeed, as Hirschkop charges, heavily influenced by "mechanical physics."

The natural sciences undoubtedly provided Bakhtin with some of his most basic systemic metaphors. One aspect of Bakhtin's early investment in Kant that stayed with him throughout his career was a sense that the question of what is real cannot be separated from the philosophy of science. But a single-minded focus on physics among Bakhtin's critics has obscured the possibly even greater role played by the life sciences in dialogism. Hirschkop asks, "[W]hy is there such a deep connection between the discovery of value and consciousness of exact physical placement [in Bakhtin]?" (13). I believe his question draws attention to a feature that has fundamental significance in dialogism, that is, its emphasis on the material ground of existence. In order for his question to work, however, it needs to be extended: not only should we wonder why placement in space and time is so important in Bakhtin's theory of the subject, but we must ask as well, *What* exactly is it that materializes situatedness in that precise physical placement. And the answer, quite clearly, is that it is the *body* of the subject that registers his or her situatedness.

Bakhtin's radical insistence on the situatedness of perception results inevitably in an emphasis on the human body. In such early texts as "Philosophy of the Act," Bakhtin is already announcing the Leitmotiv orchestrating the overwhelming bulk of his later work: "In the given unique point at which I am now located, no one else in the unique time and unique space of unique being can be located."[9] The logical result of so relentless a focus on uniqueness is to assign enormous privilege to the physical body, the marker most unambiguously indicating location in such a unique point.

From the prominence of bodies in his Rabelais book, from the central role of "embodiment" in such early works as "Author and Hero in Aesthetic Activity," from his emphasis on the physiological bases of time and space perception in the essay on chronotopes, it is obvious that Bakhtin, whose chronic osteomyelitis was a constant personal reminder of his own corporeality, was particularly engaged by bodies. Emphasis on the situatedness of the perceiving subject in Bakhtin's early works, as well as on "material bearers of culture," and "bodies of meaning" (tela cm'icla) in such late texts as the *Novy Mir* interview in 1970, have troubled some of Bakhtin's more percipient readers. Hirschkop, for instance, says, "It seems odd that Bakhtin should so often define 'situation' as one's *place* in the most literal, physical sense. There is, in fact, a kind of gross and vulgar materialism underlying the theoretical sophistication: after all the philosophical subtleties, everything depends on a concept of abstract space drawn undiluted from mechanical physics."[10] But by focusing on the body as a merely physical thing, we miss much of what is important in the key Bakhtinian concept of situatedness. For Bakhtin, what matters about bodies is not only that they are *there*, but that they are *alive*—they manifest the deed of life in that particular place.

There is a certain irony in Bakhtin's critics focusing so single-mindedly on the role of physics to the exclusion of biology in dialogism: those who emphasize the mechanical as opposed to the life sciences recapitulate the history of vexed relations between the very disciplines involved in Bakhtin's assumptions about system—the relations between physics and biology. Physics, because it was first of the disciplines we now recognize as scientific to develop, has until very recently been regarded as the model to which all exact sciences should aspire. Because biology is not reducible to mathematics, the physicist Ernest Rutherford, for example, considered it to be simply a form of "postage stamp collecting."[11]

Physics has been a developed discipline since at least the seventeenth century, while biology does not exist even as a word, much less as a science, before the nineteenth century (it was first used in 1802 [by Gottfried Reinhold in German], and in English not until 1813). It is not surprising, then, that Newton's laws, and those of such successors as Einstein and Bohr, are often regarded as coextensive with the workings of science itself.

What such a view fails to take into account is precisely that aspect of biology that made it of interest to Bakhtin: it concerns itself with *animate subjects*, while physics studies *inanimate objects*. Unlike early physics, biology insists that there is a difference between a rock and a living organism. Thus biology from the beginning had to wrestle with the charge that the nature of its subject—life (*bios*)—was a concept that did not lend itself to the same kind of hard-edged definition that "velocity," or "temperature" had in physics. In fact, biology had to overcome the suspicion that its distinctive subject, "life," had the dubious appearance of "soul," and to hardheaded nineteenth-century physicists "life" was a topic that smelled suspiciously of transcendence. Certain biologists, such as Hans Driesch, on whom Bakhtin wrote a (pseudonymous) essay in 1926,[12] and certain eminent philosophers (such as preeminently Henri Bergson[13]) did not help matters when they sought to define "life" as a "nonmechanical entelechy," a "*vis viva*," an "élan vital," or some other mysterious force.

But as George Gaylord Simpson has pointed out, "Insistence that the study of organisms requires principles additional to those of the physical sciences does not imply a dualistic or vitalistic view of nature. Life . . . is not thereby necessarily considered as nonphysical or nonmaterial. It is just that living things have been affected for . . . billions of years by historical processes. . . . The results of those processes are systems different in kind from nonliving systems. . . ."[14] The difference between living and nonliving matter, in other words, consists not in the substance out of which they are made, but *in the form of their organization.*

Thus Bakhtin's predilection for biology should not at all be read as a turning away from materialism, certainly not from the specific lessons of Einsteinian or quantum physics, which play an important role in his systematic thinking. In fact, he appropriated biology as one way to deepen the significance physics might have as a model for open-ended systems. "Biology" in this sense should not, of course, be confused with the kind of crude organicism that is attacked in the Voloshinov book on Freud, where the whole school of *Lebensphilosophie* (Simmel, Scheler, Bergson, Driesch) is denounced: "A sui generis fear of history, an ambition to locate a world beyond the social and the historical, a search for this world precisely in the depths of the organic—these are the features that pervade systems of contemporary philosophy and constitute the symptom of the disintegration and decline of the bourgeois world."[15]

Bakhtin's use of biological models, especially as they pervade his thinking about culture, does not consist in the appropriation of any particular, single doctrine taken over from the discipline of biology. Rather, his work is bathed in what might be called "biological thinking" (or, as it is sometimes called, "population thinking"), a point of view that is imposed when the world has introduced into it the phenomenon of *living* (a dynamic process, which is not the same as the static entity generations of philosophers have sought to define as the substantive "life"). I have in mind here the attributes of living as they both determine the behavior of single organisms and mandate special conditions that must be met for any system that includes them.

Using the eminent biologist and philosopher of science Ernst Mayr as our guide, we might identify among the features of living systems that make them different from nonliving systems of the kind physicists study—the features that made living systems influential in shaping Bakhtin's dialogism—the following: living systems are first of all *complex.* "Systems may have any degree of complexity, but, on the average, systems in the world of organisms are infinitely more complex than those of inanimate objects" (Mayr 1982, 53). "Complexity" has a particular meaning in a biological context, one that has been neatly summarized by H. A. Simon, who defines a complex system as one in which "the whole is more than the sum of the parts, not in an ultimate, metaphysical sense but in the important pragmatic sense that, given the properties of the parts and the laws of their interaction, it is not a trivial matter to infer the properties of the whole."[16] Quite simply, "most structures of an organism are meaningless without the rest of the organism; wings, legs, heads, kidneys cannot live by themselves but only as parts of an ensemble" (Mayr 1982, 53–54).

The *opposite* of such a system, one that would be merely mechanical, is precisely the kind of system Bakhtin begins his career by attacking. The first words in his first published piece, "Art and Answerability," are: "[A] whole is called 'mechanical' when its constituent elements are united only in space and time by some external connection and are not imbued with the internal unity of meaning. The parts of such a whole are contiguous and touch each other, but in themselves they remain alien to each other."[17] It was to avoid such reductionism that Bakhtin was driven to search for the kind of systemic connectedness biologists call complexity. It was complexity understood in just this sense that gave rise to Bakhtin's emphasis on dialogue as the only mode of interaction between elements locked into such ramifying interconnectedness.

Another special characteristic of living organisms that necessitates a particular way of looking at any world they inhabit, is that—unlike mechanical entities—they cannot be easily quantified. The qualitative aspects of biology "are particularly important in relational phenomena, which are precisely the phenomena that dominate living nature. Species, classification, ecosystems, communicatory behavior, regulation, and just about every other biological process deals with relational properties" (Mayr 1982, 55). Relational systems are those in which fine discriminations are made at a local level; such systems are, in other words, value systems. The distinction between quantitative and qualitative worldviews is what Bakhtin had in mind when he writes in a characteristic passage, "Naive positivism assumes that what we have to do with in the world . . . is a matter of . . . mathematical numbers, and that these have a bearing on the meaning and purpose of our acts. . . . Meanwhile, the only thing these concepts explain is the material of the world, the technical apparatus of the event of the world. . . . What needs to be understood, however, is not the technical apparatus, but the immanent logic of creative activity, and what needs to be understood first of all is [its] value-and-meaning structure,"[18] or, in other words, a system of values. Values impel choice, of course, an important first hint as to the closeness of dialogism and experimental method, where discrimination is fundamental.

Living systems are not only complex, they are indeterminate, or, as Bakhtin has it, "unconsummated," "unfinished" (nezaveršen). Indeterminacy is not to be thought of in terms of its role in physics,[19] but must be understood in connection with systems that grow, that are living. Remember that "complexity in living systems exists at every level form the nucleus (with its DNA program), to the cell, to any organ system (like kidney, liver, or brain), to the individual, the ecosystem, or the society" (Mayr 1982, 53). Not only is it the case that this hierarchy mandates great subtlety in understanding relations between its different planes, from nuclei to nations: what cannot be overemphasized is that *at each level*, these elements are constantly changing *in themselves*. "While entities in the physical sciences, let us say atoms or elementary particles, have constant characteristics, biological entities are characterized by their changeability. Cells, for instance, constantly change their properties and so do individuals. Every individual undergoes a drastic change from birth to death . . . from the original zygote, through adolescence, adulthood, senescence, to death" (Mayr 1982, 55).

As if all this potential randomness were not enough, living systems are characterized by a constant interplay between organisms and their physical environment. Two systems that are highly variable in themselves—unique individuals and unique ecosystems—create, when perceived in terms of their mutual influence, another order of stochastic possibilities. The way in which individual organisms interact with others of the same species, with the weather, or with populations of other animals in their environment creates a perpetual dialogue whose consequences are unpredictable in most given instances.

Living systems require that attention be paid to complexity, indeterminacy, and uniqueness. The consequence of this is that biology is deeply pervaded by history. Max Delbrück makes the point by contrasting, once again, the physical and the life sciences: "A mature physicist, acquainting himself for the first time with the problems of biology, is puzzled by the circumstance that there are no 'absolute phenomena' in biology. *Everything is time-bound and space-bound.*"[20] It is precisely this sense that everything is ineluctably historical that impels Bakhtin to assert that "the image of man is always intrinsically chronotopic."[21]

When, then, I describe Bakhtin's dialogism as being pervaded by biological thinking, I mean that such key concepts as "heteroglossia," "chronotope," and, of course, "dialogue" itself, as well as the crucial distinctions between "finished" and "unfinished," "horizon" and "environment," or "given" versus "created" relate to each other most meaningfully if they are conceived as aspects of a single worldview. The worldview they manifest is one that focuses on all relations as having complexity of a kind found in living—as opposed to mechanical—systems.

In what follows I will argue that such a system has relevance not only in explaining why consciousness is situated, but why perception located in this way inevitably leads to a particular way of coming at the world. The dialogue between organism and environment must take place as a constant *experimentation* on the part of the situated subject. The way in which these experiments are conducted, and how their results will be evaluated, will differ, of course, from place to place and from time to time. But there is enough sameness in the logic of perception that it may begin to serve as the kind of "relative universal" we need in order to mediate between authoritarian claims to uniformity (of which Eurocentric colonialism is a particularly egregious example) and the wilderness of difference in which cultural relativity, when taken to its logical extreme, must result.

III

Difference has of late been much celebrated. Epistemological and psychoanalytic aspects of the problem have famously preoccupied much of recent French thought, especially those aspects of it that have had the greatest resonance in the United States. But today an increasingly urgent dimension of alterity seems to be the question of differences between cultures. How are we to evaluate such disparities in an age when many of the traditional sources of authority have broken down? In the past, European culture represented (for Europeans, certainly, but also for many non-Europeans) a cross-cultural norm, and was felt to be superior to that of, let us say, Aztec culture. The Spanish were Christians and knew the one and only God, while the early Mexicans were inferior because they did not know the truth of Christianity. In later periods new absolutes were invoked: anthropologists, such as Lévy-Bruhl, could claim that there was a fundamental distinction between European and all traditional (or, as he said, "primitive") societies because he had a postreligious, but no-less-effective standard for making such a judgment: insofar as Europeans were "logical," and native peoples were not—Brazilian tribes were "prelogical" because they believed that they were men and parakeets at the same time—Europeans were superior.[22] They were at a more advanced stage in a cycle all societies must complete, because they recognized a truth of the world tribal cultures had not yet perceived.

In our own day the power of logic to make distinctions of this kind is, to say the least, less self-evident. Either one dispenses with it entirely as simply one more culturally, historically, and, some would argue, gendered ideology, or one argues with slightly more discrimination, as Peter Winch,[23] or the Tartu developmental psychologist Peeter Tulviste[24] recently have done, that the practice of magic is simply one of a *number* of ways of thinking that might be characteristic of a given culture, and does not at all exclude the simultaneous existence in the *same* culture of quite rational technical practices: one may *indeed* be both a man and a parakeet.[25]

While there is a great deal of confusion in recent debate among cultural critics, one thing is very clear: any point of view that claims a mediating thirdness, that is, any claim to be a standard for evaluating differences between two cultures, is now open to charges of "essentialism" or "foundationalism," an ideological blindness to the historical and culturally constructed nature of knowledge. Structuralism is widely regarded as the historically latest attempt to evade history, thus permitting a wide range of contemporary suspicions to be generalized as "poststructural," as when Catherine Belsey and Jane Moore write: "In poststructuralist theory meanings are cultural and learned, but they are also unfixed, sliding, plural. . . . Culture itself is the limit of our knowledge: there is no available truth outside culture. . . ."[26]

Such a definition of theory—and I take it to be canonical for a wide spectrum of work now being done across several professional discourses—is opposed not only to structuralism, but to the whole armature of attitudes that have been subsumed under the term "scientific method." Scientific method has been under increasing attack since 1945, when science demonstrated its power in the instantaneous destruction of whole cities. Since then, a growing number of historians and philosophers of science have joined with newly emergent feminist and anticolonialist scholars to raise further questions about the claims of scientific method.

They have done so because science is increasingly perceived not just as one more belief system, but as one that is particularly repressive. Paul Feyerabend notes, "Almost all scientific subjects are compulsory subjects in our schools. While the parents of a six year old child can decide to have him instructed in the rudiments of Protestantism, or in the rudiments of the Jewish faith, or to omit religious instruction altogether, they do not have a similar freedom in the case of the sciences."[27] It is at this point that a bit of on-the-job cultural relativism may help us to understand Bakhtin's enthusiasm for science, a position that would appear to be quite at odds with suspicions about scientific method now being raised in the West. Far from being viewed as oppressive, science has, since at least the work of the great Lomonosov in the eighteenth century, been most often seen by Russians as a liberating force. Revolutionary critics of the nineteenth century (Chernyshevsky, Pisarev, and others) used science as their primary anticlerical weapon in the ideological struggle against the czar, whose claims to authority were rooted in the Russian

Orthodox church. After the October Revolution, the exact sciences (especially physics) were the one area of activity least affected by Party dogma, although they too did not go completely unscathed. Bakhtin, of course, is drawing more specifically on the capital that science always constituted in the work of Kant himself, and even more markedly in the work of the Marburg school of neo-Kantians (Hermann Cohen, Paul Natorp, Ernst Cassirer). Suffice it to say that Bakhtin is thinking in an environment where science had a plus instead of a negative sign attached to it in general.

As I noted, the situation is quite different now in the West. Ruth Bleier sums up several papers presented at a 1985 conference on women in science by identifying scientific method as "an oral tradition and set of idealized practices . . . [which] at each step . . . is profoundly affected by the values, opinions, biases, beliefs, and interests of the scientist."[28] Lynda Birke, in *Women, Feminism, and Biology: The Feminist Challenge*, goes even further, suggesting a complicity between scientific method and a repressive genderization: "At least part of the reason why present scientific methods are held to be better than others—to give greater truth—is that . . . they have become historically associated with masculinity. Other ways of knowing have become synonymous with the feminine—and accordingly are held to be less true."[29]

Donna Haraway has shown how assailable are claims to scientific objectivity in primatology (the study of forms of life similar to, but earlier or "lower" than, *Homo sapiens*), with results that have implications not only for feminists, but for anti-colonialists as well. Haraway has written a detailed study of what has been done in the name of science to the skeleton of a three-million-year-old erect biped female, quickly dubbed "Lucy," found in Haadar, Ethiopia. Lucy is now widely regarded as the hominid ancestor of ancestors, but Haraway has no difficulty—and a great deal of naughty fun—in showing how reconstructions of Lucy's sex life and family relations flow more or less directly out of the ideology and fantasies of the mostly male primatologists who have written about Lucy. Haraway says, "In other times and places, people might have cast Lucy's bones in the rituals of necromancy for purposes Western observers called *magical*. But Western people cast her bones into "scientific" patterns for insight into a human future made problematic by the very material working-out of the Western stories of apocalypse and transcendence."[30]

Biology, of special importance in dialogism, has been a particular problem for those in the West troubled by the relation between science and ideology. This is chiefly because some of the greatest political excesses have appealed to biology for authority, as in the cases of colonialist theories of social Darwinism, "scientific" attacks directed against people of color or Jews because they are organically inferior, or the Stalinist genetics of Lysenko. The power of biology to serve such ends is based on the epistemologically privileged claims it makes about the human body. We must become naive again to remember such obvious truths as there is no politics without society, there is no society without human subjects, and human subjects—for all their differences—have in common the fact of *material embodiment*: the body is therefore a most potent force in ideology, for it is the one home we share in the world's diverse materiality.

The communality that comes with the condition of being embodied may at first blush appear to be trivial; it will perhaps seem less so if we remember as well that embodiedness — in the first of several important features it shares with language — not only joins us, but separates us as well. Politics, as the means by which claims to authority and ascriptions of responsibility are negotiated, requires a space that is social in the degree to which it is composed of interacting individuals who can figure authority and responsibility because they are simultaneously the same and different. At its most basic, a head is needed to anoint when a king is crowned, and a head is needed to chop off when a king is deposed. Each such instance, as every issue of the journal *Representations* reminds us, is only a representation of something else.

But what does the universal condition of separate embodiment have to do with science? To answer this question we might begin by recognizing that "scientific method," as a construct, is usually used interchangeably with experimental method, with selection and judging. The difference between what scientists do when they are in the laboratory, and what all of us do most of the time (including scientists when they are outside the laboratory) is one of quantity and not quality: each is a contest of differing assumptions about the world adjudicated by results judged according to their effects as registered in individual bodies, even when there are enough individual bodies together to form the kind of mass that enters politics and history. It is this aspect of having to perceive the world through the optic of values that is the root of scientific method in normal human existence, as well as the aspect of living that is a central preoccupation of Bakhtin's dialogism.

The condition of being in a body is similar to the condition of being in a language insofar as in both cases the relation between one and many, self and other, us and them, is primary. Desire and its ideologies are not individual phenomena, any more than words and their meanings can be unique. But the effects of desire are no less known in particular, separate bodies than words that belong to every speaker, and yet which are uttered by particular, separate speakers. We are texts insofar as the world writes on our bodies its judgments concerning our assumptions about it.

Stated briefly, my thesis is this: scientific method is more comprehensive, relative to other methods for adjudicating differences, because we are so constructed as to have bodies in quite the way we do. And the way we do is paradoxical: the very separateness of our bodies is the one thing we all have together. What we share is uniqueness. In this apparent contradiction is to be found a common root of both scientific method and political practice. The necessary science of everyday life consists in this: experimental method is a first condition of existence for beings who live in a world from which they are cut off by the wall of their skins, and thus a world that can be known even in its most rudimentary forms only through trial and error. And all relations between those who share the condition of bodily uniqueness are *political*, insofar as they must negotiate differences in the deployment of separate bodies, first in material and then in social space. The paradox of shared uniqueness that the body manifests for human beings constitutes in its turn another paradox: the possibility of a relative universal.

Since the term "scientific method" is so complicit with the name Francis Bacon, who also celebrated knowledge as power, thus rendering the very term of "scientific method" suspect, it might be well to clarify what is meant when I invoke it as a term. I do not mean the kind of science the demise of which was proposed at the twenty-fifth annual Nobel Conference in 1989. That conference had as its theme "The End of Science," yet another Fukuyama-ism whose egregiousness was only slightly ameliorated by the addition of a question mark ("The End of Science?"). The organizers allowed as how there is today "an uneasy feeling . . . that science, as a unified, universal, objective endeavor, is over."[31] Mary Hesse argued that "the whole imperialist aim of theoretical science to be the royal and single road to knowledge has been a profound mistake" (Hesse, 24).[32] Another philosopher of science (Sandra Harding) attacked pure science because it demanded large sums of public money while having "no apparent social value." And she added, "I'm not arguing that everybody should do socially important work. I would really be happy to play bridge all day—I love it. But I wouldn't think of asking for huge supplies of Federal and national resources in order to entertain myself" (Harding, 24).[33]

The historical, political—and, if I may say so, the scientific—bankruptcy of a science that would claim to be pure in the sense of being *wertfrei* is so patent that I'll not waste time in demonstrating that it is not what I have in mind when invoking scientific method. It is precisely the degree to which science is ineluctably bound up with values and the need to make discriminations that makes it important for dialogism. The bankruptcy of claiming that science is "value free" is so obvious that one can't help wondering what it is that motivates otherwise serious philosophers of science (as Mary Hesse certainly is) to use it even as a straw man (with all the gendered irony that term bears). Rather, the kind of science I am meditating here is an extreme case of what we all do all of the time—its ubiquitousness for humans is what makes it recognizably the aspect of science that attracted Bakhtin.

IV

We might better understand the positive charge of science in dialogism if we invoke not the Baconian and Cartesian versions of science now under attack by critics like Feyerabend, but turn rather to what Arthur Danto has called "beautiful science."[34] Danto's account of "beautiful science" begins with his gloss on the famous 1986 issue of the prestigious journal *Science* that contained two articles by Jeremy Nathans and his team at Stanford University. In these articles Nathans reported how his group had isolated the genes that control the perception of color: using DNA probes, they analyzed defects in the DNA of various categories of dichromates until they determined the precise protein moieties or "opsins" on the x-chromosome that specify the three primitives out of which all others are made, the red, green, and violet centers excited by, respectively, long, medium, and short waves. The importance of this research was not only that it clarified issues that had historically engaged figures as important as Newton, Dalton, Goethe, and von Helmholtz, but it provided overwhelming evidence that specific genes determine specific functions.

The papers by Nathans and his associates were felt to be so important that the editors of *Science* provided an introduction by the distinguished geneticist David Botstein, who praises Nathans's work not only for its contribution to chromatics and genetics, but because it illustrates so well the journey from "discovery" to "understanding." Botstein writes:

> First, the confrontation of the human mind with a natural phenomenon, then its investigation through observations and experiments, the continual proposal of theories, the testing of predictions, and finally, in the best case, the convincing demonstration of the validity of one of the theories through confirmation of its specific predictions. The process can take only a few years and involve only a few scientists or it can span centuries and involve many. The practical consequences may be revolutionary and change the course of history (for example, special relativity) or it may have little or no use. In either case, a full scientific story, especially one that has been unfolding over historic times, can be a lovely thing, like a classical symphony or a Gothic cathedral. (Quoted in Danto 1989, 370)

This, then, is what Danto is calling "beautiful science." And he begins by pointing out a curious dichotomy in scientific method so understood. There is in the work of the Stanford researchers much that would have been *un*familiar to scientists in the past:

> To all the earlier investigators in this history, beginning with Isaac Newton, John Dalton, Thomas Young, . . . von Helmholtz and James Clark Maxwell, some components in Nathans's work would have been incomprehensible in terms of the science of their day: they lacked the theoretical matrices for understanding various of its central terms [such as DNA, opsins, and so on]. All of them, on the other hand, would have . . . accepted the general picture of Beautiful Science which Nathans's work, like their own, very adequately exemplifies. (Danto 1989, 370)

And just as the science of Nathans and his colleagues is both the same (in its method), but different (in its content) from the science of Newton and Maxwell in the past, so it is that all future science will be both the same and different from what it now is. If we think of science as Botstein and Danto do, then "we really know what there is to know about the science of the future. It will be as much like it is today two centuries hence as it was two centuries ago. Nothing can be science which greatly differs from what science is today. But if we mean the future exemplars of Beautiful Science, well, we can have as dim an idea of what they will be in time to come as Newton or Dalton would have had two centuries ago . . . of the Stanford results of 1986" (Danto 1989, 372). In other words, the matter of future science will always be *other*, but experimental method will always be a *limit* (although very capacious and elastic) on what that otherness can be. If so much is granted (and not all will go so far, of course), then the question becomes, Why should the formal procedure of experimental method remain constant, while the theories it seeks to establish and the assumptions it makes about everything else will have changed so radically?

Danto is seeking to understand why it is that microbiology, for all its shaping force, cannot determine the route from genes to the content of future theories, let us say, from the microbiological gene to theories of microbiology itself. We may confidently suppose that

> our human genetic endowment . . . is invariant from Aristotle . . . to Nathans and after: it is, relative to the contents of theories, a kind of tabula rasa. . . . There may be [there will almost certainly be discovered] a microbiology of linguistic competence, which accounts for the fact that any human child can learn any natural language. But that is not the same thing as saying that in every child every language — including languages for possible worlds that never are to become actual — are stored as DNA sequences: that there are Russian, French, and Yiddish genes. So . . . we must suppose the content of Beautiful Science's microbiology will not be among the things of which it is the microbiology. So of what *will* it be a microbiology? (1989, 376)

The answer, surely is

> contained already in the familiar description of Beautiful Science given by David Botstein: it is the microbiology of what scientists do when they confront nature, propose theories, perform experiments, make observations. Now these are things we all do, at a certain level, when we perceive something, form a belief about it, infer certain propositions that must be true if our beliefs are sound, and perform certain actions to see if they are sound. . . . Small wonder then that the picture of Beautiful Science is so familiar, small wonder that it would have been familiar to Aristotle. . . . (Danto 1989, 376)

What permits allochronic exercises in science to be mutually intelligible is that the subjects who perform them are transhistorically defined as beings who make propositions, test them, and evaluate the results.

By making use of the familiar concepts of common sense of "folk psychology" — beliefs, desires, hopes, fears, intentions, and ends — we attain an enviable degree of interpersonal coordination. But this view of the human subject as constructed from beliefs, perception, and feeling has recently been assailed as a hopeless anachronism by philosophers seeking analogues between computers and brains (as in Steven Stich's book, *From Folk Psychology to Cognitive Science*).[35] As Amahl Smith has recently pointed out, "Our folk physics and our folk demonology have not withstood the test of time; why believe our folk psychology will fare any better?"[36]

One reason for thinking it might withstand such a test is that it seems to be the kind of thinking that Danto has in mind when he equates "beautiful science" with characteristically human behavior. As such, it is just such "folk psychology" (as a transhistorical, transcultural category) that is "certainly not part of the history of psychology" (Danto 1989, 378) conceived as a science. Just as experimental method transcends any of its historically instanced applications ("the content of Beautiful Science's microbiology will not be among the things of which it is the microbiology"), folk psychology will not be among the things of which it is a psychology. Now it is precisely here, in the equation of scientific method with the folk psychology that presumes belief, perception, action, inference, desire, and feeling, that Danto's work would seem to speak most cogently to what I take to be the key proposition in dialogism, that is, that we can know the world only from a unique situation in it, and yet are compelled by the nature of life to generalize our local knowledge.

V

Keeping these considerations in mind, it is possible now to turn to the question with which we began: For all its obvious kinship with cultural criticism as it is now practiced, can dialogism provide help in better conceptualizing the chief bugbear of such criticism, the problem of cultural relativity? Can dialogism help us avoid the Scylla of essentialism and the Charybdis of endless difference? We might begin by considering some of the implications that flow from translating Bakhtin's emphasis on "I" and "the other" to "us" and "them." And we will be helped in this translation by a recent article by S. P. Mohanty devoted to cultural relativism, called, not by chance, "Us and Them."[37]

Mohanty recognizes the potentially vicious effects of relativism taken to an unarbitratable extreme, and yet he is not unaware of the fallacies into which former positivisms and essentialisms have fallen: the trivializing psychologizations, the unrealistically isolated individual as subject, the unexamined assumption of authority. And, drawing on the work of Charles Taylor, he proposes as a category for mediating between cultural differences, "human agency." The definition of human agency is twofold: "If . . . we are to deal seriously with other cultures and not reduce them to insignificance or irrelevance, we need to begin by positing the following minimal commonality between us and them: the capacity to act purposefully, to be capable of agency and the basic rationality that the human agent must in principle possess" (Mohanty 1989, 21). What makes agency specifically human is "the capacity to act purposefully but also to *evaluate* actions and purposes in terms of larger ideas we might hold about, say, our political and moral world, or our sense of beauty or form. . . . It is this capacity for a second-order understanding and evaluation, which enables us to be critically and cumulatively self-aware in relation to our actions, that defines human agency and makes possible the sociality and the historicality of human existence" (Mohanty 1989, 22).

Danto and Mohanty are self-deprecating in the claims they make for the heroine of their cross-cultural scenarios: the irony of "folk psychology" as a term for Danto's transhistorical category is obvious, and Mohanty's favorite adjective is "minimal," as in "minimal tasks" (24), "the minimum basis of intelligibility" (22), or "minimal rationality" (23, 24). Such modesty is understandable in light of the notoriously inflated claims made by proponents of scientific method who perceived what is, after all, only a folk psychology as the triumph of an all-conquering reason, or those who interpreted human agency as the hallmark of "Man." Danto and Mohanty seek to avoid the partial blindness that has afflicted past attempts to formulate a thirdness capable of putting "us" and "them" into more meaningful interaction. And both do so by emphasizing the role of proposition and experiment in the principle each puts forward as common to humans across time and cultures. But what is common to the principles they put forward, what do folk psychology and human agency share in their definition of sharing? It is in answering such a question that the ineluctability of human embodiment makes itself felt with the greatest urgency.

No area of science has more radically experienced the paradox of difference and sameness than anthropology, and this is no more evident than in the 1986 volume edited by James Clifford and George Marcus called *Writing Culture*.[38] So in trying to understand the relation of bodies to theories of cultural relativity, it is perhaps fitting to conclude with some reflections on what has to be a major text for anyone preoccupied by such questions. The cover of the Clifford and Marcus volume carries a photograph of the anthropologist Stephen Tyler at work in an Indian village. Clifford uses the photo as the organizing trope for his introductory essay, describing it in these terms: "The ethnographer is absorbed in writing—taking dictation? recording an important observation? dashing off a poem? Hunched over in the heat, he has draped a wet cloth over his glasses. His expression is obscured. An [Indian villager] looks over his shoulder—with boredom? patience? amusement? In this image the ethnographer hovers at the edge of the frame—faceless, almost extraterrestrial, a hand that writes" (Clifford and Marcus 1986, 1).

This photo is indeed what Clifford would make of it: an icon of cultural difference mediated by the power of writing. But Clifford, for all his subtlety and sympathy, is perhaps premature in his assumption that it is a *hand* that writes, or that the agent of the writing is hovering, in his pregnant phrase, "at the edge of the frame." I make this suggestion under the influence of another meditation on the writing of culture, not simply as one world is recorded by a visitor from another, but as the world itself writes on the bodies of those who are objects being studied and those who think they are subjects doing the studying. I have in mind here Kafka's great parable on the writing of culture as a writing on bodies, called "In the Penal Colony."[39]

VI

The tale, you will remember, is very simple; a traveling researcher ("Forschungs-reisende") from Europe visits an island prison in the tropics, where he is shown a machine used to execute those who commit crimes on the island. The officer who demonstrates the machine is afraid the order it represents is about to be replaced by a new order instituted by a new commandant. He asks the scientist to intervene, but he refuses. The officer then releases the man who was about to be executed and takes his place in the machine himself. He is brutally killed when the apparatus breaks down. The anthropologist gets in a small boat to be taken to the ship that will carry him back to Europe, but, as the story concludes, he must beat off the released prisoner and his former guard to do so.

The apparatus at the heart of the story is a scholarly apparatus, an interpretation machine created to teach certain things about writing and reading—and bodies. The machine consists of three parts: on the top is a *designer*, which controls the work of the *harrow*, a set of needles that writes what the designer dictates into the body of the victim, who is strapped to a *bed*. It also legislates three points of view: that of the judges, who always know the sentence being inscribed into the prisoner's body; the public who never know the true sentence, for they are unaware that the machine is actually writing on its victim, much less *what* the machine is writing; and the prisoner, who begins as member of the crowd insofar as he too is ignorant of what is transpiring, but who, throughout the course of the twelve hours the machine takes to do its work, learns first that what is being inscribed in his skin is legible as a writing, and then seeks to puzzle out the specific message his body is textualizing. The execution really consists of a journey that the condemned man makes between the ignorance of the onlookers and the knowledge of the judges.

His enlightenment, that radiation that comes from his eyes in the sixth hour—or, in Kafka's twist on Dante, in the very middle of his twelve-hour journey—is the knowledge not only that he is being written on, but that a specific message is being addressed to him. The knowledge he gains, a knowledge that is so prized that the old commandant decreed that only children should be allowed close access to it (209), a transfiguration that "might tempt one to get under the harrow oneself," is first of all the awareness that what is happening to him is not a generalized experience, but a meaning with particular reference to him. He is being called and—in the most transitive sense of that verb—addressed. The spectators have only the general knowledge that "Now justice is being done" (209), but it is the privilege of the judges, and finally of the condemned man, to have knowledge of the particular form justice has taken in this specific execution. Although a man being torn by the needles struggles for the first five hours, he always grows quiet around the sixth hour: "Understanding comes to the most dull-witted [Verstand geht dem blödesten auf]. It begins around the eyes. From there it radiates. A moment that might tempt one to get under the harrow oneself" (204).

This apparatus, this *Schreibmaschine* that gives not only pain but light, defines more than the difference between those who know the sentence and those who do not. It determines as well the difference between two fundamentally opposed ways of perceiving the world. On the one hand, there are those who believe, like the proponent of Baconian science, they know a universal truth and are thus condemned always to judge, as is the officer who is the old commandant's vicar: "Guilt is never to be doubted [Die Schuld ist immer zweifellos]. Other courts cannot follow that principle, for they have several opinions. . . . That is not the case here . . ." (145). On the other hand, there are those who, like the cultural relativist, believe in the "new, mild Order" [die neue milde Richtung], and thus they can never judge another society from inside the home of its own culture. Such is "the famous Western investigator" [ein grosser Forscher des Abendlands]. Kafka goes out of his way to emphasize the degree to which the explorer occupies a point of view situated not only outside the island prison, but also outside the metropolitan "home" of which it is a colony: "He was neither a member of the penal colony nor a citizen of the state to which it belonged . . . he travelled only as an observer, with no intention at all of altering other people's methods of administering justice" (106).

The complexity of the parable is compounded by the extreme positions it deploys: the officer's status as judge for whom "Guilt is never to be doubted," and the anthropologist's status as an intercultural traveler who has "no intention at all of altering other people's methods of administering justice." But between the essentialist judge and the relativist anthropologist looms the other hero of the tale, the "remarkable piece of apparatus" that writes on bodies, which, unlike the ethnographer in Clifford's parable, hovers not at the edge of the frame, but is the limiting frame itself. It is not only the icon, but the engine of situatedness: the enlightenment it enacts is the knowledge that all our values are local to the place from which we make them, and that place is always a site established by the situation of our bodies.

The privilege of *specifically* instanced knowledge is what the machine manifests in all its parts. It is obvious in the designer, where the particular words are each time arranged differently to be sent in the message that will be inscribed into the condemned's body. The bed, with its straps and its little cup of rice pap, is arranged differently each time to fit the precise measurements of the condemned man's figure.

The harrow has features that make it particularly relevant to the machine's enactment of particularity. As the officer is first explaining the machine to the explorer, the scientist takes in the naming of the parts silently, until the officer gets to the harrow. At that point the officer asks a question by repeating what has just been said: "The harrow?" (193). The harrow, in other words, among all the other parts of the apparatus, is singled out for particular attention. One reason for such focus is that the German word for harrow is *Egge*, a word that puns *eigene*, which ineluctably conveys particularity. It can be "own," as in "My own house" (as opposed to anyone else's house) in an expression such as "Mein eigenes Haus." Or, if one wishes to specify a quality that specifically characterizes somebody or something, one uses the word *Eigenart*, as in the expression "Deutsche Eigenart," that quality that is peculiar to the Germans and no one else, or in "Eigenartbericht unserer Zeitung," meaning "a report from our own correspondent."

Kafka goes out of his way to underline the pun when the text says, "Yes, the harrow . . . a good name for it. The needles are set in like the teeth of a harrow . . ." (194), for in German this goes, "'Ja, die Egge' sagte der Offizier, 'der Name passt. Die Nadeln sind *eggenartig* angeordnet . . .'" (100). Not only is particularity the function of the harrow which writes the specific message in the condemned's body, it is the very name of the particular (*eggenartig/eigenartig*). Parallels between body structure and the means by which language organizes itself fascinated Kafka, and the pun as a trope is, of course, particularly suggestive in this regard. Using the name for sameness to nominate the difference that puns always manifest is only one of the ways in which otherness is shown to have a sameness.

Thus the opposition between the old and the new, between the tropics and Europe is read in Kafka's story as a distinction between knowledge whose authority resides in its particularity (its *Eigenartigkeit*), a uniqueness that is always situated, localized on the one side, and on the other, knowledge that is general and universal, not confined to a single site.

The story viewed in this light permits us to meditate again on the central place in it of the devilish torture machine. We are at least closer to understanding the question, "What is physical torture?" It is a setting in which subjects are reduced to the situation of the utmost localization: the victim of torture wills to be in some other place; least of all does he wish to be in the here and now of his pain, but it is in the nature of the pain torture inflicts that the victim cannot forget where he is. Torture cannot be separated from restraints needed to immobilize its victims. The whole meaning of the clamps and chains needed to bind the condemned is that, without such restraints, they would not be in the place of pain. The physical restraints, such as the straps that the victims keep tearing in their frantic struggle to escape the particular place where the needles can cut them, keep the body from being elsewhere. But it is the invisible pain that is most confining to the victim, for just as the physical restraints keep him lashed to a particular place, so the pain keeps him bound to a particular time, the constant present that will not let him forget his hurt, even in the deepest, most intimate recesses of his mind.

Not being able to get out of the time of a space that is ineluctably situated is, I believe, the situation Arthur Danto is describing when he invokes the paradox of beautiful science: that the content of experiment will always be different, local, historically specific; but the method of beautiful science will always be the same dialogue of proposition, testing, and evaluation, the end of which is a judgment made not only from the particular site of a specific body, but a judgment shaped by the effects of the test on that body. "Beautiful science" presumes an anthropology, one that might be useful in reconceiving that other science that calls itself anthropology: the subject presumed by beautiful science is one that can know only through the exercise of value discrimination, or, in other words, through a judging whose mode of being is interaction, through experiment with the environment. The characteristic space of such a subject is dialogical, or perhaps better, ecological, insofar as ecology maintains its filiations with "oikos," the house which is our home, the home of our bodies that determines the otherness of another person.

In this light, what is mysterious about Kafka's parable is not its emphasis on a gnostic, or even political, otherness. We are compelled to invert the logic of canonical Kafka criticism which parabolically assigns an abstract meaning to particular details in the stories. "In the Penal Colony" is a parable about polarity and incommensurability, alright, but it is so not in order to dramatize some abstract proposition, but to celebrate precisely the opposite condition of specificity, rootedness in a particular situation. The ruling paradox of "In the Penal Colony" is that we are all in the penal colony insofar as we are all both judges and judged. That is what is perhaps most unsettling in its proposition that particularity—situatedness with all its attendant implications for the need to experiment to know—is a universal condition for subjects that are embodied. Kafka's paradox is that uniqueness is what we all have in common.

I would like to suggest in conclusion that that is also the root paradox of anthropology, one Lévi-Strauss seems to have overlooked precisely in those studies devoted to the writing on bodies to which he addressed himself when studying the tattoos and painted designs that textualized the particularity of Brazilian Indians.[40] The abstractions of French structuralism are happily in decline. But we have recently perhaps gone too far in the other direction, as utter difference is increasingly celebrated and the will to make judgments across cultures seems to have faded in the face of arguments that the evaluation of a culture can be made only from within the center of that culture itself. We have left the place of the judges. But if we give too much weight to the particularity and uniqueness of a culture, are we not falling into the subject position of the judged? Can we, from so hopelessly situated a place as cultural relativism provides, ever experience the otherness needed to effect real differences? Must we not get out from under the harrow, the machine of seamless identity, if we are to give others the gift of our own otherness?

In light of Bakhtin's emphasis on situatedness, we may read Kafka's tale as a kind of dialogic parable about monologue, whose moral would run something like this: we must always respect the difference of cultural systems different from our own, but we are equally ethically bound to have a set of principles that will let us distinguish between various cultures effectively and coherently. What such principles might be we are still in the process of working out. If the argument that is now being made from various sides for parallels between experimental method and folk psychology has any validity at all, those cultures that are least insensitive to the biologically mandated human necessity to explore differences will provide a principle of sameness that has the beginnings of what a greater openness to difference might look like. This surely is what Bakhtin is pointing to when he insists that "in the realm of culture, outsideness is a most powerful factor in understanding. . . . A meaning only reveals its depths once it has encountered . . . another foreign meaning. . . . We raise new questions for a foreign culture, ones that it did not raise itself; we seek answers to our own questions in it; the foreign culture responds to us by revealing to us its new aspects and new semantic depths."[41] The sameness and difference of the body is something we must remember not only as a culturally produced representation, but as the root condition of our common mortality.

Notes

1. M. M. Bakhtin, "Response to a Question from the *Novy Mir* Editorial Staff," in *Speech Genres and Other Late Essays*, trans. Vern W. McGee, ed. Caryl Emerson and Michael Holquist (Austin: University of Texas Press, 1986), 3; my italics.

2. Bakhtin, "Response to a Question," 6–7.

3. Bakhtin, "From Notes Made in 1970–71," in *Speech Genres*, 147; "Toward a Methodology for the Human Sciences," in *Speech Genres*, 169.

4. Bakhtin, "Response to a Question," 2.

5. Bakhtin, "The Problem of the Text," in *Speech Genres*, 108.

6. V. N. Voloshinov, *Marxism and the Philosophy of Language*, trans. Ladislav Matejka and I. R. Titunik (Cambridge: Harvard University Press, 1986), 10–11.

7. Ken Hirschkop, "Introduction: Bakhtin and Cultural Theory," in *Bakhtin and Cultural Theory*, ed. Ken Hirschkop and David Sheperd (Manchester, England: Manchester University Press, 1989), 1–38.

8. See the essay by D. S. Neff, "In the Heart of the Heart of the Chronotope: *Dialogism, Theoretical Physics, and Catastrophe Theory*," *Yale Journal of Criticism* 4, no.2 (Spring 1991), 87–104.

9. Bakhtin, "Arxitektonia nostupka," ed. S. G. Bočarov, *Sotsiologicheskie issledoranyja* 2 (1987): 167–68. A translation by Vadim Liapunov of a more comprehensive version of this fragment (part of the larger [but incomplete] text published by the University of Texas Press in 1990 as "Author and Hero in Aesthetic Activity") will be available.

10. Ken Hirschkop, "Bakhtin and Cultural Theory," in *Bakhtin and Cultural Theory,* 13.

11. Quoted by Ernst Mayr in his *The Growth of Biological Thought: Diversity, Evolution, and Inheritance* (Cambridge: Harvard University Press, Belknap Press, 1982), 33.

12. Bakhtin, "Sovremennij vitalizm [Contemporary Vitalism]" Chelovek i priroda [Man and Nature], 1: 33–42. 2: 9–23. Trans. in *The Crisis in Modernism: Bergson and the Vitalist Controversy,* edited by Frederick Burwick and Paul Douglass. (Cambridge, England: Cambridge University Press, 1992), 76–97.

13. Cf. Michael Holquist, "The Architectonics of Answerability," in M. M. Bakhtin, *Art and Answerability: Early Philosophical Essays,* trans. Vadim Liapunov, ed. Michael Holquist and Vadim Liapunov (Austin: University of Texas Press, 1990), xxxiii–xxxv.

14. George Gaylord Simpson, *This View of Life* (New York: Harcourt, Brace, World, 1964), 106–7.

15. V. N. Voloshinov, *Freudianism: A Marxist Critique,* trans. I. R. Titunik (New York: Academic Press, 1976), 14.

16. H. A. Simon, "The Architecture of Complexity," *Proceedings of the American Philosophical Association* 106 (1986): 467–82.

17. Bakhtin, "Art and Answerability," in *Art and Answerability,* 1.

18. Bakhtin, "Author and Hero in Aesthetic Activity," in *Art and Answerability,* 193–94.

19. However, Heissenberg's work, and that of other submolecular specialists, has opened up unexpected connections between the hitherto tightly segregated disciplines of physics and biology, nowhere more manifest than in the work of Max Delbrück.

20. Max Delbrück, "A Physicist Looks at Biology," in *Transactions of the Connecticut Academy of Arts and Sciences* 38 (1949): 173; my italics.

21. Bakhtin, "*Forms of Time and the Chronotope in the Novel,*" in *The Dialogic Imagination,* trans. Caryl Emerson and Michael Holquist, ed. Michael Holquist. (Austin: University of Texas Press, 1981), 85.

22. For a more complex insight into Lévi-Bruhl's thesis than is contained in his *The Primitive Mind,* see L. Lévi-Bruhl, *The Notebooks on Primitive Mentality* (New York: Harper and Row, 1975).

23. Peter Winch, "Understanding Primitive Society," in *Rationality,* ed. Bryan R. Wilson (Oxford: Oxford University Press, 1985), 78–111. This important essay originally appeared in *American Philosophical Quarterly* in 1964.

24. Peeter Tulviste, *Kul'turno-istoričskoe razvititie verbal'nogo myšlpnija.* Tallin: Valgus, 1988.

25. See J. Z. Smith, "I am a parrot (red)," *History of Religions* 11 (1972): 391–413.

26. Catherine Belsey and Jane Moore, eds. *The Feminist Reader: Essays in Gender and the Politics of Literary Criticism* (New York: Basil Blackwell, 1989), 10.

27. Paul Feyerabend, *Against Method: Outline of an Anarchistic Theory of Knowledge* (London: Verso Books, 1982), 301.

28. Ruth Bleier, ed., *Feminist Approaches to Science* (New York: Pergamon Press, 1988), 3.

29. Lynda Birke, *Women, Feminism, and Biology: The Feminist Challenge* (Brighton, England: Wheatsheaf Books, 1986), 152.

30. Donna Harraway, "Primatology Is Politics by Other Means," in *Feminist Approaches to Science,* 114–15.

31. See "Does Ideology Stop at the Laboratory Door? A Debate on Science and the Real World," *New York Times,* 22 October 1989, p. E24.

32. "Models, Metaphors, and Myths," *New York Times,* October 22, 1989, p. 24.

33. "Value Free Research Is a Delusion," *New York Times*, October 22, 1989, p. 24.

34. Arthur C. Danto, "Beautiful Science and the Future of Criticism," in *The Future of Literary Theory*, ed. Ralph Cohen (New York: Routledge, 1989), 370–85.

35. But see the powerful defense of folk psychology by Andy Clark in his *Microcognition: Philosophy, Cognitive Science, and Parallel Distributed Processing* (Cambridge: MIT Press, 1989); also see Roland Penrose, *The Emperor's New Mind* (New York: Oxford University Press, 1989), esp. chaps. 9 and 10.

36. Amahl Smith, "The Net of Behavior," *TLS*, 9–15 March 1990, p. 259.

37. S. P. Mohanty, "Us and Them: On the Philosophical Bases of Political Criticism," *Yale Journal of Criticism* 2, no.2 (Spring 1989): 1–32.

38. James Clifford and George Marcus, *Writing Culture: The Poetics and Politics of Ethnography* (Berkeley and Los Angeles: University of California Press, 1986).

39. Texts used in the following reading will be: in German, "In der Strafkolonie," in Franz Kafka, *Das Urteil und andere Erzählungen* (Frankfurt am Main, Germany: Fischer Verlag, 1987), 98–126; in English, "In the Penal Colony," in Franz Kafka, *Kafka: The Complete Stories* (New York: Schocken Books, 1976), 140–67.

40. Claude Lévi-Strauss, "Split Representation in the Art of Asia and America," in his *Structural Anthropology*, trans. Claire Jacobson and Brooke Grundfest Schoepf (New York: Doubleday/Anchor Books, 1967), 239–63.

41. Bakhtin, "Response to a Question," 7.

Conversation as Dialogue

I

Traditionally speech act theory has a very restricted subject matter. The speech act scenario is enacted by its two great heroes, "S" and "H"; and it works as follows: S goes up to H and cuts loose with an acoustic blast; if all goes well, if all the appropriate conditions are satisfied, if S's noise is infused with intentionality, and if all kinds of rules come into play, then the speech act is successful and nondefective. After that, there is silence; nothing else happens. The speech act is concluded and S and H go their separate ways. Traditional speech act theory is thus largely confined to single speech acts. But, as we all know, in real life speech acts are often not like that at all. In real life, speech characteristically consists of longer sequences of speech acts, either on the part of one speaker, in a continuous discourse; or it consists, more interestingly, of sequences of exchange speech acts in a conversation, where alternately S becomes H; and H, S.

Now the question naturally arises: Could we get an account of conversations parallel to our account of speech acts? Could we, for example, get an account that gave us constitutive rules for conversations in a way that we have constitutive rules of speech acts? My answer to that question is going to be "No." But we can say some things about conversations; we can get some sorts of interesting insights into the structure of conversations. So, before we conclude that we can't get an analysis of conversations parallel to our analysis of speech acts, let us see what sort of regularities and systematic principles we can find in the structure of conversations.

The first principle to recognize (and it's an obvious one) is that in a dialogue or a conversation, each speech act creates a space of possibilities of appropriate response speech acts. Just as a move in a game creates a space of possible and appropriate countermoves, so in a conversation, each speech act creates a space of possible and appropriate response speech acts. The beginnings of a theory of the conversational game might be a systematic attempt to account for how particular "moves," particular illocutionary acts, constrain the scope of possible appropriate responses. But when we investigate this approach, I believe we will see that we really do not get very far. To show this, let us first consider the most promising cases, so that we can see how special and unusual they are. Let us consider the cases where we do get systematic relationships between a speech act and the appropriate response speech act. The best cases are those that are misleadingly called "adjacency pairs," such as question/answer, greeting/greeting, offer/acceptance or rejection. If we consider question and answer sequences, we find that there are very tight sets of constraints on what constitutes an ideally appropriate answer, given a particular question. Indeed, the constraints are so tight that the semantic structure of the question determines and matches the semantic structure of an ideally appropriate answer. If, for example, I ask you a yes/no question, then your answer, if it's an answer to the question, has to count either as an affirmation or a denial of the propositional content presented in the original question. If I ask you a wh-question, I express a propositional function, and your appropriate response has to fill in the value of the free variable. For example, from an illocutionary point of view, the question, "How many people were at the meeting?" is equivalent to "I request you: you tell me the value of X in 'X number of people were at the meeting.'" That is, genuine questions (as opposed to, e.g., rhetorical questions), in my taxonomy at least, are requests; they are directives; and they are in general requests for the performance of speech acts, where the form of the appropriate response speech act is already determined by the form of the question.

However, there are some interesting qualifications to be made to these points about questions. One is this: I said in *Speech Acts*[1] that questions were requests for *information*, and that suggests that every question is a request for an assertion. But that seems obviously wrong if you think about it. The point was brought home to me very forcefully when the book was in press, and one Friday afternoon a small boy said to me "Do you promise to take us skiing this weekend?" In this case, he was asking for a *promise*, not a piece of factual *information*. He was requesting me either to promise or refuse to promise, and of course, those are speech acts different from assertions.

A second qualification is this: I said that the structure of questions determines and matches the structure of answers. But an apparent counterexample can be found in the exasperating English modal auxiliary verbs. There are cases where the structure of the interrogative does not match that of the appropriate response. If I say to you "Shall I vote for the Republicans?" or "Shall I marry Sally?" the appropriate answer is not "Yes, you shall" or "No, you shall not." Nor even "Yes, you will" or "No, you won't." The appropriate answer is, oddly enough, imperative—"Yes, do" or "No, don't." That is, "Shall I?" doesn't invite a response using a modal auxiliary verb, rather it seems to require an imperative; and thus from an illocutionary point of view it requires a directive.[2]

A third qualification is this: Often a question can be answered by an indirect speech act. In such cases the answer may be semantically and pragmatically appropriate, even though the syntax of the answer does not reflect the syntax of the question. Thus, in an appropriate context, "How many people were at the meeting?" can be answered by any of the following:

Everybody who was invited came.

I counted 127.

The auditorium was full.

even though none of these sentences matches the syntactical form of the propositional function expressed in the original question. They are answers in the way the following would not normally be:

None of your business.

How should I know?

Don't ask such dumb questions.

There are other classes of speech acts besides questions that serve to determine appropriate responses. An obvious case is direct requests to perform speech acts. Utterances such as "Say something in Portuguese" or "Tell me about last summer in Brazil," are straightforward, direct requests to perform speech acts, and they thus constrain the form of a possible appropriate reply.

The above are obviously two classes of speech acts in conversations where the dialogic sequence of initial utterance and subsequent response is internally related in the sense that the aim of the first speech act is only achieved if it elicits an appropriate speech act in response. How far can we get in discovering other such classes?

Well, a third—and rather large—class, are those cases where the speaker performs a speech act that requires acceptance or rejection on the part of the hearer. For example, an offer, a proposal, a bet, or an invitation all invite a response on the part of the hearer. Their structure constrains the hearer to accept or reject them. Consider, for example, offers. An offer differs from an ordinary promise in that an offer is a conditional promise, and the form of the conditional is that the promise takes effect only if it is explicitly accepted by the hearer. Thus, I am obligated by my offer to you only if you accept the offer. Offers are commissives, but they are conditional commissives, and the condition is of a very special kind, namely, conditional on acceptance by the hearer. In the case of bets, the bet is not even fully made unless it is accepted by the hearer. If I say to you "I bet you five dollars that the Republicans will win the next election," that is not yet a completed bet. It only becomes a bet if you accept it. The bet has only been effectively made if you say "OK, you're on" or "I accept your bet" or some such.

If we consider cases such as offers, bets, and invitations, it looks as if we are at last getting a class of speech acts where we can extend the analysis beyond a single speech act, where we can discuss sequences. But it seems that this is a very restricted class. In assertions, there are no such constraints. There are indeed general conversational constraints of the Gricean sort and other kinds. For example, if I say to you "I think the Republicans will win the next election," and you say to me, "I think the Brazilian government has devalued the Cruzeiro again," at least on the surface your remark is violating a certain principle of relevance. But notice, unlike the case of offers and bets, the illocutionary point of my speech act was nonetheless achieved. I did make an assertion, and my success in achieving that illocutionary point does not depend on your making an appropriate response. In such a case, you are just being rude, or changing the subject, or are being difficult to get on with, if you make such an irrelevant remark. But you do not violate a constitutive rule of a certain kind of speech act or of conversation just by changing the subject.

There are also certain kinds of formal or institutional speech act sequences where there are rules that constrain the sequencing. Think, for example, of courtrooms, formal debates, parliamentary procedures, and such like. In all of these cases, there are a set of extra-linguistic rules that impose a series of ceremonial or institutional constraints on the sequencing of utterances. The professionals are supposed to know exactly what to say and in what order, because the discourse is highly ritualized. The bailiff says "Everybody rise!" and then everybody rises. The bailiff then says "The Superior Court of the State of California, County of Alameda, is now in session, the Honorable J. B. Smitherby presiding." And then J. B. Smitherby comes and sits down. The baliff says, "Be seated and come to order," and then we can all sit down. The judge then starts conducting the proceedings in a highly ritualized fashion. Any incorrect speech act is subject to an "objection" which the judge is required to rule on. But that is hardly a good example of natural discourse. On the contrary, if you sit through a court hearing you are struck by its unnatural, highly structured and ceremonial character. Nonetheless there is something to be learned about the nature of conversation in general from this example, and that is that conversation only can proceed given a structure of expectations and presuppositions. I will come back to this point later.

II

So far it appears that traditional speech act theory will not go very far in giving us sequencing rules for discourse. So let us thrash around and see if we can find some other basis for a theoretical account. What I am going to conclude is that we will be able to get a theoretical account, but it won't be anything like our account of the constitutive rules of speech acts. I want to turn to two efforts or two approaches to giving a theoretical account, and show in what ways I think they are inadequate. They both have advantages, but they also have certain inadequacies. First, Grice's approach with his maxims of conversation, and then some work in a subject that used to be called "ethno-methodology."

Let's start with Grice.[3] He has four maxims of quantity, quality, manner, and relation. (This terminology is, of course, ironically derived from Kant.) Quantity has to do with such things as that you shouldn't say too much or too little. Manner has to do with the fact that you should be clear; quality has to do with your utterances being true, and supported by evidence; and relation has to do with the fact that your utterances should be relevant to the conversation at hand. I want to say that though I think these are valuable contributions to the analysis of language, they really are of limited usefulness in explaining the structure of conversation. Why? To begin with, the four are not on a par. For example, the requirement of truthfulness is indeed an *internal* constitutive rule of the notion of a statement. It is a constitutive rule of statement-making that the statement commits the speaker to the truth of the proposition expressed. There is no way to explain what a statement is without explaining what a true statement is, and without explaining that anybody who makes a statement is committed, other things being equal, to the truth of the proposition that he expressed in making the statement. It is the condition of satisfaction of a statement that it should be true, and it is an internal defect of a statement if it is false. But the other Gricean features are not like that. The standards of relevance, brevity, clarity, and so on, unlike truth, are not in that way internal to the notion of the speech act. They are all *external* constraints on the speech act, external constraints coming from general principles of rationality and cooperation. It is not a constitutive rule of statement-making that a statement should be relevant to the surrounding discourse. You can make a perfectly satisfactory statement, qua statement, and still change the subject of the conversation altogether. Notice in this connection that our response to the person who changes the subject in a conversation is quite different from our response to the person who, e.g., lies.

Well, one might say "So much the better for Grice." After all, what we are trying to explain is how speech act *sequences* can satisfy conditions of being de facto internally related, in the way I was talking about earlier, without there being necessarily any internal requirement of that relation, that is, without there being any de jure requirement from inside the initial speech act, of the sort that we had for such pairs as are initiated by offers, invitations, and bets. One might say: what we want are not constitutive rules of particular speech acts but precisely maxims of the Gricean sort that will play the role for talk exchanges that constitutive rules play for individual utterances. To support this we might point out that a series of random remarks between two or more speakers does not add up to a conversation. And this inclines us to think that relevance might be partly constitutive and hence explanatory of conversation in the same way that, for example, commitment to truth is partly constitutive and hence explanatory of statement making.

The analogy is attractive, but in the end I think it fails. Given a speech act, we know what counts as meeting its conditions of success and nondefectiveness; but given a sequence of speech acts in a conversation, we don't yet know what counts as a relevant continuation until we know something which is still external to the sequence, namely its purpose. But the fact that it is a conversation does not so far determine a purpose, because there is no purpose to conversations qua conversations in the way that there is a purpose to speech acts of a certain type qua speech acts of that type. Statements, questions, and commands, for example, each have purposes solely in virtue of being statements, questions, and commands; and these purposes are built in by their essential conditions. But conversations do not in that way have an essential condition that determines a purpose. Relative to one conversational purpose an utterance in a sequence may be relevant, relative to another it may be irrelevant.

You can see this point if you think of examples. Think of what counts as relevance in a conversation involving a man trying to pick up a woman in a bar, where indirection is the norm, and contrast that with the case of a doctor interviewing a patient, where full explicitness is required. You might even imagine the same two people with the same background capacities and many of the same sentences, but the constraints of a relevant response are quite different. Thus, suppose the conversation has reached the following point:

A: How long have you lived in California?

B: Oh, about a year and a half.

One relevant response by A in the bar might be:

A: I love living here myself, but I sure am getting sick of the smog in L.A.

That is not relevant in the clinic. On the other hand a perfectly relevant move in the clinic, but probably not in the bar, might be:

A: And how often have you had diarrhea during those eighteen months?

This variability is quite general. For example in formal "conversations" such as in a courtroom a statement may be stricken from the record as "irrelevant" or an answer as "nonresponsive." But in certain other formal conversations such as a linguistics seminar similar "irrelevant" and "nonresponsive" utterances would count as relevant and responsive. Still different standards would be applied in a casual conversation among friends.

The point I am making is: in the way that, e.g., a commitment to truth is in part constitutive of statement making, and therefore explanatory of statement making, the way that relevance is "constitutive" of conversation is not similarly explanatory of conversation; because what constitutes relevance is relative to something that lies outside the fact that it is a conversation, namely the purposes of the participants. Thus, you can't explain the general structure of conversation in terms of relevance, because what counts as relevance is not determined by the fact that it is a conversation. The fact that a sequence of utterances is a conversation, by itself, places no constraints whatever on what would count as a relevant continuation of the sequence.

We can now state this point more generally, that is, we can now make a general statement of the limitations of relevance to the analysis of conversational structure. Consider the syntax of "relevant." Superficially we might say: a speech act can be said to be relevant (or irrelevant) to a topic or issue or question. But once we see that, for example, a topic must be, as such, an object of interest to the speaker and hearer, we can now state a deeper syntax of "relevant." A speech act can be said to be relevant (or irrelevant) to a purpose, and a purpose is always someone's purpose. Thus, in a conversation, the general form would be: a speech act is relevant to the purpose P of a hearer H or a speaker S. Now, the problem is that there is no general purpose of conversations, qua conversations, so what will count as relevant will always have to be specified relative to a purpose of the participants, which may or may not be the purpose of the conversation up to that point. If we insist that it be relevant to the antecedently existing purpose of the conversation, then the account will be circular because the criteria of relevance are not independent of the criteria of identity of the particular conversation; and if we don't require relevance to the conversational purpose, then anything goes provided it is relevant to some purpose or other. That would put no constraints on the structure of actual talk exchanges.

Suppose, for example, I am having a conversation with my stock broker about whether or not to invest in IBM. Suppose he suddenly shouts, "Look out! The chandelier is going to fall on your head!" Now is his remark relevant? It is certainly not relevant to my purpose in investing in the stock market. But it certainly is relevant to my purpose of staying alive. So, if we think of this as one conversation, he has made an irrelevant remark. If we think of it as two conversations, the second one which he just initiated being about my safety, then he has made a relevant remark. But in neither case does relevance explain the general structure of conversations. Rather, the purpose of particular conversations explains what counts as relevant to that purpose, but it doesn't even explain what counts as relevant to that conversation, unless "that conversation" is defined in terms of that purpose.

Of the Gricean maxims, the most promising for explaining the structure of conversations seems to be relevance, and I have therefore spent some time discussing it. His maxims concerning quantity and manner don't seem to me plausible candidates for the job, so I will say nothing further about them. They both concern efficiency in communication, but they do not provide an adequate apparatus for getting at the details of conversational structure. Efficiency is only one among many constraints on talk sequences of the sort we have in conversation.

Though I think that the Gricean maxims are very useful in their own realm, they won't give us, for conversation, anything like what the rules of speech acts give us for individual speech acts.

Let us now turn then to the efforts of some sociolinguists who have studied the structure of conversation, as they would say, "empirically." One such effort at explaining the phenomenon of turn-taking in conversations is provided in an article by Sacks, Schegloff, and Jefferson.[4] They think that they have a set of rules, indeed, "recursive rules," for turn-taking in conversations. They say,

> The following seems to be a basic set of rules governing turn construction providing for the allocation of a next turn to one party and coordinating transfer so as to minimize gap and overlap. (1) For any turn at the initial transition relevance place of an initial turn construction unit: (a) If the turn so far is so constructed as to involve the use of a current speaker's select-next technique, then the party so selected has the right, and is obliged to take next turn to speak, no others have such rights or obligations and transfer occurs at that place. (b) If the turn so far is so constructed as not to involve the use of a current speaker's select-next technique, then self-selection for next speakership may, but need not be instituted. First speaker acquires rights to a turn and transfer occurs at that place. (c) If the turn so far is constructed as not to involve the use of a current speaker's select-next technique, then the current speaker may but need not continue unless another self-selects. (2) If at the initial transition

relevance place of an initial turn constructional unit neither 1a nor 1b is operated, and following the provision of 1c current speaker has continued, then the rule set a–c reapplies at the next transition relevance place, and recursively at each next transition relevance place until transfer is effected.

That is the rule for conversational turn-taking. Now, I have puzzled over this for a while, and my conclusion (though I am prepared to be corrected) is that that couldn't possibly be a rule for conversational turn-taking simply because nobody does or could follow it. The notion of a rule is, after all, rather closely connected with the notion of following a rule. And I want to argue that nobody does or could follow the turn-taking rule. Now what exactly does the rule say when it is stated in plain English? It seems to me they are saying the following: In a conversation a speaker can select who is going to be the next speaker, for example, by asking him a question. Or he can just shut up and let somebody else talk. Or he can keep on talking. Furthermore, if he decides to keep on talking, then next time there is a break in the conversation (that's called a "transition relevance place") the same three options apply. And that makes the rule recursive, because once you have the possibility of continuing to talk, the rule can apply over and over.

Now, as a description of what actually happens in a normal conversation, that is, a conversation where not everybody talks at once, the rule could hardly fail to describe what goes on. But that is like saying that this is a rule for walking: If you go for a walk, you can keep walking in the same direction, or you can change directions, or you can sit down and stop walking altogether. Notice that the walking rule is also recursive, because if you keep on walking, then the next time you wonder what to do, the same three options apply—you can keep on walking in the same direction, you can change directions, or you can sit down and quit walking altogether. As a *description* of what happens when someone goes for a walk, that could hardly be false, but that doesn't make it a recursive *rule* for walking. The walking rule is like the Sacks, Schegloff, Jefferson rule in that it is almost tautological. It is not completely tautological because there are always other possibilities. When walking, you could start jumping up and down or do cartwheels. In talking, everybody might shut up and not say anything, or they might break into song, or they might all talk at once, or there might be a rigid hierarchical order in which they are required to talk.

But the real objection to the rule is not that it is nearly tautological; many rules are tautological and none the worse for that. For example, systems of constitutive rules define tautologically the activity of which the rules are constitutive. Thus, the rules of chess or football tautologically define chess or football; and similarly, the rules of speech acts tautologically define the various sorts of speech acts, such as making statements or promises. That is not my real objection. The objection to this kind of "rule" is that it is not really a rule and therefore has no explanatory power. The notion of a rule is logically connected to the notion of following a rule, and the notion of following a rule is connected to the notion of making one's behavior conform to the content of a rule because it is a rule. For example, when I drive in England, I follow the rule: Drive on the left-hand side of the road. Now that seems to me a genuine rule. Why is it a rule? Because the content of the rule plays a causal role in the production of my behavior. If another driver is coming directly toward me from the opposite direction, I swerve to the left—that is, I make my behavior conform to the content of the rule. In a theory of intentionality, we would say that the intentional content of the rule plays a causal role in bringing about the conditions of satisfaction. The rule has the world-to-rule direction of fit—that is, the point of the rule is to get the world (that is, my behavior) to match the content of the rule. And it has the rule-to-world direction of causation—that is, the rule achieves the fit by causing the appropriate behavior.[5] This is just a fancy way of saying that the purpose of the rule is to influence people's behavior in a certain way so that the behavior matches the content of the rule, and the rule functions as part of the cause of bringing that match about. I don't just *happen* to drive on the left-hand side of the road in England: I do it *because* that is the rule of the road.

Notice now a crucial fact for the discussion of the conventional turn-taking rule. There can be extensionally equivalent descriptions of my rule-governed behavior not all of which state the rules that I am following. Take the rule: Drive on the left-hand side of the road. We might describe my behavior either by saying that I drive on the left, or, given the structure of English cars, by saying that I drive in such a way that on two-lane roads, while staying in one lane, I keep the steering wheel near the centerline and I keep the passenger side nearer to the curb. Now that actually happens in British cars when I drive on the left-hand side of the road. But that is not the rule that I am following. Both "rules" provide true descriptions of my behavior and both make accurate predictions, but only the first rule—the one about driving on the left—actually states a rule of my behavior, because it is the only one whose content plays a causal role in the production of the behavior. The second, like the Sacks, Schegloff, Jefferson rule, describes a consequence of following the rule, given that the steering wheel is located on the right, but it doesn't state a rule. The so-called rule for conversational turn-taking, like much similar research I have seen in this area, is like the second rule statement and not like the first. That is, it describes the phenomenon of turn-taking as if it were a rule; but it couldn't be a rule because no one actually follows that rule. The surface phenomenon of turn-taking is partly explicable in terms of deeper speech act sequencing rules having to do with internally related speech acts of the sort that we talked about before: but sometimes the phenomenon of turn-taking isn't a matter of rules at all.

Let us go through the cases. Case A: "Current speaker selects-next speaker." Well, speakers hardly ever directly select a subsequent speaker. People don't normally say in conversation "I select you to speak next," or "You talk next." Sometimes they do. If a master of ceremonies gets up and introduces you as the next speaker, then you are selected to talk next. He has certainly selected you to talk. But such cases are not very common. What normally happens, rather, is that the speaker asks somebody a question, or makes him an offer. The 'rules' that determine that the second person is to speak aren't rules of "speaker selects-next technique," but they are consequences of rules governing questions or offers. The surface phenomenon of speaker selection is not the explanation; the explanation is in terms of the rules for performing the internally related speech act pairs. The "speaker selects-next" rule is not a rule; it is an extensionally equivalent description of a pattern of behavior which is also described, and more importantly explained, by a set of speech act rules.

Now consider the second case. Case B: Next speaker self-selects. That just means that there is a break and somebody else starts talking. That "rule" says that when there is a break in the conversation anybody can start talking, and whoever starts talking gets to keep on talking. But I want to say that doesn't even have the appearance of being a rule since it doesn't specify the relevant sort of intentional content that plays a causal role in the production of the behavior. As we all know, the way it typically works in real life is this: Somebody else is talking and you want very much to say something. But you don't want to interrupt the speaker because (a) it's rude and (b) it's inefficient, since with two people talking at once it's hard to get your point across. So you wait till there is a chance to talk and then start talking fast before somebody else does. Now, where is the rule?

Case C is: current speaker continues. Again, I want to say that is not a rule, and for the same reason. No one is following it. It just says that when you are talking, you can keep on talking. But you don't need a rule to do that.

Perhaps one more analogy will help to clarify the main point I am trying to make. Suppose that several researchers in ethnomethodology made empirical observations of an American football game and came up with the following recursive clustering rule: organisms in like-colored jerseys are obliged and have the right to cluster in circular groups at statistically regular intervals. (Call this the "law of periodic circular clustering.") Then at a "transition relevance place," organisms in like-colored jerseys cluster linearly (the law of linear clustering). Then linear clustering is followed by linear interpenetration (the law of linear interpenetration). Linear interpenetration is followed by circular clustering, and thus the entire system is recursive. The precise formalization of this recursion could also be stated with temporal parameters. The Sacks-Schegloff-Jefferson "rule" is like the "law" of clustering in that it finds regularities in phenomena that are explainable by other forms of intentionality. A statement of an observed regularity, even when predictive, is not necessarily a statement of a rule.

One final remark about the nature of "empirical" evidence before concluding this section. Many researchers feel that a serious study of conversation must proceed from transcriptions of real conversations that actually took place. And of course they are right in thinking that many things can be learned from studying actual events that cannot be learned from thinking up imaginary conversations alone. But it is also important to keep in mind that where theory is concerned the native speaker takes priority over the historical record. We are only willing to accept and use the transcriptions of conversations in our native culture to the extent that we find them acceptable or at least possible conversations. If some investigator came up with an impossible conversation we would reject it out of hand because we are masters of our language and its culture, and the fact that an impossible conversation might be historically actual is irrelevant. Thus the following is OK:

B: I don't know whether you have talked with Hilary about the diary situation.

A: WELL she has been EXPLAINING to me rather in rather more general TERMS . . . mmmm . . . what . . . you are sort of DOING and . . .

B: . . . what it was all . . . about . . . yes.

A: I gather you've been at it for nine YEARS . . .

B: . . . mmm . . . by golly that's true yes yes it's not a long time of course in the . . . uh . . . in this sort of . . . work . . .[6]

Because we recognize it as an intelligible fragment of a possible conversation. But if A had responded:

A: Whereof therefore maybe briny very was could of should to be.

or B had said:

B: UGGA BU BUBU UGGA

We would at the very least require some further explanation before taking the "data" seriously. The fact that the events had actually occurred would be by itself of no more theoretical interest than if one of the participants had just collapsed from a heart attack or the other had thrown up. To be of theoretical interest, the "empirical" facts have to accord with our inner abilities and not conversely.

III

Well then, if such "rules" are no help to us, let us go back to the beginning of our discussion. I said that it would be nice if we could get a theory of conversation that matches our theory of speech acts. I am not optimistic. I have examined two directions of investigation, but I think that neither gives us the sorts of results we wanted. The hypothesis that underlies my pessimism is this:

> The reason that conversations do not have an inner structure in the sense that speech acts do is not (as is sometimes claimed) because conversations involve two or more people, but because conversations as such lack a particular purpose or point.

Each illocutionary act has an illocutionary point, and it is in virtue of that point that it is an act of that type. Thus, the point of a promise is to undertake an obligation; the point of a statement is to represent how things are in the world; the point of an order is to try to get somebody to do something, etc. It is the existence of illocutionary points that enables us to get a well defined taxonomy of the different types of illocutionary acts.[7] But conversations don't in that way have an internal point simply in virtue of being conversations. Consider the similarities and differences between the following talk exchanges:

A woman calling her dentist's office to arrange an appointment.

Two casual acquaintances meeting each other on the street and stopping to have a brief chat in which they talk about a series of subjects (e.g. the weather, the latest football results, the president's speech last night).

A philosophy seminar.

A man trying to pick up a woman in a bar.

A dinner party.

A family spending a Sunday afternoon at home watching a football game on television and discussing the progress of the game among various other matters.

A meeting of the board of directors of a small corporation.

A doctor interviewing a patient.

Now, what are the chances of finding a well-defined structure common to all of these? Are they all "conversations"?

Of course, they all have a beginning, a middle, and an end, but then, so does a glass of beer; that is not enough for an internal structure. The literature on this subject is partly skewed by the fact that the authors often pick telephone conversations, because they are easier to study. But telephone conversations are unusual in that most people, adolescents apart, have a fairly well defined objective when they pick up the phone, unlike two colleagues encountering each other in the hallway of a building, or two casual acquaintances bumping into each other on the street.

Though I am pessimistic about certain sorts of accounts of conversation, I am not saying that we cannot give theoretical accounts of the structure of conversation or that we cannot say important, insightful things about the structure of conversation. What sort of apparatus would we use to do that? Here I want to mention a couple of features that I think are crucial for understanding conversation, and indeed, for understanding discourse generally.

One of the things we need to recognize about conversations is that they involve shared intentionality. Conversations are a paradigm of collective behavior. The shared intentionality in conversation is not to be confused with the kind of iterated intentionality discussed by Steven Schiffer and David Lewis, which involves what they call "mutual knowledge." In the case of mutual knowledge, I know that you know that I know that you know . . . that p. And you know that I know that you know that I know . . . that p. Schiffer and Lewis try to reduce the shared aspect to an iterated sequence, indeed, an infinite sequence of iterated cognitive states about the other partner. I think that their analysis distorts the facts. *Shared* intentionality is not just a matter of a conjunction of individual intentional states about the other person's intentional states. To illustrate this point I will give a rather crude example of shared intentionality. Suppose you and I are pushing a car. When we are pushing a car together, it isn't just the case that I am pushing the car and you are pushing the car. No, I am pushing the car as part of *our* pushing the car. So, if it turns out that you weren't pushing all along, you were just going along for a free ride, and I was doing all the pushing; then I am not just mistaken about what you were doing, but I am also mistaken about what I was doing, because I thought not just that I was pushing (I was right about that), but that I was pushing as part of *our* pushing. And that doesn't reduce to a series of iterated claims about my belief concerning your belief about my belief about your belief, etc.

The phenomenon of shared collective behavior is a genuine social phenomenon and underlies much social behavior. We are blinded to this fact by the traditional analytic devices that treat all intentionality as strictly a matter of the individual person. I believe that a recognition of shared intentionality and its implications is one of the basic concepts we need in order to understand how conversations work. The idea that shared intentionality can be entirely reduced to complex beliefs and other intentional states leads to those incorrect accounts of meaning where it turns out you have to have a rather large number of intentions in order to perform such simple speech acts as saying "Good-bye," or asking for another drink, or saying "Hi" to someone when you meet him in the street. You do, of course, require some intentional states, but once you see that in collective behavior, such as conversations, the individual intentionality is derived from the collective intentionality, the account of the individual intentionality is much simpler. On the pattern of analysis I am proposing, when two people greet each other and begin a conversation, they are beginning a joint activity rather than two individual activities. If this conception is correct, then shared intentionality is a concept we will need for analyzing conversation.

Now, there is another concept I think we need for understanding conversation, and indeed, for understanding language generally, and that is the notion of what I call "the background." Now, let me work up to that briefly. Take any sentence, and ask yourself what you have to know in order to understand that sentence. Take the sentence: "George Bush intends to run for president." In order fully to understand that sentence, and consequently, in order to understand a speech act performed in the utterance of that sentence, it just isn't enough that you should have a lot of semantic contents that you glue together. Even if you make them into big semantic contents, it isn't going to be enough. What you have to know in order to understand that sentence are such things as that the United States is a republic, it has presidential elections every four years, in these elections there are candidates of the two major parties, and the person who gets the majority of the electoral votes becomes president. And so on. The list is indefinite, and you can't even say that all the members of the list are absolutely essential to understanding the original sentence; because, for example, you could understand the sentence very well even if you didn't understand about the electoral college. But there is no way to put all of this information into the meaning of the word "president." The word "president" means the same in "George Bush wants to run for president" as in "Mitterrand is the president of France." There is no lexical ambiguity over the word "president," rather, the kind of knowledge you have to have to understand those two utterances doesn't coincide. I want to give a name to all of that network of knowledge or belief or opinion or presupposition: I call it "the network."

If you try to follow out the threads of the network, if you think of all the things you would have to know in order to understand the sentence "George Bush wants to run for president," you would eventually reach a kind of bedrock that would seem strange to think of as simply more knowledge or beliefs. For example, you would get to things like: people generally vote when conscious, or: there are human beings, or: elections are generally held at or near the surface of the earth. I want to suggest that these 'propositions' are not like the genuine belief I have to the effect that larger states get more electoral votes than smaller states. In the way that I have a genuine *belief* about the number of electoral votes controlled by the state of Michigan, I don't in that way have a belief that elections go on at or near the surface of the earth. If I was writing a book about American electoral practices, I wouldn't put that proposition in. Why not? Well in a way, it is too fundamental to count as a belief. Rather it is a certain set of stances that I take toward the world. There are sets of skills, ways of dealing with things, ways of behaving, cultural practices, and general know-how of both biological and cultural sorts. These form what I am calling "the background," and the fact that part of my background is that elections are held at or near the surface of the earth *manifests itself* in the fact that I walk to the nearest polling place and don't try and get aboard a rocket ship. Similarly the fact that the table in front of me is a solid object is not manifested in any belief as such, but rather in the fact that I'm willing to put things on it, or that I pound on it, or I rest my books on it, or I lean on it. Those, I want to say, are stances, practices, ways of behaving. This then for our present purposes is the thesis of the background: all semantic interpretation, and indeed all intentionality, functions not only against a network of beliefs and other intentional states but also against a background that does not consist in a set of propositional contents, but rather, consists in presuppositions that are, so to speak, preintentional or prepropositional.

To further illustrate the relevance of this point for semantic interpretation, consider the different interpretations given to verbs of action. Consider, for example, sentences of the form: "X cut Y." The interpretation that one attaches to "cut" alters radically in different sentences even though the semantic content doesn't alter. Consider the sentences:

1. Sally cut the cake.
2. Bill cut the grass.
3. The barber cut Jim's hair.
4. The tailor cut the cloth.
5. I just cut my skin.

The interesting thing for our present discussion about these sentences is that the same semantic content occurs in each of them with the word "cut" but is interpreted differently in each case. In 1–5, the word "cut" is not used ambiguously. Its use in these cases contrasts with sentences where it is used with a genuinely different meaning such as "The president cut the salaries of the professors" or (one of Austin's favorites) "Cut the cackle!" or "He can't cut the mustard." In these cases, we are inclined to say that "cut" is used to mean something different from what it is used to mean in 1–5. But that it has the same meaning in sentences 1–5 is shown by the fact that the standard tests for univocality apply. So for example, you can have a conjunction reduction: For example, "General Electric has just invented a new device which can cut cakes, grass, hair, cloth, and skin." But if you then add "and salaries, cackles, and mustard," it seems like a bad joke. But though "cut" means the same in 1–5, it is interpreted quite differently in each case. And thus, the semantic content by itself cannot account for the fact that we understand those sentences in radically different ways. We can see that we understand the occurrences in different ways if we consider analogous occurrences in directives. If I say "Bill, go cut the grass" and Bill goes out and stabs the grass with a knife, or attempts to slice it up the way one would a cake, or takes a pair of scissors to it, there is an important sense in which Bill did not do what I asked him to do. That is, he did not obey my literal and unambiguous request.

How is it that we are able to understand the word "cut" in sentences 1–5 so differently given that it has the same semantic content in each occurrence? Someone might claim — indeed, I have heard it claimed — that it is part of the literal meaning of the verb that we interpret it differently in different verbal contexts. "Cut" with "grass" as direct object is interpreted differently from "cut" with "cake" as direct object, and thus the explanation would be given entirely in terms of the interaction of semantic contents.

But that explanation by itself won't do either, because if we alter the background in the right way, we could interpret the "cut" in "Cut the grass" as we interpret "cut" in "Cut the cake." For example, in California there are firms that sell instant lawns. They simply roll a lawn up and load it into your pickup truck. Now, suppose I am the manager of one of these sod farms and you order a half an acre of grass, and I tell my foreman "Go out and cut half an acre of grass for this customer." If he then gets out the lawnmower and starts mowing it, I'll fire him. Or imagine that we have a bakery where we have a super strain of yeast that causes our cakes to grow up all the way to the ceiling and for that reason we have to employ a man to chop the tops off the cakes. Suppose I tell him "Watch out they are going toward the ceiling again. Start cutting the cakes!" If he then starts cutting the cakes in neat slices, I'm going to fire him as well. I want to say there is no obvious way that the traditional context-free conception of semantic interpretation of sentences can account for the indefinite range of such facts.[8]

What then is different about these different sentences? What enables us to interpret them differently? Well, we have certain background practices. We know what it is to cut grass; we know what it is to cut cake; and we know that each is quite different from cutting a cloth. But those are human practices. The knowledge we have about such matters is either knowledge from the network or is so fundamental that it is not quite right to construe it as a propositional "knowing that . . ." at all. These are just ways we have of behaving.

Now notice a further point. There are many syntactically acceptable English sentences containing the word "cut" that we can't interpret at all. Suppose I say to you "Go cut that mountain!" or "Sally cut the coffee." In the sense in which we interpret 1–5 effortlessly, I don't know how to interpret these other examples. I can *invent* an interpretation for each of these, but when I do that, what I do is invent a background practice that fixes an interpretation. It doesn't take much imagination. Suppose we run a big freeway building crew and we are making interstate highways. We have two ways of dealing with mountains; we either level them or we cut right through them. So if I say to my foreman "Go cut that mountain," he just cuts a freeway right through it.

Many of my students immediately attach a metaphorical interpretation to "Cut the coffee." They interpret it as meaning: dilute the coffee in some way. But we could invent other interpretations. We could invent literal interpretations if we imagine ourselves engaging in certain sorts of practices. Notice that in the case of "The president cut the salaries," we immediately give it a metaphorical interpretation. But with a little ingenuity and an idiosyncratic president, we could give a literal interpretation. Suppose the salaries are always in the form of wads of dollar bills and an eccentric president insists on cutting the end off of each person's salary before handing it over. This would be an odd case, but we could in such a case imagine a literal interpretation of "cut." Now why is it that we so effortlessly attach a metaphorical interpretation as the normal case? The answer, I believe, is that we always interpret a sentence against a background of practices and within a network of other beliefs and assumptions which are not themselves part of the semantic content of the sentence. We assume that the speaker's utterance makes sense, but in order to make sense of it we have to fit it into the background. In this case, the metaphorical interpretation fits the background easily, the literal interpretation requires generating a new background.

One of the ways in which the background is crucial for understanding conversation is in the role that the background plays in determining conversational relevance. We saw earlier that relevance was in general relative to the purpose of the conversation; but we can now, I believe, deepen that point if we see that the purpose itself, and what constitutes relevance relative to that purpose, will depend on the shared backgrounds of the participants. One reason that we cannot get a non-circular account of "relevant" just by looking at a conversation is that what the participants in the conversation take as relevant, what counts as relevant, will always be relative to the cognitive apparatus they bring to bear on the conversation. That is to say, it will always be relative to their network and background.

In order to illustrate the operation of the background in the production and comprehension of conversation, I want to consider an example from real life. The following conversation took place on British television immediately after the Conservative party victory that brought Mrs. Thatcher to power as Prime Minister for the first time.[9]

FIRST SPEAKER: I think you know the question I'm going to ask you. What's the answer?

SECOND SPEAKER: We'll have to wait and see.

FIRST SPEAKER: Would you like to?

SECOND SPEAKER: It all depends.

Two things are clear from this brief snatch of conversation. First, the amount of information contained in the lexical meanings, that is, in the semantic contents of the words and sentences uttered, is very minimal. Literally speaking, neither party says much of anything. Secondly, it is clear that the two participants understand each other perfectly well, and that a great deal is being conveyed. Now what is it that the two speakers have to know in order to understand each other so well on the basis of such minimal semantic content? And, what would we have to understand as spectators in order to understand what was being communicated in this conversation? Well, we might begin by listing the propositional contents which were known by British television viewers as well as by the two participants and which enabled them to understand the conversation. The list might begin as follows: The first speaker is Robin Day, a famous British television news broadcaster. The second speaker is Edward Heath, the former Conservative Prime Minister. It is well known that Mr. Heath hates Mrs. Thatcher and Mrs. Thatcher hates Mr. Heath. Now, the question on everyone's mind at the time of this conversation was, "Would Heath serve as a minister in a Thatcher cabinet?" It is obvious that the conversation construed simply as a set of utterances carrying literal semantic content is unintelligible. The natural temptation is to assume that it is made intelligible by the fact that these additional semantic contents are present in the minds of the speaker, the hearer, and the audience. What I am suggesting here is that they are still not enough. Or rather, that they are only enough because they themselves rest on a set of capacities that are not themselves semantic contents. Our ability to represent rests on a set of capacities which do not themselves consist in representations.

In order to see how this works, let us imagine that we actually plugged in the semantic contents that we think would fix the interpretation of the conversation. Suppose we imagine the participants actually saying,

FIRST SPEAKER: I am Robin Day, the famous British television news broadcaster.

SECOND SPEAKER: I am Edward Heath, the former British Conservative Prime Minister, and I hate Mrs. Thatcher, the present British Conservative Prime Minister. She hates me, too.

Now, if we plug in such semantic contents as these, it looks as if we have converted the conversation from something that is almost totally mysterious on the face to something that is completely intelligible on the face. But if you think about it for a moment, I think you will see that we have not overcome our original problem. The original conversation was intelligible only because the participants and the viewers had a lot of information that wasn't explicit in the conversation. But now this new conversation is similarly intelligible only because the participants and the observers still have a lot of information that is not explicit in the conversation. They understand the conversation as revised only because they understand what sorts of things are involved in being a Prime Minister, in hating other people, in winning elections, in serving in cabinets, and so on. Well, suppose we plugged all that information into the conversation. Suppose we imagine Heath actually stating a theory of the British government, and Day actually stating a theory of human hostilities and their role in personal relationships. So now we imagine the conversation enriched in something like the following fashion:

FIRST SPEAKER: Hatred normally involves a reluctance to engage in close association with or appear to be accepting favors from the hated person.

SECOND SPEAKER: The authority of the Prime Minister in the British constitution has altered considerably since the days when the Prime Minister was considered *primus inter pares*, prior to the time of Walpole. The Prime Minister now has an authority which enables him or her to appoint and dismiss cabinet ministers almost at will, an authority tempered only by the independent popularity and political standing of other members of the party in the country at large.

Now that is the sort of thing people have to know in order to understand this conversation properly. But even if we plugged all of these propositions into the conversation, even if we filled in all of the information which we think would fix the right interpretation of the original utterances, it would still not be enough. We would still be left in our original position where the understanding of the conversation requires prior intellectual capacities, capacities which are still not represented in the conversation.

The picture we have is this. We think that since the original semantic contents encoded in the literal meaning of the sentences uttered are not all sufficient to enable communication to take place, then communication takes place because of prior collateral information which speaker, hearer, and observer possess. This is true as far as it goes, but the problem still remains. The prior collateral information is no more self-interpreting than the original conversation. So it looks as though we are on the start of a regress, possibly infinite. The solution to our puzzle is this. Both the original utterances and the prior collateral information only function, that is, they only determine their conditions of satisfaction, against a background of capacities, stances, attitudes, presuppositions, ways of behaving, modes of sensibility, and so on, that are not themselves representational. All interpretation, understanding, and meaning, as well as intentionality in general, functions against a background of mental capacities that are not themselves interpretations, meanings, understandings, or intentional states. The solution to our puzzle, in short, is to see that all meaning and understanding goes on against a background which is not itself meant or understood, but which forms the boundary conditions on meaning and understanding, whether in conversations or in isolated utterances. In the conversation we considered from British TV, the richness of the shared background enables a very minimal explicit semantic content to be informative and even satisfying to the participants and the audience. On the other hand some of the most frustrating and unsatisfying conversations occur between people of radically different backgrounds, who can speak at great length and achieve only mutual incomprehension.

Notes

This article is reprinted from *(On) Searle on Conversation*, by John R. Searle et al., compiled and introduced by Herman Parret and Jef Verschveren, Amsterdam and Philadelphia: John Benjamins, 1992. It originated in a lecture I gave at the University of Campinas, Brazil, at a conference on Dialogue in 1981. A later version was given at a conference at Michigan State University in 1984. Much of this version is simply a transcript of the Michigan State lecture. Since that lecture was delivered without a text and without notes, it is somewhat more informal than is generally the case with published articles. The original version was published as "Notes on Conversation" in *Contemporary Issues in Language and Discourse Processing*, edited by D. G. Ellis and W. A. Donahue, Hillsdale, New Jersey: Lawrence Erlbaum Associates, 1986. I am indebted to Dagmar Searle, Yoshiko Matsumoto, and Robin Lakoff for comments on the original transcript. I have made additions, revisions, and clarifications for this version, hence the change in the title.

1. John R. Searle, *Speech Acts: An Essay in the Philosophy of Language*, Cambridge University Press, Cambridge, 1969, p. 66.

2. I am indebted to Julian Boyd for discussion of this point.

3. H. P. Grice, "Logic and Conversation," in *Syntax and Semantics, Volume 3, Speech Acts*, Peter Cole and J. L. Morgan (eds.), Academic Press, New York, 1975.

4. H. Sacks, E. A. Schegloff, and G. Jefferson, "A simplest systematics for the organization of turn-taking for conversation," *Language*, 1974, 50, 696–735.

5. For a further explanation of these notions, see John R. Searle, *Intentionality: An Essay in the Philosophy of Mind*, Cambridge University Press, Cambridge, 1983.

6. From J. Svartvik and R. Quirk (eds.), *A Corpus of English Conversation*, Lund: Gleerup, 1980, 408–411, as cited in Ronald Wardhaugh, *How Conversation Works*, Oxford: Basil Blackwell, 1985, 202–203.

7. John R. Searle, "A Taxonomy of Illocutionary Acts," in *Language, Mind and Knowledge*, Minnesota Studies in the Philosophy of Science, 11, K. Gunderson (ed.), University of Minnesota Press, 1975. Reprinted in *Expression and Meaning: Studies in Theory of Speech Acts*, Cambridge University Press, 1979.

8. For more on this and other examples, see John R. Searle, "The Background of Meaning", in *Speech Act Theory and Pragmatics*, J. R. Searle, F. Kiefer, and M. Bierwisch (eds.), Dordrecht: D. Reidel, 1980, 221–232. Also, *Intentionality: An Essay in the Philosophy of Mind*, chapter 5.

9. My attention was called to this conversation by Philip Johnson-Laird.

Extracts from a *Heteroglossary*

Readers of Bakhtin are aware of his tendency not to define his terms explicitly, but rather to illustrate them by use, often by passing them through many different contexts. It is a technique that makes maximal demands on the reader, and has often led to misunderstandings (about which he sometimes complained). To make matters still more confusing, Bakhtin sometimes used the same word (most notoriously, "dialogue") in different senses, each of which would really require a separate definition to distinguish it from the word's other senses.

One reason we are engaged in writing the *Heteroglossary*, then, is to clarify Bakhtin's neologisms, special phrases, and idiosyncratic way of introducing concepts. Another is to call attention to some of Bakhtin's most intriguing ideas, which frequently occur in digressions or tangents from his main arguments, and therefore are often overlooked. Tied to specific coinages, these concepts have been included in the *Heteroglossary*. A third reason concerns existing English translations, made by different people at different times, that have often rendered a single key term variously, or various terms by a single one, thus creating further difficulties for those who want to determine Bakhtin's meaning by usage in context. We have therefore indicated how the English translations correspond to the Russian and to each other. Where we feel that significant mistranslations have occurred, we have indicated what we believe to be better renditions. Omitted from the present selection is a fourth feature of the *Heteroglossary*, a list of the passages in which a term significantly figures.

As we explain in *Mikhail Bakhtin: Creation of a Prosaics* (Stanford University Press, 1990) and in the introduction to our anthology *Rethinking Bakhtin: Extensions and Challenges* (Northwestern University Press, 1989), an integral understanding of Bakhtin is hindered by the dubious attribution to him of the "disputed texts" published by his friends Voloshinov and Medvedev. For reasons we have specified in those two books, we do not believe that Bakhtin wrote the disputed texts. We think it more likely that Voloshinov and Medvedev were deeply influenced by Bakhtin, recast his ideas in a Marxist and semiotic framework with which Bakhtin was uneasy, and then in turn influenced him. It seems sensible to posit a lively dialogue among the members of the Bakhtin group, which should not be "crammed into a single consciousness," as Bakhtin would say; all the more so, since there is no convincing evidence of Bakhtin's authorship of the disputed texts.

The *Heteroglossary* therefore includes terms from Voloshinov and Medvedev, but is careful to distinguish their usages from Bakhtin's. Voloshinov and Medvedev coined a number of important terms and concepts not found in Bakhtin's works; moreover, they use some of his terms in a different sense attributable to their own different intellectual agendas. A distinction between Bakhtin and his colleagues should be helpful not only to those who believe that Voloshinov and Medvedev wrote the books published under their names, but also to those who regard the question of attribution as open. The practice of drawing these distinctions might even be helpful in resolving that vexing question.

The *Heteroglossary*, of course, presents terms in alphabetical order. Here we thought it more useful to arrange (abbreviated) entries in a format more conducive to sequential reading.

The following abbreviations are used:

BSHR "The *Bildungsroman* and Its Significance in the History of Realism." In *Speech Genres and Other Late Essays*, translated by Vern McGee, edited by Caryl Emerson and Michael Holquist. Austin: University of Texas Press, 1986.

DiN "Discourse in the Novel." In *The Dialogic Imagination: Four Essays by M. M. Bakhtin*, translated by Caryl Emerson and Michael Holquist, edited by Michael Holquist. Austin: University of Texas Press, 1981.

N70–71 "From Notes Made in 1970–71." In Bakhtin, *Speech Genres*.

PDP *Problems of Dostoevsky's Poetics*. Translated and edited by Caryl Emerson. Minneapolis: University of Minnesota Press, 1984.

PT "The Problem of Text in Linguistics, Philology and the Human Sciences." In *Speech Genres*.

RQ "Response to a Question from the *Novy Mir* Editorial Staff." *Speech Genres*.

TF1929 "Three Fragments from the 1929 Edition, *Problems of Dostoevsky's Art.*" In *Problems of Dostoevsky's Poetics*, Appendix 1.

TRDB "Toward a Reworking of the Dostoevsky Book." In *Problems of Dostoevsky's Poetics*, Appendix 2.

V:MPL Voloshinov, *Marxism and the Philosophy of Language*. Translated by Ladislav Matejka and I. R. Titunik. New York: Seminar, 1973.

(Translations of cited passages have sometimes been amended by comparison with the Russian texts.)

Polyphony (*polifoniia*) and polyphonic novel (*polifonicheskii roman*)

Arguably Bakhtin's most original and counterintuitive concept, the term has often been misunderstood by both his admirers and his critics. Bakhtin observed that this term in particular "has more than any other given rise to objections and misunderstanding."

Polyphony is NOT:

1. An attribute of all novels. In *Problems of Dostoevsky's Poetics*, Bakhtin writes that the creator of polyphony was Dostoevsky; no works before his were polyphonic. DiN does *not* amend Bakhtin's earlier position to say that all novels are polyphonic; this common misinterpretation perhaps derives from the conflation of polyphony and heteroglossia.
2. A theory postulating that the author should be passive, uninvolved, lacking a point of view, or purely "objective" and dispassionate. Bakhtin explicitly stresses that the polyphonic author has a point of view, is involved in the work's dialogues, and is active to a high degree. The difference between the monologic and polyphonic kinds of authorship is rather to be found in the *kind* of activity characteristic of each.
3. A theory endorsing extreme or categorical relativism: "the polyphonic approach has nothing in common with relativism (or with dogmatism). But it should be noted that both relativism and dogmatism equally include all argumentation, all authentic dialogue, by making it either unnecessary (relativism) or impossible (dogmatism)" (PDP, 69).
4. Equivalent to heteroglossia or dialogized heteroglossia. "Polyphony" and "heteroglossia" describe entirely different classes of phenomena. Heteroglossia, a term Bakhtin developed in his essays on the theory of the novel in the early 1930s, refers to the diversity of speech styles in a language; polyphony, a product of Bakhtin's thinking about authorship and responsibility in the 1920s, pertains to a specific sense of truth coupled with a specific relation of author to heroes. Confusion of the terms is something like treating *heterodoxy* as synonymous with *polymer*.
5. Dialectics (see entry on **Dialectics**, below). For Bakhtin, dialectics is a form of monologism and is therefore incompatible with polyphony.

Bakhtin is less careful to specify what polyphony *is*. A sense of this term must be derived from numerous characterizations in context.

Polyphony is an approach to narrative that embodies a dialogic sense of truth (see entry on **Dialogue**, Sense 3, below). Or as Bakhtin sometimes puts the point, a remarkable idea—that truth is the sort of thing that can be represented not by a proposition but only by an unfinalizable conversation—is the "form-shaping force" (or "form-shaping ideology" or "form-shaping idea") of polyphony. That force is realized by a method of creating that involves a special relation of the work's author to its heroes.

In monologic (nonpolyphonic) works only the author has the "direct power to mean." All views at odds with his or her own are either refuted or, more commonly, represented as merely typical of a character's psychology. The reader is not asked to engage directly with the character's idea, nor to enter into dialogue with it; rather, the reader is asked to appraise it in terms of the character's life and the work's structure. The reader is invited to enter into dialogue only with the author's idea, as conveyed by the whole work. In this sense, the ideas of characters in a monologic work are "objectified."

By contrast, in a polyphonic work, the reader is asked to engage directly with the ideas of characters, much as the reader engages with the ideas of the author. Characters' ideas are not just traits: they "mean directly," and they therefore can be said to lie on the "same plane" as the ideas of the author. Because the direct power to mean belongs to many people in a polyphonic work, major characters are in a position analogous to that of the author in a monologic work. Thus the tendency of so many of Dostoevsky's critics to engage directly with characters—to argue directly with Myshkin, for example, or Raskolnikov—as if they were independent agents, is not the same sort of error as it would be if such a procedure were applied to a monologic work. The tendency to engage characters this way is itself indicative of polyphony at work, because only in polyphonic works do (major) characters possess the power to mean directly.

In a polyphonic work the author expresses his own position in *two* ways. As the creator *of* the work he embodies (through the very act of creating a polyphonic rather than a monologic work) a dialogic sense of truth. The author may also express ideas *in* the work, as Dostoevsky often does (say, through a character with ideas similar to Dostoevsky's own). In this case, his views enjoy no special privilege over those of other characters. Those views compete in an equal and truly open-ended dialogue with the views of other characters; and the victory of the author's views is anything but assured.

Polyphony is therefore a way of representing human freedom. Bakhtin compares the polyphonic author to "Goethe's Prometheus," who "creates not voiceless slaves (as does Zeus) but *free* people capable of rebelling against him" (PDP, 6). In monologic works the true freedom of the character is impossible, because what the character will do or say is planned by the author in advance. Thus, although monologic works can be designed to assert human freedom (and many have been), the very form of the monologic work is in implicit contradiction to that assertion. The creation of polyphony allowed Dostoevsky—for the first time in literary history, according to Bakhtin—not only to assert freedom, but actually to represent characters as free beings.

Because the author must not know the outcome of the work's dialogues in advance, polyphony is necessarily a theory of the *creative process*. To be truly polyphonic, a work must be created in a different way from a monologic work. Otherwise, instead of a true dialogue, the author will produce only a "finalized image" of a dialogue, which is quite a different thing. Such a finalized image is a mere "stenographer's report of a *finished* dialogue, from which the author has already withdrawn and *over* which he is now located as if in some higher decision-making position" (PDP, 63).

The difference between a true dialogue and a finalized image of a dialogue is analogous to that between the creation of free characters and the creation of characters destined, planned, and forced to assert human freedom.

To create characters who are free, the author must renounce his or her "essential surplus": the author must not know more about the character than the character knows about himself or herself. Above all, the author must not know the characters' destiny in advance. He or she must not have preplanned what they will say in crucial situations that test their identity and their fundamental convictions. The polyphonic author imagines a character as an integral point of view on the world, as a voice with its own special registers, and then the author places the character in situations that will provoke the character to outgrow himself or herself in ways the author cannot foresee in advance. He or she sets up the dialogues without foreseeing their outcome.

Although the author renounces an "essential surplus," he or she necessarily retains and makes use of a "purely information-bearing surplus" (the power to set up the dialogues or provoke incidents). [The *Heteroglossary* will contain a detailed entry on **Surplus**, a crucial concept for Bakhtin.]

It follows that a polyphonic work cannot be "plotted" in the usual way, and that plot must play a new role in a polyphonic work. Specifically, plot is no longer the "clamps" holding the novel together; the "clamps" are the great dialogues. In a polyphonic work, plot (1) is (in a way roughly analogous to stage directions in a drama) the way of setting up the dialogues, and (2) is, when taken as a whole from the beginning of the work to the end, merely the record of whatever happened to result from the great dialogues and free utterances (or actions) of the characters.

A closely related consequence of polyphony is that the work lacks *structure* in the usual sense, that is, a pattern designed to be contemplated (after the process of reading is over) synchronically. What appears to be a structure is simply the unplanned outcome of the work's dialogues; to see a structure in a polyphonic work is to transform it into a monologic work. Instead of structure, polyphony depends on and preserves the "eventness" of each event, its open-endedness in its own present moment. [The *Heteroglossary* also devotes an entry to **Eventness**, another key concept of Bakhtin's.]

There is a fundamental difference between a finalized image of eventness or of process (as in such metaliterary classics as *Tristram Shandy* and "The Overcoat") and the genuine eventness that is to be found in polyphonic works. Polyphonic works must have real, not scripted, unfinalizability. In a polyphonic work the dialogues take place "right now, that is, in the *real present* of the creative process" (PDP, 63).

Polyphony affects not only plot and structure but also unity, which can no longer be a consequence of structure. The successful polyphonic work does not lack unity, but has a different kind of unity, a "unity of the event." By this phrase, Bakhtin seems to have three concepts in mind:

1. What he calls "unity of a higher order" or "unity of the second order," which he never adequately defines. But we might explain it this way: Because each character is in a position analogous to the author of a monologic work, each could in principle supply a monologic order to the whole. Hence the polyphonic unity of all these characters is a unity of potential unities, which is to say, a unity of a second (or higher) order. In this sense, the "unity of the event" is a "unity of co-being" (as Bakhtin seems to pun on the Russian word for event, *sobytie*).

2. The event of the dialogue itself. In this sense, the unity of the polyphonic work is the unity of an ongoing conversation, a unity that participants may sense even before they know its outcome (if they ever do).

3. The unity of the event of the creative process producing the work. In a polyphonic work, we sense that process as ongoing, as somehow evolving simultaneously (though in a different kind of time) with the dialogues of the characters. This sort of unity derives from the reader's sense of a set of consistent methods used to create the work; that is, the unity derives from the reader's apprehension of a coherent process rather than of an organized product.

These are the defining features of polyphony. Bakhtin also describes specific ways in which Dostoevsky realized polyphony, that is, special features that may, but do not have to, accompany polyphony. Sometimes it is not clear whether a specific feature is definitive or characteristic only of Dostoevsky. But nondefining features would seem to include carnivalization, the use of Menippean satire, and a special sense of time. [The *Heteroglossary* refers the reader to its entry on **Cross-section of a single moment**.]

The final chapter of the Dostoevsky book, devoted to double-voiced words, has prompted readers to presume that polyphony is present whenever double-voicing is. However, double-voicing is also common in monologic works. It is not unique to polyphonic works, but is exploited by them (or at least by Dostoevsky) in an especially powerful way.

Dostoevsky was the first polyphonic author, but "after Dostoevsky polyphony burst powerfully into world literature" (PT, 112). Unfortunately, Bakhtin provides no examples, which is one reason it is difficult to know precisely which features are definitive of polyphony and which were Dostoevsky's own ways of realizing polyphony. Bakhtin also believed that polyphony and the dialogic sense of truth may be destined to replace monologism and theoretism. "After my book (but independently of it) the ideas of polyphony, dialogue, unfinalizability, etc., were widely developed. This is explained by the growing influence of Dostoevsky, but above all, of course, by those changes in reality which Dostoevsky (in this sense prophetically) succeeded in revealing earlier than others" (TRDB, 285). [For a discussion of **Theoretism**, see the introduction to *Rethinking Bakhtin*; an entry will also appear in the *Heteroglossary*.]

The proper antonym of polyphony is "homophony," but Bakhtin also uses "monologism." The justification of this usage is that polyphony incorporates a dialogic sense of truth (**Dialogue** in the third sense—see below). Consequently, in these contexts monologism is used in only one of its senses (as the opposite of the dialogic sense of truth). In other contexts the term "monologism" (or "monologic") also functions as the opposite of "dialogue" in the second sense, thus leading to more confusion.

[A fuller discussion of polyphony occupies chapter 6 of *Mikhail Bakhtin: Creation of a Prosaics.*]

Dialectics (*dialektika*)

For Bakhtin, the dialectics of the Socratic dialogues contained a dialogic understanding of the world. That sense is lost in Hegelian or Marxist dialectics, which Bakhtin criticizes and contrasts with dialogue. In Hegelian (and Marxist) dialectics, dialogicality is absent, because the whole dialectical process can take place within a *single* consciousness, whereas true dialogue requires at least two different people and two irreducibly different perspectives. Dialectics is a manipulation of moribund abstractions; dialogue is a kind of interaction that requires live and unfinalizable people. "Dialogue and dialectics. Take a dialogue and remove the voices . . . remove the intonations (emotional and individualizing ones), carve out abstract concepts and judgments from living words and responses, cram everything into one abstract consciousness—and that's how you get dialectics" (N70–71, 147). "Dialectics is the abstract product of dialogue" (TRDB, 293).

In dialectics, contextual meaning is reduced to an abstraction, and so thought becomes like a fish in an aquarium that "knocks against the bottom and the sides and cannot swim farther or deeper. Dogmatic thoughts" (TRDB, 293).

Dialogic relations cannot be reduced to logical ones, a statement that applies to dialectical logic as well.

Neither can polyphony be reduced to dialectics, because polyphony demands both unfinalizability and the plurality of distinct voices. But a common way in which critics "monologize" Dostoevsky's polyphony is to transform it into a "philosophical monologue unfolding dialectically" (PDP, 26). "The idea in Dostoevsky is never cut off from the voice. For this reason it is radically wrong to claim that Dostoevsky's dialogues are dialectical. . . . Such an understanding is absurd" (TF1929, 279).

By contrast, Voloshinov always uses the term "dialectics" in a complimentary sense, as the proper approach to solving problems in the social and human sciences. For example, we may consider Voloshinov's criticism of "abstract objectivism" for being unable to arrive at "the dialectical combination of the unity of meaning with its multiplicity" (V:MPL, 80). Second example: Voloshinov's argument against seeking a compromise between "individual subjectivism" and "abstract objectivism": "We believe that in this instance, as everywhere else, the truth is not to be found in the golden mean and is not a matter of compromise between thesis and antithesis, but lies over and beyond them, constituting a negation of both thesis and antithesis alike, i.e. constituting a *dialectical synthesis*" (V:MPL, 82).

Potential meanings (*potentisal'nye smysly*); semantic possibilities (*smyslovye vozmozhnosti*); intentional potentials (*intentsional'nye vozmozhnosti*)

Concepts Bakhtin develops to explain how great works develop in meaning over time. He is trying to avoid two positions unacceptable to him: (1) reducing a text's meanings to those intended (in the narrow sense) by its author or discovered by its original readers, and (2) expanding its meanings to include whatever any reader or group of readers might choose to find in it. Bakhtin calls the first of these two positions "enclosure [of a work] within the epoch" of its creation and calls the second "modernization and distortion" (RQ, 4).

Bakhtin argues that authors put two *kinds* of meaning into a (great) work. First, the work contains meanings that the author intends (in the usual sense) and which contemporaries can (in principle) find; second, the work contains "potential meanings," put there by the author. The author senses these potentials for meaning, can sense a work's rich potential, but he or she senses it precisely *as* potential, as the capacity for meanings the precise nature of which he or she is not and cannot be aware. Learning to recognize such potentials is a part of learning to be an author. (Bakhtin presumably would attribute the weakness of most modern theories to the recognition of only one kind of intention. Bakhtin is trying to enrich the concept of intention, to credit authors with the intention to intend more than could be immediately extracted from their work.)

Semantic potentials can be realized only dialogically. What is required is genuine alterity or "outsideness," a perspective shaped by cultural experiences the author could not know. The two perspectives—of the work and of readers with these experiences—may generate new meanings that (as in all true dialogue) neither side could arrive at without the other.

Thus readers from another culture or a later epoch may enter into dialogue with the work and, responding to its potentials, produce meanings that depend on *both* the readers' conceptual horizon (*krugozor*) and the potentials in the work. The process may be repeated by readers from still later epochs, and so the work may grow in meanings over time (or across cultures). Because the new meanings depend on readers as well as the potentials of the work, rich potentials may generate many different kinds of readings as the work figures in different cultures and epochs.

This model therefore identifies three broad kinds of interpretation:

1. One may seek to discover the author's meanings intended (in the narrow sense) by the author or discovered by its original readings. One places oneself as much as possible within the horizon of the writer and his epoch; this kind of interpretation requires something resembling "empathy."
2. One can forget about the author's intended readings and read the work according to the interests of one's own group or time; this is "modernization and distortion." If the first type of reading suppresses one side of dialogue (the reader), the second suppresses the other (the author).
3. One can respond dialogically to the work and exploit its potentials. Bakhtin calls this process "creative understanding." Both sides of the dialogue are active, which is why something genuinely new can be produced. One seeks to address not only the intended meanings (in the narrow sense) but also the potentials; one recognizes the text as genuinely other and one's own interests as having something to contribute if used in the appropriate way. One might begin with "empathy," for instance, but then make use of one's "outsideness" and "surplus" for an act of "live entering" (*vzhivanie*) in order to achieve "creative understanding."

The same three kinds of interpretation pertain to anthropological research into other cultures.

Of the three types of interpretation, the most valuable is creative understanding. But "enclosure within the epoch" is preferable to "modernization and distortion" because the former at least reveals an other, and may be the basis for creative understanding in the future.

It is important to emphasize that the potentials are really *in* the work. They are *intentional* potentials, placed there by the author, who senses them in the material he or she uses. "Semantic phenomena can exist in concealed form, potentially, and be revealed only in semantic cultural contexts that are favorable for such disclosure" (RQ, 5). Thus Shakespeare "has grown because of that which actually has been and continues to be found in his works, but which neither he himself nor his contemporaries could consciously perceive and evaluate in the context of their epoch" (RQ, 4).

Because the potentials are genuinely in the work, a purely relativist account of value is inadequate. One measure of a work's greatness is the richness of its potentials.

"Favorable conditions" for the activation of potentials may arise through a change in the "dialogizing background." [The *Heteroglossary* contains pertinent entries on **Dialogizing background** and **Reaccentuation and canonization**.] A great writer is able to produce rich potentials because the very "bricks" he or she uses to create his or her work are themselves rich in accumulated meanings and potentials produced in past epochs. Any great work is really created not just by the author in his or her own time, but over "great time"; and any truly historical criticism must recognize this extended time frame. For example, the genres an author uses "remember" meanings of the past because genres are really forms of thinking and ways of visualizing the world that have themselves developed over "great time." In effect, the concept of "potential meanings" is a correlate of the concept of "genre memory"; what the latter does in relation to the past, the former does in relation to the future.

Other cultures and past epochs also have "potential meanings." "Antiquity itself did not know the antiquity that we know now. . . . [The time since then was] filled with increasing discoveries of new *semantic* values in antiquity, values of which the Greeks were in fact unaware, though they themselves created them" (RQ, 6). By entering into dialogue with these potential meanings, scholars can assist "in the great cause of liberating antiquity from the captivity of time" (RQ, 6).

Dialogue (*dialog*) versus **monologue** (*monolog*)

Frequently misunderstood terms of Bakhtin. He cautions that dialogue is not to be confused with the alternation of speakers (in life or in a drama), with mere "compositionally expressed dialogue." Neither can it be reduced to logical contradiction (which may provide the material for a dialogue, but is not itself dialogic). It cannot properly be identified with disagreement, which is only one type of dialogic relation; agreement is no less dialogic than disagreement. Dialectics in the Hegelian or Marxist sense is not dialogic.

Bakhtin uses the term "dialogue" in at least three distinct senses, and he is not careful to specify which he has in mind on a given occasion, a lapse that has obscured his meaning.

Common to all uses is the sense that dialogue involves two or more distinct speakers, each with a special voice, set of experiences, complex of attitudes, and outlook on the world. Logical contradiction is not dialogic because it requires no specific voices (and can be expressed by one voice). The process of dialectics can be expressed by a single voice and contained within a single consciousness, so it too is not dialogic. However complex the relations in a trope, one voice is all that is required to use it; tropes may be extremely rich, but their richness is not dialogic in nature. For similar reasons, ambiguity is not to be confused with dialogue. It is characteristic of monologic thinkers who encounter dialogic phenomena to transform them into these and other essentially nondialogic phenomena.

"'Hunger, cold!'—one utterance of a single speaking subject. 'Hunger!'— 'Cold!'—two dialogically correlated utterances of two different subjects: here dialogic relations appear that did not exist in the former case" (PT, 117–18). What Bakhtin calls traditional linguistics, poetics, and stylistics do not recognize dialogue. That is because, strictly speaking, dialogue is not a linguistic phenomenon. "Dialogic relations presuppose a language, but they do not reside within the system of a language. They are impossible among elements of a language" (PT, 117). Dialogic relations are metalinguistic in nature. Traditional linguistics treats relations among elements of language, such as sentences, but metalinguistics treats relations among utterances; and utterances require distinct speakers. "When an utterance is used for purposes of linguistic analysis, its dialogic nature is ignored, it is regarded within the system of the language . . . and not in the larger dialogue of speech communication" (PT, 118). Language provides resources for dialogue, but someone must be communicating with someone for dialogue to exist.

Within this broad framework, we may distinguish three distinct senses of dialogue in Bakhtin's work:

1. *Dialogue in the first sense* applies to all utterances, which are dialogic by definition. Hence, this sense of the term does not admit of the possibility of monologic utterances. All utterances are dialogic in the first sense because they presuppose (at least) two participants, and the utterance is shaped *from the outset* by both speaker and listener (whether present or potential). Bakhtin therefore rejects the telegraphic model of communication, according to which the speaker makes the utterance and the listener simply decodes it, a model that makes the listener in principle unnecessary. This case is also argued by Voloshinov in V:MPL. Bakhtin locates other sources of the dialogism of all utterances, specifically the "superaddressee" and the orientation to earlier utterances on the same topic or using the same words (see entry on **Third person** below).

2. *Dialogue in the second sense* allows for the existence of nondialogic (or monologic) utterances. In this case, the orientation to the listener or to earlier utterances on the topic are part of the "task" of the utterance. In parody, for example, one is intended to hear a second voice sounding within the utterance; if one does not, one will not appreciate the fact that the utterance is designed as a parody. All "double-voiced" utterances are dialogic in the second sense. On the other hand, one can shape an utterance as if no one could possibly dispute it, indeed as if no one has the right even to agree with it. In this case, the listener is expected to accept

it passively. ("Monologue as speech that is addressed to no one and does not presuppose a response. Various degrees of monologicity" [PT, 117].) Such monologic utterances are nevertheless dialogic in the first sense (because all utterances by definition must be). [The first two senses of dialogue are discussed in detail in chapter 4 of *Bakhtin: Creation of a Prosaics.*]

3. *Dialogue in the third sense* is not a term applied to utterances per se. Rather, it is a vision of the world and of truth. This sense of the term also admits of the opposition dialogic to monologic. Bakhtin criticizes the legacy of European "rationalism," which understands truth monologically, that is, it understands truth as the sort of thing that can best be represented by impersonal propositions. By contrast, it is possible to conceive of truth as something that can only be represented by a conversation, as something that by its very nature demands many voices and points of view. Such an image of truth is present in a rudimentary way in some early Platonic dialogues, but received its fullest development in Dostoevsky's polyphonic novels. Dialogue in the third sense is essential to the "form-shaping idea" of polyphony. Thus, the very form of Dostoevsky's novels has profound philosophical significance. Depending on the situation, we may need either a monologic or a dialogic conception of truth.

Third person (*tret'e litso, tret'e soznanie*); **absence of the third person** (*otsutstvie tret'ego*)

This term is used in several distinct senses in Bakhtin's work. The frequency (and diversity) of these usages perhaps reflects Bakhtin's suspicion of thinking in terms of binary oppositions, as the Russian Formalists tended to do. It also marks a difference between Bakhtin and Voloshinov; the latter tends to formulate binary oppositions and then, having described the opposition as "dialectic," to derive a synthesis. Bakhtin's "third person" (or third category) is normally not synthetic, and Bakhtin does not tend to think in terms of dialectical oppositions. The tone with which he usually introduces a "third person" is not one of resolution, but of new opening and new complexity, perhaps with a suggestion that still more complexity and still more "persons" are to be found. Main uses of the term include:

1. In PT, the third person is the "superaddressee," the perfectly understanding listener to which every utterance is oriented. This orientation is constitutive of the utterance, just as a real (present or potential) listener is. Therefore, there is nothing more terrible than a situation in which one becomes convinced that there can be no such listener, even conceptually; for then discourse, even to oneself, is sensed as frustrated in its very shaping. Such a situation, according to Bakhtin, is hell, "the absolute absence of a third person" (PT, 126), as represented in Thomas Mann's *Dr. Faustus.*

2. At the beginning of DiN, the "third person" is the topic of an utterance. The topic is "already spoken about," and earlier utterances on the topic enter into dialogue with the present utterance as a "third person." The speaker must orient himself or herself to the third person; the utterance must interact dialogically with earlier utterances on the topic.

3. Later in DiN, the term is used to describe the role of the author in a novel. The language of the novel is a style of styles. "It is as if the author has no language of his own, but does possess his own style, his own organic law governing the way he plays with languages and the way his own real semantic and expressive intentions are refracted in them" (DiN, 311). For example, the author may choose a narrator with a "language" of his own that differs from the "normal" literary language that serves as a dialogizing background to the narrator's speech. The author is not to be found in either of these languages. He is always switching among, orchestrating, and dialogizing languages "at every point of his work in order that he himself might remain as it were neutral with regard to language, a third party in a quarrel among two people (although he might be a *biased* third party" (DiN, 314).

4. In PDP, a third person is a viewer, audience, or reader of an artistic work who remains detached from it and does not "participate" in it. The polyphonic novel does not permit this kind of audience. Because its great dialogues are radically unfinalized, the audience must participate in them to comprehend the work. This use of the term is clearly related to Bakhtin's concept of "footlights": in the polyphonic novel, as in carnival, there are no "footlights," no nonparticipating third persons. Neither can the author of a polyphonic novel be a third person: he speaks *with* the heroes, not *about* them. In a polyphonic work, "everything must be felt as *discourse about someone actually present,* as the word of a 'second' and not of a 'third' person" (PDP, 64; Bakhtin's italics). By contrast, in a monologic novel, words about a character are "third person's" words, which "the hero himself cannot hear . . . he cannot make of them an aspect of his own self-consciousness, cannot respond to them. . . . Such words would materialize and debase the human being-personality" (TRDB, 296).

Truth of one's own self-consciousness (*pravda sobstvennogo soznaniia* or *pravda samosoznaniia*) versus **secondhand truth** (*zaochnaia pravda*) and **secondhand evaluation** (*zaochnaia otsenka*).

The core idea behind these terms is that no external characterization of oneself (no secondhand truth) can be the same as one that is freely spoken by oneself about oneself, even if the characterizations are otherwise the same. "In the mouth of another person, a word or definition identical in content would take on another meaning and tone, and would no longer be the truth" (PDP, 55). Such a secondhand truth tends to *finalize* one, tends to treat one as a fixed image or as a known quantity incapable of surprise. And to the extent that a secondhand characterization is accurate, it carries with it a condescending superiority potentially offensive to one's dignity, no matter how careful the second person is to avoid offense. The only way to avoid this danger is to approach the other *dialogically,* as someone who can respond unexpectedly, and so has the capacity to render untrue all definitions of himself or herself.

Ultimately, secondhand truth is not true at all. "The truth about a man in the mouths of others, not directed to him dialogically and therefore a *secondhand* truth, becomes a *lie* degrading and deadening him, if it touches upon his 'holy of holies,' that is, 'the man in man'" (PDP, 59). By contrast, "the truth of one's own self-consciousness" is spoken out of a sense of one's own unfinalizability, one's capacity to change and to make untrue even self-descriptions. Only a free confession preserves that sense of unfinalizability and true freedom. This line of reasoning is central to Bakhtin's approach to ethics, and central to the ethical argument of PDP.

In literature, secondhand definitions are adequate for representing "characters" but not "personalities." [The *Heteroglossary* contains an entry on **Character versus personality**.] *Zaochnyi* literally means "taking place in the absence of the interested party," as in *zaochnyi prigovor*, "sentence delivered in the absence of the accused."

Bakhtin may be punning on the root meaning of *zaochnaia pravda* as "the truth beyond one's eyes"; he may thus be alluding to his concepts of "outsideness" and "the field of vision," which he illustrated in spatial terms.

Innerly persuasive discourse or innerly persuasive word *(vnutrenne ubeditel'noe slovo)*

A key concept in Bakhtin's (meta)linguistically based account of selfhood. Selfhood is understood in terms of the complex of voices that sound within us and in terms of our way of orienting ourselves among these voices (with all their attendant values, tones, special registers, ways of conceptualizing the world). We think in "inner speech," inner dialogues with voices we have learned. Two broad categories of voices within us may be distinguished: "authoritative" and "innerly persuasive." The two may coincide, but usually do not. Even when authoritative voices are innerly persuasive, the two aspects are distinct. There are degrees of authoritativeness and inner persuasiveness.

Both authoritative and innerly persuasive voices are "other" or "alien" to us, but the latter group are much less alien. An innerly persuasive voice is halfway to becoming "our own" (it is "half-ours and half-someone else's" [DiN, 345]). Thus, an innerly persuasive voice is not identical with "our own word" (*svoe slovo*).

In a person's psychic development, there is usually a conflict between authoritative and innerly persuasive discourses. (These terms name whole groups of voices.) Authoritative discourse — "the word of a father, of adults and teachers" (DiN, 342) — is not usually experienced as truly persuasive but rather demands *unconditional* allegiance simply because it derives from an authoritative source. By contrast, innerly persuasive discourse is denied such authority or privilege. Its importance comes only from its persuasiveness. "The struggle and dialogic interrelationship of these categories of ideological discourse are what usually determine the history of an individual ideological consciousness" (DiN, 342).

In contrast to the authoritative word, the innerly persuasive word functions in a realm of "familiar contact"; consequently, it lends itself to complex interactions with other "words." In the psyche, it organizes various discourses, develops in response to new experiences, and interacts with other innerly persuasive discourses. The intense struggle of discourses, with the values and attitudes they carry, are essential to our psychic development; and the struggle is both highly creative and productive of new experience. In short, innerly persuasive discourse "is not *finite*, it is *open*;

in each of the new contexts that dialogize it, this discourse is able to reveal ever new *ways to mean*" (DiN, 346; Bakhtin's italics).

Because novelistic discourse has developed the subtlest and most complex "hybrid constructions" of various discourses, that genre is especially well adapted to representing psychic life as Bakhtin understands it . Conversely, it would be possible to say that Bakhtin has devised a novelistic theory of the psyche.

In the novel's hybrid constructions, a character's inner speech interacts with authorial discourse. Either may predominate: at times the inner speech of the character is invaded by authorial discourse; at other times the process is reversed (in "character zones," for instance). Indeed, the novel allows the inner speech of characters who have not encountered each other to interact, producing complex hybrids and philosophically rich dialogues.

Inner persuasiveness is not permanent. A discourse may begin to lose its persuasiveness; it may become less "one's own" and more than half "someone else's." In such cases psychic life may involve play and experiment with the discourse; one may make an objectified "image" of it and (in the manner of a novelist) join it to the image of a possible speaking person. In this way, one can examine it at a distance and so discover more of its limitations. "The importance of struggling with another's discourse, its influence in the history of an individual's coming to ideological consciousness, is enormous. One's own discourse and one's own voice, although born of another or dynamically stimulated by another, will sooner or later begin to liberate themselves" (DiN, 348). On the other hand, once a discourse has been persuasive, it may unexpectedly regain that persuasiveness (perhaps marked with a new polemical tone).

First stylistic line of the European novel *(pervaia stilisticheskaia liniia*
   evropeiskogo romana) and **Second stylistic line of the European novel**
   (votoraia stilisticheskaia liniia evropeiskogo romana)
The final chapter of DiN is devoted to identifying, characterizing, evaluating, and tracing the development of these two traditions of prose art.

For Bakhtin, the novel as a genre (and therefore both of its stylistic lines) depends on a "Galilean linguistic consciousness," by which he means a sense that no way of speaking (or viewing) the world is self-sufficient. There always are, and one always needs, many "languages of truth," and to understand the world one must be able to comprehend and participate in many competing languages of heteroglossia (each with its attendant worldview, habits of perception, and ways of assigning value). One language may be better than another for certain purposes, but others are bound to be better for other purposes; and even this relative privilege is constantly tested and open to further testing. The Galilean language consciousness is the genre's "form-shaping ideology."

The two stylistic lines of the novel are distinguished by their *ways* of exploiting heteroglossia and embodying the Galilean language consciousness.

The first line reached fruition earlier. In antiquity, it found "a sufficiently full and finished expression" in the "Sophistic novel." Retrospectively, one can also see elements that prepared for the second line, but it did not reach fruition in antiquity.

The second line more fully and more richly exploits the "generic potential" of the novel; that is, it embodies the Galilean language consciousness and utilizes the resources of heteroglossia better than the first line. This is presumably why Bakhtin sometimes describes a given quality as characteristic only of the second line and proceeds to say that it also exhibits the essence of "novelness." At such moments, he speaks as if the first line could be treated as a mere approximation to true novelness.

The two lines remained largely distinct until the nineteenth century (although there are some significant examples of their combination before then). In the nineteenth century, the two lines merged fully (to produce "the novel" in the narrower sense we sometimes have in mind). In this mixture, the second line clearly predominates.

The two lines exploit heteroglossia differently. In the second line, heteroglossia is incorporated into the novel; in the first, it remains outside in "the dialogizing background." The language of the novel of the first line is dialogized because it is perceived against that background; we sense the *contrast* of its language with the heteroglossia of the surrounding world.

The primary characteristic of the first line "is the fact that it knows only a single language and a single style (which is more or less rigorously consistent): heteroglossia remains *outside* the novel, although it does nevertheless have its effect on the novel as a dialogizing background in which the language of the world and of the novel is polemically and forensically implicated" (DiN, 375). A highly stylized "literary language" predominates in the text, but we are meant to perceive that style as dialogized with respect to the background of social heteroglossia. For example, the literary language in the work may polemically ignore (and therefore implicitly pay attention to) the "crude" language of daily life. The linguistic energy of the work derives from the interaction of the language of the text with the presumed language of the social context. Novels of the first line are dialogized (and are designed to be dialogized) not by what is in them, but by what is presumed by them.

For this reason, the precise nature, or even the very existence, of dialogization may be lost for later generations who do not know the background that the author and initial readers took for granted. "Except in those cases where it is grossly apparent, the presence of parody is in general very difficult to identify (that is, difficult to identify precisely in literary prose, where it is rarely gross), without knowing the background of alien discourse against which it is projected, that is, without knowing its second context. In world literature there are probably many works whose parodic nature has not even been suspected" (DiN, 374). For such reasons, the whole range of dialogic phenomena in novels of the first line (not just parody) is difficult to detect.

By contrast, the second stylistic line, "to which belong the greatest representatives of the novel as a genre (its greatest subgenres as well as the greatest individual examples), incorporates heteroglossia *into* a novel's composition, exploiting it to orchestrate its own meaning and frequently resisting altogether any unmediated and pure authorial discourse" (DiN, 375). Whereas the first line presumes a dialogizing background, the second line incorporates and dialogizes heteroglossia in the work. Thus, it is the second line that developed the most complex forms of novelistic discourse: various hybrid constructions, interilluminated languages, double-voicing combined with double-languagedness. This is why the form-shaping ideology of the genre (its Galilean language consciousness) is realized better in the second line, which exploits the genre's "potential" more fully.

A few important differences between these two types of novels follow from the basic distinction between them. Whereas novels of the first line cultivate a general "extrageneric literariness of language," novels of the second line tend to treat "literary language" as just another language of heteroglossia, to be orchestrated along with all the rest. It may do so by including "'literary people' with their literary way of thinking and their literary way of doing things—that is, such a novel transforms them into authentic characters" (DiN, 383).

Novels of each line often include inserted genres, but the two lines use inserted genres for different purposes and with different effects. Novels of the first line include genres that are highly "literized" and linguistically "ennobled"; hence these inserted genres are easily detached and used as models for daily behavior or respectable speaking and writing. Novels of the second line often include inserted genres in order to orchestrate the nonliterary kinds of discourse they bring with them. The first line avoids discourse saturated with "practical" purposes, "philistine" associations, and "specific contexts," all of which are cultivated by the second line. Whereas the second line perceives objects and expressions as part of "the ever-changing world view of a living and mobile human being," the first line seeks to escape from such a world, and turns to it "one and the same immobile pose." It is a pose a person might assume "not in order better to see, but quite the opposite—he moves so that he may turn *away*, not notice, be distracted" from heteroglossia and "crude real life" (DiN, 385).

Plot and character also differ. For the first line, the most characteristic plot is one of "testing" (of fidelity, piety, professional experience). The second line developed the plot of gradual becoming. In the first line, character is either already given or present from the start in embryo. Experience can test or reveal it, but cannot shape it. In the second line, character more often undergoes genuine becoming. It is possible for novels of the second line to use testing as a way to provoke becoming, thus integrating and transforming the devices inherited from the first line.

Novels of the first line include the ancient Sophistic novel, the chivalric romance, the high baroque novel, and the adventure novel, among others. Classic examples of the second line include the satire novella and the parodic epic. *Amadis* belongs to the first line, Rabelais's works and *Don Quixote* to the second; in the first we find Rousseau and Richardson, in the second Fielding and Sterne. In BSHR, Bakhtin characterizes the novel from a different standpoint, and his description of novelistic "becoming" appears somewhat inconsistent with his account of it in DiN.

Unnovelistic novel *(neromannyi roman)*
A work that is intended to be a novel but is not written out of a genuine "prosaic consciousness." For example, the author may lack a "Galilean linguistic conscious-

ness" (DiN, 327), may be "deaf to organic double-voicedness" and to the potentials of dialogized heteroglossia. Such an author "may, of course, create an artistic work that compositionally and thematically will be similar to a novel, will be 'made' ["*sdelano*"] exactly as a novel is made, but he will not thereby have created a novel. The style will give him away. . . . We quickly sense that such an author finds it easy to purge his work of speech diversity" (DiN, 327). The language of such works may resemble mere stage directions in a closet drama (or may be poetic rather than prosaic).

The reference to an unnovelistic novel as "made" is a (double-voiced) criticism of the Russian Formalists, who used the term in analyzing literary works as assemblies of "devices." For Bakhtin, genres were not a particular way of combining devices but an outlook on the world. Each genre has a "form-shaping idea" that typically is realized by the aid of certain devices; an unnovelistic novel imitates the devices but does not manifest the form-shaping idea. It lacks "prosaic consciousness." In general, Bakhtin does not regard the creative process as a matter of "making"; this argument about creativity is another significant difference between Bakhtin and the Russian Formalists, to which he perhaps alludes here.